Corruption and Development

Palgrave Studies in Development

Titles include:
Sarah Bracking (*editor*)
CORRUPTION AND DEVELOPMENT
The Anti-Corruption Campaigns

Tanja Schümer
NEW HUMANITARIANISM
Britain and Sierra Leone, 1997–2003

Palgrave Studies in Development
Series Standing Order ISBN 978-0-230-52738-6

You can receive future titles in this series as they are published by placing a standing order. Please contact your bookseller or, in case of difficulty, write to us at the address below with your name and address, the title of the series and the ISBN quoted above.

Customer Services Department, Macmillan Distribution Ltd, Houndmills, Basingstoke, Hampshire RG21 6XS, England

Corruption and Development

The Anti-Corruption Campaigns

Edited by

Sarah Bracking
University of Manchester, UK

With a Foreword by Deryck R. Brown
Commonwealth Secretariat, UK

First published 2007 by
PALGRAVE MACMILLAN
Houndmills, Basingstoke, Hampshire RG21 6XS and
175 Fifth Avenue, New York, N.Y. 10010
Companies and representatives throughout the world

PALGRAVE MACMILLAN is the global academic imprint of the Palgrave Macmillan division of St. Martin's Press, LLC and of Palgrave Macmillan Ltd. Macmillan® is a registered trademark in the United States, United Kingdom and other countries. Palgrave is a registered trademark in the European Union and other countries.

ISBN-13: 978-0-230-52550-4   hardback
ISBN-10: 0–230–52550–4   hardback

This book is printed on paper suitable for recycling and made from fully managed and sustained forest sources. Logging, pulping and manufacturing processes are expected to conform to the environmental regulations of the country of origin.

A catalogue record for this book is available from the British Library.

A catalog record for this book is available from the Library of Congress.

10   9   8   7   6   5   4   3   2   1
16   15   14   13   12   11   10   09   08   07

Printed and bound in Great Britain by Antony Rowe Ltd, Chippenham and Eastbourne

Contents

List of Tables   *vii*

List of Figures   *viii*

Foreword   *ix*
Deryck R. Brown (Commonwealth Secretariat)

Editor's Preface   *xii*
Sarah Bracking

Acknowledgements   *xiv*

Notes on the Contributors   *xv*

List of Abbreviations   *xviii*

Part I: Introduction   **1**

1   Political Development and Corruption: Why 'Right Here,
    Right Now!'?   3
    Sarah Bracking
2   The Limits of a Global Campaign against Corruption   28
    Kalin S. Ivanov
3   Economic Models of Corruption   46
    Vincent G. Fitzsimons

**Part II: Corruption, Political Development and
            Anti-Corruption Campaigns**   **75**

4   Tickling Donors and Tackling Opponents: the
    Anti-Corruption Campaign in Malawi   77
    David Hall-Matthews
5   Corruption and Reform in Nigeria   103
    Paul Okojie and Abubakar Momoh
6   Challenges to the Philippine Culture of Corruption   121
    Edna Estifania A. Co
7   Challenges of Anti-Corruption Policies in
    Post-Communist Countries   138
    Anastassiya Zagainova

8   Political Corruption in Georgia   155
     Nina Dadalauri
9   Corruption Scandals and Anti-Corruption Institution   167
     Building Interventions in Jamaica
     Philip Duku Osei
10   Governance, Neoliberalism and Corruption in Nicaragua
     Ed Brown, Jonathan Cloke and José Luis Rocha   182

**Part III: Development Policy and Anti-Corruption
              Initiatives**   **203**

11   Fighting Public Sector Corruption in Ghana:
     Does Gender Matter?   205
     Namawu Alhassan Alolo
12   Upgrading Democracy in Mozambique: the Question
     of Party and Election Finance   221
     Bruno Wilhelm Speck
13   Accountability in Development Finance Projects:
     Between the Market and a Soft Place   236
     Sarah Bracking
14   Why Anti-Corruption Initiatives Fail: Technology
     Transfer and Contextual Collision   258
     Richard Heeks
15   Strengthening Checks and Balances in Financial Governance:
     the Evolving Role of Multilateral Banks in Latin America   273
     Carlos Santiso

Part IV: Conclusion   **293**

16   Conclusion   295
     Sarah Bracking and Kalin Ivanov

Index   *304*

List of Tables

1.1	Different types of corruption	5
3.1	Direct costs of corruption	56
3.2	Internal policies to deter corruption	60
3.3	Environmental deterrents to corruption	63
3.4	Economics of institutions (NIE view)	66
5.1	Misappropriation by ministry, 2000–2001 fiscal year	108
5.2	International anti-corruption law, codes of conduct and conventions	111
7.1	Typology of corruption forms in post-communist countries	142
7.2	Main indicators of countries by group	143
9.1	Some corruption scandals in Jamaica	172
9.2	Post-2000 anti-corruption reform in Jamaica	175
14.1	The design inscriptions of a democratisation project in West Africa	261
15.1	WB diagnostic instruments in public financial management	280
16.1	A summary of the global anti-corruption policy package	300

List of Figures

3.1   Corruption and income – 2005 CPI against
      2004 PPP$pc income   53
3.2   Corruption and income – non-OECD countries   54
3.3   Boxplot of regional variation in corruption   55
7.1   Corruption's level in the transition countries   141
11.1 Model for corrupt behaviour   217
13.1 A concessionary business environment in Lesotho   246
14.1 Anti-corruption initiatives and context – inscription
      and insertion   262
14.2 Reciprocating accommodations between initiative
      design and reality of deployment context   266
14.3 Deep- vs. shallow-inscribed anti-corruption initiatives   267

Foreword

The tide of world opinion has turned against corruption, and the international development community is today far less tolerant of it than they were just a few short decades ago. There is now unanimity that corruption is detrimental to the interests of society in general, and the poor in particular, and its eradication has become the *cri de coeur* of a number of multilateral and intergovernmental organisations. The pervasive view, as articulated by outgoing United Nations Secretary-General Kofi Annan in a message to the First Conference of the States Parties to the UN Convention against Corruption (UNCAC), is that:

> In ways large and small, corruption hurts us all. It impedes social and economic development. It erodes the public's trust, hurts investment and undermines democracy and the rule of law. It facilitates terrorism, conflict and organized crime.

Some decades ago, in a famous article entitled 'What is the problem about corruption'? published in the *Journal of Modern African Studies*, Professor Colin Leys argued that an element of corruption might be justified in post-colonial states – particularly in Africa – given their levels of development and their many and varied problems. Leys noted the role that corruption had played in eighteenth- and nineteenth-century Britain where votes were openly bought and sold in the so-called 'rotten boroughs'; as well as in nineteenth-century America where electoral machine bosses and 'robber barons' held sway, and where money was used to integrate newly-arrived immigrants into the then existing political process. Indeed, some might argue that corruption helped build modern America. Similar arguments have been made about the role of corruption in the development of Japan and the Asian Tigers.

Professor Leys argued that newly-independent African states faced problems and challenges not unlike those experienced by the old nations at an earlier stage in their development, and that corruption could in certain circumstances prove to be functional to national integration, institution-building and economic development. Given the low salaries paid to public officials in these countries, for example, bribes could be viewed as an incentive or bonus to get things done, especially in over-regulated societies with undue bureaucratic and judicial red tape. Bribes lowered transaction costs by reducing delays that consume management and/or investor time.

In today's world this type of thinking would be viewed not only as eccentric or heretical, but downright dangerous. The international climate against corruption has indeed changed. A body of empirical and other work done over the past decade shows the impact of corruption on investment, growth and poverty. There is compelling evidence that corruption tends to fuel poverty by subverting the normal means of distributing economic gains, only enriching the procurer of the graft and the person who commits it while impacting negatively on public spending programmes that benefit the poor, like health and education. On this basis, both bilateral and multilateral development agencies have placed anti-corruption strategies at the heart of their efforts to strengthen governance in beneficiary countries.

Is corruption better or worse now than it was in earlier periods? For those working in the field – as well as in the broader area of governance – it is flattering to believe that because corruption has become so central to governance and is receiving much more attention than it did in the past, that it is less likely to occur. However, this question is difficult to answer for obvious reasons. A casual trawl through the global press would lead one to the conclusion that corruption is still very much present. And it is not restricted to any particular group of countries: there is as much evidence of corruption in the developed as there is in the developing world. Whether it is the 'cash for peerages' scandal in the United Kingdom or the corruption of local mayors and councillors by the Spanish construction industry; whether it is the Anglo-Leasing affair that shook the National Rainbow Coalition (NARC) government in Kenya or the conviction of a former Prime Minister in the small Caribbean country of Trinidad and Tobago for failing to declare a London bank account – the prevalence of corruption cannot be in doubt. What is different today is that, because the world is less tolerant of large-scale corruption and because democracy, free and fair elections and press freedom have become the norm even in the developing world, corrupt officials have to find ever more daring ways of concealing their improprieties and the proceeds thereof, which makes it all the more difficult to gauge actual levels of corruption with any real degree of accuracy.

The conference on 'Redesigning the State: Political Corruption in Development Theory and Practice', organised by the *Global Poverty Research Group* at the University of Manchester on 25 November 2005, the proceedings of which form the basis of this volume, was both relevant and timely, coming, as it did, mere days before the *United Nations Convention Against Corruption* (NCAC) came into force. The UNCAC provides, for the first time, a global framework for effective action to combat corruption. As at December 2006, over 140 countries had signed the Convention and 80 had ratified it. Many of the themes and issues covered in the contributions to the conference – and presented in this book – resonate with the provisions of the Convention. Issues such as transparency in government procurement and the management of public finances (fiscal governance), codes of conduct for public officials, asset disclosure, witness/ whistleblower protection, money laundering, asset forfeiture and repatriation are all vitally important in the fight against corruption. Of interest, too, is the proliferation of anti-corruption agencies and institutions, many of which are shells that lack the resources to effectively carry out their mandates.

How successful could we expect these international and local anti-corruption initiatives to be? Success will depend partly upon the answers to three major questions, i.e.:

a) who owns the anti-corruption efforts being undertaken?
b) is leadership being provided from the highest levels of government? and
c) does the state have the capacity to implement anti-corruption strategies and campaigns through effective detection, investigation and prosecution?

The effectiveness of any anti-corruption measures will also depend on the fundamental underlying assumptions we make about the nature of people. Do we assume that human beings are inherently good and will see the merit in avoiding graft and corruption because of its negative impact on society? Or, do we assume that people are inherently evil and that we live in a Hobbesian 'state of nature' in which life is 'solitary, poor, nasty, brutish and short'? There are those who would argue that corruption, like prostitution and poverty, will never be eradicated and that, while bureaucracy and its rules are essential safeguards, there are special occasions when in order to make an omelette, many bureaucratic eggshells must be broken. This volume can help us decide on which side of this dilemma we fall.

Deryck R. Brown
Adviser, Governance and Development
Commonwealth Secretariat

Editor's Preface

This book began at a conference on 'Redesigning the State: Political Corruption in Development Theory and Practice' held in Manchester in November 2005. A multidisciplinary agenda invited participants, variously and not exclusively, to unravel the normative labelling and ontological embedding of corruption and anti-corruption in development theory and practice; examine the incidence and effects of corruption on firm behaviour and competition; evaluate and deconstruct donor policy in the area of anti-corruption; and look at new institutional initiatives to build transparency and accountability in government. Such was the success of the conference that this book was planned to share the wealth of global and local research examined, from every continent and in politics, economics and social theory.

The inspiration for the conference, in turn, came a few years earlier, as corruption began to dominate accounts of politics and development in Africa, with little historical context, contributing to Afro-pessimism. I thought it time for a comprehensive review of anti-corruption policy and practice to counter the over-generalisations of the industry. After all, as Dr John Githongo noted at the conference, there are now, for the first time, a group of 'ex-African leaders who are enjoying their retirement'. So why was everything written about politics in Africa so bleak?

There is no singular message which emerges from this book, but instead a number of nuanced observations, analytical developments and policy suggestions, not least that incremental improvements in governance are apparent across Africa, Latin America and East and central Europe, and that anti-corruption work is making ground, although not always or everywhere. There is also however, a cautionary tale for donors about anti-corruption intervention. While it is clear that corruption in government remains everywhere, the privileging of corruption as the 'central problem' by development policy organisations such as the *Commission for Africa*, may be counterproductive.

There are many challenges ahead in the complex relationship between policy, conditionality, political development and corruption. Northern governments need to go beyond punitive conditionalities, be more deeply reflective, and consider the global networks of corruption, the role of their own nationals, and the corruption enhancing or reducing effects of Northern foreign and development policy. Many chapters here question the efficacy of moralist discourse and argue instead for well established processes of democratisation as a long-term strategy for reducing corruption.

Also, policy which disaggregates anti-corruption into smaller elements may also work better: continued work in a number of fields such as international standards, institution and capacity building, knowledge transfer and cooperation, smart economic regulation and the reduction of Northern originated financial incentives may be more efficacious policies than tendencies towards deepening donor interventionism and a rejuvenated moral campaign. The knowledge generated here reiterates the importance of nuance, context and caution in the policy process.

The support of the *Economic and Social Research Council* (ESRC UK) is gratefully acknowledged: the work was made possible by a grant from the ESRC to the Global Poverty Research Group (GPRG) at the Universities of Manchester and Oxford (grant no. M571255001), which included sponsorship for the conference held in Manchester 2005. An academic debt is owed to numerous people, particularly Morris Szeftel, who had the task of supervising my Ph.D., and has been a source of great wisdom ever since, Paul Cammack and Martin Minogue at Manchester, for working with me in *Politics and Development*, Ray Bush, a long-standing inspiration and source of encouragement, and Patrick Bond, Mark Duffield, Lloyd Sachikonye, Anand Kumar and Giovanni Arrighi, for variously supporting my work. All errors are obviously mine. The editor would also like to thank the contributors for being a pleasure to work with, and my own family, particularly Christine and Colin, Pascal and Louie and the Makoneses in Zimbabwe. If the book is dedicated to anyone it is to these latter, and to Sekuru Paul in particular, who sadly left us too early.

Sarah Bracking

Acknowledgements

Chapter 10 contains material reprinted from *Political Geography*, 24, Ed Brown and Jonathan Cloke, 'Neoliberal reform, governance and corruption', 612–30, 2005, with permission from Elsevier.

Chapter 16 contains material reprinted from *Public Budgeting & Finance*, 26, Carlos Santiso, 'Banking on Accountability? Strengthening Budget Oversight and Public Sector Auditing in Emerging Economies' 66–100, with permission from Blackwell Publishing.

Notes on the Contributors

Namawu Alhassan Alolo is currently a Policy and Research Analyst at Islamic Relief. She spends half of her time at the International Development Department, University of Birmingham where she is part of a research team exploring the role of faith in development. Her current research interests are the gender-corruption nexus, anti-corruption initiatives, monitoring governance in sub-Saharan Africa, gender and HIV/AIDS.

Sarah Bracking is a Senior Lecturer in Politics and Development, University of Manchester, and member of the *Review of African Political Economy* Editorial Group and Democratic Audit UK.

Ed Brown has been a Lecturer in Geography at Loughborough University since 1991. His publications include *Structural Adjustment: Theory, Practice and Impacts* (co-author, 2000) and articles in various journals. He is also Chair of the Leicester Masaya Link group, an NGO promoting links between the cities of Leicester and Masaya in Nicaragua.

Jonathan Cloke is currently a Lecturer in the University of Newcastle's Geography Department. He was awarded his Ph.D. in 2003, after a career in the voluntary sector. Jon is also a member of different activist groups working under the umbrella of the European Social Forum, part of the World Social Forum movement set up as a progressive counter-balance to the World Economic Forum at Davos.

Edna Estifania A. Co has a doctorate in Public Administration from the University of the Philippines where she is Professor of Public Administration and Governance. Dr Co heads the Philippine Democracy Audit, a project under the Philippine Political Science Association which conducts a comprehensive assessment of the state of Philippine democracy, inspired by International IDEA. Dr Co also serves widely as a consultant.

Nina Dadalauri is a Research Fellow at the Transnational Crime and Corruption Centre Caucasus Office in Tbilisi, Georgia (TRACCC-CO). Her main research interests are the post-Soviet bloc countries, political corruption, political elites and informal institutions.

Vincent G. Fitzsimons is a Senior Lecturer in Economics, Department of Business Studies, University of Huddersfield, UK.

David Hall-Matthews is a Lecturer in International Development in the School of Politics and International Studies at Leeds University. His main research interest is famine and food security in both contemporary Africa and nineteenth-century India. He has published a number of articles on the subject as well as a book, *Peasants, Famine and the State in Colonial Western India* (2005).

Richard Heeks is a Senior Lecturer in Development Informatics at the University of Manchester, UK. His work focuses on four main areas: the relation between ICTs and public corruption and accountability; success and failure of e-government projects; public health information systems; and understanding e-government from an organisational behaviour/ politics perspective. His publications include *Reinventing Government in the Information Age* (2001) and *Implementing and Managing eGovernment: an International Text* (2005).

Kalin S. Ivanov is a doctoral candidate in International Relations at the University of Oxford where he is researching the impact of EU accession on the politics of anti-corruption in Bulgaria and Romania.

Abubakar Momoh is Senior Lecturer in the Department of Political Science at Lagos State University. He holds a Ph.D. in Political Theory. He has been studying youth, social movements, pan Africanism and democracy in Africa. He is currently the Vice-President of the African Association of Political Science (AAPS).

Paul Okojie is a Senior Lecturer in Law at Manchester Metropolitan University and Chair of the Board of Trustees, Ahmed Iqbal Ullah Race Relations Archives, Manchester University. His teaching and research interests are international criminal law, and good governance and international humanitarian law, with recent contributions in the *Routledge Encyclopedia of International Development*.

Philip Duku Osei is a Fellow of the Sir Arthur Lewis Institute of Social and Economic Studies at the University of the West Indies, Mona, Jamaica. He specialises in public policy, governance and international development. He has provided research and advisory services for the governments of Jamaica, Saint Lucia and the United States of America, the Organisation of American States, European Commission, the Organisation of Caribbean Utility Regulators, and the UNDP.

José Luis Rocha works at the Universidad Centroamericana in Managua, Nicaragua, where he is also on the editorial boards of *Envío* and *Encuentro*, UCA's academic journals. He is well known in Central America for his research on youth gangs in Nicaragua, local governments, natural disaster preparedness, the coffee crisis and migration. He also coordinates the *Regional Migration Analysis and Policies in Central America* research project for the Jesuit Service for Migrants in Central America.

Carlos Santiso is a governance and public finance adviser with the Department for International Development (United Kingdom), founding member of the board of the Centre for Democratic Governance (Burkina Faso) and non-resident fellow of the Centre for the Implementation of Public Policies Promoting Equity and Growth (Argentina).

Bruno Wilhelm Speck, Ph.D., holds a doctorate in political science from the University of Freiburg and currently works as a Professor of Political Science, State University of Campinas (Unicamp), Brazil. He has undertaken consultancy for INWENT in Bad Honnef, Gesellschaft für Technische Zusammenarbeit (GTZ) in Brazil, the Carter Center in Atlanta and the Christian Michelsen Institute in Bergen (Norway), and is currently a Senior adviser for the Americas Department, Transparency International, Berlin.

Anastassiya Zagainova is a researcher at PEPSE – Espace Europe Institute, University Pierre Mendès France, Grenoble, France. Her research interests concentrate on development and transition economics, the political economy of transition, specificities of post-Soviet economies, and links between institutionalised forms of corruption and growth.

List of Abbreviations

ACB	Anti-Corruption Bureau (Malawi)
ADMARC	Agricultural Development and Marketing Corporation, (Malawi)
ALPE	Georgian NGO conducting Public Opinion Research
ANC	Anticorruption Network for Transition Economies
ATP	Aid and Trade Provision (UK)
BAMER	Banco Mercantil (Nicaragua)
BANCAFE	Banco de Café (Nicaragua)
BIR	Bureau of Internal Revenue (Philippines)
BWI	Bretton Woods Institutions
CABS	Common Approach to Budget Support (Malawi)
CAS	Country Assistance Strategy
CDC	Commonwealth Development Corporation (UK)
CEEC	Central Eastern European countries
CEO	Chief Executive Officer
CFAA	Country Financial Accountability Assessment
CIS	Community of Independent States
CNE	Comissão Nacional de Eleições (Mozambique)
COA	Commission on Audit (Philippines)
COMESA	Common Market for East and Southern Africa
CPC	Commission for the Prevention of Corruption (Jamaica)
CPI	Corruption Perception Index
CPIA	Country Policy and Institutional Assessment
CSC	Civil Service Commission (Philippines)
DAC	Development Assistance Committee of the OECD
DANIDA	Danish International Development Agency
DAO	Differential Association and Opportunity Theory
DAP	Development Academy of the Philippines
DFI	development finance institution
DFID	Department for International Development (UK)
DGI	Dirección General de Ingresos (Nicaragua)
DOJ	Department of Justice (Philippines)
DP	Democratic Progressive Party (Malawi)
DPP	Director of Public Prosecutions (Malawi)
DTI	Department of Trade and Industry (UK)

EBRD	European Bank for Reconstruction and Development
ECA	Export Credit Agency
ECGD	Export Credit Guarantee Department (UK)
EDF	European Development Fund
EIB	European Investment Bank
ENEL	Empresa Nicaragüense de Electricidad
ENITEL	Empresa Nicaragüense de Telecomunicaciones
EU	European Union
FCPA	Foreign Corrupt Practices Act (US)
FOI	Freedom of Information
FRELIMO	Frente de Libertação de Moçambique (Mozambique)
FSLN	Frente Sandinista de Liberación Nacional (Nicaragua)
GEL	Georgian Lari (currency)
GES	Ghana Education Service
GNP	gross national product
GOCC	Government Owned and Controlled Corporations
GON	Government of Nicaragua
GORBI	Georgian Opinion Research Business International
GPS	Ghana Police Service
GRECO	Group of States Against Corruption
HC	House of Commons (UK)
HIPC	Highly Indebted Poor Countries
IADB	Interamerican Development Bank
ICC	International Chamber of Commerce
ICRG	International Country Risk Guide
IDA	International Development Association
IDB	Interamerican Development Bank
IDC	International Development Select Committee (UK)
IDR	Integrity Development Review
IFC	International Finance Corporation
IFI	International Financial Institution
IGR	Institutional and Governance Review
IISMI	Iligan Integrated Steel Mills, Inc. (Philippines)
IMF	International Monetary Fund
INAA	Instituto Nicaragüense de Acueductos y Alcantarillado Sanitario
INDEM	Information Science for Democracy
INTERBANK	Banco Intercontinental (Nicaragua)
IPS	Industrial Promotions Services (Kenya) Ltd
IRIN	Integrated Regional Information Networks (UN)
IRN	International Rivers Network

IT	Information Technology
K	Kwacha, Malawi unit of currency
KKM	Daniel Kaufmann and Aart Kraay, Massimo Mastruzzi (WB)
LHDA	Lesotho Highlands Development Authority
LHDC	Lesotho National Development Corporation
MCA	Millennium Challenge Account
MCP	Malawi Congress Party
MIA	Ministry of Interior Affairs (Georgia)
MNC	Multinational Corporation
MODULTECSA	Módulos Técnicos y Servicios (Nicaragua)
MRA	Malawi Revenue Authority
MSCE	Malawi Schools Certificate of Education
NGO	Non-governmental Organization
NHDC	National Housing Development Corporation (Jamaica)
NPM	New Public Management
NSWMA	The National Solid Waste Management Scandal (Jamaica)
OAS	Organization of American States
OECD	Organization for Economic Co-operation and Development
OGCC	Office of Government Corporate Counsel (Philippines)
OSI	Open Society Institute
PAC	Parliamentary Public Accounts Committee (Malawi, Jamaica)
PAGC	Presidential Anti-Graft Commission (Philippines)
PAL	Philippine Air Lines
PBMA	The Public Bodies Management and Accountability (Act) (Jamaica)
PC	personal computer
PCAGC	Presidential Commission against Graft and Corruption (Philippines)
PCIJ	Philippine Centre for Investigative Journalism
PCPEA	President's Committee on Public Ethics and Accountability (Philippines)
PDD	Partido para a Paz, Democracia e Desenvolvimento (Mozambique)
PEA	Public Estates Authority (Philippines)
PEFA	Public Expenditure and Financial Accountability Programme
PEIR	Public Expenditure and Institutional Review

PER	Public Expenditure Review
PETRONIC	Empresa Nicaragüense del Petróleo
PETS	Public Expenditure Tracking Survey
PIMO	Partido Independente de Moçambique (Mozambique)
PLC	Partido Liberal Constitucionalista (Nicaragua)
PNP	People's National Party (Jamaica)
PRI	Institutional Revolutionary Party (Mexico)
PRIDE	The Programme for Resettlement and Integrated Development Enterprise (Jamaica)
PRS	Political Risk Services Group
RA	Republic Act (Philippines)
RENAMO	Resistência Nacional Moçambicana (Mozambique)
RN	Republic of Nicaragua
ROSC	Reports on the Observance of Standards and Codes
SA	South Africa
SGR	Strategic Grain Reserve (Malawi)
SHG	Self-help Group
SIDA	Swedish International Development Agency
SSA	Sub-Saharan Africa
STAE	Secretariado Téchnico de Administração Eleitoral (Mozambique)
SWS	Social Weather Stations
TCTA	Trans-Caledon Tunnel Authority (Lesotho/South Africa)
TI	Transparency International
UDF	United Democratic Front, political party in Malawi
UN	United Nations
UNCAC	United Nations Convention Against Corruption
UNDP	United Nations Development Programme
UNO	Unión Nacional Opositora (Nicaragua)
UNODCCP	United Nations Office for Drug Control and Crime Prevention
US	United States (of America)
USAID	United States Agency for International Development
USD	United States' dollars
USSR	Union of Soviet Socialist Republics
WAS	World Aid Section (UK, DTI)
WB	World Bank
WBI	World Bank Institute

Part I
Introduction

1

Political Development and Corruption: Why 'Right Here, Right Now!'?

Sarah Bracking

The anti-corruption campaign is a paradox, with both inspiring and tragic elements. On the one hand, it would only be possible alongside the rise of global social movements and a new and vibrant civil society which articulates the cosmopolitan language of political reform and a better world, and catalyses such strategic victories as the 'Rose' and 'Orange' revolutions. On the other, the campaign may be one of the final episodes in a redundant development intervention paradigm, illustrating as it does the weaknesses in conception, delivery, resources and context that accompany the expert-led, sanitised, technocratic and medicalised view of the development subject and process. It has produced, in a fifteen-year period, an industry of consultants, organisations, and technologies bounded in the discourse of combat and high moral velocity. People have been urged to 'fight' corruption, to 'combat' its causes and effects, to wage a 'war' against the degradation of the social fabric, and to rally around a moral standard of integrity and principal. To accompany the effort, new field technologies, rather like an army's tools and weapons, have been designed and propagated: integrity workshops, peer review workshops, disclosure of assets, anti-corruption codes and best practice for civil servants, guidelines on conflict of interest, summarised within the iconic Transparency International (TI) *Sourcebook* (2000; for practical handbooks see also, Organisation for Economic Cooperation and Development (OECD), 2002, 2005; Spector, ed., 2005). The mode of policy transfer has been largely vertical from North to South, but with staged and boxed examples of where best practice has been found in the lands of the 'Other' (see Minogue, 2002).

What is unusual about this is that such a great effort should be mobilised around a concept – corruption – which, while morally loaded, actually refers to a wide range of discrete and differing social practices (Williams,

3

1999: 511; Hutchcroft, 1997; Brown and Cloke, 2004: 282–4). When these are disaggregated and the war fought against its components the effort of language looks rather more precocious: 'the war against small acts of theft by civil servants', or 'combating the pilfering of business expenses by senior executives'.

Indeed much corruption looks rather mundane in comparison, and while its victims are nonetheless real, in that all diversion of resources in a socialised space to a private pocket is at the expense of the public as a whole, victims are not necessarily immediately apparent. Table 1.1 summarises the many different social practices that 'corruption' refers to, and the work of aggregation and summary that the concept is being required to do.[1] Olivier de Sardan, for example, would include 'nepotism, abuse of power, embezzlement and various forms of misappropriation, influence peddling, prevarication, insider trading and abuse of the public purse' (1999, 27; cited in Andvig et al., 2001, 49), while others, following Scott (1972, 7–8) delineate other behaviours tending toward corruption as 'proto-corruption'.

The most perennial definition of corruption, however, makes it sound very neat and simple, the abuse of public office for 'private economic gain' (Rose-Ackerman, 1999: 75). This is the definition preferred by the World Bank (1997: 8), although it is now a well established critique of this definition that it consigns corruption spacially quite firmly in the public sector (see Polzer, 2001; Brown and Cloke, 2004, 283–4), and within a positivist neoliberal world view where rational economic behaviour is embedded epistemologically in self-interested perpetrators who have succumbed to temptation because of inadequate regulation and sanction.[2] This book will instead use the concept in a sociological sense, understanding behaviour as socially located and purposive, rather than a problem of 'natural' human nature (see also Jain ed., 2001; Szeftel, 2000: 291– 5). This chapter will now progress by examining the definition of corruption further, by academic discipline; and then by reviewing donor and IFI use of the concept, before returning to the central contribution of this book and its chapters. The concluding chapter then returns to reviewing the work of the global package of anti-corruption solutions on offer, summarising hazards in the donor approach, before offering some possible means to reduce corruption globally.

Definitions of corruption by academic discipline

Politics

The mainstream view of corruption has long historical routes in traditions of classical republicanism and neoclassical political economy, wherein

Table 1.1: Different types of corruption

	Definition	Involves
Administrative corruption or bureaucratic corruption	Illicit payments required from users by civil servants in the (often distorted and arbitrary) implementation of existing regulations, policies and laws.	A wide constituency is usually involved, experienced by citizens as harassment in their efforts to obtain even small administrative goods. Companies typically seek tax advantages, licences or influence on the formation of rules and law.
Petty corruption	Refers to these small acts, or rent-taking actions, by civil servants. Bribery, influencing, and gift giving are sometimes seen as different forms of petty corruption.	Public administrators, particularly those with direct encounters with members of the public, who accept bribes for expediting documents or, in the case of the police, not charging a suspect.
Graft	Involves the utilisation of public resources to serve individual or private interests.	Use of resources, time or facilities by a staff member (without a transaction with an external person). Often used interchangeably with corruption.
Influencing	Forcing a decision in one's favour.	Political lobbying is a form of influencing and is legitimate, but secretive contacts or suspicion of favouritism or influence that are suspected to be disproportionate to public interest may be considered as corrupt.
Bureaucratic corruption		'[W]here individuals pay money . . . to get in or to get on . . . (and) a moneyless form of corruption, where officials insert friends, relatives, political supporters and so on into public jobs which, without the official's influence, they would not obtain . . . moneyless corruption, called "patronage" here, is important and insidious.' (U4, 2005)

(Continued)

Table 1.1: (Continued)

	Definition	Involves
Political corruption	Often conflated with grand or high-level corruption: the misuse of entrusted power by political leaders. More specific meaning is corruption within the political or electoral process.	The use of resources, machinery, personnel, and authority to perpetuate one's position, such as during electoral campaigns, corruption in political finance such as vote buying, the use of illicit funds, the sale of appointments and abuse of state resources (TI, 2004)
Political patronage (clientelism) and nepotism	Government resources are directed to patrons, clients, family or ethnic clan of office holders.	'[I]n many countries the "patron" can present himself or herself as a social altruist, discharging an obligation to political supporters, family members and others.' (U4, 2005)
High-level corruption	The misuse of high public office, public resources or public responsibility for private, personal or group gain.	This term is often used interchangeably with grand corruption, or endemic corruption.
State capture	Private payments to public officials, and the 'capture' of their area of jurisdiction, in order to affect laws, rules, decrees, regulations or capture resources, for example, contracts.	Firms, who need to pay, and the public in general, whose interests are sidelined

the classical binary dichotomies of public and private, and economic and political first become central to what later emerges as social science epistemology. For example, Skinner summarises that Machiavelli asserts:

> we are generally reluctant to cultivate the qualities that enable us to serve the common good. Rather we tend to be 'corrupt', a term of art the republican theorists habitually use to denote our natural tendency to ignore the claims of our community as soon as they seem to conflict with the pursuit of our own immediate advantage . . . how can naturally self-interested citizens be persuaded to act virtuously, such that they can hope to maximise a freedom which, left to themselves, they will infallibly throw away? (Skinner, 1999: 170)

In this 'men' are seen to have a self-interested nature, such that institutional and legal regulation is foregrounded: Machiavelli's solution is that 'it is laws that make them (men) good' (cited in Skinner, 1999: 170). In the later tradition of contractarian political thought (Hobbes and Locke), a similar conclusion arises, although the basis of human nature has shifted somewhat in conception, in that law is seen to preserve individual liberty from threats of corruption.

Modern political science borrows heavily from these traditions, and with a strong institutionalist tradition, tends to define and explain corruption within the ambit of the abuse of public trust and power, within weak political institutions, sometimes very convincingly (see Johnson, 2005; Nicholls et al., 2006). A series of deficiencies are associated with corruption, such as weak political competition, underdeveloped civil society, insufficient public service integrity and ethics, and weak democratic structures (see della Porta and Vannucci, 1999; Doig and Theobald, eds, 2000; Heidenheimer and Johnston, eds. 2001). In classic political development texts corruption is seen as a by-product of modernisation (Huntington, 1968). Unsurprisingly, this explanatory base leads to policy emphasis on strengthening institutions and voice mechanisms. More composite explanations collect a number of factors together in explanation, such as the policies of a particular country, its bureaucratic traditions, 'cultural factors', political development, and political system as well as historical trends (Collier, 2005).

In the politics and development subdiscipline of development studies, or in the political development tradition more generally, there are also specific texts concerning corruption, which, during the last fifty years or so, have changed dramatically from a pragmatic or normatively neutral position, toward the current orthodoxy that corruption is an anathema to development (see Chapter. 3). For example, in 1973, the eminent Sir Arthur Lewis argued that:

> corruption is just a payment for service. Provided that the required bribes are reasonably small, having regard to the profit involved in the transaction to which they relate, and provided also that they can be foreseen when entering into contracts, they are just a form of costs like any other and they are passed on to the consumer in prices. (Lewis 1973: 409)

Later, Theobald argued that corruption could assist in capital formation, foster entrepreneurial abilities and allow business interests to penetrate bureaucracy (Theobald, 1990). Many of the more positive texts were written during the dominance of economic approaches in development (see Toye, 1993). Now, however, overwhelming evidence is said to exist that corruption is a major obstacle to economic development, good governance and development; and that countries with high levels of corruption experience poor economic performance (World Development Report, 2000).[3]

There are also theories of corruption, principally within studies of African politics which are not strictly within the development discipline, which explain corruption in relation to the supposed specificity of African political systems, using the concept of patrimonialism, (or *neo*patrimonialism for those who view this specificity as a return to an earlier pre-colonial system of authority). A comprehensive definition of this was given by Bratton and van de Walle:

> In neopatrimonial regimes, the chief executive maintains authority through personal patronage, rather than through ideology or law . . . relationships of loyalty and dependence pervade a formal political and administrative system and leaders occupy bureaucratic offices less to perform public service than to acquire personal wealth and status. The distinction between private and public interests is purposely blurred . . . personal relationships . . . constitute the foundation and superstructure of political institutions. The interaction between the 'big man' and his extended retinue defines African politics, from the highest reaches of the presidential palace to the humblest village assembly. (1994: 458–9)

Developing the theme of the difference and distinction of the public and private spheres still further, Bayart wrote similarly that:

> African political societies are duplicated between, on the one hand, a *pays legal*, a legal structure which is the focus of attention for

multilateral donors and Western states, and on the other hand, a *pays reel* where real power is wielded. In extreme cases this duplication can lead to the existence of a hidden structure which surrounds, or even controls, the official occupant of the presidential throne, rather like a board of directors which appoints an executive to carry out its decisions. (2000: 229–30)

These, and a plethora of other authors, see a 'deep' or endemic corruption embedded in the systemic mode of everyday life and resident in political institutions in so far as these are separate at all from the private realm, in neopatrimonial African regimes (for example Bayart, et al., 1999; Chabal and Daloz, 1999; reviewed in Bracking, 2006). Reno now famously gave the hidden or *pays réel* realm of politics the term 'shadow state' (1995, 2000).

Arguably, where states differ most from the forms expected within hegemonic (neo)liberal political theory the task of the political scientist in understanding corruption becomes the most challenging. For example, countries under the yoke of the Soviet system until 1991 were not then termed corrupt, since other concepts were used of a grander and more totalising magnitude, such as 'authoritarian', or 'totalitarian'. Similarly, the older generation of African dictatorships of, for example Mobuto Sese Seke, HK Banda, Idi Amin or Sani Abacha, were not termed corrupt so much as more generally defined as dictatorships. In other words, where a regime is truly nefarious and mendacious, anti-corruption policy is a luxury relative to the need for more wholesale interventionism, of whatever problematic form, to arrest suffering caused by warlordism, kleptocracy, ethnic cleansing, political violence and torture, or deliberate government-sponsored famine.

In this sense, it is worth remembering that relative to a fairly recent past the 'Third Wave' of democratisation of the 1990s has ushered in for many a new more democratic dispensation, which in historical terms makes further work on reducing corruption meaningful and possible, because certain essential standards of polity have been already met. Theories of 'socialist corruption' are now retrospectively possible, while a generation of African dictators are sliding into retirement, without either dying in post or being removed by military coups. Similarly, in Latin America, a new wave of democratic social democracy, although obviously not free of corruption, is, nonetheless, slowly sweeping aside traditions of elite or military rule. In Europe, meanwhile, the problems of corruption have clearly resurfaced in established democracies, such that theories of political development and democratisation do well to finally and conclusively jettison modernisation approaches, which viewed corruption as a residual characteristic of the historical stage of under-development, in favour of the view that corruption, like democracy, is a matter of degree in all polities (Neild, 2002; Beetham et al., 2002).

Economics

A classical economic theory of corruption sees it as one way among several of allocating scarce resources, where the rational behaviour of market actors in respect to incentives and rents explains corruption outcomes (see Mishra, 2005; Fitzsimons, Chapter 3). New institutional economics has broadened analysis of economic agency to further identify the role of institutions, in addition to individuals, in producing corrupt transactions, opportunism and transactional costs (Lambsdorff et al., 2004; Fitzsimons, Chapter 3).

Within the classical approach, an 'optimal amount of corruption' is possible, in terms of 'marginal social cost', whereby

> Corruption is a variant of economic choice, and like any other economic choice is determined by its price on the market' . . . [and] corrupt incentives are the nearly inevitable consequences of *all* government attempts to control market forces – even the 'minimal' state. (Caiden cited in de Leon 1993, 13)

Here, corruption is explained as a species of rent-seeking, which in the functionalist school is further theorised in terms of potential benefits to 'getting things done'. Caiden further summarises that:

> the availability of personal gain via public corruption recruits skilled personnel into an otherwise unattractive, unrewarding bureaucracy, motivates an otherwise lackadaisical administrative system into the timely actions necessary for economic development, and provides socialising services to otherwise disenfranchised parts of the political system. (Caiden cited in de Leon 1993, 13)

While the functionalist school is less in vogue during the current anti-corruption campaign, since its observations sit uneasily with the moral proselytising therein, the basis of the economic approach does still underpin dominant donor explanations of corruption.

The policy implications of such a dominance are manifold, leading to anti-corruption policy which aims to cut back government's role in the economy; stop, or privatise, as many government functions as possible (with plural myopias with regard to the actual opportunities for corrupt behaviour that this widespread privatisation policy has created); and legalise or formalise bureaucratic transactions which were previously a source of rents. In short, the political culture of a country is largely left intact, ready to exploit the renewed opportunities for corruption that a globalising neoliberalism creates (Brown and Cloke, 2005). The civil service devolution and downsizing that often results from marketisation is also not the panacea for reducing rent-seeking opportunities that neoclassical economic theory suggests (McCourt, 2000; Nunberg, 1994), while in sub-Saharan Africa, civil service downsizing and the reduction of government functions creates a particular threat to the security and reproduction of elites (Szeftel, 2000).

Political economy

The definition of corruption in political economy is particularly problematic, given that 'economy' and 'politics' themselves eschew stable ontological referents. This assertion has been similarly argued by Castree for the concepts' economy' and 'culture', who continues that it is better to view them (these latter) as 'two performative signifiers', performing in many contexts rather than simply, or easily referent to one corresponding 'real-world' phenomenon (2004: 206–8). In a similar methodological turn, it is useful to interrogate 'economy' and 'politics' cognisant that economics is culturally embedded (following Granovetter, 1985) and also politically grounded; and that the economic is re-presented in culturally specific discourses (for example, Barnes, 1996) and also in political discourse. Thus post-structuralist political economy examines conceptual interrelationships, which is a different task to the mainstream positivist study of 'real-world' phenomena, limited generally to how the institutions of market and state affect economic performance. Needless to say, current work in political economy is split between these two positions, or schools, with the majority of work still carried out in the latter.

Here, corruption is explored using post-structuralist methodology, where we examine how different actors have attempted to fix 'cultures of corruption' or 'corrupt' behaviour within structures of global power and political economy, or as an expression of particular political conflicts (Szeftel, 2000: 291, citing Colin Leys 1965). In short, what the concept *is* is less interesting that what it *does*, a shift in emphasis which also allows us to put aside the somewhat stale debate about which features of corruption are universal or culturally relative. Thus Polzer (2001) deconstructs ideas of corruption within World Bank documentation to reveal the instrumentality and contradictory governmentality in terms of the South, wherein 'corruption' is used to assign normative culpability singularly with the 'Other' (2001). Despite promises to seek out the 'rogue' traders in World Bank projects, corruption is only viewed as systemic in non-Western cultural contexts.

Corruption becomes a strategic resource within World Bank discourse, because of its polysemism. More generally, as several chapters here illustrate, corruption is a key global signifier in contemporary political discourse, as much as in development discourse, and acts to indicate illegitimacy, while its use is also a barometer of geopolitical position. It is a disciplinary governance concept, following the Commission for Africa report, in the latest chapter of the 'short history' of corruption in development (Tesh, 1999, cited in Polzer 2001). It is also, from the perspective of the not so powerful, the key signifier in popular political discourse when discussing the relative merits of rulers and their opponents in situations of contested authority in sub-Saharan African states. The moralisms it invokes are the pegs on which people's political views are hung, whether elite Northern institutional 'views' or popular ones: was his or her wealth, or the government of a country's power, legitimately secured, or corruptly engineered? In sum, the concept of corruption has become a ubiquitous normative labeller of different economic behaviours, within contested political discourses on privilege and power.

Economic anthropology

According to Andvig et al., who cite Olivier de Sardan (1996), some social norms and behavioural logics studied by anthropology facilitate corruption. They include:

> fluid and always negotiable 'rules of the game', multiple norm systems, the many brokers and middlemen, gift-giving practices, networks of solidarity and collusion, extended family solidarity and predatory (neo-patrimonial) forms of authority. (2001: 46)

They continue that the narrowness of the rational-legal paradigm for defining corruption – as private abuse of the Weberian public space – is clear when compared to the anthropological insights gained by examining these socio-cultural logics informing everyday practices. Thus, while the rational-legal paradigm understands corruption as the non-respect of the distinction between public and private, the notion of public office is located, and derives from, the Weberian model of public administration, which may differ from understandings of space elsewhere. For example, the public space within many new state formations is often governed by the liberationist party which sees itself as owning 'public resources' for the benefit of the erstwhile nationalists (see Speck, this volume; Bracking, 2005).

Anthropologists have a long history of examining how the public might be understood in a non-Weberian sense to explain practices of resource allocation. Myrdal began with the observation that actual bureaucratic rules might not correspond to official rules and may be more innovative (1968); Wood wrote of the non-transferability of Weberian rationality to other societies (Wood, 1994: 520); while Price argued that the Indian civil servant responds to demands using competing codes of practice which may or may not correspond to bureaucratic norms, and may occlude them (1999: 318). Ward even suggested that corruption humanises the workings of bureaucracy (1989), while Gupta, again in reference to the Indian civil servant, found that the 'state' and 'society', as categories, 'are descriptively inadequate to the lived realities that they purport to represent' (1995: 384, cited in Andvig, 2001: 50). As Andvig et al. point out, the legal public definition is problematic because it assumes that laws prohibit corrupt behaviour; that legal frameworks are neutral and non-political (citing Williams, 1999); that all corrupt behaviour is covered by laws; and that there is an invariant correspondence between legality and morality (2001: 48–9). In fact, the legality of various practices will vary; corruption is a 'social act', a transaction which 'is now a legal one, now illegal, depending upon the social context' (2001: 49).

Ethnographers have studied examples of different sociocultural logics of gift giving and solidarity networks to show how habits and commonplace practices inform actors' perception of legitimacy. In Bangladesh, for example, there is reported an almost general obligation of mutual assistance (Andvig et al., 2001: 57), while in Russia, 'blat' signifies 'the use of personal networks and informal contacts to obtain goods and services in short supply and to find a way around formal procedures' (Ledeneva, 1998: 1; cited in Andvig et al., 2001: 58). While no money is involved here, exchanges are still reportedly grounded in actors' mutual utility and are viewed as legitimate. Interestingly, in this volume, Co and Dadalauri both note the importance of cultural 'gift-giving' in common explanations of corruption in the Philippines and Georgia respectively, but suggest that the good nature of the people is here abused, since corruption more correctly and centrally involves the abuse of high political and economic position. It may be that the anthropological approach served to point out the importance of the social and cultural context, seen from actors' own points of view, but that without the insights from political economy the pervasive role of power and discourse in conditioning these contexts is missing.

Discourse theory and corruption

It is not unreasonable to argue that common (mis)representations of developing states underpin development policy on corruption, the strategic use of the concept, and the way it is understood within a racialised development discourse. For example, the differences between the North and South are still commonly represented by binary descriptions and characterisations, with the South suffering from deficits and a 'lack of' attributes of the North, while the latter remains pristine despite evidence to the contrary (see Bracking, 2006). When development is understood as a discourse, knowledge can be seen to compete in different paradigms to create 'reality', or 'fix' our meaning of corruption in a strategic manner. Here, development is a 'political technology', *a constructed collective discourse* which aligns and subjects countries into particular 'fields of action' (Foucault, 1983: 221; Foucault, 1994: 237) where corruption is used to signify their deficiency. Within this discourse, statistical data, such as within the *Corruption Perception Index* (CPI), creates intelligibility in an abstracted ahistorical manner, supporting the dominant view of reality, such that knowledge is created conditioned by the power and positionality of those party to constructing the index.

Thus, the Corner House asked the International Development Select Committee in Britain to consider:

the institutionalized racism that assumes the Third World to be inherently corrupt and corruptible and which thereby underwrites bribery even where nominally accountable procedures are in place. (HC, 2001)

And compares this to the:

Evidence presented to the committee from pressure groups suggested western businesses paid bribes conservatively estimated at £53bn a year, with the arms and construction industries the worst offenders. (*Guardian*, 4, April 2001)

The explanation of such inconsistencies is found in discourse theory, that representations of 'crisis' and problems in the South serve the powerful: they demand intervention from the development industry while reassuring superiority (see Crush, 1995; Cowen and Shenton, 1995). In this, the invocation of 'a crisis of corruption', such as when corruption is portrayed as the most significant dysfunction of developing states (Commission on Africa, 2004), follows a similar pattern to crises discovered elsewhere, in terms of poverty, governance or economic growth (Escobar, 1997).

Development knowledge retains contradictions because sometimes causation is depicted in a culturally relative manner, and sometimes universally, depending on the strategic interests of those actors exercising power. Thus, more often than not, corruption is seen as culturally relative (to the South), while expertise is given a universal value (but principally resides in the North!). We can see how heuristic contradictions exist in development practice: as argued in Bracking (Chapter 14), development project contracting is inscribed with various meanings for similar anthropological practices and business behaviours, but these are *obscured* by discursive universalisms. Thus, developmental concession (closed tenure systems for development projects for western experts) is understood as benevolent expertise; while Southern state policy on empowerment (closed tenure systems for development projects which build African economic and political elites) is viewed as corrupt, despite their anthropological similarities.

What is particular to the political economy of development, from the vantage point of discourse theory, is that the spatial context of economic activity is central to classification and meaning, including in corruption discourse. The pathology of the corrupt Southern state, which key donor documents such as the Commission for Africa report perpetuate, contributes to the construction of a residual 'spacial sink' in poor countries, where country risk assessment, shaped by perceptions of endemic corruption, prevents 'free' (incoming) associational economic activity, including investment, thus guaranteeing continued economic residuality and dependence.

Donor views of corruption

The meanings of corruption which are strategically used by international financial institutions (IFIs) and the governments of rich 'donor' governments in international development, coalesce around the 'abuse of public office for private gain' (World Bank, 1997: 8). Corruption is largely understood in a neoliberal, economistic anti-state paradigm which emphasises politics as a source of rents, such that anti-corruption policy unduly relies on deregulation (to reduce opportunities for officials to collect bribes) and privatisation. Policy on corruption is thus deeply embedded within the wider constructions of global neoliberal governance (see Szeftel, 2000b; Marquette, 2003; Brown and Cloke, 2004; 2005), and replicates the contradictions therein between the sacrosanct avowed protection of sovereignty, and the indirect abuse of sovereignty that conditionality incurs in practice. Political conditionality and policy on anti-corruption have become central within good governance programming, with anti-corruption policy used to positively encourage greater accountability and democracy, and conditionality employed as a punitive driver to persuade recalcitrant governments into better governance practice (Doig and Marquette, 2004). The historiography and detail of the anti-corruption campaign is further detailed by Ivanov, in the next chapter.

Suffice to say, that corruption was not always viewed as such a bad thing, but that views have coalesced around its infamy in a quite recent past. Following the end of the Cold War, key international donors and the IFIs redefined their missions to include anti-corruption work, for both self-interested and wider, more altruistic reasons (reviewed in Doig and Marquette, 2004: 200–2). The effort of turning the old Soviet Union into a succession of capitalist economies created huge opportunities for new elites, under the not very watchful eye of international custodians, to steal, bribe and plunder their way to sustainable privilege, while the ousting of many of the old dictators in Africa, with some notable exceptions, caused enough light to fall on the institutions of the state for wider corrupt practices to come into view. The 'free market' conception of economic development within *Poverty Reduction Strategy* processes (as in their forerunner, the discredited structural adjustment processes) continued to stymie the state's ability to regulate the anarchic and amoral business practices of both international firms and local equivalents. Scandals and corruption grew, and were eventually 'discovered' by the World Bank and other donors (Polzer, 2001; Tesh, 1999), strangely without any associated epiphanies in relation to their own implicated roles, but certainly pushed by the ever growing influence of a vociferous international civil society toward the end of the century.

Now, corruption is perceived as being inimical to national development, but critically, similarly nationally sited, 'over there'. For example, the British Department for International Development (DFID), in its 1997 White Paper on Eliminating World Poverty, proposed measures to help build sound and accountable government in a bid to help poor people (1997: 30). The consequences of corruption advanced by DFID for the poor are higher prices, fewer employment opportunities (due to market distortion), payments for public services which are supposed to be free, diversion of budgetary resources from poverty reduction into unproductive expenditure and repayment of debt accumulated by corrupt leaders, loss of tax and customs revenue, lowered economic growth as uncertainty puts off prospective investors, and reduced political representation as elites cling to power to exploit corruption opportunities (ibid.). Although some of these associations have been contested historically, the litany of negative effects has since reached hegemonic status, catalysing an unquestioned moral campaign. This book is designed to critically review policy and practice in the field of corruption and anti-corruption, which is not to say that the negative effects of corruption are denied. However, it is not the purpose of this book, as the methodology dictates, to assess the costs and benefits of corruption *per se*. Nor is it the book's intention to imply that *all* anti-corruption policy is flawed, or that *all* anti-corruption policy comes from the IFIs: developing countries' governments are initiators of policy in their own right, with a range of observable outcomes.

The structure of this book

The book will explore corruption and anti-corruption policy in various countries, from within and outside the development paradigm. It asks 'why now?', 'who does what?', and in 'what ways?' corruption is addressed in international development policy in countries and regions of East and Central Europe, Africa, Asia and Latin America where donors are more (for example in Ghana or Malawi) or less (in Russia, Georgia or Nigeria) influential, although influence, in its turn, is notoriously difficult to measure. The book finds that experiences of corruption and anti-corruption are plural, that interpretations of the problem are not fixed but culturally and spatially variant, and that policy itself is fluid and sometimes contradictory. We find no singular or universal outcome to correspond with the universal donor policy package.

Concluding the introductory Part I

In Chapter 2 Ivanov provides an historical overview of why corruption has become salient to development since the mid-1990s. It problematises the sense of novelty portrayed in development publications and the efficacy of the salience given to corruption in overall governance policy. Ivanov argues that anti-corruption policy can have a number of unintended and adverse effects on politics and society, which include a tendency to delegitimise and pathologise government in East and Central Europe. In Chapter 3, Fitzsimons reviews economic theories of corruption; how governments can act to reduce economic corruption; and then reviews the experience of anti-corruption policy from an economic perspective, suggesting that a 'wider institutional economics' would assist policy success. The overly economistic and traditional view of economic agency taken by the IFIs has reduced the impact of their regulatory interventions.

Part II: Anti-corruption policy and political change in case study countries

In Part II, we examine the historical development of political systems in Africa (Hall-Matthews, Okojie and Momoh), Asia (Co), East and Central Europe (Zagainova and Dadalauri), the Caribbean (Osei) and Central America (Brown, Cloke and Rocha) at varying levels of external influencing, in order to review how the institutionalist focus of donor reform has been mediated within structures of power and political economy. A pattern emerges whereby the overly moralist tones of the anti-corruption campaigns have met with resistance, particularly in the Eastern and Central Euroepan and African context; and where the overly insitutionalist approach has been rendered impotent in societies with powerful political and economic elites.

Hall-Matthews, in Chapter 4, examines the recent complex interplay of donor influence and domestic political manoeuvring around the anti-corruption campaign central to current Malawian political discourse. He questions how far this campaign actually serves anti-corruption and not individual political ambition, and how far donors are prepared to pursue anti-corruption above other objectives. In Malawi, a relatively new independent state, government office remains financially rewarding, and political society a source of personalistic scandal and intrigue into which donor influence and institutional monitoring are weakly integrated. In a regional context, and compared to a recent past, progress in accountability is in evidence, although the moralism of the anti-corruption campaign seems also to have encouraged a pre-existing proclivity for overly personalistic politics, accusation and counter-accusation, and displaced a more procedural oversight of generic policy.

In Chapter 5, on Nigeria, Okojie and Momoh explore aspects of recent anti-corruption institution-building in historical perspective, and question how far law and institution have actually arrested systemic corruption. The contest between the forces of democracy and autocracy is fully joined, but its outcome still remains difficult to predict, for the reasons Okojie and Momoh outline, not least because of the strategic integration of the Nigerian economy and its wealthy elite into world markets. Similarly to Co on the Philippines, Okojie and Momoh echo concerns that institutions *per se* may have little effect, where an (internationalised) political economy of corruption, built up historically under the infamous Marcos, or several Nigerian dictators, retains significant conditioning effects on the polity. Thus, in the Philippines, Chapter 6, the insitutional focus has had limited effect, due to a political economy dominated by unaccountable privilege and excessive wealth enjoyed by an economic and political elite outside the purview of the formal institutions of state. The long process of holistic democratisation required to bring economic power to account, has, however, begun. In the case of the Philippines, even the constitutional crisis of late 2005, is arguably overshadowed by the excesses of the Marcos era.

In Jamaica, Osei shows how the Westminster model of executive government, inherited from the era of British occupation, has resulted in political factions and cronyistic networks more powerful than the central institutions of state, which can effectively bypass new insitutional initiatives. The 'winner takes all' model of first past the post elections and executive government has encouraged just that to occur, as Osei presents us with an overview of the plethora of anti-corruption initiatives undertaken, alongside an account of recent high-level scandal. He suggests that wholesale institutional reform, in an additive process, has failed to recapture cronyistic power. Anti-corruption policy has been compromised by an inability to enforce pre-existing legislation; too much institutional initiative doing too little to change underlying culture and behaviour.

The questions arising from these chapters on Nigeria, Malawi, the Philippines and Jamaica, are whether there now *appears* to be more corruption because of the growth of institutional oversight and the hard work of civil society in monitoring government; whether corruption does indeed remain endemic and systemic; or whether the first signs of a reduction can be evinced due to the work of institutional reform and normative programming. However, a central problem also emerges, related to the two patterns noted above, that, in short, the anti-corruption campaign and policy package assumes an authoritative and benevolent central state, (authoritative in the sense that it can dominate other sites of power, and benevolent in the sense that its purpose is the pursuit of the public good) whereas in practice, and in various ways, this simply does not exist.

Zagainova and Dadalauri, in Chapters 7 and 8, develop the analysis of how economic corruption is embedded in social processes and cultural signification more generally, in reviews of the post-communist economies (Zagainova), and Georgia in particular (Dadalauri). They illustrate how particular processes of marketisation and the introduction of economic and political liberalisation are related to, and can generate corruption,[4] although trends in these countries show a decline in corruption overall, particularly in Georgia after the Rose revolution.

More specifically, Zagainova and Dadalauri agree that policy leverage from IFIs to rapidly conform to economic liberalisation measures led to corruption, while the same institutions were doing much to foreground the role of domestic political systems. While the binary divide between national and international influence is untenable, there are clearly complex processes at work to recruit the public to differing interpretations of social reality, guilt and blame. Nowhere is this underlined as adeptly as in Chapter 10, on Nicaragua (Brown, Cloke and Rocha), where the anti-corruption campaign was initially weakly pursued for geopolitical reasons, and then belatedly came alive only as evidence of grand corruption was forced into the public gaze by the persistent reporting of a resilient independent press. The inconstancy of donor influence, in contrast, was breathtaking.

The culpability of the 'global anti-corruption campaign' (Ivanov, Chapter 2) is thus found particularly well illustrated in these latter chapters on the former Soviet countries, evidenced in the standardisation and zeal of anti-corruption policy advice, despite the evidence of perverse effects. There is also in evidence a lack of coherence, rooted in the corrosive assumption that other external policy pressure, principally that advocating wholesale privatisation, is exogenous to anti-corruption policy and not within the remit of the institutions leading the governance campaign. This is despite the obvious role of privatisation policy in undermining public service regulation in the transition economies. In the case of Georgia, there is also the strategic decision to support a government brought to power on an anti-corruption agenda, and with significant investment of donor and Western interest, for geostrategic reasons, despite increasing failings with regard to integrity issues in the subsequent post-election period.

Relatedly, in most countries covered by this volume the discursive sense given by donors is that anti-corruption is their principal concern, as well as self standing in relation to others. However, in the Nicaraguan case in Chapter 10, as in the Georgian case in Chapter 8, the geopolitical agenda clearly overrides the anti-corruption and governance agendas, serving to unline that it is donor preference which is behind the forgrounding and/or de-emphasis of anti-corruption within a wider foreign policy remit. This failure to transparently depict anti-corruption policy as only one element in a broader process of social change, which itself is framed within several competing governance concerns, is most apparent when strategically important countries are being considered. This leaves an expedient lack of coherence and consistency to the anti-corruption campaigns in Georgia and Nicaragua, but also to a lesser extent in Malawi, as described in Chapter 4. We return to these issues during the course of the book and conclusion.

Part III: Donor policy in anti-corruption work by sector and issue

Part III contains chapters on donor intervention in governance, to assess how anti-corruption policy is practised in different sectors and policy areas: Alolo on gender and public management reform in Ghana; Speck on political finance in Mozambique; Bracking on the regulation of development finance; Heeks on technology transfer and Santiso on assistance to budgetary auditing in Latin America. The chapters variously illustrate two potentially contradictory conclusions: that 1) at the meso and micro policy levels intervention in anti-corruption is harvesting positive results, particularly illustrated within the chapters by Speck, Heeks and Santiso, as long as these are locally owned and initiated; but that 2) flaws in policy implementation are also still in evidence, particularly where anti-corruption policy is fashionable rather than part of a longer process of political reform and democratisation (Alolo, Heeks, and Bracking). When corruption policy is clumsily attached to other generic policy processes, such as within programmes of gender in public management (Alolo), but not adequately integrated, its implementation is flawed.

These implementation problems derive from various causes, illustrated here in the work of Alolo and Bracking, as, respectively: due to a fickle pursuit of fashionable trends, such as using gender mainstreaming to 'carry' anti-corruption policy (Alolo); and due to contradictory and limited perceptions of who is likely to be corrupt rooted in racialised worldviews, such as in pursuing development projects with ineffective regulation of Northern consultants (Bracking). These causes have in common the institutional and discursive weaknesses of international development policy and practice: its rarification and separateness from other policy areas; its spacial and racial divorce from comparable, complimentary and catalysing processes sited in the North; and its post-colonial mindset and pathologising of the 'Other'. Despite this context, however, the social agency of democratic change still, as in conclusion 1) has chances to breathe, leading to the contradictions of policy negotiation in practice.

Alolo looks in particular at the genealogy of intervention in the African public sector and modes of civil service reform, critically assessing the latest fashionable inclusion of 'gender mainstreaming' as the panacea for previous failure. In this, women are seen as less prone to corrupt behaviour than men, such that their very presence is predicted to reduce corruption. Alolo deconstructs this essentialist association, arguing that in fact women are not less prone overall to corrupt behaviour than are men, but that the justification and type of behaviour differs by gender, at least in her case study group of Ghanaian public servants. Similarly, Heeks provides a model of the inherent problems in transferring policy without consideration to domestic policy context, drawn from e-government interventions, but applicable to anti-corruption initiatives more generally. These problems of policy transfer and design seem to severally confound donor implementation, despite evidence that they are ubiquitous and could be tackled.

Meanwhile, Bracking writes of a policy sector, development finance, particularly sensitive to corrupt abuse, where an anti-corruption consideration built into generic policy is long overdue. Recent efforts to provide increased oversight of contracts and derivative business within the aid industry share the 'adjunct' model of policy transfer, (described above in relation to the chapters by Alolo and Heeks) where anti-corruption oversight is a poor relation of generic development policy and practice. Relatedly, Bracking's chapter illustrates a general myopia about the role of donor intervention *itself* in generating opportunities for corruption, which then remain unregulated and separate from other areas of policy. This exclusivity of anti-corruption policy from other areas of donor intervention is not restricted to the aid-generated private sector (as described in Bracking), but has been observed in other donor sectors and policy areas, notably, within poverty measurement and relief programmes in India (see Mukherjee, 2005). For example, research by Mukherjee (2005) has illustrated how a poverty measurement, targeting and relief exercise in West Bengal was pursued singularly and mechanically during 2002, despite evidence of widespread corruption, illustrating donor myopia in relation to the opportunities created by a poverty programme.

Speck, in this volume, reflects on the impact of accountability systems in regulating the political economy of party financing in Mozambique, in contradistinction to much Africanist literature which stresses the pathology of the African state in a generalist manner. Speck's chapter serves as a reminder that political reform did not start, and nor will it end, with the current phase of anti-corruption reform, and that democratisation of polities in their plural aspects remains the best insurance against corrupt practice. Catalysed at the end of the civil war in 1992 by global best practice in this area, political finance in Mozambique is relatively well-regulated, albeit in a political system retaining elements of cronyism. In a similar vein of illustrating institutionalised accountability processes which are established methods of improving government integrity, Santiso then provides a comprehensive overview of donor support to processes of improving fiscal governance in Latin America. He illustrates that development assistance has reflected increasing technical capacity and enhanced analytical capabilities in the area of managing public finances. IFIs here have shown a growing understanding of the importance of parliaments and wider political process, as opposed to merely the 'adjunct' external institutions, to enacting accountability. However, using the example of Nicaragua, he also illustrates how these substantial improvements can be emasculated by adverse political developments. These latter two chapters provide the best evidence to support proposition 1) above, that anti-corruption reform at an institutional and meso-level can produce positive results, and that the perverse effects of the anti-corruption campaign, in 2) above, are sited instead predominantly in the implementation of development policy, and more widely within the discursive and ideological framing of political change within global development discourse.

Part IV: Concluding the volume

The concluding chapter in Part IV reflects on the perverse effects of anti-corruption policy in political development, themes and issues that the chapters bring to the fore and possible remedies for an improved global integrity policy (Bracking and Ivanov). It remains difficult to assign any positive gains of more prudent and accountable government to anti-corruption policy, although we are reluctant to abandon the effort altogether in view of the considerable harm corruption does. Also, at such a level of aggregation, assigning social change to a particular public policy is inherently and generically difficult. Thus, this review of the campaign against corruption ends with a call for more contextual understandings of the politics and political economy of different countries and areas; reform of policy to include the role of Northern states and global governance practices in perpetuating corruption, including consideration of the role of Northern-originated development policy in framing the field of action of social agents in the South more generally; and more consistent policies of solidarity with those clearly abused by corruption and malevolent governance.

Notes

1. Many of the contributors to this volume, and Osei, Co and Zagainova in particular, contributed to this table.
2. There are numerous books, which adopt a positivist methodology and then propose practical activities and policies through which corruption can be 'solved', many concentrating on Asia. For example Bhargava and Bolongaita (2003); Kidd and Richter (eds) (2003).
3. Thanks to Philip Osei for these citations, which appeared in a draft of his chapter.
4. Similar to Holmes (2006), although Holmes' conclusion, that neoliberalism has both caused the increase in corruption, while being simultaneously the panacea for solving it, is not shared by our authors, who give weight to communist structures in causing corruption, and little weight to neoliberalism in solving it.

References

Andvig, Jens Chr. and Odd-Helge, Fjeldstad with Amundsen, I., Sissener, T. and Soreide, T. (2001), *Corruption: a Review of Contemporary Research*, R 2001: 7, Chr. Michelsen Institute

Barnes, T. (1996), *Logics of dislocation*, New York, Guildford

Bayart, J-P. (2000), 'Africa in the World: a History of Extraversion', *African Affairs*, 99, 217–267

Bayart, J-P., Ellis, S. and Hibou, B. (eds) (1999) *The Criminalization of the State in Africa*, Oxford, Bloomington and Indianapolis: International African Institute, in association with James Currey; Indiana University Press

Beetham, D., Bracking, S., Kearton, I. and Weir, S. (2002), *International IDEA Handbook on Democracy Assessment*, Kluwer Law International and International IDEA (as above)

Bhargava, V. and Bolongaita, E. (2003), *Challenging Corruption in Asia: Case Studies and a Framework for Action*, Washington, World Bank

Bracking, S. (2005), 'Development Denied: Autocratic militarism in post-election Zimbabwe', *Review of African Political Economy*, 32, 104/5, 341–57

Bracking, S. (2006) 'Contemporary political economies of sub-Saharan Africa: the post-colonial legacy of multiple narratives', *Afriche e Orienti*, Special Issue II, Occidente e Africa: Democrazia e nazionalismo dalla prima alla seconda transizione, pp. 85–102

Bratton, M. and van de Walle, N. (1994), 'Neo-patrimonial regimes and political transition in Africa' in *World Politics*, vol. XLVI, pp. 453–89

Brown, E. and Cloke, J. (2004), 'Neoliberal Reform, Governance and Corruption in the South: Assessing the International Anti-Corruption Crusade', *Antipode*, 36, 2, 272–94

Brown, E. and Cloke, J. (2005) 'Neoliberal Reform, Governance and Corruption in Central America: Exploring the Nicaraguan Case', *Political Geography*, 24, pp. 601–30

Caiden, N. (1979), 'Shortchanging the Public', *Public Administration Review*, 39, 3, 294–303

Castree, N. (2004), 'Economy and culture are dead! Long live economy and culture!', in *Progress in Human Geography*, vol. 28, no. 2, pp. 204–26

Chabal, P. and Daloz, J-P. (1999), *Africa works: disorder as political instrument*, Oxford, Bloomington, Indiana; James Currey; Indiana University Press

Collier, P. (2005), *Political Corruption in the Caribbean Basin: Constructing a Theory to Combat Corruption*, London, Routledge

Commission on Africa (2004), *Our Common Interest: a Report of the Commission for Africa*, Commission for Africa

Cowen, M. and Shenton, R. (1995), 'The Invention of Development', in Crush, J. (ed.) *Power of Development*, London, Routledge, pp. 27 –43

Crush, J. (ed.) (1995), *Power of Development*, London, Routledge,

de Leon, P. (1993), *Thinking about Political Corruption*, New York, M. E. Sharpe

Della Porta, D. and Vannucci, A. (1999) *Corrupt Exchanges: Actors, Resources, and Mechanisms of Political Corruption*, New Jersey, Aldine Transaction

Department for International Development (DFID), (1997) *White Paper on Eliminating World Poverty*, Cm 3789, London, HMSO

Doig, A. and Marquette, H. (2005), 'Corruption and democratisation: the litmus test of international donor agency intentions?', *Futures*, 37, pp. 199–213

Doig, A. and Theobald, R. (eds) (2000), *Corruption and Democratisation*, Frank Cass

Escobar, A. (1997), 'The Making and Unmaking of the Third World through Development', in Rahnema, M. and Bawtree, V. (eds), *The Post-Development Reader*, London, Zed Books, pp. 85–93

Foucault, M. (1983), 'Afterword: the Subject and Power', in *Michel Foucault: Beyond Structuralism and Hermeneutics*, Hubert Dreyfus and Paul Rabinow, University of Chicago Press, 208–39

Foucault, M. (1994), *Dits et écrits*, vol. 4, Paris, Éditions Gallimard

Granovetter, M. (1985), 'Economic action and social structure: the problem of embeddedness', *American Journal of Sociology*, 91: 481–510

Gupta, A. (1995), 'Blurred boundaries: the discourse of corruption, the culture of politics, and the imagined state', *American Ethnologist*, 375–402

Heidenheimer, A. J. and Johnston, M. (eds) (2001) *Political Corruption: Concepts and Contexts*, New Brunswick, Transaction Publishers

Holmes, L. T. (2006), *Rotten States? Corruption, Post-communism and Neo-liberalism*, Durham, Duke University Press

House of Commons (HC) (2001), Fourth Report, *Corruption*, 4 April 2001, HC 39 I Report and Proceedings of the Committee, and HC-39 II Minutes of Evidence and Appendices, accessed at www.publications.parliament.uk/pa/cm/cmintdev.htm 20 June 2001

Hutchcroft, P. (1997), 'The politics of privilege: Assessing the impact of rent, corruption and clientalism on Third World development', *Political Studies*, 45, 3, 639–58

Huntington, S. (1968) *Political Order in Changing Societies*, London, Yale University Press

Jain, A. K. (ed.) (2001), *The Political Economy of Corruption*, London, Routledge

Johnson, R. A. (2005) *The Struggle Against Corruption: a Comparative Study*, Basingstoke, Palgrave Macmillan

Kidd, J. B. and Richter, F-J. (eds) (2003), *Fighting Corruption in Asia: Causes, Effects and Remedies*, Singapore, World Scientific Publishing

Lambsdorff, J. G., Taube, M. and Schramm, M. (2004), *The New Institutional Economics of Corruption: Norms, Trust and Reciprocity*, London, Routledge

Ledeneva, A. V. (1998), *Russia's Economy of Favours: Blat, Networking and Informal Exchange*, Cambridge, Cambridge University Press

Lewis, W. A. (1973), 'The Development Process: the Lessons of Two Decades', in *Sir William Arthur Lewis: Collected Papers 1941–1988*, Vol. III, edited by Patrick A. M. Emmanuel. ISER, Eastern Caribbean, University of the West Indies, Barbados

Leys, C. (1965), 'What is the Problem about Corruption?', *Journal of Modern African Studies*, 3, 215–30

Marquette, H. (2003), *Corruption, Politics and Development: the Origins and Development of the World Bank's Anti-Corruption Agenda*. Basingstoke, Palgrave Macmillan

McCourt, W. (2000), Public Appointments: From Patronage to Merit, *Working Paper No. 9*, Human Resources in Development Group Working Paper, pp. 1–15

Minogue, M. (2002), 'Power to the People? Good Governance and the Reshaping of the State', in Kothari, U. and Minogue, M. (eds), *Development Theory and Practice*, Basingstoke, Palgrave – now Palgrave Macmillan, pp. 117–35

Mishra, A. (2005) *The Economics of Corruption*, Oxford, Oxford University Press

Mrydal, G. (1968) *Asian Drama: an Enquiry into the Poverty of Nations, Vol. II*, New York, The Twentieth Century Fund

Mukherjee, N. (2005), 'Political Corruption in India's Below the Poverty Line (BPL) Exercise: Grassroots' Perspectives on BPL in Perpetuating Poverty and Social Exclusion and Good Practice in People's Participation from Bhalki Village, West Bengal', conference paper to the Global Poverty Research Group (GPRG) conference 'Redesigning the State? Political Corruption in Development Policy and Practice' held at the University of Manchester, 25 November, available from: www.sed.manchester.ac.uk/idpm/research/events/PoliticalCorruption/documents/Mukherjee.doc

Neild, R. (2002) *Public Corruption: the Dark Side of Social Evolution*, London Anthem Press

Nicholls, C., Daniel, T., and Hatchard, J. (2006), *Corruption and Misuse of Public Office*, Oxford, Oxford University Press

Nunberg, B. (1994), *Managing the Civil Service: Reform Lessons from Advanced Industrialised Countries*, Washington, World Bank

OECD (2002), *Public Sector Transparency and Accountability: Making it Happen*, with the Brookings Institution, Paris

OECD (2005), *Fighting Corruption and Promoting Integrity in Public Procurement*, OECD, Paris

Olivier de Sardan, J-P. (1996), 'L' économie morale de la corruption en Afrique' in *Politique Africaine*, 63, 97–116

Polzer, T. (2001), Corruption: Deconstructing the World Bank Discourse, Destin, Working Paper Series, no. 01–18, London School of Economics, Available at: www.lse.ac.uk/collections/DESTIN/pdf/WP18.pdf

Price, P. (1999), 'Cosmologies and corruption in (South) India', *Forum for Development Studies*, 26, 2: 315–27

Reno, W. (1995), *Corruption and State Politics in Sierra Leone*, Cambridge, Cambridge University Press

Reno, W. (2000), 'Clandestine Economies, Violence and States in Africa', *Journal of International Affairs* 53, 2, 433–59

Rose-Ackerman, S. (1999), *Corruption and Government: causes consequences and reform*, Cambridge, Cambridge University Press

Scott, J. C. (1972), *Comparative Political Corruption*, Englewood Cliffs, NJ, Prentice-Hall

Skinner, Q. (1999) 'The Republican Ideal of Civil Liberty', in Rosen, M. and Wolff, J. (eds) *Political Thought*, Oxford, Oxford University Press, 161–71

Spector, B. I. (ed.) (2005), *Fighting Corruption in Developing Countries: Strategies and Analysis*, Bloomfield, CT, Kumarian Press

Szeftel, M. (2000), 'Between Governance and Underdevelopment: Accumulation and Africa's 'Catastrophic Corruption', *Review of African Political Economy*, 27, 84, 287–306

Szeftel, M. (2000b), 'Misunderstanding African Politics: Corruption and the Governance Agenda', in Robert Williams (ed.) *Explaining Corruption*, Aldershot, Edward Elgar

Tesh, S. (1999), 'A Short History of Anti-Corruption Activities in the World Bank' in 1818 Society Newsletter, no. 70, Jan/Feb

Theobald, R. (1990), *Corruption, Development and Underdevelopment*, London, Macmillan

TI (2004) *Global Corruption Report 2004*, London, Pluto Press

Toye, J. (1993), *Dilemmas of Development: Reflections on the Counter-revolution in Development Economics*, Oxford, Blackwell, 2nd edn

Transparency International (TI) 2000, *Confronting Corruption: the Elements of a National Integrity System*, TI Source Book 2000 available from: www.transparency. org/publications/sourcebook accessed 3 January 2007

U4 (2005), *Corruption Glossary*, available from: www.u4.no/document/glossary. cfm#principalagenttheory accessed on 3 January 2007

Ward, P. M. (1989) 'Introduction' in Ward, P. M. (ed.) *Corruption, Development and Inequality: Soft Touch or Hard Graft?* London, Routledge

Williams, R. (1999), 'New concepts for old?', *Third World Quarterly*, 20, 3, 503–13

Wood, G. D. (1994), *Bangladesh: Whose Ideas, Whose Interests?* Dhaka: University Press Limited

World Bank (1997), *World Development Report 1997: the State in a Changing World*, New York, Oxford University Press

World Bank (2000), *Anticorruption in Transition: a Contribution to the Policy Debate*, Washington, DC, World Bank

World Development Report (2000), *Attacking Poverty*, Oxford University Press, World Bank

2
The Limits of a Global Campaign against Corruption

Kalin S. Ivanov

Introduction

This chapter begins by tracing the origins of the global anti-corruption agenda, which emerged in the mid-1990s from the US government's perception of foreign corruption as a commercial and security threat. The World Bank and the IMF repackaged their policy advice, prescribing deregulation to reduce opportunities for officials to collect bribes. Founded by a former World Bank official in 1993, Transparency International began to publish a corruption perception index to raise awareness about the problem. Economists seized on such quantifications of corruption (despite their problematic methodology), to produce econometric studies in support of the largely neoliberal global agenda.

The global agenda diverges from local understandings of corruption in developing and post-communist countries. Although the global agenda aims to be 'multipronged' and tailored to local circumstances, it still prescribes similar policies from Nigeria to Bulgaria. Also, the international anti-corruption industry focuses on institutional reform to prevent future corruption, whereas popular sentiment is based on egalitarian norms and on demands for the punishment of wealthy officials. The vague and emotive term 'corruption' has masked the gap between global and local discourses, a gap that Western-funded NGOs have struggled to bridge. The global anti-corruption agenda succeeded in drawing attention to a previously neglected problem. Yet, it did so in ways that have proven counterproductive, especially in post-communist and developing countries. This chapter raises doubts about the feasibility of a global fight against corruption, divorced from the local context.

Origins of the global anti-corruption agenda

The global anti-corruption agenda tends to represent itself as a grass-roots movement, giving a voice to ordinary people around the world who are victims of corruption. Transparency International, self-consciously styled after the international human rights movement, long featured on its website images of protesters carrying banners against corruption. Likewise, US ambassadors often speak in the name of the host country's population when they denounce corruption. In his groundbreaking 'cancer of corruption' speech, World Bank president James Wolfensohn (1996) declared, 'In country after country, it is the people who are demanding action on this issue.'

Anti-corruption does enjoy popular appeal, which explains why it is a tempting topic for both serious and 'muckraking' journalists and politicians. The global anti-corruption agenda did strike a chord with the masses in many parts of the world, partly because of the semantic elasticity and affective load of 'corruption'. Yet, the emergence of a global anti-corruption agenda was not the work of banner-waving protesters. The global agenda's origins lie in the interests of the US government, multinational companies, and multilateral donors. Over time, the universally negative connotation of the term 'corruption' helped to enlist a wider constituency with seemingly shared goals.

The second half of the 1990s witnessed the 'globalization of American-style anti-corruption standards' (Boeckmann, 2004: 630). US companies had long complained that the US Foreign Corruption Practices Act (1977), prohibiting the bribery of foreign officials, offered an unfair advantage to competitors from OECD countries without such laws. Some OECD countries even allowed bribes paid to foreign officials to be counted as a tax-deductible expense. According to intelligence estimates, US businesses lost contracts worth billions of dollars to competitors who paid bribes (Lewis, 1996). Sympathetic to such concerns, the trade-mined Clinton administration endeavoured to 'level the playing field' (Glynn et al., 1997: 20).

In addition, Washington came to view foreign corruption as a threat to US security, emanating especially from weak states overwhelmed by wealthy criminals (Smale, 2001). Latin American corruption was demon-strably linked to drug violence in the US; the bribery of post-Soviet officials could lead to nuclear proliferation, and in NATO's new member states, corruption threatened to cause intelligence leaks (Wallander, 2002: 6). Generally, corruption and organised crime appeared to imperil US interests by destabilizing the *status quo*. In recognition of such concerns,

Vice-President Al Gore convened a global forum on fighting corruption among justice and security officials.

Both commercial and security considerations led the US to champion the adoption of the OECD Convention on Combating Bribery of Foreign Public Officials in International Business Transactions (1998). During the negotiations, the US used public pressure to embarrass European governments into accepting anti-bribery rules. Previously, Europeans had resisted such rules as illegitimate claims of extraterritoriality, or as an example of 'America's Puritanism and penchant for international moralizing' (Glynn et al., 1997: 20–2). Now, moral pressure was instrumental in the rise of the global anti-corruption agenda, as nobody wished to be seen as a proponent of corruption. The OECD convention approximated the legal framework of signatory countries to the US model. It was further extended in a UN Convention against Corruption (2003) which included new commitments to transparency in public works procurement. The UN convention's standards apply not only to OECD countries but also to so-called 'demand' countries – countries whose officials extort bribes from multinational companies.[1]

Multinationals themselves supported the anti-corruption drive, as, concerned about 'reputational risk', branded corporations sought to level the playing field with firms that had no reputation to lose. In Eastern Europe, multinationals found corruption to be a hidden form of protectionism. Local companies had superior information and access to informal networks, allowing them to offer the right bribe to the right official at the right time (Krastev, 2000: 30). Corporate complaints of corruption as a non-tariff barrier increased international awareness of corruption. This trend was reinforced by globalisation, which 'brought individuals from countries with little corruption into frequent contact with those from countries where corruption is endemic' (Tanzi, 1998: 561).

The global agenda insists on 'zero tolerance' for corruption, departing from prior lenience. For instance, it is no longer acceptable for a prime minister to say, as the Greek one did in 1985, that a public enterprise executive is entitled to make himself a small 'gift' (Koutsoukis, 1995: 140). In a similar vein, the dictator of then-Zaire Mobutu Sese Seko is reputed to have told civil servants in the mid-1970s to steal, but steal a little (Wrong, 2001). Such lenience was openly shared by Western businesses and governments, which turned a blind eye in order to secure lucrative deals. When it was revealed that a Canadian crown company had bribed South Korean and Argentinean officials, Jean Chrétien, then still trade minister, remarked publicly that 'commercial practices in other countries sometimes are different from ours . . . It would be very presumptuous for

Canadians to tell other people how to conduct their morals' (Adams, 1991: 141). That such a reaction would be unthinkable today (at least in public) is a testament to the growing dominance of anti-corruption discourse.

The global agenda against corruption became conceivable only after the end of the Cold War, when the West no longer needed to support corrupt dictators in an effort to contain communism. During the Cold War, Western financiers knowingly tolerated irregularities in the public projects that they funded throughout the 'Third World', as it was then known. Western lenders were well aware that President Marcos of the Philippines was diverting development funds to his cronies. The Asian Development Bank allowed its monies to be lent to Bangladeshi businessmen who had no serious intention of pursuing the projects they proposed. As Adams (1991: 142) summarises, 'Corruption in the Third World required complicity from those in the West who, one way or another, benefited from the Third World's status quo.'

Politely silent about corruption during the Cold War, the World Bank and the IMF came to include it in their conditionalities. The two Bretton Woods institutions repackaged their policy advice, prescribing deregulation to reduce opportunities for officials to collect bribes. Such a shift required the depoliticisation of corruption into a technocratic problem, rather than the stuff of partisan scandal. 'I visited a number of countries,' recalls World Bank president James Wolfensohn, 'and I decided that I would redefine the [previously unspeakable] "C" word not as a political issue but as something social and economic' (Wolfensohn, 1999). Reinvented in this way, anti-corruption could be reconciled with World Bank and IMF statutes that prohibited entanglement in the domestic politics of recipient countries.[2]

Inaugurated at the 1996 annual meeting of the IMF and World Bank, the new focus on corruption was part of a broader campaign for 'good governance', which emerged in reaction to criticism of the Washington Consensus. Corruption, as part of a 'weak institutional environment', provided an explanation for the disappointing results of market reforms advocated by the IMF and World Bank. Anti-corruption also fortified the Bank's mission statement at a time when its *raison d'être* was being questioned. New IMF guidelines singled out corruption in state regulation of foreign direct investment, as such corruption ran 'counter to the IMF's general policy advice aimed at providing a level playing field to foster private sector activity'. To promote transparency, the Fund set out to remove 'unnecessary regulations and opportunities for rent seeking' (International Monetary Fund, 1997).

The IMF and the World Bank could now withdraw from countries where corruption was feared to be so rampant as to jeopardise economic recovery. In August 1997, the IMF suspended a $220 million loan to Kenya because the government had not done enough to curtail bribery. The World Bank also delayed loans to Nairobi for the same reason. Following the IMF's decision, Kenya's currency lost 20 per cent of its value (Bonzom, 1997). President Daniel Arap Moi challenged the loan suspension as 'purely political' (Bonzom, 1997).

The Kenyan response echoed the concerns of other developing country governments about interference in their domestic affairs. Malaysian central banker Dato' Seri Anwar bin Ibrahim insisted that the IMF and the World Bank should not pressure recipients to acquiesce to demands on 'noneconomic' matters. His Pakistani counterpart V. A. Jafarey (1996: 174) warned:

> Given their apolitical mandate, the Fund and the Bank need to proceed with extreme caution, being drawn into an area which defies easy quantification, entails subjective evaluation, and requires symmetry of treatment between debtor and creditor governments, especially in the two-sided area of corruption.

Civil society and the quantification of corruption

If the governments of some developing and transition countries had doubts about external pressure regarding corruption, their populations often welcomed such pressure (Miller et al., 2001: 32). 'Civil society', embodied primarily in NGOs, has played a central role in the global anti-corruption agenda. The World Bank (2000, xxiii) sees civil society as 'essential in constraining corruption'. The OECD (2003) published a 27-page report on the role of civil society in fighting corruption, while the *Anti-Corruption Toolkit* issued by the UN Office on Drugs and Crime (2004) mentions 'civil society' 151 times.

The archetypal anti-corruption NGO is Transparency International, founded by former World Bank official Peter Eigen. In 1995, TI began to publish its corruption perception index, a 'poll of polls' ranking countries on the basis of how corrupt they were perceived to be by international businesspeople. Updated annually and cited widely, the index left an indelible mark. It was instrumental in the construction of corruption as a global problem requiring global solutions. Journalists sometimes ignored the caveats contained in the index, and interpreted it as measuring actual, rather than perceived corruption.

Scholars have questioned the validity of the index, given the nebulous and clandestine nature of corruption. Perceptions are often based on 'group think', hearsay, or generalised sentiment rather than specific personal experiences of corruption. The most fundamental charge is that the CPI reflects the prejudices of outsiders who misunderstand local customs. For instance, Western businessmen in Russia, as caricatured by Burgess (1997: 10), are hardly a reliable source:

> Never having left the hotel throughout their hundreds of business trips for fear of violence, they might just as well be on Mars for all they know about what is around them. Nevertheless, lack of experience and knowledge invariably do not prevent them from pontificating at length (given the chance) on the ways of the mysterious Russians.

Surveys comprising the CPI may offer just such a 'chance'. Likewise, a study of Swedish businessmen in Eastern and Central Europe found that their perceptions of local bribery were shaped by 'conventional images of Eastern Europe' (Wasterfors, 2004). Local perceptions too are not immune from distortion.

To smooth out random oscillations, the CPI averages data over three consecutive years, and may thus reinforce stereotypical opinions, acting as a self-fulfilling prophecy (Sík, 2002: 110). In physics this problem is known as the Heisenberg effect: in the course of measuring, the observer interacts with the object and reveals it not as it is but as a function of measurement (Todorova, 1997: 10). TI has improved the index over the years but never to the complete satisfaction of critics.

In fact, the CPI is more about public relations than about scientific measurement. TI uses the index to rally support for anti-corruption. In the words of Eigen (Transparency International, 1998), 'Governments that have sought to brush this debate aside can no longer do so, as the whole world sees how their nations rank.' TI Vice-Chairman Frank Vogl (Transparency International, 1998) added,

> The CPI scores, with their shocking portrayal of so many countries perceived to be home to rampant corruption, will spur Transparency International to be even more aggressive in mobilising initiatives to counter corruption world-wide.

TI's head of research Fredrik Galtung left in 2003 to establish a new organisation, TIRI, aiming to move beyond awareness raising and into practical solutions. Galtung (2006) criticised the CPI for its unfair focus on bribe takers (rather than givers or abettors), irregular and uncontrolled country coverage, biased samples, and inability to measure trends and reward genuine reformers (see also Andvig, 2006). TI admits the index does not allow for comparisons across time, yet TI's own press releases speak of worsening or improving trends.

Competing for a newly discovered 'niche', the World Bank, the OECD and many others published their own rankings and indices of good governance, including corruption. A survey in 2003 counted no fewer than 52 initiatives to develop indicators for good governance (Landman and Häusermann, 2003). Some of these rankings are variations on the same theme, with, for example, the World Bank's index correlating almost perfectly with the TI one, or developed to provide a particular agency or NGO with a 'signature' index to attract visibility and funds.

Despite the questionable reliability of the CPI and other governance rankings, economists seized on the 'hard' data to perform regressions showing that corruption obstructs growth (Mauro, 1995), exacerbates inequality (Gupta et al., 1998), and expands the unofficial economy (Johnson et al., 2000). Economists also found that countries which 'restrict the freedom of international trade' are 'more corrupt' (Ades and Tella, 1994). Using the CPI and other quantitative indices, such studies helped bring corruption into the spotlight as an economic and institutional issue, increasingly divorced from its local context. Contemporary economic studies are not unanimous on every issue, but they share a tendency to condemn corruption as the root of all evil.[3]

Econometric studies, some sponsored by research institutes attached to the IMF and the World Bank, became another pillar of the neoliberal agenda against corruption. The essence of economic wisdom was encapsulated in the *Business Week* columns of Nobel laureate Gary Becker (1994) under titles such as 'To Root Out Corruption, Boot Out Big Government'. For Becker (1995) and many other economists, 'the source of official corruption is the same everywhere: large governments with the power to dispense many goodies to different groups'. Therefore, smaller and more 'businesslike' government is 'the only surefire way to reduce corruption' (Becker, 1995).

Such views rested on a pre-Enron assumption that business was by nature cleaner than government. Economic analysis tended to have a blind spot for corruption in the private sector, as well as for bribe-payers. William Easterly (2001: 252) warned, 'Knowing that governments are corrupt, we should be cautious about relying on them to do interventions on behalf of growth.' Economists acknowledge that insufficient regulation may also invite corruption, but the focus has been on excessive regulation as creating bottlenecks at which bureaucrats extract bribes.

Econometric research on corruption became part of a larger discourse delegitimising the state.[4] Such research discounted evidence that the countries ranked as least corrupt (North European countries and Canada) were not the ones with smallest governments. When Robert Leiken (1996) suggested that privatisation may open new opportunities for bribery and that culture is not irrelevant, the World Bank Institute's Daniel Kaufmann (1997) denounced him as an apologist for corruption.[5] In a backlash against 'revisionism', Kaufmann went on to establish 'the facts', embodied in econometric data. The facts unfailingly pointed to deregulation and privatisation, as well as greater international involvement in fighting corruption in emerging economies.

The measurement of corruption facilitated the dominance of economics, marginalising the policy relevance of qualitative approaches that treat corruption in its specific local context (Krastev, 2000: 38). Despite some internal disagreements, the various elements of the global anti-corruption agenda are interlinked. As TI (1998) notes, the CPI 'influences the policies of major aid agencies and is a factor in the foreign investment decisions of multinational corporations'. Since 2004, the index is formally among the criteria used by the US government to determine whether developing countries qualify under the Millennium Challenge Account, leading to the exclusion of Kenya solely on the basis of its corruption 'score', although TI itself discourages this type of use of its index. There have been calls to use TI's index as a benchmark for the conditionalities of international financial institutions (Buiter, 2005: 31). Galtung (2006: 16–17) opposes such 'misuse' of the CPI and even urges TI to stop publishing the index.

The global agenda has circumvented questions not only about measuring corruption but also about defining it. The definition of corruption is a complex and thorny problem. Most econometric studies and global policy projects tend to sidestep definitional debates by referring to the World Bank's (1997: 8) standard and pithy 'abuse of public office for private gain'. Studies and projects often begin with a caveat about the contested definition of corruption, and then proceed to treat it as though it were an unproblematic concept.

Generally absent from the global agenda's technocratic definitions is an understanding that corruption may reflect alternative normative frameworks such as familial duties, ethnic or religious loyalties, fidelity to friends, or norms of reciprocity (Philp, 2002: 71). The global approach tends to ignore deeply rooted traditions of clientelism and nepotism. Thus, universal definitions espoused by TI and the IMF have come into conflict with local cultures where gifts are not easily distinguishable from bribes (Shore and Haller, 2005: 16–17). The definitional distinction between public and private is also questionable, especially in post-communist countries where the lines are blurred between legitimate and illicit redistribution of state property. In parts of Africa too, the distinction between a public and a private sphere has not been internalised, especially since in the colonial regimes which introduced modern bureaucracy, the 'public' sector was devoted to seeking and extracting profit (Theobald, 1990). In India as well, Gupta (1995) found the dichotomy between officials' public and private roles to be largely irrelevant.

In response to revelations of private sector corruption in several Western countries, TI broadened its definition to 'the abuse of entrusted [rather than just "public"] power for private gain'. It also published a bribe payer's index in 1999, 2002 and 2006, ranking countries according to the degree to which their companies are perceived to be paying bribes abroad. TI's chapter in Denmark went even further by removing the definition of corruption from its statutes, because it was considered unhelpful. Nevertheless, the main focus has remained on state failure rather than market failure.

Exporting the anti-corruption agenda

Separately from the Bretton Woods institutions, the European Commission drew attention to corruption in countries applying for EU membership. The Commission's influential regular reports referred to corruption frequently, if unsystematically and without explicit benchmarks. The Commission's approach was also vulnerable to charges of a double standard, as candidates were required to ratify conventions that not all EU members had yet ratified. At times EU pressure resulted in formalistic anti-corruption efforts in candidate states, raising concern that 'ineffective measures will undermine the credibility of all anti-corruption efforts' (Open Society Institute, 2002: 17). Another limitation was the absence of explicit anti-corruption language in the *acquis communautaire* and thus in the accession negotiations. Despite such limits, the EU threatened to delay the accession of Bulgaria and Romania if these countries failed to do more to address corruption.

Even though occasional scandals revealed corruption within Western governments and institutions themselves (including the World Bank and the European Commission), they took the high moral ground in relation to developing and post-communist countries. Officials in those countries have been eager to emulate the West, even if not always in the prescribed ways. For instance, Nepalese parliamentarians who visited Western capitals to observe democratic procedures at work, learned a different sort of lesson. 'With every trip to a foreign parliament in an affluent country', Thomas Carothers (1999: 201) reports,

> the members of Nepal's parliament are more impressed by the luxurious offices, cars, and fancy equipment, and they return to Nepal yet more determined to increase still further their own perquisites and benefits – or simply to steal more money – so that they can live like 'real' parliamentarians.

As we have seen, the global anti-corruption agenda stems from the post-Cold War economic and security interests of the United States, from World Bank and IMF efforts to remain relevant, and from international NGOs and agencies competing for attention. Not all elements of the global anti-corruption movement are in agreement on all questions, but they share a 'definite social construct of what corruption is about and how to challenge it' (Krastev, 2000: 39). The global agenda is premised on a shared understanding of corruption as a measurable problem requiring global, technocratic solutions, including a smaller role for the state and a larger one for 'civil society'.

Civil society has been crucial in legitimating the global anti-corruption agenda, through Transparency International and its 85 chapters, as well as additional advocacy NGOs funded by USAID, the World Bank and others. Such NGOs have sometimes been more responsive to the concerns of their donors than to those of their presumed constituents. They transmit the global anti-corruption discourse into their local political environments. This function parallels the role of civil society in 'manufacturing consent' in African countries with Poverty Reduction Strategy Papers (Fraser, 2005).

Like other Western-funded advocacy NGOs, these specialised elite groups are assumed to represent the core of civil society. For example, Carothers (1999: 210) notes that it is common for US aid officers in transition countries, while describing NGO activities they are funding, 'to say grandly, "Civil society has decided to do this" or "Civil society disagrees with the government on that." Thus, as few as one or two dozen people who happen to have close relations with the donors are . . . characterized as deciding and acting for the entire civil society of the country.' In the words of a harsher critic, the staff of Western-funded NGOs are 'under no pressure to win respect from the citizenry whose concerns they . . . allegedly represent' (Burgess, 1997: 176).

Evaluations of NGO anti-corruption projects, like evaluations of Western democracy assistance, belong in a 'culture of success', focusing on quantifiable results, exaggerating benefits, and overlooking potential drawbacks. Corruption fighters, like democracy promoters, often shrink from acknowledging their own mistakes and thus fail to make substantial progress along Carothers's learning curve. Both kinds of activists are more inclined toward action than retrospective reflection – a tendency reinforced by the bureaucratic imperative to move from one project to the next. Like democracy promotion as described by Carothers (1999: 8–9), anti-corruption is pervaded by missionary zeal, 'bringing with it a disinclination for self-doubt and a reflexive belief in the value of the enterprise'. Furthermore, competition among anti-corruption NGOs discourages tough-minded reviews of their own performance.

Global anti-corruption slogans did capture the popular imagination. Anti-corruption NGOs achieved real successes in mobilising public support by drawing on people's disgust with corruption. Yet, donor (global) and popular (local) visions of corruption are often at variance. Steven Sampson (2005) brings attention to 'conflicts between global elites and grass roots, between the moral imperatives of fighting against corruption and the grant-getting intrigues involved in procuring funds for projects'. Such conflicts are often pushed under the rug by the 'anti-corruption community', but they have deep roots and serious consequences.

At the international level, corruption is construed primarily as an economic problem requiring liberalisation, deregulation, and institutional reform. Local publics, on the other hand, are eager to see corrupt officials and politicians punished and replaced by ones more responsive to the electorate. The international anti-corruption agenda has tended to conceal such divergences. In practice, as Ernest Harsch (2002: 18) puts it, 'not everyone considers corruption in the same way, nor opposes it for the same reasons'. Harsch examines popular sentiments in Ghana and Burkina Faso, which diverge from the standardised anti-corruption agenda. Ghanaians and Burkinans 'favored a state free of corruption, but also strong, effective, and capable of ensuring social welfare and equity' (Harsch, 2002: 3). Such perspectives are typically ignored by the prevalent anti-corruption discourse. In another sign of a disconnect between global and local concerns, surveys in the Czech Republic, Slovakia, Bulgaria and Ukraine found that corruption was not citizens' biggest complaint in dealings with public officials (Miller et al., 2001).

Adverse side effects of global anti-corruption

Few would dispute that donors have a legitimate interest in ensuring that their funds are disbursed properly. But the 'good governance' agenda has reached further, eliciting scholarly debate about the benefits and costs of anti-corruption. Corruption fighters typically fail to acknowledge that their efforts may involve negative side effects, despite abundant evidence (Anechiarico and Jacobs, 1996).

For example, if anti-corruption rhetoric lacks tangible results, it may reinforce popular cynicism about politics. A corruption scandal that leads to resignations and prosecutions serves as a ritual of catharsis and relegitimation. However, if their protagonists remain unpunished, corruption scandals become part of a delegitimising spiral in which the credibility of democratic norms is ever further undermined (Chubb and Vannicelli, 1988: 138–9). The global campaign against corruption has raised enormous, and yet unfulfilled, expectations for catharsis.

Moreover, global anti-corruption has added to the appeal of demagogues and extremists whose rhetoric pits an innocent 'people' against a corrupt elite. Mainstream politicians have also unscrupulously manipulated popular fixations on corruption. In Russia, anti-corruption campaigns became so distorted that:

> everyone who denounced corruption was now perceived as corrupt himself, eager to use anti-corruption campaigns as a means to denounce political rivals and therefore acquire power. (Coulloudon, 2002: 203)

Obsession with corruption can also drain political life of its content. Political discussion has degenerated from substantive policy issues into accusations of corruption and promises of integrity throughout Central and Eastern Europe (Bogdanov, 2005). Mark Philp (2002: 79) finds that:

> Western agencies have often shown a lack of sensitivity is in their willingness to supply a lexicon of corruption to political forces in transition states which, rather than assisting in the process of cleaning up government, has simultaneously armed political groups with a resource that they have no incentive to use responsibly and has further weakened the legitimacy of these states both domestically and in the international community.

By weakening state legitimacy, anti-corruption rhetoric has proven counterproductive. James Jacobs (2002: 83) concurs that 'Countries going through a political transition from dictatorship to democracy may be especially vulnerable to too much corruption and too much anti-corruption ideology.' Communism was premised on ideals of equality, which were contradicted by a reality of privileges for the nomenklatura. Egalitarian norms and resentment survived the fall of the Berlin Wall. Many citizens of post-communist counties have remained suspicious of private wealth, which is automatically attributed to illicit means. In these circumstances, local anti-corruption discourse is based on social envy. The global agenda provided a catch-all category, and open signifier, for citizens to air their grievances.

For example, the prevalence of anti-corruption rhetoric led many Romanians who lost civil trials to suspect that the judge had been bribed (Sampson, 2005). In general, for ordinary Romanians, to denounce corruption was to lament 'their own experience and their inability to deal with it' (Sampson, 2005). Like an earlier narrative about witchcraft, corruption provides an all-embracing trope that explains the inexplicable and channels social resentment. In the words of Krastev (2004: 43), corruption:

> explains why industries that were once the jewels of the communist economies have bankrupted. Corruption explains why poor are poor and why rich are rich. Blaming corruption for the post-communist citizen is the way to express his disappointment with the present political elites, to mourn the death of his 1989 expectations for better life, and to reject responsibility for his own well being. Talking about corruption is the way post-communist public talks about politics, economy, past and future.

In much of Central and Eastern Europe, successive governments won elections on promises of curbing corruption, but before long came to be seen as corrupt themselves. Meanwhile, western-funded NGOs successfully raised public awareness of corruption, but their technical and consensual approach to anti-corruption brought them too close to government to be effective (Tisné and Smilov, 2004). Anti-corruption has thus floundered at the implementation stage, confronted with the divergence of global discourse and local realities.

Even initial enthusiasts now harbour doubts about the global anti-corruption agenda. Moisés Naím (1995) was once optimistic that new global trends would shrink corruption to a 'historical minimum', leading to a 'catharsis' of world politics. Ten years later, Naím (2005) observed that global efforts against corruption had proven ineffective or even counterproductive: 'Today, the war on corruption is undermining democracy, helping the wrong leaders get elected, and distracting societies from facing urgent problems.'

Corruption too easily became a universal diagnosis for a nation's ills, stealing the spotlight from other pressing areas in need of reform.

Obsession with corruption also encouraged the illusion that removing the venal officials currently in power would automatically generate progress. In many countries, political stability suffered as leaders ousted their predecessors on charges of corruption, only to face similar accusations themselves. Meanwhile, authoritarian regimes in China, Vietnam, Pakistan and elsewhere have used anti-corruption as a pretext to repress domestic opponents.

Conclusion

Of course, developing and transition countries face different problems, most of which would have existed even without a global discourse against corruption. The point is not to question the good intentions of anti-corruption activism but to shed light on its problematic side effects. These side effects are often linked to a mismatch between global and local views about the nature of corruption.

Donors view corruption as an economic problem, which to be min-imised by altering officials' incentives. Citizens condemn corruption in order to air frustration with social stratification, and to demand the pun-ishment of wealthy bureaucrats and politicians. Citizens who criticise a privatisation deal as 'corrupt' may view the very policy of privatisation as a form of 'looting'. It was the vague and emotive term 'corruption' that allowed Western-funded NGOs to mobilise popular support initially. The lack of convicted officials undermined public confidence in the political process.

Contrary to the global agenda, John Girling (1997) argues that the solu-tion to corruption 'is not more neo-liberalism, but more democracy'. He holds neoliberal policies responsible for the collusion of political and economic elites, increasingly distant from the 'concerns of ordinary peo-ple' (Girling, 1997: 173). Critics have also pointed to other limitations of the neoliberal perspective on corruption, especially its 'blindness to the complex interplay between economic liberalization, political power and institutional reform' (Brown and Cloke, 2004: 275).

Further research is needed to uncover the full complexity of the global anti-corruption agenda. Such research should ideally refrain from uncon-ditional endorsement or wholesale dismissal of anti-corruption, but instead adopt a Carothers-like (1999: 60) perspective of 'constructive critical inquiry'. Qualitative knowledge about corruption in its context has yet to prove its policy relevance. To do that, it must avoid romanticising graft or falling prey to the maxim that 'to understand all is to forgive all'.[6] Well-informed strategies against corruption in different countries may well borrow from one another, without forgetting that corruption means different things to different people, and mindful of the risk of negative side effects.

Corruption is a value-ridden concept that should not be treated as though it were essentially the same phenomenon around the world. Global efforts to address corruption in a cultural vacuum have backfired. The pursuit of 'universal' statistical knowledge about corruption is partly responsible for flaws in the global anti-corruption agenda. A more contextualised analysis of corruption as a social construct could inform more successful policies.

Notes

1. The term 'demand' countries, used within the global anti-corruption discourse, betrays an underlying view of multinationals as the passive victims of corrupt officials in developing and transition countries.
2. The IMF's new guidelines stated that although 'the IMF's mandate and resources do not allow the institution to adopt the role of an investigative agency or guardian of financial integrity in member countries, and there is no intention to move in this direction,' its staff should 'address governance issues, including instances of corruption, on the basis of economic considerations within its mandate' (International Monetary Fund, 1997).
3. Such scholarly consensus was absent in the 1960s and 1970, when it was still legitimate to refer to corruption as contributing to capital formation, diminishing red tape, mitigating conflict, and 'lubricating' development. (See for example Leff, 1964 and Huntington, 1968).
4. For a critical examination of dominant economic wisdom about corruption, see Chapter 3 by Vincent Fitzsimons.
5. See also Leiken's (1997) response.
6. In the French original – *tout comprendre, c'est tout pardonner*.

References

Adams, P. (1991), *Odious Debts: Loose Lending, Corruption, and the Third World's Environmental Legacy*, London and Toronto: Earthscan

Ades, A. and Di Tella, R. (1994) 'Competition and Corruption', Oxford University Institute of Economics and Statistics *Discussion Paper 169*

Andvig, J. C. (2006) 'The Challenge of Poor Governance and Corruption – Opponents' Views'. In *How to Spend $50 Billion to Make the World a Better Place*, edited by Bjorn Lomborg, 90–4: Copenhagen Consensus Center

Anechiarico, F. and Jacobs, J. B. (1996), *The Pursuit of Absolute Integrity: How Corruption Control Makes Government Ineffective*, Chicago: University of Chicago Press

Becker, G. S. (1994) 'To Root out Corruption, Boot out Big Government', *Business Week*, 31 January, p. 18

—— (1995), 'If You Want to Cut Corruption, Cut Government', *Business Week*, 11 December, p. 26

Boeckmann, A. (2004), 'Taking a Corporate Stand against Public Corruption', Vital Speeches of the Day 70, 20, 630–34

Bogdanov, L. (2005) 'Politicheskiat Risk Raste s Otkaza ot Ideologia v Partiite', *Dnevnik*, 10 February

Bonzom, M-C. (1997) 'IMF – Anti-Corruption Champion?', *African Business*, November, p. 14

Brown, E. and Cloke, J. (2004), 'Neoliberal Reform, Governance and Corruption in the South: Assessing the International Anti-Corruption Crusade', *Antipode*, 36, 2, 272–94

Buiter, W. H. (2005), 'Country Ownership: a Term Whose Time Has Gone', in *Conditionality Revisited: Concepts, Experiences, and Lessons*, edited by Stefan Koeberle, Harold Bedoya, Peter Silarsky and Gero Verheyen, pp. 27–32, Washington, DC: World Bank

Burgess, A. (1997), *Divided Europe: the New Domination of the East*, London, Pluto Press

Carothers, T. (1999) *Aiding Democracy Abroad: the Learning Curve*. Washington, DC: Carnegie Endowment for International Peace

Chubb, J. and Vannicelli, M. (1988), 'Italy: a Web of Scandals in a Flawed Democracy', In *The Politics of Scandal: Power and Process in Liberal Democracies*, edited by Andrei S. Markovits and Mark Silverstein, pp. 122–50, New York: Holmes & Meier

Coulloudon, V. (2002), 'Russia's Distorted Anti-corruption Campaigns'. In *Political Corruption in Transition: a Sceptic's Handbook*, edited by Stephen Kotkin and András Sajó, pp. 187–206. Budapest: Central European University Press

Easterly, W. R. (2001), *The Elusive Quest for Growth: Economists' Adventures and Misadventures in the Tropics*. Cambridge, Mass.: MIT Press

Fraser, A. (2005), 'Poverty Reduction Strategy Papers: Now Who Calls the Shots?' *Review of African Political Economy*, 32, 104, 317–40

Galtung, F. (2006), 'Measuring the Immeasurable: Boundaries and Functions of (Macro) Corruption Indices'. In *Measuring Corruption*, edited by Charles Sampford, Arthur Shacklock, Carmel Connors and Fredrik Galtung, pp. 101–30. London: Ashgate, 2006

Girling, J. (1997), *Corruption, Capitalism and Democracy*, London: Routledge

Glynn, P., Kobrin, S. J. and Naím, M. (1997), 'The Globalization of Corruption'. In *Corruption and the Global Economy*, edited by Kimberly Ann Elliott, pp. 7–27. Washington, DC: Institute for International Economics

Gupta, A. (1995), 'Blurred Boundaries: the Discourse of Corruption, the Culture of Politics, and the Imagined State'. *American Ethnologist* 22, 2, 375–402

Gupta, S., Davoodi, H. and Alonso-Terme, R. (1998), 'Does Corruption Affect Income Inequality and Poverty?' *IMF Working Paper 98/76*

Harsch, E. (2002) 'Cleaning House: Anti-corruption Struggles in Ghana and Burkina Faso'. PhD Thesis, New School University

Huntington, S. (1968) *Political Order in Changing Societies*. New Haven: Yale University Press

International Monetary Fund (1997), 'The Role of the IMF in Governance Issues: Guidance Note', Washington

Jacobs, J. B. (2002), 'Dilemmas of Corruption Control'. In *Political Corruption in Transition: a Sceptic's Handbook*, edited by Stephen Kotkin and András Sajó, pp. 81–90. Budapest: Central European University Press

Jafarey, V. A. (1996), 'Statement by the Governor of the Bank for Pakistan'. Summary Proceedings of the Fifty-First Annual Meeting of the Board of Governors, pp. 171–74

Johnson, S., Kaufmann, D., McMillan, J., and Woodruff, C. (2000), 'Why Do Firms Hide? Bribes and Unofficial Activity after Communism'. *Journal of Public Economics* 76, 3, 495–520

Kaufmann, D. (1997), 'Corruption: the Facts'. *Foreign Policy*, no. 107, pp. 114–31

Koutsoukis, K. S. (1995), 'Greece'. In *Sleaze: Politicians, Private Interests and Public Reaction*, edited by F. F. Ridley and Alan Doig, pp. 140–48. Oxford: Oxford University Press

Krastev, I. (2000), 'The Strange (Re)Discovery of Corruption'. In *The Paradoxes of Unintended Consequences*, edited by Ralf Dahrendorf, Yehuda Elkana, Aryeh Neier, William Newton-Smith and István Rév, pp. 23–41. Budapest: CEU Press

—— (2004), *Shifting Obsessions: Three Essays on the Politics of Anti-corruption*. Budapest: Central European University Press

Landman, T. and Häusermann, J. (2003), *Map-Making and Analysis of the Main International Initiatives on Developing Indicators on Democracy and Good Governance*. Colchester: University of Essex

Leff, N. (1964), 'Economic Development through Bureaucratic Corruption'. *The American Behavioral Scientist* 8, 3, 8–14

Leiken, R. S. (1996), 'Controlling the Global Corruption Epidemic'. *Foreign Policy*, no. 105, pp. 55–73

—— (1997), 'Corruption Revisited'. *Foreign Policy*, 108, pp. 184–85

Lewis, P. (1996), 'A World Fed up with Bribes; Nations Begin Following U.S. Curbs on Corruption'. *New York Times*, 28 November, p. D1

Mauro, P. (1995), 'Corruption and Growth'. *Quarterly Journal of Economics* 110, 3, pp. 681–712

Miller, W. L. (2001), Åse B. Grødeland, and Tatyana Y. Koshechkina. *A Culture of Corruption?: Coping with Government in Post-Communist Europe*. Budapest: CEU Press

Naím, M. (1995) 'The Corruption Eruption'. *Brown Journal of World Affairs* 2, 2, pp. 245–61

—— (2005), 'Bad Medicine'. *Foreign Policy*, pp. 95–96

OECD (2003), *Fighting Corruption: What Role for Civil Society? The Experience of the OECD*. Paris

Open Society Institute (2002), *Monitoring the EU Accession Process: Corruption and Anti-Corruption Policy*. Budapest

Philp, M. (2002), 'Political Corruption, Democratization, and Reform'. In *Political Corruption in Transition: a Sceptic's Handbook*, edited by Stephen Kotkin and András Sajó, pp. 57–80. Budapest: Central European University Press

Sampson, S. (2005), 'Integrity Warriors: Global Morality and the Anti-corruption Movement in the Balkans'. In *Corruption: Anthropological Perspectives*, edited by Dieter Haller and Cris Shore, pp. 103–30. London: Pluto

Shore, C. and Haller, D. (2005), 'Introduction – Sharp Practice: Anthropology and the Study of Corruption'. In *Corruption: Anthropological Perspectives*, edited by Dieter Haller and Cris Shore, pp. 1–28. London: Pluto

Sík, E. (2002), 'The Bad, the Worse and the Worst: Guesstimating the Level of Corruption'. In *Political Corruption in Transition: a Sceptic's Handbook*, edited by Stephen Kotkin and András Sajó, pp. 91–113. Budapest: Central European University Press

Smale, A. (2001), 'The Dark Side of the Global Economy'. *New York Times*, 26 August, p. 3

Tanzi, V. (1998), 'Corruption around the World: Causes, Consequences, Scope, and Cures'. *IMF Staff Papers 45*, 4, pp. 559–94

Theobald, R. (1990), *Corruption, Development and Underdevelopment*. London: Macmillan

Tisné, M. and Smilov, D. (2004), *From the Ground Up: Assessing the Record of Anti-corruption Assistance in Southeastern Europe*. Budapest: CEU Center for Policy Studies

Todorova, M. N. (1997), *Imagining the Balkans*. New York: Oxford University Press

Transparency International (1998), '1998 Corruption Perceptions Index'. Press Release, 22 September

UN Office on Drugs and Crime (2002), *Anti-Corruption Toolkit*. Vienna, 2004.

Wallander, C. (2002), 'Nato's Price: Shape Up or Ship Out', *Foreign Affairs*, 81, 6: 2–8

Wasterfors, D. K. (2004), 'Stories about Bribes: the Social and Moral Meaning of Corruption among Swedish Businessmen in Eastern Central Europe'. Fildr thesis, Lunds Universitet, Sweden

Wolfensohn, J. D. (1996), 'Speech to the World Bank/IMF Annual Meeting'. Washington, DC: World Bank

—— (1999), 'Remarks at a Global Forum on Fighting Corruption', Washington, DC, 24 February 1999, web.worldbank.org/WBSITE/EXTERNAL/NEWS/0„ content MDK:20024339~menuPK:34472~pagePK:34370~piPK:34424~the Site PK:4607,00.html

World Bank (1997) 'Helping Countries Combat Corruption: The Role of the World Bank', Washington, DC, September, www.worldbank.org/publicsector/anticorrupt/corruptn/corruptn.pdf

—— (2000), *Anti-corruption in Transition: a Contribution to the Policy Debate*. Washington, DC: World Bank

Wrong, M. (2001), 'The Leopard'. *Washington Post*, 28 November

3
Economic Models of Corruption

Vincent G. Fitzsimons

Introduction

Corruption is something of a conundrum to economists. Whilst clearly being economic in its nature and principle motivation, that of personal gain, it is also clearly determined by a range of institutional, psychological, cultural and social factors which challenge the narrow assumptions that economics uses to model economic behaviour. The idea of 'unethical' behaviour is difficult for economists to analyse given their assumption that all individuals and organisations simply pursue self interest opportunistically. Also, their tendency to maintain in practice that 1) government cannot be trusted and should be restricted from intervening in markets, whilst 2) until recently, in theory, assuming them to be neutral or even conscientious in their provision of essential services, caused obvious problems for judgements on corruption issues. The work of Krueger (1974) and Tullock (1989) brought corruption to the attention of the academic community, but the problem remains one primarily addressed by the 'policy community' rather than pure theorists. Although generally keen to promote neoliberal and free-market policies based on classical economics, the Bretton Woods Institutions (BWI) have also been interested in the further analysis of the specific economics of corruption, in line with their role as provider of finances to developing countries, but also because, in their lending capacity, they have been subject to some remarkable losses through corruption themselves. This chapter reviews the progress of economists, and the BWI, in defining, analysing and tackling corruption from an economic perspective.

The chapter then argues, referring to the evidence presented later in this volume, that corruption has proved largely resistant to the packages of anti-corruption policies implemented in developing and transitional countries, causing grave concern over the suitability of the anti-corruption strategies advocated by the Bretton Woods institutions (BWIs). The failures of existing approaches towards corruption may partly be explained by their failure to incorporate elements of institutional analysis that appear to have direct relevance to corruption and the design of anti-corruption strategies.

The tendency of BWIs to recommend broadly similar packages of reform for a wide range of problems, as outlined in the first part of the chapter, stems from their fundamental belief in the advocacy of neoliberal policies, where neoliberalism includes:

> institutionalized normative principles favoring free-market solutions to economic problems [and] includes institutionalized cognitive principles, notably a deep, taken for granted belief in neoclassical economics. (Campbell & Pedersen, 2001: p. 5)

The standard anti-corruption packages include an emphasis on competitive, but simply regulated private sectors and decentralised decision making (World Bank, 2000). While additional features have been incorporated from the New Institutional Economics (NIE), emphasising the need for transparency if corruption is to be avoided, and also a belief in the role of an independent judicial system to provide institutional constraints on the actions of all individuals, these remain insufficient in relation to further possible measures to reduce the relative attractiveness of corruption.

Economic approaches to corruption

Corruption has not always been viewed negatively by academics and the popular view that 'grease money' was necessary in some way to the operation of business has been difficult to dismiss conclusively. Huntington's (1968) analysis of political decision making presented a case for corruption when governments failed to provide effective legal systems and protection of individual rights. The role of inadequate legal institutions in causing persistent market failures has also been emphasised by Coase (1988) and in the work of the NIE. In this way, corruption may be 'positively' viewed as a response to market failure. This interpretation has been largely abandoned, however, due to the significant evidence showing corruption's negative impacts in developing countries and also in developed economies, as well as the consequent emergence of new models of corruption.

Analyses of corruption have subsequently taken a variety of approaches to the problem. Some consider determinants of individual decision-making in the general economic, social and political environment whilst others focus more specifically on influences within organisations, considering personal motivating and de-motivating factors. A further division exists between theories that consider corruption to be a consequence of agents' decisions, in principal–agent relationships, who abuse their positions of trust, and those that consider it to be a consequence of the activities of vested interests. At one extreme, poor individuals may be forced to pay bribes to opportunistic officials in order to receive essential public services where these are provided by state monopolies. At the other, large corporations may approach key government officials at various levels of government to acquire preferential provision of state services, or persuade selective application of regulations or provisions in favour of themselves. Thus, whilst there is a general concern with the damaging nature of corruption, there is still no clear agreement on the nature of its causes.

Public choice economics, which studies the optimal and actual behaviour of government institutions, has contributed several models of corruption. Stigler's (1971) '*capture*' theory of regulation has been one highly influential model of the determination of corruption. In this theory, firms will attempt to corrupt their regulators, or 'capture' them, due to the potential for firms to gain from particular forms of regulation that may be in the regulators' power. Strict regulations on standards, for instance, enforce significant compliance costs on firms that may form barriers to the entry of new firms, thus reducing the level of market competition and permitting established firms to extract additional 'rents', or unearned surpluses in value, which incumbent firms share. This also constitutes one of the few models that views firms as the 'perpetrators' of corruption, rather than public administrators.

The 'Public Interest Theory' of regulation (or PIT) grew from the traditional view held by economists, that regulation was essential for the protection of the welfare of the general public, given the existence of market-failures that can be compensated by corrective government action (Pigou, 1938). This provided a general rationale for government intervention that complemented Keynesian interventionist theory. However, PIT was subsequently heavily criticised by authors such as Stigler, who noted that regulation appears not to vary in any systematic way with the extent of failure of market institutions. An alternative explanation has developed that, rather than regulation benefiting the public interest, it instead creates 'shadow prices' for publicly provided services which generally deviate from market prices (which would be expected to reflect the value to consumers of services). This creates the potential for *rent-seeking* from bureaucrats to extract bribes from firms or individuals due to the excess of the value of services over their state-administered price (Krueger, 1974). Regulated societies are therefore likely to experience problems of corruption.

This theory has been developed further into what Djankov et al. (2002) call the '*tollbooth*' view of corruption. The rent-seeking theory of regulation is compatible with the view that regulation is established by well-intentioned governments intending to solve problems of market-failure. In the tollbooth view, however, opportunistic bureaucrats and politicians realise the potential for rent-seeking in the presence of regulation and accordingly create unnecessary regulations in order to take advantage of the opportunities created (McChesney, 1987). Public services become littered with unnecessary administrative processes for which officials extract charges. This theory appears to offer a good explanation of the systemic corruption that undermines whole economies such as in the case of Peru (De Soto, 1990) or Brazil (De Souza Martins, 1996). In this influential rent-seeking model, low regulation and high competition can be expected to reduce the 'gap' between market values and shadow prices, thus reducing the potential size of 'economical' bribes and levels of corruption.

The work of the New Institutional Economics, with authors such as Coase (1988), Williamson (1985), and North (1990) has also focused attention on the quality of public institutions. This analysis starts from its consideration of the costs of any form of economic transaction in an economy, typically neglected in traditional economic theory. According to North (1990), these constitute a significant proportion of all costs of economic activity, and significantly affect patterns of behaviour.

Coase examines the development of institutional systems, particularly legal or organisational systems, in the context of the minimisation of costs and externalities involved in economic activity. A transaction is made costly by the need to gather information on available exchanges, the establishment of satisfactory 'contract' commitments and constraints (whether written, unwritten or implicit) and costs due to the risk that performance of the contract's provisions may deviate from those specified, for example due to opportunism. Coase (1988) uses Dahlman's (1979) categorisation of the consequent transaction costs into 'search and information costs, bargaining and decision costs, policing and enforcement costs' (Coase, 1988: 6). The balance of these will be affected by the nature of the exchange, i.e. the institutional environment in which it takes place such as personal exchange, impersonal exchange in markets, etc., as well as by the nature of the product, and security of property rights. The problems of measurement or monitoring of compliance (Lancaster, 1966) and enforcement pose significant practical difficulties in any economy, and particularly in those undergoing reform (EBRD, 2003). Reduction of these costs to the organisation is difficult or even impossible. The process of search for information relevant to decisions is of course difficult, but in addition 'ineradicable uncertainty' exists where the information simply does not exist, regardless of the need or desire to acquire it. Instead organisations may seek to avoid rather than reduce these costs by 'internalising' transactions. In terms of government regulatory activity, this could be via the formation of corrupt relationships with officials for direct provision of state services.

Corruption leads to general difficulties for state and private organisations ('principals') who need to delegate tasks to their 'agents', whether members of their organisation or external contractors. When corruption is known to be present, detailed contract constraints and compliance monitoring measures are necessary to reduce this risk of opportunistic behaviour. Inevitably, costs will be incurred in the contractual, monitoring, or compliance-measurement devices used to insure against this behaviour, which will increase the general costs of the activities being delegated to the control of the agent. In known high-corruption and low-trust economies levels of transaction costs may be increased to an extent that deters individuals and firms from entering economic activity, particularly when legal institutions of enforcement are similarly undermined by corruption.

The regulatory environment will affect the model through two channels. The quality and attitude of legal institutions will affect the expected probability of detection as well as that of successful enforcement and the associated punishments consequently expected. In addition, as suggested by Krueger (1974), the extent of government regulation and intervention in the economy constitutes the fundamental scope of corrupt 'capture' activity: without government intervention, no potential 'rents' exist as all resources would trade at market values (Ehrlich & Lui, 1999). Even in relatively low corruption economies particular state functions such as procurement, in which administrators may exercise significant discretionary choice in decisions with large financial implications, appear particularly susceptible to corruption. The extent to which corruption constitutes a problem should depend, therefore, on the balance between the effectiveness of internal or external controls, and the extent of deviation of the price and availability of state-provided 'public goods' from their market equivalent.

The economic models above present us with a number of determining factors for corruption, with certain themes recurring such as the administrators' or firms' desire to create restrictions that will enable them to profit from their position. Investigators in practice approach the existence of corruption from a different angle, however, concentrating much more on the psychology of the individual and their position within the organisation. Whilst economic approaches clearly address the likely extent of systemic corruption, these models may also contribute to our understanding and consequent prevention of corruption. We will return to the contribution of NIE and 'wider institutionalism' in the concluding part of this chapter.

Examples of economic corruption

Corruption may occur in private or public sector organisations, but often involves some interaction or exchange between the two sectors. Firms may attempt to purchase licences at below official prices with the help of a bribe; or equally politicians may solicit bribes in order to favour certain business interests over others. The problem of corruption has many possible forms. In some of the most complex and difficult forms to break, politicians both receive bribes and make disbursements to companies in complex corruption structures such as those that existed in many South American countries, where the line between private and public activities of politicians was often blurred in a system of traditional patronage that conflicted with modern democratic political institutions (De Souza Martins, 1996: 195). Such complexity, by disguising the true nature or overall pattern of exchanges in an economy, inevitably creates a tendency towards corruption.

Corruption, therefore, appears to be a general abuse of position that is frequently helped by lack of transparency in the organisations involved, and also lack of clearly stated and separated roles within those organisations. It may exist in one of many forms, or in a more complex combination, at various levels of administration, and with varying degrees of 'acceptance' from the population subject to the corrupt institutions. Once such general problems exist, a range of specific issues may arise. The UNODCCP list of corruption issues demonstrates a range much wider than simple bribe-taking and selective exercise of powers, and includes fraud, embezzlement, favouritism, extortion, abuse of discretion and conflict of interests (2002: 3).

In addition, corruption can build on itself. Once an elite or interest group demonstrates to others the clear benefits from their corruption

it is likely to alter the typical ethical culture of an economy. The accumulation of private wealth by corrupt leaders often leads to a decline in the general attitude against corruption in practice (World Bank, 1992: 16; Liu, 1983: 617) even though it may still be objected to in principle – one model explains how the 'rationalisation' of corruption on the basis of perceived fairness is a common, or even essential part of individuals' justification of their own corrupt acts (Ramos, 2003). Examples abound of this more general phenomena where unacceptable conditions, not necessarily simply corruption of elites, leads to an endemic corruption.

Two examples from the socialist era in Central Eastern Europe come from Poland and the Czech Republic. One popular Polish 'joke' of the time was 'They pretend to pay us: we pretend to work.' Shirking is a form of abuse of trust by employees. Meanwhile, a saying amongst some industrial workers in Czechoslovakia was 'if you don't rob the state, you rob your family'. Similarly the People's Republic of China suffered considerable problems of reported corruption (Liu, 1983), due to the common practice of the state imposing targets without providing sufficient resources to fulfil them ('planning gaps'), such that 'Corrupt deeds such as bribery, illegal exchange of goods, and even speculation grow' (Liu, 1983: 617). In addition the state's under-provision of many consumer goods exacerbated the corruption problem as 'scarcity, years of poverty, and the examples set by privileged Party cadres combine to perpetuate . . . the traditional attitude of regarding public property as legitimate loot' (ibid.). Such 'fairness' rationalisation is a frequent reason behind 'popular' corruption across an entire culture.

This combination of poor state provision of a (monopoly) service, poor behavioural example of superiors, and individual poverty provides a strong combination of incentives to participate in corrupt practices. Unfortunately, the removal of such 'bad government' causes of corruption can provide alternative motivations for corruption. Privatisation of state industries provides those in administrative positions, who are used to receiving a small income stream from corruption in the industry, the opportunity to make significant one-off, lump sum gains instead (Stiglitz, 2002). The introduction of market reforms is therefore often accompanied by cases of complex frauds, deliberate under-pricing in returns for shares or bribes, and other serious cases of mal-administration that start new corruption trends that potentially overcome the new private sector (see Russian and CIS cases for examples of this – such as in EBRD, 2003 analysis of legal problems in transition). Such economic crime is often aided by the disruption of the social institutions in which economic activity is embedded (Granovetter, 1985) making a holistic understanding necessary.

The economic effects of corruption

Corruption affects economies at a number of levels. As Reinikka and Smith state, studies on corruption have demonstrated the significant:

> negative impact of corruption on the economic, social and political development of countries, due to the increased transaction costs, the reduction in the efficiency of public services, the distortion of the decision-making process, and the undermining of social values. They have also shown a strong correlation between corruption and poverty. (2004: 7)

However, the economic evidence for these associations is weaker than one might expect. For example, Reinikka and Smith assert that corruption shows a strong negative connection to national levels of income, but as is demonstrated in Figure 3.1, some countries lie far off the associated regression line, a long way outside the 95 per cent confidence limits, some with significantly better corruption levels than expected, some worse. Figure 3.2 is derived from Transparency International's *Corruption Perceptions Index* (CPI), measured on a scale from 1 for poor to 10 for excellent, plotted against per capita incomes, and shows a positive correlation with an R^2 of 0.74. The central line on the diagram represents a linear regression line, the outer lines represent a 95 per cent confidence interval.

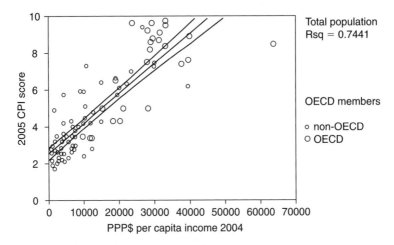

Figure 3.1: Corruption and income – 2005 CPI against 2004 PPP$pc income
Sources: Transparency International and IMF *World Economic Outlook*

A large number of OECD members lie above the regression line, with better than predicted levels of corruption, and so it may be useful to examine non-OECD countries on their own to take out this group of OECD outliers. When shown separately, as in Figure 3.2, non-OECD countries can be seen to have a similar regression line, but much higher levels of variation around it (with a wider band for the 95 per cent confidence interval around the central fitted line) and accordingly having a much lower R^2 at only 0.58. It appears that for those lower income countries that are typically thought to suffer most corruption, income is not as powerful an explanatory factor as it is for more highly developed economies.

However, no particular regional group appears to consistently over- or under-perform in terms of corruption, with wide degrees of variation apparent. This variation, despite the overall link between income levels and corruption, suggests that corruption is highly specific in its determinants. It therefore demands very careful analysis on a case-by-case basis and cannot be presupposed on either regional or income grounds. The degree of regional variation within the CPI dataset is shown in Figure 3.3.

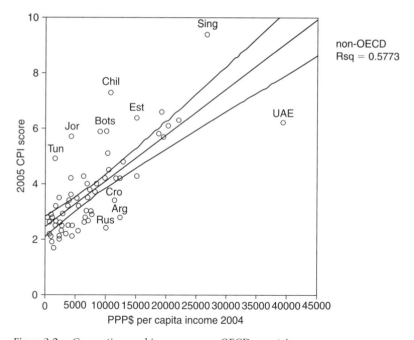

Figure 3.2: Corruption and income – non-OECD countries

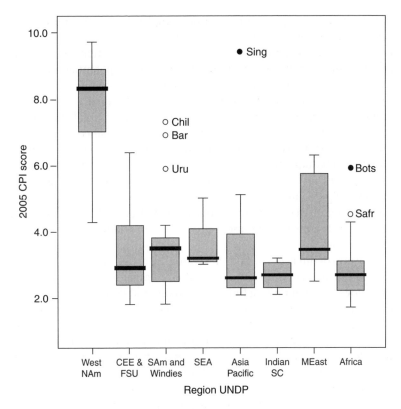

Figure 3.3:   Boxplot of regional variation in corruption

As can be seen in the boxplot (showing the mean and range of corruption scores for the different regions as defined by the UNDP) regional groups' ranges of corruption significantly overlap, meaning that no reliable assumptions can be made on the basis of a country's location alone about the nature or extent of their corruption problems. It is also worth remembering that these measures of perceived corruption are subject to the bias of members of the sample, which may give a partial explanation for the remarkably good performance of OECD countries despite the evidence that many of the highest value acts of fraud and corruption in fact occur in OECD countries (see data on the costs of corruption, below).

Costs of corruption

No definitive estimate has been produced of the total impact of corruption in economic terms. This is partly because of the constantly changing nature of globalising economies, and rising levels of hidden economic activity (Schneider, 2002). However, two general types of cost of corruption exist, which are direct costs or expenditures on corruption, and indirect or 'opportunity costs' of corruption in terms of lost potential incomes.

Direct costs may well show up in organisations' accounts or in figures for national income, but are in fact 'bads' or negative impact expenditure/ earnings which in principle should be excluded from calculations of economic value. Indirect costs do not show in national economic data, but may be estimated as the shortfall from potentially higher income or growth levels due to the existence of corruption. Typical explanations of this suggest that corruption acts as a deterrent to investment activities domestically (Mauro, 1995) and internationally (Wei, 2000), thus costing economies growth of economic activity which they might otherwise have enjoyed. It is a measure of under-production in relation to the capacity of economies.

Measures of direct costs, from the reasoning above, should be relatively easy to calculate, but unfortunately different organisations use different and indeed overlapping definitions of fraud and corruption, making it difficult to produce comprehensive measures of total corruption on a global scale. Fraud examiners typically include corruption as a type of fraud: corruption analysts generally include fraud as a form of corruption. Some estimates exist at the national level for certain economies, however, which suggest the true scale of the problem of corruption is vast even in the most developed economies (see Table 3.1).

Whilst corruption is not only a problem of public services, these appear particularly vulnerable to damaging impacts of corruption.

Table 3.1:   Direct costs of corruption

Description	Costs	Source
Fraud	$600 billion in USA in 2002 (6% of revenues annually). Some estimates show 20% rate likely based on employee surveys.	Association of Certified Fraud Examiners (2004); Ernst & Young (2002)
Bribery (one element only of corruption, excluding standard interpretation of fraud)	$ 1 trillion annually (global) from 2001–2 data.	World Bank (2004)

Embezzlement from public funds, or diversion from their specified uses, can significantly impact on the provision of public services. The development of public expenditure tracking surveys (PETS) has permitted aid donors and governments to measure the extent to which funding is 'captured' by incumbents within the system rather than delivered to intended beneficiaries. For example, Reinikka & Smith (2004, table 2.1, p. 36) collected data from a range of PETS to assess the level of capture of non-wage funds in primary education in Uganda (1995), Ghana (1998), Tanzania (1998), Peru (2001), and Zambia (2001, 2 surveys). With reasonable sample sizes they recorded levels of capture ranging form a low of 10 per cent (fixed school grants in Zambia) to a high of 78 per cent (per student capitation grants in Uganda), with an average level of capture of 50 per cent of funding (not weighted by sample size). Thus the problem of capture is obviously of great significance, but also not uniform in its occurrence or in its impact. Capture of state monies appears to have clear connections to the risks involved to those participating in the corruption, and these vary with a range of social characteristics of the victims. The evidence shows that expropriation risk varies according to the level of wealth of the ultimate 'clients' as well as their levels of organisation and access to the media. These latter may affect information at clients' disposal on their entitlements and their subsequent ability to publicise problems with corrupt officials (Reinikka & Svensson, 2002).

Measures of the indirect costs of corruption vary enormously due to their dependence on the nature and specification of variables within the statistical models used to estimate them. It appears generally that an improvement of one point in the corruption perceptions index scale of 1 to 10 is associated with incomes higher by approximately PPP\$2,000 per capita per annum or more. This potentially dwarfs the direct costs of corruption shown above. This impact is explained by the general difficulty of doing business, and the lower incentives to invest that exist in corrupt environments (Mauro, 1995) where costs of doing business are inflated and individuals' property is relatively less secure than in less corrupt economic environments. Corruption generally 'leads to competitive bribery, instead of fair competition based on price, quality and innovation' (Transparency International, 2006).

Johnson et al. (1997) and Djankov et al. (2002) show that higher levels of corruption are associated with a withdrawal into the unofficial economy, to avoid the costs of corruption on businesses in the formal economy derived from regulations associated with costly bribe-paying. This withdrawal reduces the size of the official economy open to taxation, with implications for spending programmes. Developing economies (which typically suffer the highest levels of corruption) are least capable of bearing high rates of taxation, and the state's attempts to levy taxes in order to compensate for a falling tax-base may lead to avoidance by both under-reporting of legitimate business as well as the further withdrawal into the hidden economy. One argument for neoliberal economic policies, such as the reduction of government spending and taxation, is that it will encourage the voluntary 'formalization' of informal activities, implicitly assuming that these are predominantly caused by high burdens of taxation and regulation.[1]

These enormous economic costs of corruption, however, still understate the extent of the wider impact of corruption. Its negative influence on democratic institutions and associated loss of individuals' voice in democratic societies is difficult to quantify, but no less significant: corruption threatens fundamental human and political rights as much as it threatens economic rights.

Anti-corruption strategies

Ideally, anti-corruption policies need to be addressed to the fundamental causes of corruption. However, the analyses above suggest a range of factors that may influence corruption, while the economic models for dealing with corruption frequently deal with only a small number of these in, by necessity, simplified models of actual behaviour. Arguably, strategies to reduce corruption from the field of economics most heavily rely on, and are most adept at, understanding motivation, incentive and reward at the level of the individual. For example, the widely influential efficiency wage model of corruption is based on the principle of 'efficient' wages, or those that elicit the desired productivity from employees, and suggests that wages above expected or market levels may yield increased productivity following evidence from developing countries in the 1950s. This principle has been developed into several different forms of efficiency wage model, but the 'shirking' model specifically addresses the problems of employers attempting to overcome principal–agent (abuse of position) problems when designing compensation packages (Becker & Stigler, 1974; Shapiro & Stiglitz, 1984).

An adaptation of this model may enable us to examine the 'principal–agent' problem in corruption, although this will only apply within the restrictive assumptions of economic modelling. We assume that individuals are calculating, rational, and maximising, and in this particular model suggest that they form subjective expectations of the probability of future benefits from their actions. Finally we assume that individuals are rationally corrupt in their actions, i.e. that they have the choice whether or not they act corruptly or not, and calculate which is the more beneficial strategy. All individuals will receive a wage, but those who are corrupt receive benefits in addition to this whilst undetected, while on detection corrupt individuals make losses equal to the wage and corruption benefits (rents/bribes), plus any penalties imposed for the offence. The balance of these factors will determine whether individuals act corruptly.

Technically, the expected outcome for corrupt workers will be a probability-weighted average of the outcome if caught and the outcome if not caught. In other words the expected outcome = [p × penalties if caught] + [(1 − p) × (wages + benefits)], where p equals the probability of being caught given existing scrutiny arrangements. To deter corruption, this should be made to look as undesirable as possible. The main recommendation is to increase the probability of detection and prosecution as much as possible by use of monitoring processes, as well as raising the size of penalties imposed. Raising wage levels also makes the alternative – honesty – relatively more attractive. This principle is reflected even in the UK legal system, where judges' compensation is intended not to create dissatisfaction, and place them 'beyond temptation' so that they are unlikely to be corrupted.

Whilst the model assumes that the benefits of corruption cannot be controlled, the implications of the regulation theory discussed above suggest that this is possible. By reducing the potential rents created through the regulatory process, the potential size of 'rational' bribes that might be paid by consumers to officials are also reduced. To do this, a government should aim to ensure that state services' 'shadow prices' and their level of provision are close to those for a free market.

Some anti-corruption models closely mirror some of the efficiency wage model's factors. For example, the Australian approach to anti-corruption (Gorta, 1998), is based on criminological research and work on fraud examination, but lists as the general forms of corruption deterrence:

i) Increasing the perceived effort required by the offender; ii) Increasing perceived risks; iii) Reducing the anticipated rewards; iv)Increasing social controls; [and] v) Inducing guilt. (1998: 81)

It also states a range of specific examples of policy under each of these headings (see Gorta, 1998: 81, Table 2). Whilst factor (ii) relates to the probability of capture and prosecution from above, which depends on the monitoring and effectiveness of legal institutions, and (iii), directly relates to the level of benefits, (i), (iv) & (v) also relate to benefits as they

Table 3.2:   Internal policies to deter corruption

1. *Monitoring expenditure,* such as internal and external audit procedures.
2. *Internal checks and balances* (audit approach):
    a. segregation of responsibility and co-signatory;
    b. limited authority requiring approvals of transactions from senior management;
    c. 'stop limits' when budgets, authorised transactions, etc., go beyond predetermined levels;
    d. close monitoring of data and enforcement of rules.
3. *Whistleblower policies*
4. *Management policies:*
    a. Clear procedures, guidelines, and contract requirements;
    b. Ethical codes of conduct and encouragement of ethos;
    c. Hire those with good ethical behaviour (*less* likely to offend);
    d. Be aware of networks that enable co-operation to create 'corruption structures' (Liu, 1983) such as using vertical authority-based networks or horizontal peer networks – and be aware of recruitment out of external social groups;
    e. Investigate suspicions – if it looks dodgy it very probably is (the 'Swan' effect – most of the interesting activity is below the surface);
    f. Suspect round numbers;
    g. Educate employees – misfeasance and malfeasance prosecutions should be publicised; compliance training and separate clearly designated reporting officers with responsibility for money-laundering problems, etc.

reduce the attractiveness of the reward from corruption. The approach incorporates a strong reliance on strategies to combat the common justifications and moral neutralisations used by offenders to rationalise their acts (Gorta, 1998: 75), as suggested by the work of Cressey (1953). These models combine to provide us with a range of anti-corruption strategies that can be implemented at an organisational level (see Table 3.2).

Beyond the individual to structural models

An alternative type of model that takes a very different approach to corruption deterrence is the 'environmental' model. This type is used by several agencies when expressing their approach to anti-corruption strategies, and often reflects the concerns expressed by the NIE over the negative impacts of inadequate legal, social and cultural institutions. In essence environmental models analyse the influences on corruption at a societal level, equivalent to 'macroeconomic' reasoning in mainstream economic policy. The most influential model of this type is Klitgaard's

(1988) anti-corruption approach which is based on both the theoretical literature in political economy, and also on practical experience of the implementation of anti-corruption strategies. It is stated in the form of an equation that predicts the extent of corruption given the size of three different variables:

CORRUPTION = MONOPOLY + DISCRETION − ACCOUNTABILITY

This model, whilst misleadingly brief, covers many aspects of the corruption problem, and forms the basis of the original USAID anti-corruption strategy (USAID, 2005: 13), with, in most cases, each factor acting as an indicator of several others.

The extent of monopolisation of a country will reflect a range of influences, such that significant state-run monopolies, private sector monopolies or oligopolies would suggest corruption problems, but for different reasons. Significant state-sector monopoly could imply that the price structure of the country contained many 'shadow prices' that created the incentive to pay bribes to administrators for preferential provision of the relatively cheap goods and services produced. This would be associated with rent-seeking behaviour by administrators. On the other hand, private sector monopolies, if they existed, would have the incentive to 'capture' regulators and influence them to maintain or raise the regulatory burden on organisations that constituted barriers to the entry of new potential competitors. Anti-corruption policies would therefore aim to reduce the extent of monopolisation in the state and private sectors.

The extent of bureaucratic or executive discretion would of course indicate the degree of 'agency' problems that existed in the control of those in administrative posts. The problem of limiting the extent of agents' discretion has been discussed above, but it is one that is costly to solve due to the high costs of constructing effective restrictions within employment contracts, and monitoring and enforcing them. This also reflects Cressey's (1953) identification of the need for perpetrators of corruption to feel that they had the ability to commit corrupt acts (as well as get away with them). Although the costs of restricting this are high, the costs of corruption shown above indicate that these are worth incurring. Audit professionals will recommend a range of strategies to restrict the potential abuse of power of individuals, and these must be mindful of the fact that even those who must, due to their position, have executive powers can be 'kept honest' to some extent by 'checks and balances' – procedures that make abuse difficult to perpetrate and hide. This may involve the separation of duties so that individuals must make decisions over large financial transactions jointly with others. Whilst 'co-signatory' policies do not appear particularly effective, it reduces the likelihood of corrupt acts, as it requires a co-incidence of two or more corrupt individuals in a decision-making group (see Table 3.2).

Whilst the restriction of administrative discretion is an important anti-corruption device, the effectiveness of this strategy will be greatly reduced in the absence of a system of oversight capable of detecting deviation from proper behaviour in the organisation. Audit procedures are essential internally, to verify that accurate records are kept that will permit investigation of corrupt practices. External scrutiny is equally likely to act as a deterrent, and so the encouragement and education of civil society groups is likely to improve the efficiency of provision of services and reduce corruption. This is supported by the evidence of the Public Expenditure Tracking Surveys as reported above (see Reinikka & Svensson, 2002).

USAID, World Bank and environmental models

Whilst the early USAID anti-corruption strategy was closely based on the Klitgaard approach, this has been complemented with wider environmental analysis in subsequent versions (USAID, 2005: 15). The revised model suggests four general determinants of corruption: those from political competition, economic competition, social attitudes and behaviour, and the bureaucratic and regulatory environment. These again appear largely justified by the theoretical models, although additional elements are introduced. Bureaucratic and regulatory environment and the extent of economic competition, for instance, relate clearly to the problems of regulation and monopoly discussed above. A range of 'environmental' policies can be implemented by regulators, however, that do not promote monopolisation of markets as much as improve the quality of governance in organisations (see Table 3.3). Whilst these will still incur compliance costs which will constitute deterrents to new firms entering industries, their overall impact would be expected to be positive, from the experience of practical corruption investigators (see Wells, 2001).

The fourth general determinant of the revised USAID model, 'Political competition', is assumed to make for more responsive governments that, due to the existence of active and credible opposition parties, are forced to behave better. In this model, the government is always exposed to the scrutiny of its opposition party at any particular time. This also, coincidentally, provides a justification for the 'democratisation' policy pursued under US foreign policy. In the form stated during the worst years of the Russian transition, the principle had originally been that wealth-creation would lead eventually to democracy-creation, which can be justified by

Table 3.3:   Environmental deterrents to corruption

1. Legal requirements for transparency – recording and publishing information on decisions processes, and outcomes.
2. Court 'efficiency' – juries and judges are not susceptible to bribery.
3. Participation of NGOs in oversight activity.
4. Independent media to inform stakeholders of abuse.
5. Limit structural reforms, which permit large 'one-off gains' in bribes to administrators, and should be avoided or highly transparent, e.g. privatisation.
6. Money laundering law and regulation (reduces likelihood of gain).
7. Specialist units to gather evidence and prosecute.
8. Penalties that must be proportionate.

examination of historical cases such as Britain (see World Bank, 2000). Consequent events, however, have demonstrated that a more active approach may be necessary. Similarly, social attitudes and behaviour are of obvious significance as the determinants of individuals' interpretation of corrupt acts. All economic acts are embedded on, and constrained or partly determined by social institutions (Granovetter, 1985), and social factors are as likely to rationalise corrupt actions, in the individuals' minds, as economic ones. Problems of endemic, systemic corruption, as discussed above, are likely to lend acceptability to individuals' decisions to participate in corruption that would not otherwise exist (see Liu, 1983).

A more complex model of anti-corruption policy is outlined in the World Bank's report *Anti-corruption in Transition* (2000), which has since been frequently quoted in the literature. In particular it expands the range of environmental considerations in the determination of corruption, recognising several institutional factors that had not been prominently recognised in previous models (see figure, World Bank, 2000: xxii). It considers explicitly

> Institutional restraints, political accountability, competitive private sector, public sector management, independent media, and civil society participation. (xxii)

In addition, it emphasises the importance for transparency and accountability of fostering an independent media (World Bank, 2000: xxiii). In practice, however, it simply lists more of the detail that the Klitgaard model leaves as implicit.

Whilst this 'institutional' emphasis is valuable, as emphasised in the reform of the transition countries of the former Soviet Union and Central and Eastern Europe, the model fails to emphasise an important lesson learnt in the transition. Despite the implicit assumption that institutional changes can be simultaneously created (and even in some cases naively assuming that they will naturally evolve themselves due to pressure from interest groups who will benefit from the reforms), institutional reforms in fact require careful introduction that logically builds the new framework of control. Often, for instance, the legal reforms are seen as the most fundamental if others are to develop effectively. Secondly, institutional reforms are interrelated, just as social or political institutions are, so that significant interaction effects exist between the elements of the institutional structure that are, and those which are not, shown in the reform model. These neglected problems of sequencing and interactions or spillovers caused significant problems in the process of reforms during economic transition, as illustrated in Chapters 7 and 8 by Zagainova and Dadalauri in this volume. Thus, while valuable for its clarity, the model should therefore be viewed with some caution.

Further developments within NIE

Whilst the NIE is broadly neoliberal in its approach, incorporating many aspects of the neoclassical economic consensus into its analysis, it also gives limited recognition to the role of fundamental, underlying institutions upon which the economic, organisational, and legal institutions that constitute its main focus all depend. This is the basis of the World Bank model as described above. In contrast, the approaches of the 'wider institutionalism', as demonstrated in the Old Institutional, post-Keynesian and Austrian economics, recognise significant features from the wider institutional environment that would significantly augment the analytical power of NIE, creating in turn a more effective approach for the analysis of problems of corruption. In particular, the focus of the latter schools on 'realist' economics creates an inherent advantage over the NIE which adopts many of the tenets of orthodox theory that are largely at odds with reality.

Some of those involved in the NIE's revival of institutional economics do recognise the relevance of the wider set of institutions explicitly in their analysis. Coase (1988) contributed greatly to the realism of economics due to his reconsideration of the nature of organisations and their function, which 'opened the black box of the firm' and enabled re-interpretation of the behaviour of and within firms. The orthodox view of the firm was of a simple technical mechanism dominated by logical 'rules' where 'each business firm maximises profits subject to its demand and cost conditions' (De Alessi, 1983: 65), with little, if any, weight given to the firm's embeddedness in and influence on the institutions which make up the socio-economic system. As De Alessi (1983: 65–6) shows, a range of dissatisfied economists extended this interpretation significantly by incorporating limits on the rationality of decision-making as well as including a wider range of motivations. This has provided economics with some ability to see the strategic nature of firm decision making in a more realistic light.

The strategic nature of corruption emerged as firms' motivations were better understood, such that corruption may be seen as a normal business behaviour in certain circumstances (Hellman et al., 2000) and is subject to the usual calculative criteria such as in the problem of calculating optimal bribes given corrupt environments (Lui, 1985). Baumol has also recognised that entrepreneurial decision-making includes choices between legitimate ('productive') activity such as competitive innovation and illegitimate ('destructive') forms of activity such as rent-seeking (1990: 893). These appear to complement closely the institutional analysis of Williamson (2000) who reviews the opportunistic behaviour of individuals in organisations and in the wider economy, which requires the imposition of structures to ensure the compliance of individuals with the duties of their positions within organisations. In the broader context it would also suggest the need for external mechanisms to ensure that such opportunistic behaviour does not lead the firm to corrupt behaviour.

Williamson, unlike many in the NIE, also recognises the wider context of institutions that influence individual behaviour (see Table 3.4). Here, market and organisational institutions are understood to depend crucially on social and cultural institutions that are relatively intractable and influence behaviour at the most fundamental level. Social and cultural institutions are interpreted as the most influential by many 'Old Institutionalists' in determining both the legal and political institutions that NIE charges with providing the system of institutional checks upon the aberrant behaviour of firms and individuals.

This recognition of 'crossover' between the fields of social, political, and economic activity has fundamental and wide-ranging implications for economic analysis which have only begun to be explored in any detail. Only limited attempts, but with the notable exception of North (1971, 1990), have been made in the New Institutionalism to explore the opportunities presented for firms' behaviour outside the limited field envisaged for the firm by neoclassical theory, which include the potential for businesses to indirectly influence formal legal institutions, and for society to either support or undermine the operation of legal institutions in practice. There remains a relatively blind trust in the ability of the

Table 3.4:   Economics of institutions (NIE view)

Level		Frequency (years)	Purpose (NIE view)
L4: Neoclassical economics/ agency theory	Resource allocation and employment (prices and quantities; incentive alignment)	Continuous	Get the marginal conditions right. 3rd order economising
L3: Transaction cost economics	Governance: play of the game – esp. contract (aligning governance structures with transactions)	1 to 10	Get the governance structures right. 2nd order economising
L2: Economics of property rights/positive political economy	Institutional environment: formal rules of the game – esp. property (polity, judiciary, bureaucracy)	10 to 100	Get the institutional environment right. 1st order economising
L1: Social theory	Embeddedness: informal institutions, customs, traditions, norms, religion	100 to 1000	Often noncalculative; spontaneous

Source: adapted from Williamson (2000) p. 597. Each level determines the institutions of the level above, and is in turn susceptible to feedback effects from those institutions. North (1971) calls levels 1&2 fundamental/primary and level 3 secondary institutions. The classification of the formal, hierarchical and market levels as 'economising', and the social level 'non-calculative' reflects the NIE, and particularly not the OIE, view of social institutions.

legal system to correct economic problems which significantly restricts the ability of the NIE to make realistic contributions to the debate on corruption. Those attempts that have been made from the NIE side have been quite atypical of their work in general (see Graf Lambsdorff et al., 2004). As a consequence there persists a view that corruption is a problem involving 'the firm as innocent victim', simply requiring a small state and the design of a robust set of legal institutions to enable free market economics to correct the problem.

New theoretical opportunities

It is only recently that more detailed analysis has been conducted into patterns of corruption and the differences between forms of, and motivations for, corruption. Many types of economic agents in the mainstream analysis are implicitly constrained in their activities only to within prescribed roles. Corruption and opportunism must, more realistically, be at least considered a possibility in all institutional structures, and *in relation* to all other institutional structures. Thus, previous approaches have analysed the firm's 'corruption decision', where it has been considered at all, in isolation, with little recognition of its position within the complete range of strategic opportunities open to the firm, themselves conditioned by other institutional influences.

This failure reflects the shortcomings in the NIE which has dominated institutional analysis in recent years. The institutional structure of the society overall has impacts on the economic elements of individual interactions, and a wide and complexly evolving range of institutional forms exist in any modern economy (see Table 3.4). Whilst the NIE has concentrated on transaction costs and the theory of formal political, legal and organisational institutions, the neglected social institutions interact with these others in a way which affects both their fundamental character and the resulting patterns of behaviour directed by them. Logically, these institutional levels might each offer avenues of strategic behaviour for individuals or organisations to enhance their earnings. Firms may participate in 'good works' in order to prove social credentials that may ultimately create some pay-back for the business. Similarly the firms may specifically target legal or political institutions for their concerted or individual action. Many of the firm's activities in the purchase of political or social capital are largely, although not universally, interpreted as corruption, but these are in fact only some of a wider range of strategies that firms may use, both legitimate and illegitimate, or perhaps constructive and destructive, to produce gains for themselves. The firm is therefore likely to adopt a combination of strategies across a range of different institutional forms, social, political and economic, in its pursuit of profit, creating a considerably more complex view of the potential behaviour of the firm, and the requirements of anti-corruption policy.

Once we have recognised the wider set of opportunities available to firms, it is possible to extend the scope of the standard corruption models incorporating some of these factors, such as social institutions, whose omission was most puzzling from the standard theories. Applying standard economic logic, if we view the firm as the 'consumer' of corruption, or more specifically of the under-supplied or discretionary public services which provide firms with potential gains if corruption is possible, then a consumer equilibrium (Jevons, 1888) will occur across a range of types of institutional strategy which would accrue gains for the firm. Other authors have generalised the principle of consumer equilibrium before, with benefits to the accuracy of their models. Dorfman and Steiner (1954) apply the concept of general consumer equilibrium to the firm's decision on its 'consumption' of marketing when faced with a range of strategies capable of maximising profits. Similarly we can extend the concept of competitive equilibrium to the problem of corruption, viewing it as one of a range of strategic approaches to acquisition of property rights.

This principle would lead to similar outcomes to that of a consumer equilibrium if the benefits of a strategic course decline as its use increases, similar to the decline in utility return to consumption as levels rise; and more controversially, if marginal costs of these strategies rise in line with their use (which is not always assumed to be the case). In this case, use of each strategy would increase until the ratio of marginal benefits to marginal costs (MB/MC) was equal for each type of strategy or institutional type of behaviour. In considering this 'equilibrium' for competitive firms, these strategic behaviours could take any form, not simply the pursuit of profit through normal market competition. Any institutional avenue may be open to the firm in practice, not excluding ones that are technically proscribed, if we view this in its practical application. Firms may consider expenditures in lobbying for self-beneficial changes in legal codes, open market competition, public relations and promotions all to be comparable strategic behaviours.

Implications of using wider institutionalism in anti-corruption policy design

The treatment of corruption as a largely institutionally determined behaviour and the recognition of the firm as a potential consumer of corruption, rather than being necessarily an innocent victim of it, rectify some of the problems in the existing analysis. Several issues obviously remain, however, that require further examination, such as a corresponding detailed analysis of the demand for corruption in terms of the relative costs and benefits of all the forms of institutional strategy of which corruption is one. Of course, several such factors have already been examined in the theoretical and empirical literature, such as the nature and effectiveness of legal systems following North (1990), although strong evidence of legal corruption and also legal ineffectiveness still tends to be ignored in much institutional analysis of corruption. Also, the supply side of corruption needs to be comprehensively re-examined, including in the demand and supply side interrelationships. For example, if lax legal institutions encourage both the demand for, and supply of corruption, the impact on the overall incidence of corruption caused by this particular factor would remain unclear overall. However, such interrelationships, once exposed, could at least help inform policy in holistically dealing with both.

The model has implications for the generally hostile approach of BWIs to state regulation in their analysis of corruption. Corruption, taxation and regulation, have generally been viewed as a restrictive factor in the performance of economies (see Mauro, 1995; Wei, 2000; Jaffe et al., 1995 respectively), and deregulation credited with the role of enhancing efficient markets, including by the World Bank (2000: xxiii).The general hostility of IFIs towards regulation often leads to excessive reduction of state powers needed for anti-corruption work and other key state objectives. More fundamentally, simple deregulation ignores the demand for corruption from the perspective of the firm, and may in turn privatise or change the strategy adopted by the firm for particularistic gain. Instead, we must view regulation as a universal requirement of economies, a complex and difficult task that needs to be done sensitively in order to address its potentially destructive impacts.

Overall, corruption is doubly linked to regulation. Regulation (in price or market entry interventions) does create rents that attract firms to corrupt behaviour (despite this straying outside the typical model of firm behaviour!) but it is also required by the existence of other corruption patterns that would exist independently of the existence of such regulations. It is a market failure that cannot be reduced entirely by deregulation. This confusion requires us to examine the causes or motivations for corruption within the wider purview of 'old' institutionalism, linking explanation of why it occurs to the different forms it might take.

Conclusion

Generally corruption is seen as a problem of developing countries, but the analysis presented here reveals that to be a massive over-simplification. In fact corruption is determined by individuals' decisions and their motivations, as well as a complex range of factors in the environment around them. Even assuming that every individual is a selfish opportunist, economic modelling suggests that there are a range of strategies that can combat this tendency to corruption. Using a combination of models we have derived a range of policies that can be implemented in organisations to combat corruption. While no model is ever a complete fit with the world it seeks to approximate, much criticism of economists has its roots in claims to predictability that the original modeller has not, in fact, made. Instead, models have a more nuanced effect on successful policy and should be applied with due regard to externalities.

Using wider institutionalism to further theorise the 'demand' for, or consumption of, corruption counters the mainstream assumption that corruption is primarily a problem of the state. Evidence from the transition economies (Hellman et al., 2000; Gray et al, 2004) suggests that the relationship between enterprises and the state is both less uniform and more complex. Moreover, an analysis of the decision making process for 'consumers' of corruption suggests that levels of corruption are not just dependent on specific anti-corruption strategies, or even the costs and benefits of specific cases of corruption, but are in fact dependent on a more complex set of factors across the institutional forms which firms may participate in for the purpose of gain. The narrow conception of the activity of the firm and the entrepreneur within economic institutions is dangerously simplistic and accordingly produces flawed anti-corruption policy. A broader, institutional view of economic activity provides the potential to open up the analysis of corruption and the construction of policy in constructive new ways.

This analysis extends the examination of the 'demand' side for corruption by placing it against alternative strategies that firms may adopt using different institutional routes: through forms of activity seeking to win advantage within the market, political and legal institutional structures of the economy. In this perspective, the attempts of firms to perform acts of 'state capture' (Hellman et al., 2000) rather than simple bribing of administrative or judicial officials (see Kaufmann and Wei, 2000) appears more a rational strategy to pursue competitive advantage by use of the most efficient institutional arrangements. This approach recognises the inevitability of corruption from opportunistic firms operating in an environment where redistribution of property rights need not only be pursued through the 'pursuit of profit', as assumed in orthodox economic analysis.

The inevitability of corruption provides strong grounds for the imposition of (considered) regulation rather than its removal as often advocated by neoliberal economists working in both academic environments and within the Washington institutions. As demonstrated here for the case of the firm's demand for corruption, a more general integration of 'wider institutional' analysis has the potential to extend models of corruption significantly. It will enable the design of more effective anti-corruption strategies, specifically designed within social and political context, rather than taken off the shelf in a 'one size fits no-one' approach.

The examination of the costs of corruption here also found that it still predominantly impacts on the poorest, least educated and least informed, even within individual societies. The impact of general education across the society as a whole and also specific 'corruption education' within organisations may offer possible supporting strategies for the deterrence of corruption. It remains a systemic, self-perpetuating problem, however, that will be resistant to any policies, no matter how wisely formulated, such that reducing corruption cannot rely on any 'quick fixes'. Anti-corruption policies, as demonstrated by the prominent cases of corruption in rich industrial countries, are essential in all societies, and must be permanent features of the environment of government and business, rather than the subject of an emotive, fashionable campaign.

Note

1. The tax revenues seem inevitably to deteriorate in transition or reform of an economy. See Casson (1994) who points out that tax revenue is particularly badly hit by the fall in real incomes which significantly reduces both the affordable margin of income tax, and the potential to raise funds through borrowing during transition. In addition, Wei (2001) indicates that taxation of foreign firms to correct a budget deficit is a significant discouragement to FDI (in fact more so than corruption), which is another important source of income to host country governments.

References

Association of Certified Fraud Examiners (2004), Report to the Nation on Occupational Fraud and Abuse. available at www.cfenet.com/pdfs/2004RttN.pdf accessed 24/3/06

Baumol, William J. (1990) 'Entrepreneurship: productive, unproductive and destructive,' *Journal of Political Economy*, 98/5: 893–921

Becker, G., and Stigler, G. (1974), 'Law enforcement, malfeasance and the compensation of enforcers,' *Journal of Legal Studies*, 3, 1–19

Campbell, J. L., and Pedersen, O. K. (2001) The rise of neoliberalism and institutional analysis' in Campbell, J. L. & Pedersen, O. K. (eds) *The Rise of Neoliberalism and Institutional Analysis*. Princeton NJ: Princeton University Press, pp. 1–24

Casson, M. (1994), 'Enterprise culture and institutional change in Eastern Europe', in Buckley, P. J. & Ghauri, P. N. (1994) *The Economics of Change in East and Central Europe: Its impact on international business*, London, Academic Press, pp. 33–54

Coase, R. H. (1988), *The Firm, the Market and the Law*, Chicago, University of Chicago Press

Cressey, D. R. (1953), *Other People's Money: a study in the social psychology of embezzlement*, Glencoe, Free Press

De Alessi, Louis (1983) 'Property rights, transactions costs, and X-efficiency: an essay in economic theory,' *American Economic Review*, 73/1 (Mar): 64–81

De Soto, H. (1990), *The Other Path*, New York, Harper & Row

De Souza Martins, J. (1996), 'Clientilism and corruption in contemporary Brazil', chapter 9 in Little, W. & Posada-Carbó, E. (eds) *Political Corruption in Europe and Latin America*, London, Macmillan / Institute of Latin American Studies, University of London, pp. 195–218

Djankov, S., La Porta, R., Lopez-De-Silanes, F., & Shleifer, A (2002), 'The regulation of entry,' *Quarterly Journal of Economics*, 117/1, 1–45

Dorfman, Robert and Steiner, Peter O. (1954) 'Optimal advertising and optimal quality,' *American Economic Review*, 44/5: 826–36

EBRD (2003), *Transition Report 2003: Integration and regional cooperation*, London, European Bank for Reconstruction and Development

Ehrlich, I. & Lui, F. T. (1999), 'Bureaucratic corruption and endogenous economic growth,' *Journal of Political Economy*, 107/6 (Part 2: Symposium on the Economic Analysis of Social Behavior in Honor of Gary S. Becker): S270–S293

Ernst & Young (2002), 'Fraud study' available at: www.ey.com/global/Content.nsf/US/Media_-_Release_-_08-05-02DC, cited at www.icpas.org (Indiana Chartered Public Accountants Society) 'Fraud 101' accessed 12/6/2006

Graf Lambsdorff, J., Taube, M., & Schramm, M. (eds) (2004) *The New Institutional Economics of Corruption*, London, Routledge

Granovetter, M. (1985), 'Economic action and social structure: the problem of embeddedness,' *American Journal of Sociology*, 91, 481–510

Gray, C. Hellman, J. and Ryterman, R. (2004) *Anticorruption in Transition 2: Corruption in Enterprise-State Interaction in Europe and Central Asia 1999–2002*, (Washington, World Bank)

Gorta, A. (1998), 'Minimising corruption: applying lessons from the crime prevention literature,' *Crime, Law and Social Change*, 30, 67–87

Gujarati, Damodar (2003), *Basic Econometrics*, London, McGraw Hill Higher Education

Hayes, A. F. (2005), *Statistical Methods for Communication Science*, Mahwah NJ: Erlbaum

Hayes, A. F. and Cai, L. (2005), 'Using heteroscedasticity-consistent error estimators in OLS regression: an introduction and software implementation', Unpublished manuscript, School of Communication, Ohio State University

Hellman, J. S., Jones, G. and Kaufmann, D. (2000) 'Seize the State, Seize the Day: State Capture, Corruption and Influence in Transition.' (World Bank Policy Research Working Paper 2444)

Huntington, S. (1968), *Political Order in Changing Societies*, London, Yale University Press

ITIM (2005), 'Geert Hofstede cultural dimensions' available at www.geert-hofstede.com accessed 5/2/2005

Jaffe, A. B., Peterson, S. R., Portney, P. R., & Stavins, R. N. (1995) 'Environmental regulation and the competitiveness of U.S. manufacturing: what does the evidence tell us?,' *Journal of Economic Literature*, 33/1: 132–63

Jevons, W. S. (1888) *The Theory of Political Economy*, 3rd edn, London: Macmillan

Johnson, S., Kaufmann, D., & Shleifer, A. (1997), 'The unofficial economy in transition', *Brookings Papers in Economic Activity*, Issue 2, 159–239

Kaufmann, D. and Wei, S-J. (2000) 'Does "Grease Money" Speed Up the Wheels of Commerce?', IMF Working Paper WP/00/64

Klitgaard, R. (1998), *Controlling Corruption*, Berkeley, University of California Press
Krueger, A. O. (1974), 'The political economy of the rent-seeking society,' *American Economic Review*, 64/3 (June), 291–303
Lancaster, K. (1966), 'A new approach to consumer theory,' *Journal of Political Economy*, 74, 132–57
Liu, Alan P. L. (1983), 'The politics of corruption in the People's Republic of China,' *American Political Science Review*, 77/3, 602–33
Lui, F. T. (1985) 'An equilibrium queuing model of bribery,' *Journal of Political Economy*, 93/4: 760–81
Mauro, P. (1995), 'Corruption and Growth,' *Quarterly Journal of Economics*, 110/3, 681–712
McChesney, F. S. (1987), 'Rent extraction and rent creation in the economic theory of regulation,' *Journal of Legal Studies*, 16, 101–18
North, D. C. (1971) 'Institutional change and economic growth,' *Journal of Economic History*, 31/1: 118–25
North, D. C. (1974), 'Beyond the New Economic History,' *Journal of Economic History*, 34/1, March, 1–7
North, D. C. (1990), *Institutions, Institutional Change and Economic Performance*, Cambridge, Cambridge University Press
Pigou, A. C. (1938), *The Economics of Welfare*, 4th edn., London, Macmillan
Ramos, M. (2003), 'Auditors' responsibility for fraud detection,' *Journal of Accountancy* (Online issues: January 2003) available at www.aicpa.org/PUBS/JOFA/jan2003/ramos.htm accessed 07/06/2006
Reinikka, R. and Smith, N. (2004), *Public Expenditure Tracking Surveys in Education*, Paris, UNESCO International Institute for Educational Planning
Reinikka, R. and Svensson, J. (2002), 'Measuring and understanding corruption at the micro level.' Chapter 8 in Della Porta, Donatella and Rose-Ackerman, Susan (eds) *Corrupt Exchanges: empirical themes in the politics and political economy of corruption*, Baden-Baden, Nomos Verlagsgesellshaft
Schneider, F. (2002), 'The size and development of the shadow economies and the shadow economy labor force of 22 transition and 21 OECD countries: what do we really know?' paper presented at OECD Round Table Conference 'On the Informal Economy', Sofia, Bulgaria, April
Shapiro, C., & Stiglitz, J. E. (1984), 'Equilibrium unemployment as a worker discipline device,' *American Economic Review*, 74/3, 433–44
Stigler, G. J. (1971), 'The Theory of Economic Regulation,' *Bell Journal of Economics and Management Science*, 2, 3–21
Stiglitz, J. (2002), *Globalization and its Discontents*, London, Penguin Books
Transparency International (2006) 'About Corruption' available at www.transparency.ie/about_cor/default.htm accessed 13/6/06, 2002
Tullock, G. (1989), 'Controlling corruption,' *Journal of Economic Literature*, 27/2, 658–9
UNODCCP (2002), 'Global Dynamics of Corruption, the role of the United Nations helping member states build integrity to curb corruption.' Global programme against corruption conferences. Vienna, October 2002 (CICP 3, prepared by Petter Langseth, Centre for International Crime Prevention, ODCCP)
USAID (2005), *USAID Anti-corruption Strategy*, Washington DC, USAID PD-ACA-557
Wei, S-J. (2000), 'How taxing is corruption on international investors?', *Review of Economics and Statistics*, 82/1, 1–11

Wells, J. T. (2001), 'Why employees commit fraud,' *Journal of Accountancy* (Online issues, February) available at www.aicpa.org/PUBS/JOFA/feb2001/wells.htm accessed 30/6/06

Williamson, O. E. (1985), *The Economic Institutions of Capitalism*, New York, Free Press

Williamson, O. E. (2000) 'The new institutional economics: taking stock, looking ahead,' *Journal of Economic Literature*, 38/3 (September): 595–613

World Bank (1992), *Governance and Development*, Washington DC, World Bank

World Bank (2000), *Anticorruption in Transition: a contribution to the policy debate*, Washington DC, World Bank

World Bank (2004), 'News and Broadcast: the costs of corruption' available at web.worldbank.org/WBSITE/EXTERNAL/NEWS/0,,co...4457~pagePK:34370~ piPK:34424~theSitePK:4607,00.html accessed 13/06/2006

Part II
Corruption, Political Development and Anti-Corruption Campaigns

4
Tickling Donors and Tackling Opponents: the Anti-Corruption Campaign in Malawi

David Hall-Matthews[1]

Introduction: Mutharika's anti-corruption campaign

Boos rang out from supporters of the United Democratic Front (UDF) as their own candidate, Bingu wa Mutharika, was sworn in as President of Malawi on 24 May 2004. During his inauguration speech, Mutharika upset his party followers – but won cheers from other sections of the audience – with the following provocative statement of intent:

> Fellow Malawians, an important aspect of economic reform in our country is to stamp out corruption. Corruption is the enemy of growth and prosperity. It robs the government and the people of Malawi – especially the poor – of their legitimate right to economic prosperity by diverting resources away from economic and social development into the coffers of a few. Therefore there will be zero tolerance of corruption. I shall . . . ensure swift investigation, prosecution and punishment of public officers at all levels – and I repeat, at all levels – who are found guilty of corruption, theft, mismanagement [and] abuse of power in all its forms. (Mutharika, 24 May 2004)

The speech launched Mutharika's unexpected anti-corruption campaign, which can be seen to have three related motivations: to create an effective developmental state; to emasculate his political rivals; and to restore suspended aid flows. Thus, presidential rhetoric of reform to enable development may be sincere, but is also aimed to woo the reluctant donor community, while attacking Mutharika's predecessor, Bakili Muluzi, with the aim of reducing his capacity for political interference. By examining the context of widespread corruption and following the bumpy trajectory of Mutharika's ongoing campaign against it, this chapter will consider the relative significance of, and relationships between, these three motivations. The chapter evaluates Mutharika's level of commitment and prospects for success by analysing the highest profile cases within the anti-corruption campaign, and interrogates the wider implications for Malawian politics, development and relationships with donors. The chapter illustrates how anti-corruption interventions meet with complex and competing political motivations in the country charged with reform, some of which share the normative framework of the blueprint donor programme, others of which are more contextual and expedient. A central motive for domestically-driven anti-corruption campaigns seems to be to undermine and delegitimise political opponents, at least in systemically clientelist polities such as Malawi.

The history of corruption in Malawi

Hastings Kamuzu Banda was typical of postcolonial leaders in East and Southern Africa in ruling via a one-party system and strongly repressing civil society and media during his 30-year regime. As a result, widespread corruption was never publicly discussed before his democratic deposition in 1994 (Hussein, 2005) and not seen as the most important of his failings subsequently. Muluzi's regime created the possibility of civil society scrutiny, yet it was also characterised by endemic corruption. In an earlier era, his credentials as a business-friendly democrat may have been enough for this to be overlooked by cynical donors as 'typically African'. However, by maintaining a clientelist system at a time when donors had started to focus on good governance after the end of the cold war, Muluzi left himself open to allegations of undisguised abuse of office, even though it may have been on a lesser scale than Banda's disguised activities. Muluzi's patrimonial style finally backfired when he hand-picked Mutharika to succeed him, thinking him amenable to influence and unlikely to emulate Levy Mwanawasa in neighbouring Zambia, who had ordered the arrest of his predecessor, Frederick Chiluba. Mutharika used the anti-corruption campaign against Muluzi nonetheless, although the structure of Malawi as a clientelist state, and political office as a source of wealth, are likely to survive the current battle.

  When Banda's monolithic Press Trust Corporation was broken up after his defeat in 1994, Muluzi and his closest political allies were quick to gain control of its most profitable aspects, such as the Illovo Sugar Corporation and Shire Buslines Company. Coupled with Banda's repression of entrepreneurialism and the failure of several privatised companies, this encouraged the perception that politics offered ambitious Malawians the best domestic opportunity for financial gain. During the 2004 election campaign, for instance, the owner of a successful abattoir business standing on the UDF ticket, Sidik Mia, estimated having spent 17 million kwacha (K) (£85,000) to win the Chikwawa Mkombezi constituency – more than most parties spent on their national campaigns. While this was an extreme example, it reflected both Muluzi's campaigning style – in which cash and maize were routinely handed out at UDF rallies – and the perceived profitability of a parliamentary seat. Though MPs' salaries are not enormous, generous allowances often exceed the costs of transport or accommodation. A culture of impunity, especially for ministers in Muluzi's bloated cabinet (which stood at 46 by the end of his regime), led to frequent accusations of over-claiming, as well as of non-payment of utility bills and rent. The Malawi Housing Corporation has declared that 'senior officials' built up six million kwacha (£30,000) in unpaid arrears ('Comment', *The Chronicle*, 4 October 2005).

Though Muluzi had created an Anti-Corruption Bureau (ACB), its capacity to deter and even investigate corruption was severely hampered by the need to get permission from the Director of Public Prosecutions (DPP) before bringing any charges. Despite himself estimating that 30 per cent of public funds were lost each year to corruption, mismanagement and fraud ('Backbencher', *The Nation*, 24 June 2006), DPP Fahad Assani failed to approve any prosecutions of ministers during the Muluzi era, despite public ACB investigations into several serious cases (Hussein, 2005). As a result, rumours of unchecked high-level corruption abounded. An unofficial report by a former associate of Muluzi's, Kalonga Stambuli, alleging the use of corrupt activities to finance Muluzi's rise and maintenance of power, was widely circulated in December 2003 before Stambuli's sudden death (Stambuli, undated). Transparency International (TI)'s Corruption Perception Index ranked Malawi 90th out of 146 in 2004, with a score of 2.8, signifying the presence of 'serious corruption'.

The extent of state losses to corruption was confirmed by the National Audit Office report for the 2002–03 financial year, for example, which revealed huge volumes of unrecovered 'dubious payments for goods, services, salaries and allowances' – particularly involving the Ministries of Finance, Education, Labour and Agriculture as well as the Malawi Electoral Commission and even the chronically under-funded ACB – which almost entirely accounted for a budget overspend of K346.4 million (£1.732m) (Langa, 7 January 2006). This was made possible through over 3,000 bank accounts which, according to the current Finance Minister, Goodall Gondwe, were opened and run by government ministries and departments without the Accountant General's knowledge (Kakwesa, 10 November 2005).

More significant than the waste itself, in financial terms, this environment angered the donor community. The IMF suspended payments under the Poverty Reduction and Growth Facility in 2000, followed by the withholding of bilateral budget support in 2001 because, in the subsequent undiplomatic words of DfID Economic Adviser Allan Whitworth, the entire government was 'corrupt and wasteful' (Kasunda, 7 December 2005). Following the disappearance of a grant worth £5000, the Danish government withdrew DANIDA permanently from Malawi. With 80 per cent of the national development budget financed by aid, Muluzi could scarcely fail to take such sanctions seriously, but he was unable to reduce donor hostility to his regime.

Motives for Mutharika's anti-corruption campaign

Mutharika is a technocrat with virtually no political base in Malawi, having worked for the World and African Development Banks, been Secretary-General of the Common Market for East and Southern Africa (COMESA) (until his dismissal for alleged abuse of office) and latterly Governor of the Reserve Bank of Malawi. Muluzi's analogy that together they represented an ideal partnership as an economic 'engineer' and a political fixer was not, therefore, unrealistic. Nonetheless, their different perspectives conspired to tear them apart from the beginning – even though Muluzi was key to securing Mutharika's victory – with a row over the size of the cabinet, which could not both be 'lean', as Mutharika had declared it would, and accommodate all those to whom Muluzi had made promises. Increasingly irked by Muluzi's undisguised back seat driving, Mutharika resigned from the UDF in February 2005 and formed his own party, the Democratic Progressive Party (DP), thus formalising the standoff between the two. The UDF responded by laying impeachment charges against the president. Predictably, both the charges and Mutharika's stated reasons for leaving the party featured allegations of corruption and cheating, ironically including the rigging of the presidential elections (which almost certainly occurred, though it was probably not critical in determining the outcome, and certainly not material in settling any dispute between Mutharika and the UDF, as both had gained by it).

In the context of this high political drama, it seems likely that Bingu wa Mutharika was attracted by all three potential motivations for extending his anti-corruption campaign. First, it is easy to argue that reduction of current levels of corruption is prerequisite for development in Malawi and it is perfectly possible that Mutharika, with his multilateral background, was sincere in seeing it as his first step towards successful economic reform. The theme of an 'Anti-Corruption Day' in February 2006 was 'Fight Corruption: Develop Malawi', which undoubtedly chimed with the donor community, raising the second motive for Mutharika. In the current aid environment (see for example DfID, 2005; Killick, 2004; Mosley, Hudson & Verschoor, 2004), setting out a stall against corruption was the most obvious way to restore external confidence in Malawi – and encourage the resumption of aid streams. Indeed, so donor-friendly were his dictums of good governance, with attacks on corruption juxtaposed with promises of tight budgets and investment in diversification of agricultural exports, that UDF supporters spread the implausible rumour that parts of the speech had been written by British High Commissioner Norman Ling and World Bank Country Representative Dunstan Wai.

The third motive can be seen most clearly of all, however. A campaign designed to clear up the existing culture of corruption inevitably focused attention on the sins of Muluzi and his cronies, giving Mutharika the opportunity to subdue his political opponents through arrests and repeated threats. He began with the dismissal of as many as eighteen senior public servants, including DPP Assani and Inspector-General of Police Joseph Aironi – both seen as too close to Muluzi – and toothless ACB Director Michael Mtegha. This left Mutharika open, however, to accusations of cronyism of his own. The stakes were raised when UDF MPs voted with the opposition to block the ratification of his nominee as the new police chief, Mary Nangwale. Mutharika's resignation from the UDF then exacerbated his isolation in parliament, setting in train a bitter power struggle. Under Muluzi and Banda, parliament had been entirely subservient to government, but the threat of impeachment and absence of a majority – indeed initially of any DP MPs at all – forced Mutharika to resort to other means to reassert his authority.

Investigations into corruption by UDF politicians – starting as early as July 2004 with the arrest of Muluzi's former publicity secretary Humphrey Mvula – were therefore widely understood in the context of this ongoing escalation of political hostilities. When the aggressive new DPP, Ishmael Wadi, declared that he was investigating more than ten unnamed senior ministers and government officials for the theft of a combined total of $80m, for example, an atmosphere of fear was created among the UDF hierarchy. In response, another of Muluzi's closest henchmen, Dumbo Lemani, called Wadi's bluff by carrying an overnight bag around with him in anticipation of imprisonment, while there were frequent rumours from the start – some deliberately started by the UDF – that Muluzi himself was about to be arrested.

Mutharika himself was affected by the mood of hostile paranoia as much as anyone. In January 2005, shortly before leaving the party, he accused three UDF committee members of treason when weapons were alleged to have been found in their cars on arrival for a party meeting, only to 'forgive' them before the evidence could be examined (Banda, 6 January 2005). Two months later, two prominent journalists were arrested after reporting the apparently innocuous story that the president believed his official residence in the capital Lilongwe to be haunted (Sonani & Liwanda, 16 March 2005). In his address to the nation to mark the end of 2005, Mutharika accused both the media and the opposition not only of relentless attacks, but of setting 'treacherous traps' to undermine him (Mutharika, 31 December 2005).

During a speech in the Scottish parliament (after First Minister Jack McConnell had been criticised for choosing so controversial a figure as the beneficiary of a charitable fund (MacDonell, 22 October 2005)), Mutharika again argued that it was the response to his campaign against corruption that was politicised: 'It is for this reason that the opposition cooked up impeachment charges against me, as a way of removing me from power. Their grand idea was to re-install the corrupt government to continue plundering our economy' (Mutharika, 6 November 2005). All three potential motives for the anti-corruption drive can be seen to be linked here, notwithstanding Mutharika's attempt to play down his political aims. Indeed Mutharika's language during the anti-corruption campaign closely echoes normative donor discourse on corruption. The introduction to this volume suggests that a false binary has been propagated between the clean and efficient donor community and corrupt, clientelist African governments (Bracking, 2007). Mutharika, showing his understanding of donor logic, has used a similar approach in attempting to cast the DP as developmentalist and bureaucratic and the UDF as the embodiment of criminal cronyism. At a time when being seen to attack corruption has become a *sine qua non* (Commission for Africa, 2005: 35–7), Mutharika can thus lay claim to be pro-development by the fact of making arrests *per se*, no matter how selectively or ineffectively.

This suggests, nonetheless, that the third motive – undermining his political opponents – was primary. His accusations openly equated the targets of his campaign with his political enemies. Days later, Mutharika unwisely went on to admit that arrests of opponents were not only the cause of the impeachment attempt, but in 'revenge' for it: proclaiming, 'Is that politics? No, it's tit for tat' (Liwanda, 8 November 2005). Cabinet minister Hetherwick Ntaba was even less circumspect: 'If they say the arrests are politically motivated, then we will also say, the impeachment issue is politically motivated. To every action there is a reaction. So Mr President, please continue arresting them' (Nkawi, 18 November 2005).

Corruption cases

Local analysts have tended to categorise corruption according to the level of harm done to the public purse, such as Hussein's distinction between 'petty' and 'systemic' corruption (Hussein, 2005; Khembo, 2005), without breaking it down by type or aims. However, it is useful to use five broad categories in analysing some of the prominent cases that have arisen in Malawi since Bingu wa Mutharika's election: acceptance of bribes during procurement processes; direct theft of public money or goods; abuse of power to subvert rules or avoid costs; use of public (or notionally private) resources for political ends; and minor or technical infringements. Looking at examples that fit under each of these headings may help to reveal Mutharika's priorities. However, given that several high-profile arrests have been made in relation to corrupt activities alleged to have taken place well before his accession – despite the fact that the backlogged ACB and courts cannot keep up with current allegations (the ACB has received over 3000 accusatory reports since its inception in 1997) – the way in which cases have emerged can not be seen to have been systematic.

Nor were they necessarily arbitrary. The initial *modus operandi* of Mutharika's DPP Ishmael Wadi, Attorney General Ralph Kasambara and new ACB Director Gustave Kaliwo was telling. Suspects were arrested in full view of the media and taken to police stations, often in cities far from their homes, for questioning, then released on bail after a few days. At that point, the ACB proceeded to investigate, frequently pointing out that this would be delayed by a lack of staff, before suggesting formal charges, usually some weeks later. This is in spite of suggestions that the ACB had already gathered enough evidence for many cases to proceed, pending approval. Wadi rarely withheld consent. A few cases reached court relatively quickly, but many were buried in a series of appeals and counter-claims. The unhelpful tendency of Kaliwo, Wadi, Kasambara and even Mutharika to finger individuals publicly, before a watertight case had been developed, both increased defendants' chances of acquittal on technical grounds and gave weight to the UDF's claim that the anti-corruption campaign was an excuse for political persecution.

Procurement scams

The first high profile UDF politician to be arrested for corruption was its research director and one of Bakili Muluzi's close allies, Humphrey Mvula, in late July 2004. Despite his clumsy attempts to destroy company records, evidence suggested that he had procured vehicle parts for the national coach company, Shire Buslines – of which he was Chief

Executive – from his cousin, rather than cheaper suppliers. In return, a deposit was alleged to have been paid to the Malawi Housing Corporation on Mvula's behalf (Chilobwe, 15 March 2005). His arrest was the first indication of the seriousness of the rift between Mutharika and the UDF and lent early credibility to the anti-corruption drive itself (Chapalapata, 3 August 2004). Before charges had been formally made, Mutharika fired Mvula from his post, to demonstrate the importance of being above suspicion. Mvula, however, succeeded in winning an injunction against his dismissal – and also in delaying his trial – on the grounds that Shire Buslines was no longer a parastatal, but a government owned private company, and therefore not within Mutharika's purview. His lawyers argued that this ruling meant Mvula could not be guilty of abuse of public office, nor his relatives of bribery (Chilobwe, 15 March 2005).

The obvious switch to a charge of fraud and embezzlement was not made. Instead, the waters were muddied by two bizarre developments. First Mvula was implicated in the 2002 murder of Sheikh Bugidad, Leader of the Sunni Supreme Council of Malawi, who was said to have been 'a thorn in Muluzi's side' and re-arrested, though no evidence was made public (Africa Confidential, 19 November 2004). Then, after visiting Mvula in prison hospital, another Muluzi ally, Dumbo Lemani, claimed that the real motive for the arrests was that Mvula had enough evidence to support a legal challenge by the opposition Malawi Congress Party (MCP) to the presidential election result (Nyirenda, 19 November 2004). Lemani, who died shortly afterwards, claimed that Mvula had confessed to having personally 'stolen' 362,000 votes to Mutharika's advantage, though Mvula himself denied it. When released on bail in February 2005, Mvula announced that he was retiring from politics. Though charges of abuse of office remained against him, no further court hearings took place for over a year, suggesting that his silence – combined with his potential to embarrass Mutharika in the election case – may have earned him a reprieve.

The second high profile politician to be arrested was Sam Mpasu, on 4 November 2005, in relation to an earlier procurement scam involving a contract worth £1.9 million with a British company, Fieldyork International, to supply exercise books when he had been Education Minister in the Muluzi regime (see Jamieson, 4 November 2005; Stambuli, undated). Mpasu had subsequently been appointed as official spokesman both for the UDF and for Muluzi personally during the rift between the party and Mutharika in 2004. It could be argued that it would have been inappropriate to take action earlier, given that an enquiry report, initially commissioned by Muluzi, had only relatively recently been published, under

Mutharika's orders. However it is striking that the timing of Mpasu's arrest coincided with those of several other key figures, at a critical point in Mutharika's attempt to defeat the impeachment case against him. A warrant for Mpasu's arrest was issued the day after an open letter was published by the major donors cautioning MPs against 'precipitate action' against the president, as outlined below (Eastman et al., 27 October 2005). Within the next three weeks, outspoken former UDF minister Clement Stambuli (no relation) was also charged with paying 14 million kwacha (£70,000) to City Motors for repairs to government vehicles that were not fully carried out in 2001 (Ng'ambi, 31 October 2005), while the two UDF MPs most directly involved in the impeachment case were accused of breaching the electoral code. Even the Vice-President, Cassim Chilumpha, who had refused to follow Mutharika out of the party, was briefly arrested on suspicion of a separate education procurement scam, in which K187 million (£935,000) was alleged to have been paid in 2000 for uncompleted school building work (Chiumia, 16 November 2005).

As impeachment pressures reduced, most of these old cases also fell quiet. Even when Mutharika later attempted to dismiss Chilumpha (despite having no constitutional right to do so), the grounds were alleged neglect of duty, with no mention of corruption (BBC, 10 February 2006). Mpasu's trial did commence in February 2006, only to be adjourned after two days. Incriminating evidence was heard against him in that time from senior civil servants, though it was somewhat undermined by defence claims that the most important of them, former Education Principal Secretary Samuel Safuli, had been promised that charges against him relating to the school building scam would be dropped in return (Liwanda, 22 February 2006). Safuli was later sentenced to two years (Theu, 29 March 2007). Thus despite alleged involvement by senior political figures in high value procurement scams, the actual results of these trials was not conviction and public catharsis, but a reconfiguration of relative power among severally mired individuals, who traded influence, position and knowledge to avoid accountability.

Theft of public resources

The first senior figure actually to be convicted of corruption during Mutharika's regime was another close political ally of Muluzi's, John Chikakwiya, the mayor of Blantyre. Chikakwiya was found guilty by Blantyre Magistrates' Court in April 2005 of stealing 400,000 kwacha (£2,000) intended for road maintenance and sentenced to 38 months' imprisonment, reduced to 24 months on appeal. His defence – that he had actually spent K50,000 (£250) on cement and was only guilty of not getting round to using the remaining money (which he produced in court) – was given little credence because road maintenance was not his responsibility but that of the City Assembly Works Department (Chilobwe, 13 December 2005). However, the fact that Chikakwiya was punished despite paying back the arrears, albeit only under trial and two months late, set a precedent that proved hard to sustain, given the climate of allowance payments, which are rarely linked to actual receipts or expenditure. Examples involving members of Mutharika's cabinet were raised by the media, notably Health Minister Ntaba and Labour Minister Ken Lipenga, who had accepted K500,000 (£2,500) and K183,000 (£915) respectively for cancelled overseas trips but were not prosecuted because they offered to repay the sums when they became public knowledge (Kasunda, 6 December 2005; Ng'ambi, 6 December 2005). Such apparent double standards served to confuse the issue of what constitutes corruption, with the result that in December 2005 the Supreme Court quashed Chikakwiya's conviction for theft, while upholding that for abuse of office. His reduced sentence of nine months meant that he was released immediately.

A far more serious case of theft, dating from the Muluzi period, has not yet resulted in any conviction. In 2001, the IMF recommended a reduction in the size of the Strategic Grain Reserve (SGR) (Owusu and Ng'ambi, 2002). When a severe food shortage became apparent later that year, however, it transpired that the entire maize stock had been sold, with the result that hundreds died of starvation (Devereux, 2003). Inquiries instituted both by the British High Commission and the Parliamentary Agriculture Committee were not published, but were widely believed to name senior politicians as beneficiaries. Indeed it was only after they were presented to Muluzi that payment was received for much of the missing maize. Though this meant that it was again not strictly theft, the food crisis ensured that the value of grain increased exponentially, guaranteeing large profits for those who had acquired the SGR supplies at the expense of the population. This incident was critical in breaking the donors' trust for the Muluzi regime.

Suspicion fell particularly on the Managing Director of the Agricultural Development and Marketing Corporation (ADMARC), Friday Jumbe, who had ultimate responsibility for the SGR. Unlike Mpasu, however, Jumbe was not even temporarily penalised by Muluzi. Instead, he was appointed as Finance Minister in the next cabinet reshuffle, effectively giving him oversight over subsequent investigations. His guilt was virtually admitted two years later, however, when he succeeded in blocking Mutharika's attempts to publish the Agriculture Committee's report.

Parliamentary reports are not allowed to implicate individuals in criminal activities without first giving them an opportunity to rebut the accusations, so Jumbe was able, in effect, to plead the Fifth Amendment by not making himself available to the committee (Munthali, 25 April 2005). He was arrested nonetheless, dramatically, at Chileka airport when trying to leave the country in October 2004. He was charged with the misappropriation of K2.9 billion (£14.5m) from ADMARC and the corrupt acquisition of the five-star Superior Hotel in Blantyre with some of the proceeds (Kasunda, 28 October 2004).

Despite, or perhaps because of, the highly emotive nature of the maize scandal and huge sums involved, the case then proceeded very slowly. After Wadi had surprisingly announced that he had no grounds for prosecuting anyone else involved (Semu-Banda, 4 March 2005), Jumbe formally denied four counts of theft and corruption in May 2005, but his trial remains adjourned. Following Mvula's example, Jumbe meanwhile tacitly distanced himself from the UDF, and the government-sponsored *Weekly News* even reported that he was considering joining Mutharika's DP party (9 January 2006).

Abuse of power

Allegations in all of these cases were sufficiently serious to justify the arrests made, though it is also apparent that senior UDF figures had been deliberately targeted. However, Mutharika initially stopped short of apprehending Muluzi himself. The main allegations circulating against him were not of accepting bribes, but of regarding himself as above the law. For example, the presidential right to buy vehicles for personal use without paying hefty import duties was stretched by the purchase of over 150 vehicles in his name, most of which were painted in UDF colours and lent indefinitely to party workers, along with thousands of imported t-shirts and caps bearing party logos. A retrospective demand by the Malawi Revenue Authority (MRA) for over K111 million (£555,000) in duty was circumvented in the absence of documentary evidence that Muluzi was their importer (as opposed to their owner) and by a claim that they had been cleared by the MRA at the time (Banda, 20 August 2005; Namangale, 22 February 2006). Similar questions surround the multi-million kwacha Keza Business Park, built on prime land in the commercial capital, Blantyre, and subsequently leased by one of Muluzi's companies to the MRA. This was sold after the lifting of an injunction obtained by the ACB, which had wanted to investigate how the construction and letting of the lucrative site had been authorised and financed (Chilobwe, 10 November 2005).

Use of resources for political ends

Matters came to a head after two of Muluzi's properties were raided (BBC, 27 October 2005), although subsequent investigations were again painfully slow. The ACB felt it necessary to fly in a computer specialist from the UK to analyse the records, which took two and a half months just to arrange (Nyangulu, 12 January 2006). The investigation established that, during his regime, K1.4 billion (£7 million) had been paid into his personal account from foreign organisations and governments, including Libya, Morocco, Rwanda and Taiwan (Munthali, 31 December 2005). Muluzi smartly devised a political defence, claiming that he was merely channelling party campaign resources. All of the money, according to UDF leader in parliament George Nga Mtafu, was spent on the 2004 election campaign, with Mutharika, therefore, its prime beneficiary (Sonani, 19 October 2005). Without rules against overseas funding of political parties, this would not have been illegal, as long as it could be shown that the donations were intended to be political, which Muammar Gaddafi said Libyan money had been. Thus the UDF was able to reinforce its complaint that the anti-corruption campaign is an excuse for persecution by arguing that Mutharika had ordered the investigation of normal political activity.

Nonetheless, the ACB remained convinced that they had an overwhelming case in relation to the diversion of foreign aid. Kalonga Stambuli (undated), for example, had claimed in his 2003 report that Muluzi commandeered $2 million specifically donated by Taiwan for the construction of military barracks. When they finally moved to arrest Muluzi, on 27 July 2006, however, it immediately became obvious that political contingencies matter more than the weight of evidence. Within hours, ACB director Kaliwo was suspended by Mutharika, who was reported to be furious at the timing of the arrest, during the critical budget session of parliament. This reduced the impact of accusations that Mutharika had sought to distract the opposition from voting against the budget, but undermined any notion of the ACB's independence and damaged the credibility of the anti-corruption campaign as a whole. This was exacerbated four days later when DPP Wadi dropped all 42 counts against Muluzi, amid unsubstantiated rumours that Taiwan (a significant donor to Malawi, which has repeatedly supported its claim to UN recognition as a state) would stop aid if it were to be scrutinised in court. As if to confirm that Muluzi had demonstrated his continuing strength, the situation then descended into farce when Mutharika publicly demanded Wadi's resignation, proclaiming that he had 'done the country more harm than he realises' (BBC, 10 August 2006).

The dismissal of key agents in the anti-corruption campaign is likely to weaken it, as is Mutharika's gauche and contradictory handling of his predecessor's arrest. The political power battle that ensued also confirmed suspicions about the nature of the campaign. Throughout, anti-corruption activities have tended to coincide with periods when Mutharika felt most politically secure. For example, in April 2006, the ACB had upped the political ante by appealing for witnesses that Muluzi had paid bribes to over 40 MPs, in the course of two failed attempts to change the constitution to allow himself to continue in office after his second term expired (Banda, 11 April 2006; and see Hussein, 2005). It can be argued that this type of directly political corruption is the most harmful for democracy and development, because it perpetuates clientelism and encourages greed throughout the political system, even when it does not work. Indeed the failure of the Open and Third Term Bills is often cited as evidence that there is hope for greater democracy in Malawi. Yet Mutharika remains cautious in attacking political abuses, with his anti-corruption speeches and arrests, including Muluzi's, focusing on theft. This may be strategically sensible – and political manipulation of public resources is necessarily hard to redress – but it is also possible that he sees personal gain as the greater sin.

Minor infringements

Mutharika is certainly not averse to using the rules to his own political advantage. The targets of the pettiest charges during the anti-corruption campaign could not have been more nakedly political. As outlined above, several arrests were used to unsettle the opposition at the height of the impeachment campaign in October and November 2005, in a strategy the president himself described as 'tit for tat'. Among these were UDF backbenchers Lucius Banda, who had initiated the setting up of impeachment procedures, and Maxwell Milanzi, who had presented the formal motion to impeach Mutharika. Both were arrested and threatened with disqualification from parliament for providing false information to the Malawi Electoral Commission before being elected in 2004. Milanzi was charged with concealing a prior criminal conviction; Banda with forging a Malawi Schools Certificate of Education (MSCE), which MPs are required to hold. Civil Society organisations were quick to condemn Mutharika for his confrontational attitude and blatant selectivity, which vindicated opponents of the drive against corruption (Liwanda, 9 November 2005). Sure enough, the UDF alleged that six members of Mutharika's cabinet had no valid MSCE either (Phiri, 27 November 2005). Nonetheless, the tactics proved effective. Milanzi withdrew the impeachment motion in January 2006, claiming that it had proved unpopular nationally and internationally – and, incidentally, that he had felt unsupported by the UDF (Sonani, 12 January 2006). Banda – a popular musician before entering parliament – ended up as the highest profile victim of the anti-corruption campaign to date when his relatively trivial offence earned him an astonishing 21 month prison sentence (BBC, 31 August 2006), only for his conviction to be unexpectedly overturned on appeal (BBC, 7 November 2006).

Allegations against Bingu wa Mutharika's allies

Mutharika's use of threats, ostensibly as part of the anti-corruption campaign, has not been confined to political pawns, or even opponents. He has also used them to shore up obedience in his own ranks. For example, in the early months of his regime, his closest confidante was Ken Zikhale Ng'oma, a civil servant promoted to the new post of Chief of Staff for State Residences and, despite the obvious conflict of interest, also made Secretary General of the new DP party on its inception. After falling out with Mutharika on being demoted, Ng'oma published a long resignation letter containing detailed criticisms of the president's 'ungrateful' management style and warning that he was losing popularity (Ng'oma, 25 September 2005). Days later, the ACB announced an enquiry into his purchase of several expensive farms on a civil service salary (Kumwenda, 6 October 2005).

Gwanda Chakuamba – who came third in the 2004 presidential election, then switched to support first the UDF then the DP, before resigning after losing his job as Agriculture Minister – also regretted making a parting shot. At a rally soon after being sacked from the cabinet – ironically in part for spending K15 million (£75,000) on a ministerial BMW during a food crisis and refusing to return it when moved to another department – Chakuamba lambasted Mutharika as 'a brute, stupid and a drunk'. In the absence of a more meaningful charge, he was arrested under the archaic Protected Names and Emblems Act for insulting the president (Chilobwe, 15 September 2005). Such cases give the impression that Mutharika seeks to retain – and also induce – loyalty through a combination of threats and promises. Targeting UDF bigwigs and exiles thus not only politicised the anti-corruption campaign; it failed to address the perceived culture of impunity within the current corridors of power. Indeed, in some respects, it encouraged it. Many DP leaders and cabinet members have well-known skeletons in their closet, which may even have been used to persuade them to back the government.

The most damning indictments of any anti-corruption campaign are claims of ongoing theft and bribery. Many such allegations in Malawi have merely been part of the political discourse created around the issue of corruption, but others merit further investigation. Mutharika's response to accusations against his government has been interesting. Some powerful individuals have been quietly dropped from cabinet or senior civil service posts with the implied threat that charges may be brought if they make a fuss. This strategy has enabled him to weed out some corrupt activities – suggesting that his distaste for it may be genuine, or at least that he is responsive to credible allegations – while giving the impression to the wider world that his team was far cleaner than Muluzi's had been, because it is the latter who were in court. Yet several cabinet ministers remained untouched. The parliamentary Legal Affairs Committee demanded an explanation, for example, why Wadi had not started cases against Ntaba, Lipenga, Agriculture Minister Uladi Mussa and Information Minister Patricia Kaliati (Liwanda, 21 February 2006).

In a couple of cases, however, Mutharika had no option but to allow investigations into corruption within his own cabinet. Indeed the first politician to be jailed as a result of the crackdown on corruption was Yusuf Mwawa, who followed Mutharika out of the UDF and became Education Minister. In February 2006 he was convicted and sentenced to five years for theft, forgery and misuse of office, after paying K160,550 (£803) for his own wedding from the Ministry of Education Special Client Account (Liwanda, 15 February 2006). His trial ended the day before Mutharika's high profile Anti-Corruption Day, allowing the president to claim that no one was immune from his campaign, but making Mwawa look like a convenient scapegoat. While his conviction was praised as evidence of Mutharika's seriousness, Mwawa is not a big fish politically. He has even attracted some sympathy, given the relatively small scale of his offence, and it is likely that his sentence will be reduced on appeal, as Chikakwiya's was.

The sense that Mwawa was a fall guy is significantly enhanced by his revelations about the nature of the Special Client Account from which he stole. Both before the parliamentary Public Accounts Committee (PAC) and during his trial, he claimed that it was set up 'to promote government business' after Mutharika left the well-financed UDF. The PAC report claims Mwawa confessed that MPs were paid up to K15,000 (£75) each to attend meetings with himself and Finance Minister Goodall Gondwe, in which they were urged to back Mutharika in parliament. In court, Mwawa argued that paid caucuses involving ministers and potentially supportive MPs were held with Mutharika's full knowledge and that when allegations of bribery surfaced, the meetings were falsely declared to have been to plan an education conference (Liwanda, 10 November 2005).

Parallel to the Special Client Account, it is alleged that Secretary to the Treasury Milton Kutengule opened a K20 million (£100,000) Government Credit Scheme Account at a private bank, for which he was the sole signatory, using an undeclared dividend from the nationalised Malawi Telecommunication Limited. He was arrested in October 2005 after it emerged that K15,765,565 (£78,828) had been withdrawn but not accounted for (Munthali, 21 October 2005). Once again, a PAC enquiry suggested that a task force of senior ministers – including Gondwe and Mutharika himself – was involved and that the money had been used to identify possible government supporters in parliament (National Assembly, 2005). Although this report was widely circulated, its formal publication was blocked – first by Kutengule's arrest, rendering its contents *sub judice*, and then by parliament because it contained allegations against named individuals who had not been invited to answer them (Langa, 29 October 2005). Kutengule, who still awaits trial, told PAC that he was unwilling to be a 'sacrificial lamb' (National Assembly, 2005: 26), though he has never spoken in public about the matter. Mutharika initially distanced himself, insisting that he was willing to see further prosecutions. Investigations slowed down after Mwawa's conviction, however, despite the latter's own incriminating evidence. In April 2006, Kutengule was bizarrely appointed to the Office of the President and Cabinet while remaining suspended from the civil service (Langa, 15 April 2006). As with Mvula, Kutengule appears to have understood that staying silent about the dangerous information he held could help to keep him out of court. Mwawa, on the other hand, paid the price for failing to keep his powder dry.

The two cases also corroborate the view that Mutharika is serious in his campaign against theft and abuse of office for personal gain, but less so about diversion of public resources for political purposes. Indeed his own frequently undemocratic behaviour suggests that he believes that no holds are barred when fighting to retain power. The irony is that the difficult political circumstances Mutharika faced – largely because his anti-corruption campaign made so many enemies – arguably forced him to behave corruptly himself in order to survive. After the initial impeachment attempt failed in November 2005, Mutharika refused to release funds for the National Assembly to sit until April 2006, when the government was able to declare more MPs as supporters – 74 – than either the UDF or MCP (Sonani, 5 April 2006). Six of these were elected on the

DP ticket in by-elections in December 2005 after elaborate campaigns; the rest were actual or de facto defectors, even though the practice is not permitted under the constitution. If the PAC reports are to be believed, at least K2.8 million (£14,000) of public money was spent on clandestine bribery (National Assembly, 2005: 43–4). The response from Mussa was telling: 'Is K30 thousand [£150] worth anything for it to buy a Member of Parliament?' (Gondwe, 24 January 2006). Open promises of extra resources for development in constituencies whose MPs back the government may have been more persuasive, and some are alleged to have been awarded food distribution contracts.

It is possible that MPs were not bought or bullied so much as convinced by the unprepossessing Mutharika – or by the advantages of being on the government side *per se*. Nonetheless the president's arguments while in the UDF that government and party functions should be clearly demarcated were abandoned after the formation of the DP. So weak did his respect for the separation of powers become that in March 2006, with a spate of politicised corruption cases at various stages in the courts, he invited senior judges to lunch at New State House (Banda & Liwanda, 3 March 2006).

Implications

This chapter has attempted to illustrate the combination of motives that have driven the anti-corruption campaign in Malawi, and weigh their relative significance: genuine condemnation of constraints on development, desire to please wary donors and political opportunism. The aim of the concluding section is to evaluate the extent to which the campaign has satisfied each of these goals in its first two years, by considering what impact it has had in each arena.

Politics

The political ramifications are by far the most significant. The legislature had been given an opportunity to reassert itself against an overbearing executive by the 2004 parliamentary election results – and again by Mutharika's defection from the UDF. Despite successfully flexing its muscles by rejecting the appointment of Nangwale and insisting on alterations to budgets, overall parliamentary credibility and influence have been damaged by skirmishes over the anti-corruption campaign and impeachment proposal. When substantial parliamentary scrutiny could have enhanced policy-making and implementation, political debate has instead been reduced to mutual destabilisation and persecution. Scare tactics proved effective against the impeachment motion, but also against legitimate opposition and, ironically, against some serious allegations of abuse of office. The UDF therefore played into Mutharika's hands by attempting to impeach him. The initial grounds (failure to prevent hunger and lack of due process in dismissing public servants) were so weak that the riposte that their real objection was to the anti-corruption campaign itself was effective. It was a double irony that as Mutharika fought to prevent a two-thirds majority from coalescing against him in parliament, he appeared to make the charges of abuse of office self-fulfilling, but at the same time succeeded in defeating them.

The upshot is that myriad threats, promises and cover-ups have determined political allegiances and infected wider political discourse. In a young democracy with weak party structures, loyalty is such a rare commodity that everything revolves around rewarding or ensuring it, such that Mutharika can rarely afford to prioritise criteria like competence, or integrity, in selecting his cabinet. The most optimistic conclusion possible is that the anti-corruption campaign has started a process of political catharsis from which a more stable and balanced system can emerge. This will require actors outside government – whether from media, civil society, parliament or judiciary – to take ownership of the anti-corruption agenda. Mutharika's campaign does not attempt to change the aggressive, patrimonial, winner-takes-all culture that has characterised Malawian politics as much since the introduction of democracy as under dictatorship. Indeed the two in many ways reinforce each other, except inasmuch as Mutharika seeks to distinguish himself from Muluzi – in the eyes of both donors and voters – by using corruption as an easily recognised signifier of bad governance. While they may well accept such a distinction, they must also question Mutharika's own legitimacy. Effectively elected under a false flag, he has responded increasingly autocratically to democratic opposition.

If Mutharika's primary aim when launching the campaign was to win political battles, however, results have been mixed. He has succeeded in throwing off the reins that Muluzi doubtless intended to keep on him indefinitely, but his enemies have just been quietened, and the attempt to deliver a knockout blow backfired spectacularly. The only convictions have been in minor cases, one of them for corruption under his own watch. The biggest problem the UDF faces, fittingly, is a chronic lack of resources now that they are out of power. Conversely, the security of Mutharika's position has improved the longer he has been in the presidency, but his success in retaining it has been less because of his anti-corruption stance than, at several levels, in spite of it. It will be interesting to see whether he can sustain the upper hand and, if so, whether he will use it to pursue corruption with more or less vigour.

Development

In the first three years of the anti-corruption campaign, Mutharika's rhetoric about the harm done to Malawi's development potential failed to convince civil society organisations that he intends serious reform. Unequal treatment of political opponents, major delays in investigations after arrests were made and a lack of transparency in the process (the ACB is accountable solely to the president) combined to give the impression that the government was still dragging its feet against corruption. In the 2005 and 2006 TI Corruption Perception Indices, Malawi came lower (97th and 105th respectively) than in 2004, with its score reduced to 2.7. Muhammad Sharif, Chair of the Public Affairs Committee, which represents faith communities on political affairs, summed up the mood of cynicism: 'Are we saying that we can steal and remain safe as long as one is in government?' (*The Chronicle*, 21 November 2005).

It is indeed moot whether sitting ministers and civil servants have significantly stronger incentives for probity as a result of the campaign. Despite both loyalty and influence having been seen to reduce the likelihood of successful prosecution, little has been done to strengthen the ACB's powers or the law. A really credible anti-corruption campaign might have focused on constitutional and legal reform rather than on high profile but frequently empty arrests. Loopholes whereby criminal investigations can be stopped by court injunction or repayment of stolen sums have hugely undermined the whole process. When Jumbe and Mvula applied for a constitutional review of their charges, they even succeeded in persuading the judges to invalidate Section 25 of the Corrupt Practices Act. In a legal solipsism of the highest order, the clause that 'Any public officer who . . . corruptly solicits, accepts or obtains . . . any gratification . . . shall be guilty of an offence" was deemed to presume guilt without trial (Paliani-Kamanga, 23 October 2005). The weakness of existing laws was partially explained when parliament delayed discussion of a Money Laundering Bill because it contained jargon that MPs outside the Legal Affairs Committee could not understand (Sonani, 19 January 2006).

Given the frequency with which Mutharika proclaims development to be his priority, the early stages of his regime showed few material improvements. In his speech opening parliament in April 2006, which focused entirely on development and made no reference to corruption, the president acknowledged that the economy was contracting and that headline policies such as a fertiliser subsidy had proved more expensive and difficult to implement than expected (Mutharika, 4 April 2006). Other schemes offering rural loans and free treadle pumps have transparently been distributed unevenly, favouring government-supporting MPs. Attempts to address ongoing food shortages have been hampered by widespread thefts of grain from ADMARC depots and allegations that local managers have sold stocks to private traders. It would be unreasonable to expect even an effective attack on corruption to have an immediate effect on development but, rather than freeing government to concentrate on it, the political battles Mutharika has fought over corruption have arguably distracted him from development concerns. Moreover, endless talk about corruption has, if anything, reduced popular trust in government programmes.

Relationship with donors

If the anti-corruption campaign has not yet unambiguously reduced corruption, enhanced development or aided Mutharika politically, one of his apparent goals when launching it – indeed perhaps his prime motivation – has borne significant fruit. Rightly or wrongly, Malawi's main donors have been sufficiently impressed by his intentions and governance to restore substantial aid flows. DfID announced increased budget support of £60 million for 2005–06 (IRIN, 25 July 2005), with others following suit soon after. The IMF, whose assessments are heavily relied upon by bilateral donors (Killick, 2004), relaunched the Poverty Reduction and Growth Facility at the start of 2006 (Munthali, 27 February 2006) and declared that Malawi had made enough progress to reach completion point under the Enhanced Highly Indebted Poor Country initiative by September, prompting the cancellation of $1.7 billion of debt. This gave Mutharika considerable breathing space.

Very unusually, donor interventions were not all restricted to conditional aid. After British High Commissioner David Pearey had warned that 'in a turbulent political environment the donors could find it increasingly difficult to play the part they want' (Banda, 5 October 2005), most of the bilateral donors to Malawi (UK, US, Norway, Germany, France and South Africa, plus the EU) published an open letter warning against Mutharika's impeachment (Eastman et al., 27 October 2005). Without commenting directly on the grounds, they criticised parliament for prioritising the issue over the food crisis and highlighted the risk that further instability would reduce international confidence. This had a huge political impact. Whereas earlier donor pressure to pass the budget on time had forced government and parliament into a constructive compromise, the open letter clearly tipped the balance in Mutharika's favour. As outlined above, the boost to his confidence was manifested by an immediate spate of arrests and the raid on Muluzi. It may or may not be a coincidence that Pearey, who appeared to have initiated the letter, was reassigned a fortnight later, after only a year in post.

Whatever the ethics of intervening in domestic politics, it is interesting that donors were so keen to support Mutharika. At around the same time, Bob Geldof and Martin Bell publicly objected to his visit to the Scottish parliament (Macaskill & Allardyce, 6 November 2005). This may have been an ill-informed reaction to the impeachment motion, but several questions remain over his presidential record. As well as the allegations of bribery and corruption against his DP party, Mutharika has often been profligate and undemocratic. On the pretext of focusing all government activity in Lilongwe, he moved out of Sanjika Palace in Blantyre and took up residence in the opulent New State House, forcing parliament to make room. He then ordered a £325,000 Maybach as his official vehicle (IRIN, 16 June 2005), though he backed down before Finance Minister Gondwe formally apologised to the World Bank for using £75,000 from its Emergency Drought Recovery Programme on Chakuamba's car (Sonani & Liwanda, 14 October 2005). Donors have also expressed displeasure at the cost of frequent overseas trips, the prolonged suspension of parliament, the unconstitutional attempt to remove Vice-President Chilumpha and tardiness in prosecuting corruption cases.

If common good governance criteria were applied (DfID, 2005; Mosley et al., 2004), a *prima facie* case for resuspending aid to Malawi could be made. It is easy to see, however, why donors do not want to undermine Mutharika, least of all on corruption grounds. Had he been impeached and convicted, he would either have been replaced by Chilumpha or by a proposed (though again unconstitutional) National Governing Council, potentially including any or all of Mpasu, Jumbe and Chakuamba, but headed by Tembo, who was accused of ordering political murders during the Banda era. A new election might even have seen Muluzi return, as the constitution only proscribes more than two *consecutive* terms. Donors have therefore taken a qualified and normative but reasonable view that Mutharika is the least bad option available.

There are two problems with normative assessments, however. First, they carry as much weight as any other. Thus when the government is accused of corruption, it can respond that sustained donor funding implies probity. This creates the potential, if not an incentive, for Mutharika to talk the talk on corruption without seriously redressing it. Second, normative assessments pose awkward questions about criteria.

How high a priority is corruption at all? For all its prominence in DfID or NEPAD mission statements and the Commission for Africa Report, reduced corruption may be seen as just one of several essential prerequisites for development. Where other elements are missing, it is not necessarily the most critical. The Common Approach to Budget Support group (CABS) has emphasised the importance of balanced budgets and macroeconomic stability in Malawi as much as acceleration of anti-corruption cases (Phiri, 4 October 2005; Nyirenda, 18 November 2005).

Corruption is most unacceptable for donors where it involves direct misuse of their own aid. This seems reasonable but can cause confusion. It would be hard to argue that the purchase of a ministerial vehicle or the naming of an EU-funded road after Robert Mugabe are the worst examples of abuse, but both caused furores, the latter being described by western diplomats as 'suicidal' (Munthali, 15 April, 2006). Root and branch attacks on endemic domestic corruption are certainly encouraged by donors, but their difficulties are recognised. Too rapid cutting of the Gordian knot could destabilise the entire political system. It could be argued, for example, that the culture of allowances to MPs attracts a better calibre of candidates, which is much-needed. However, such recognition makes reducing corruption less important than political stability, as argued by Muluzi, let alone Mutharika.

While donors still prefer Mutharika to Muluzi because of his anti-corruption agenda, they may also have to offset their support by silence on other issues. For example, Mutharika's invitation to host Mugabe suggests that he now thinks that donors will support him whatever he does. Aping the Zimbabwean president would test that confidence, but Mutharika has shown more wit. Declaring he would 'like to be called a dictator to protect my people', he has encouraged supporters to call him 'Kamuzu number two' (Liwanda & Makata-Kakwesa, 28 March 2006). Thus, while the attachment of good governance prerequisites to aid showed itself to be helpful in triggering an anti-corruption campaign in Malawi, once aid had been restored, conditionality became a much less effective lever. Malawi's extreme dependence on aid for development and poverty reduction has not forced the government to bend over backwards to keep it. As Dijkstra (2002) has argued, both aid and conditions can encourage governments to do less not more. So long as Mutharika shows willing, it is actually the donors who will put up with almost anything to avoid pulling out. With Britain's budget support targeted at the provision of basic health needs, for example, Mutharika could arrest a lot more opponents and protect government supporters for a long time before DfID would countenance suspending it again. That does not mean that he necessarily will, but at the time of writing he is in a strong position vis-à-vis political enemies and donors alike. Despite the paucity of convictions and still low TI ranking, Bingu wa Mutharika must feel that his anti-corruption campaign is going very well indeed.

Note

1. I am very grateful to the British Academy for funding my research in Malawi.

References

Commission for Africa, 2005, *Our Common Interest*, Penguin
Devereux, S., 2002, 'The Malawi Famine of 2002', *IDS Bulletin*, 33 (4), pp. 70–8
DfID, 2005, 'Partnerships for poverty reduction: rethinking conditionality', www.dfid.gov.uk/pubs/files/conditionality.pdf
Dijkstra, A., 2002, 'The effectiveness of policy conditionality: eight country experiences', *Development and Change*, 33 (2), pp. 307–34
Eastman, A., Foreland, G., Gisy, A., Lavroff, S., Mariani, A., Pearey, D., Tsheole, N. & Wilson, R., 27 October 2005, *Open letter to Malawi's political leaders from the donor community*
Hussein, M., 2005, 'Combating corruption in Malawi: an assessment of the enforcing mechanisms', *African Security Review*, 14 (4), pp. 90–101
Khembo, N., 2005, 'Scratch my back and I scratch yours: institutional analysis of democratic accountability and the anti-corruption agenda in Malawi (1994 –2005)', unpublished, Centre for Social Research, Zomba
Killick, T., 2004, 'Politics, evidence and the new aid agenda', *Development Policy Review*, 22 (1), pp. 5–29
Mosley, P., Hudson, J. & Verschoor, A., 2004, 'Aid, poverty reduction and the "new conditionality"', *The Economic Journal*, 114, pp. 217–43
Mutharika B., Speeches, 24 May 2004, 6 November 2005, 31 December 2005 & 4 April 2006
National Assembly [of Malawi], Public Accounts Committee, 2005, *Report on the investigation into the operation and management of credit scheme account in the Ministry of Finance*, unpublished
Ng'oma, K., 25 September 2005, *Circumstances leading to my resignation tender as campaign director and member of the Democratic Progressive Party*, Memorandum to His Excellency the State President
Owusu, K. & Ng'ambi, F., 2002, *Structural Damage: The causes and consequences of Malawi's food crisis*, World Development Movement
Stambuli, K., undated [2003], *Corrupt Activities by Muluzi*, unpublished
Transparency International, Corruption Perception Index 2004, 2005 and 2006, www.transparency.org/policy_research/surveys_indices/cpi/

Media sources

Africa Confidential, 19 November 2004, 'Malawi: Government versus party', *Africa Confidential*, 45 (23), pp. 4–5

'Backbencher', 24 June 2006, 'Adhering to budget just the starting point', *The Nation*, www.nationmalawi.com/

Banda, M., 6 January 2005, 'Three from UDF re-arrested for treason', *The Nation*, p. 1

Banda, M., 20 August 2005, 'Muluzi challenges MRA over 150 vehicles', *The Nation*, p. 2

Banda, M., 5 October 2005, 'UK says political crisis threatens aid', *The Nation*, p. 3

Banda, M., 11 April 2006, 'ACB wants more witnesses against Muluzi', *The Nation*, p. 1

Banda, M. & Liwanda, Z., 3 March 2006, 'Bingu invites judges to lunch', *The Nation*, p. 2

BBC, 27 October 2005, 'Malawi agents raid Muluzi's home', news.bbc.co.uk/1/hi/world/africa/4382318.stm

BBC, 10 February 2006, 'Malawian judge halts VP sacking', news.bbc.co.uk/1/hi/world/africa/4699912.stm

BBC, 10 August 2006, 'Malawi prosecutor told to resign', news.bbc.co.uk/1/hi/world/africa/4781117.stm

BBC, 31 August 2006, 'Malawi musician jailed on forgery', news.bbc.co.uk/1/hi/world/africa/5303250.stm

BBC, 7 November 2006, 'Malawi musician wins court appeal', news.bbc.co.uk/1/hi/world/africa/6125544.stm

Chapalapata, M., 3 August 2004, 'Mvula out on bail', *Daily Times*, pp. 1–3

Chilobwe, H., 15 March 2005, 'Court acquits Mvula's cousin', *Daily Times*, p. 3

Chilobwe, H., 15 September 2005, 'Gwanda arrested', *The Nation*, pp. 1–2

Chilobwe, H., 10 November 2005, 'Court allows Muluzi to sell Keza', *The Nation*, p. 1

Chilobwe, H., 13 December 2005, 'Chikakwiya free', *The Nation*, pp. 1–2

Chiumia, T., 16 November 2005, 'Chilumpha obtains injunction', *Daily Times*, p. 1

The Chronicle staff reporter, 21 November 2005, 'Civil society accuse ACB of bias', *The Chronicle*, p. 2

'Comment', 4 October 2005, 'Pay rental arrears now', *The Chronicle*, p. 4

Gondwe, G., 24 January 2006, 'DPP denies buying MPs for K30,000 each', *The Chronicle*, p. 2

IRIN, 16 June 2005, 'Malawi: Govt purchases expensive presidential vehicle despite food shortages', www.irinnews.org/Report.aspx?ReportId=54938

IRIN, 25 July 2005, 'Malawi: Britain releases £20 million in budget support', www.irinnews.org/Report.aspx?ReportId=55573

Jamieson, R., 4 November 2005, 'Mpasu arrested over Fieldyork scam', *The Chronicle*, pp. 1–3

Kakwesa, T., 10 November 2005, 'Government uncovers fraudulent accounts', *The Nation*, p. 1

Kasunda, A., 28 October 2004, 'Police ambush Jumbe at Chileka', *Daily Times*, p. 1

Kasunda, A., 6 December 2005, 'Govt playing tricks on Ntaba issue', *Daily Times*, p. 1

Kasunda, A., 7 December 2005, 'Diplomat attacks UDF', *Daily Times*, p. 5

Kumwenda, O., 6 October 2005, 'ACB closing in on Zikhale', *The Nation*, p. 1

Langa, J., 29 October 2005, 'House throws away Kutengule report', *The Nation*, p. 5

Langa, J., 7 January 2006, 'Audit exposes dubious account', *The Nation*, www.nationmalawi.com/

Langa, J., 15 April 2006, 'Kutengule posted to OPC', *Weekend Nation*, p. 1

Liwanda, Z., 8 November 2005, 'Bingu says arrests are tit for tat', *The Nation*, p. 1

Liwanda, Z., 9 November 2005, 'Civil society wants all MPs probed', *The Nation*, p. 1

Liwanda, Z., 10 November 2005, 'Mwawa implicates Bingu, cabinet', *The Nation*, pp. 1–3

Liwanda, Z., 15 February 2006, 'Mwawa jailed for 5 years', *The Nation*, pp. 1–2

Liwanda, Z., 21 February 2006, 'Legal Affairs Committee wants four ministers prosecuted', *The Nation*, pp. 1–2

Liwanda, Z., 22 February 2006, 'Mpasu lawyer says Safuli being used', *The Nation*, p. 1

Liwanda, Z. & Makata-Kakwesa, T., 28 March 2006, 'Bingu ready to be called "dictator"', *The Nation*, pp. 1–2

Macaskill, M. & Allardyce, J., 6 November 2005, 'Malawi claims sour visit', *The Sunday Times* (UK), www.timesonline.co.uk/tol/newspapers/sunday_times/scotland/article587177.ece

MacDonell, H., 22 October 2005, 'Row over Malawi president's visit', *The Scotsman*, thescotsman.scotsman.com/index.cfm?id=2128652005

Munthali, G., 25 April 2005, 'Former finance minister blocks maize report', *The Nation*, p. 3

Munthali, G., 21 October 2005, 'Kutengule faces 3rd charge', *The Nation*, pp. 1–2

Munthali, G., 31 December 2005, 'Muluzi's fate January 10', *The Nation*, p. 1

Munthali, G., 27 February 2006, 'IMF gives Malawi over K951m', *The Nation*, pp. 1–2

Munthali, G., 15 April 2006, 'Mugabe's visit to Malawi: ZANU-PF, DPP to sign pact', *The Nation*, pp. 1–3

Namangale, F., 22 February 2006, 'Govt allowed Muluzi to import vehicles', *Daily Times*, p. 1

Ng'ambi, M., 31 October 2005, 'ACB probes Stambuli', *Daily Times*, pp. 1–3

Ng'ambi, M., 6 December 2005, 'Lipenga in allowance scandal', *Daily Times*, p. 1

Nkawi, M., 18 November 2005, 'Ntaba urges Bingu to make more tit-for-tat arrests', *Daily Times*, p. 1

Nyangulu, D., 12 January 2006, 'Muluzi K1.4bn case evidence under scrutiny', *Daily Times*, p. 1

Nyirenda, D., 19 November 2004, 'Mvula rigged for Bingu', *Daily Times*, pp. 1–3

Nyirenda, D., 18 November 2005, 'Donors warn govt on trips', *Daily Times*, p. 5

Paliani-Kamanga, P., 23 October 2005, 'Court declares section 25 of Corrupt Practices Act unconstitutional', *The Sunday Times*, pp. 1–3

Phiri, P., 4 October 2005, 'Norway gives Malawi K7b in budget support', *The Chronicle*, p. 3

Phiri, P., 27 November 2005, 'Six ministers under probe for fake MSCEs', *The Chronicle*, pp. 1–3

Semu-Banda, P., 4 March 2005, 'State closes maize scam', *The Nation*, p. 3

Sonani, B., 19 October 2005, 'UDF admits Muluzi banked donations', *The Nation*, pp. 1–2

Sonani, B., 12 January 2006, 'Tembo not concerned with Milanzi's action', *The Nation*, p. 2

Sonani, B., 19 January 2006, 'Muluzi's K1.4b case: Absence of Laundering Act concerns ACB', *The Nation*, pp. 1–2

Sonani, B., 5 April 2006, '74 MPs join government', *The Nation*, pp. 1–2

Sonani, B. & Liwanda, Z., 16 March 2005, 'Govt arrests 3 journalists', *The Nation*, pp. 1–2

Sonani, B. & Liwanda, Z., 14 October 2005, 'Gondwe says sorry for Gwanda's "sins"', *The Nation*, pp. 1–2

Theu, R., 29 March 2007, 'Safuli awaits ruling on appeal', *The Nation*, www.nationmalawi.com/

Weekly News staff reporter, 9 January 2006, 'Jumbe considers quitting UDF for govt', *Weekly News*, p. 1

5
Corruption and Reform in Nigeria

Paul Okojie and Abubakar Momoh

Introduction

Nigeria has a reputation as a country of graft. The sum of £220 billion, the equivalent of six Marshall Plans has been estimated as the amount stolen since 1966 from public funds (Blair, 2005). The most serious aspect of the culture of corruption concerns the most powerful, those who may also enjoy constitutional immunity. Recently two state governors jumped bail while awaiting trial for money laundering offences in London, one by dressing as a woman, knowing they would arrive home in Nigeria to legal immunity (Soniyi, 2005).[1] This chapter uses the term 'economic crimes' and 'economic criminals' to describe those who commit grand corruption. It notes the ability of the economic criminals to protect themselves, including by the misuse of banking law, and the slow and inadequate speed at which both municipal and international legal authorities respond to their activities. In light of the difficulties experienced by a number of countries in securing repatriation of stolen funds deposited in overseas banks, it is proposed that a solution to the problem lies in the establishment of an International Court for Economic Crimes (ICEC). This would make the prosecution of economic criminals more effective, speed up the recovery of stolen assets and to deny them sanctuary in foreign countries.[2]

What is clear is that powerful national economic criminals can become part of an internationalised system of corruption, such that the current emphasis by donors on country-based solutions fails to adequately regulate these international networks. Recent convincing efforts by the Federal Government of Nigeria (FGN) in institutional anti-corruption initiatives require international extra-territorial support to be successful. Additionally, if sums in secret bank accounts were to be returned to the countries from which they were stolen, a substantial contribution would be made to the development of the economies concerned.[3]

Economic corruption

We describe corruption as a crime against society, a term much wider than the World Bank definition of the 'use of public office for private gain' (Huther & Shah, 2000: 1), to indicate the egregious and insidious role it has in undermining development. The distinction between 'grand' and 'petty' corruption (United Nations on Drugs and Crime (UNODC), 2004a) is used here, in that the former are discussed, or more accurately those economic crimes which are of a 'grand' nature. Grand corruption is defined as an act which is widespread and systematic in scale, and which may involve the transfer of funds and assets to foreign countries, producing international ramifications. A further cost to the forum country is the consequences of the stigma as a country of graft, which is exemplified by Nigeria's experience. Here, because 'corruption' suffers from overuse, 'economic crime' is used to underscore the specificity of these behaviours; an attempt simultaneously to fix and underscore their universality and illegality.

Corruption in Nigeria

Transparency International (TI) *Corruption Perception Index* for 2005 places Nigeria as the sixth most corrupt country in the world (TI, 2005). This placing has been questioned by Nigerian authorities who argue that it does not take account of the effort being made to bring the abusers of public funds to account. It could equally be argued that for the persistence of grand corruption in Nigeria, lasting over a period of fifty years and with each decade seeing more audacious crime, the country's position in the TI's league table is probably generous, while recent reforms may take some time to take effect.

A historical pattern of corruption exists in Nigeria which shows it to be systemic and widespread. For example, after the regime of General Yakubu Gowon, deposed by a coup in 1975, a Commission of Inquiry found 10 of the 12 state governors guilty of corruption and the misuse of funds totalling over 16 million naira (Ayittey, 2006) A decision to enact the Public Officers (Protection Against False Accusations) Decree 11 of 1977, but with retroactive effect to July 29 1975 (see Odekunle, 1986: chap. 1), began a pattern of impunity. This Decree provided protection for erring public officials, and diminished the public service component of whistle-blowing, much of which is generally proved well-founded. Indeed, a tribunal set up in 1984 led to the eventual conviction of 51 public office holders of embezzlement and other abuses of public office on a grand scale.[4]

During the 1970s oil boom a 'frantic grab of the well-placed for easy wealth' and 'hideous displays of affluence' occurred (Diamond, 1989; cited in Ayittey, 2006). This pattern continued unabated throughout the 1980s, with billions of dollars worth of scandals reported involving:

> the illicit auction of much of the $2,500 million annual allocation of import licenses; the arrest of several top officials of the Federal Capital Development Authority in Abuja over an alleged $20 million fraud; and the revelation by a federal minister that Nigeria was losing $50 million a month to ghost workers and other forms of payroll fraud. (Ayittey, 2006)

Thus throughout the post-Independence period, and before, a group of economic criminals have proved relentless in their pillage of the public purse, unremitting in their determination to continue to do so and confident of their ability to control risk of capture by their manipulation of the public interest deficiency (PID).[5]

General Sani Abacha, President between 1993 and 1998, has been accused of the systematic looting of Nigeria's Treasury, and is estimated to have embezzled at least $5 billion, according to the late Bola Ige, Nigeria's former Attorney General, amassed through:

> misappropriation of funds from the Central bank of Nigeria, bribes received from foreign companies and kickbacks on inflated contracts with Nigerian companies under the control of the Abacha family. (Ige, 2002: 111)

Typical of the Abacha period were fake public contracts for phantom projects, such as a steel mill at Ajaokuta, which was under construction for over seventeen years at a cost of $7 billion, but which never produced steel, and an aluminium plant in Alscon that cost $3 billion without production (Hussain, 1999: 57). According to Hussain, over two-thirds ($200 billion) of the $300 billion from oil revenue earned by Nigeria over a period of twenty years was lost through fraud, waste and mismanagement (1999: 68). Hussain believes a further sum of $50 billion was stolen by various officials (ibid.).

Stolen funds are said to be in over 130 banks internationally (The African Network for Environment and Economic Justice, 2006, citing a Special Investigation Panel report, which though missing, is similarly cited in TI (2004)).[6] Significantly, the 1990s provided a lax international money system in which simple bank transfers, without due diligence, were sufficient to expedite the crime, with one banking official reportedly describing Mohammed and Ibrahim Abacha as the sons of a 'well known and respected member of the northern Nigerian community' and found them to be 'unfailingly charming, polite and, above all, reliable' (UNODC 2002; 113; quoting Ige who cites the US Senate Report, 1999).[7]

After the return to civilian rule in 1999, the effort to recover the internationalised funds stolen by erstwhile President Sani Abacha exposed the weaknesses in the law against corruption in municipal and international law (see below). Not only was the civilian government reduced to bargaining with the Abacha family to secure some returned funds, with a staggering N65.96 billion eventually returned (Nwankwo, supra 124) , but internationally, Nigeria found that in the absence of mutual legal assistance treaties (MLAT), recovering stolen assets in foreign countries was prohibitively expensive and thwarted by privacy law.

Transparency International reported embezzlement of up to N140 billion by top officials of the Nigerian National Petroleum Corporation (NNPC) (TI, 2004: 9), while the head of the NNPC chose to live in a five star hotel at a cost of N240 million per year to the corporation instead of living in his private house (ibid.). Allegedly, only thirteen of 500 contracts rushed through in the latter days of the military regime in 1998, before it handed power to a civilian government, were awarded in accordance with proper procedure (Kolade, 1999). Arson is also periodically alleged as a means to destroy records, with famously, the Republic Building deliberately set on fire in 1983 by employees of the Ministry of External Affairs who wanted to 'destroy vital evidence pertaining to [the Ministry's] accounts . . . to cover up possible fraud' (Federal Government of Nigeria (FGN), 1983).

During the current Government, corruption persists and amounts of embezzled funds continue to rise. However, there is also a pattern emerging of personnel being brought to account. For example, after EFCC investigations following reports in *The News* (Olubi, 2003; Attah, 2003), the former Chief of Police, Mr Tafa Balogun, was indicted for improperly enriching himself to the tune of N13 billion or $128 million in 2005 (Oham, 2005; Adeniyi, 2005; Ebelo, 2003).[8] The Chief of Police claimed that the allegations were malicious and made by his enemies in the police seeking to promote their self interest.

Meanwhile, the Minister of Education was dismissed, as was the President of the Senate, for agreeing to bribe the latter up to N55m or $417,000, in return for the Senate voting for an increase in the Ministry's budget (Obanikoro, 2005). While the Minister threatened action against the federal government for unfair dismissal, the threat was never carried out. The Federal Minister of Housing was also dismissed for allocating prime government houses to favoured purchasers without complying with correct tender procedures in 2005, while the Minster of Internal Affairs (now deceased) was indicted for his involvement in a national identity card scam in 2003. These dismissals are at least tentative evidence that due legal process has some punitive effect.

The National Assembly and graft

The National Assembly is notoriously a focal point for corrupt practice, since it has the power to award its own contracts. This has led to allegations of corrupt payments in terms of the misuse of the award of contracts by 'anticipatory award', in other words, advance payments, or 'mobilization fees', to the contractors up to 50–70 per cent of the contract value; inflated contracts; and non performing contracts – after receipt of mobilisation fees (TI, 2004). Additionally, several public officials were individually involved in a number of cases: the permanent secretary of the Ministry of Defence was dismissed in 2004 for an alleged embezzlement of N420m; three top officials of the Educational (*sic*) Tax Fund (ETF) were accused of embezzling N40 billion from the ETF between 1993 to 2000; and the Minister of the Federal Capital Territory alleged two senators demanded a bribe of N54m as a condition of approving his ministerial appointment (TI, 2004: 15).

A report by the Acting Auditor General of the Federation in 2001 revealed the extent of misappropriation of funds in at least ten ministries, summarised in Table 5.1. The Auditor General's Report for 2003 found a familiar pattern among economic criminals: over-invoicing, lack of audit inspection, payment for jobs not done, double-debiting, contract inflation, lack of receipts for purchases, non-compliance and payments made without authorised approval (Nwaobi, supra, footnote 9, p. 32).

Corruption and state governors

The state governance system is also particularly porous to manipulation and corrupt practice. A Minister of State for Finance in the federal

Table 5.1:   Misappropriation by ministry, 2000–2001 fiscal year

Ministry	Amount misappropriated N (million naira)
Cooperation and Integration in Africa	10.45
Power and Steel	4,394.7
Works and Housing	2,262.8
Defence	1,785.9
Education	1,265.3
Police Affairs	1,209.2
Information	664.1
Commerce	640.1
Health	465.1
Industry	356.1
Total	**23,860.7**

Source: Compiled from Nwaobi (2004), rounded up to nearest 100,000.

government decided to expose how regularly pillage occurs by state governors, by proposing that:

> Three to four days after the FAAC (Federation Allocation Accounts Committee) meeting, exchange rates go up. Which means they [the state governors] are using them [the allocations] to buy foreign exchange. If you look at the states, the states that get so much, you can hardly see anything to show for it.

The minister issued this challenge:

> *Make telephone calls to any of the states and ask after the governor and you will be told that he has gone abroad. Not only the governors, even the Commissioners of Finance.* (*Guardian*, 29 November 2005)

The implication is that the governors leave the country to bank stolen monies abroad misusing section 308 of the 1999 Nigerian constitution which was intended to protect governors against malicious allegations whilst in office. Governors cannot be prosecuted in Nigeria because section 308 confers them immunity while in office. This also applies to their deputies, the President and Vice-President (ibid.) of the Federal Republic of Nigeria. Referring to the bail-jumping Bayelsa state governor, Nnanna noted that even arrest outside the country, followed by due process, did not affect the impotence of the Nigerian government in this respect (2004).

Although the Independent Corrupt Practices Commission has statutory powers to investigate state governors, offenders cannot be prosecuted until they have left office. Under section 52 of the ICPC Act 2000, the ICPC can make an application to the Chief Justice of Nigeria requesting him to appoint an independent counsel to conduct a probe. The process, however, is considered to be cumbersome and rarely leads to a satisfactory outcome. For example, when the ICPC investigated the Governor of Bayelsa state, Chief DSP Diepreye Alameyeseigha, accused of embezzling N1.7 billion, the Chief Justice of Nigeria, Justice Muhammad Lawal Uwais, after receiving the report of the ICPC's investigation found himself unable to order a probe because the Governor had obtained a restraining order.

Nigerian regulation of corruption

In Nigeria, until recently, the practice was to use panels of fact-finding investigators to investigate corruption, instead of involving the police or public prosecutors. This enables the culprits to avoid prosecution in return for forfeiting a part of their illicit enrichment. These deals are not an effective deterrent, a fact made worse by the fact that in some cases, key investigations into corruption are not published. An example is Dr Okigbo's Report, an investigation of the Central Bank of Nigeria following the loss of the windfall revenues of the Gulf War of 1991–2 (Okigbo, 1994). The report revealed how only General Ibrahim Babaginda, the then President, and the Governor of the Bank, the late Mr Ahmed, controlled a Dedicated Account into which $12.4 billion was paid, an amount representing a third of the country's foreign debt at the time, but at the time of the inquiry only $206 million was left (*News Magazine*, 2005: 1, citing Keeling, 2005). It had been spent on a wide variety of personal items, certainly not public goods, and between $3 billion of the $5 billion windfalls could not be accounted for at all, according to Keeling, a reporter from the *London Financial Times*, who was deported for his effort (ibid.).

The Okigbo inquiry report is one of at least fourteen major 'probes' instigated by the government, the results of which remain unpublished, spread between the three different categories of inquiry: the Judicial Commission of Inquiry, the Administrative Panel of Inquiry, and the Tribunal of Inquiry under the Tribunals of inquiry Act (National Conscience Party, 2006).[9] However, there have been repeated demands for the Obasanjo government to publish the Okigbo report. It has been turned into a test of the administration's commitment to its 'anti-corruption crusade' and some commentators see the non-publication of the report as undermining the government's anti-graft policy (Hussain, 2005).

According to Punch (2003), probes rarely lead to punishment or deepened transparency, but are used to 'divert the public from official corruption, ineptitude and other crimes, or to intimidate and blackmail political opponents' (18 November 2003). While President Obasanjo claimed that copies of the report could not be found in the government's archives, the credibility of the story is doubtful[10] as the government has also refused to publish the Human Rights Violations Inquiry, known as the 'Oputa Report' which it itself commissioned in 2000.

International regulation

Current international legal instruments to combat corruption are listed in Table 5.2, although many of these are precatory and therefore easily ignored by economic criminals, who also often enjoy privileges and status in respectable society regardless of the magnitude of the serious harm they cause their fellow citizens. As frequently reported by Transparency International (see for example 2004) , prosecutions for grand corruption are rare. The Paul Volcker report into the 'oil for food' programme in Iraq exposed serious weaknesses in the policing of corruption at local and international levels, and calculated that Saddam Hussein received $1.8 billion in bribes for awarding contracts, from 2,200 companies prepared to bribe (United Nations, 2005: chap. II). That taking bribes from foreign companies is not unique to Saddam Hussein is well illustrated by reports of the loss of development funds in Iraq after the fall of his regime (Le Billon, 2005).

Despite international disapproval of corrupt practices, business contracts founded on graft continue to flourish, particularly in international networks linking forum countries and Europe or North America. According to estimates by the World Bank Institute, more than $1 trillion a year is paid in bribes (cited in Van Zant, 2004). Corporate organisations from Europe and the USA were, until recently, allowed to treat bribes in foreign countries as tax deductable expenses, while economic criminal gangs function between jurisdictions and exploit deficiencies in regulation. In spite of the criminalisation of some economic crimes under the new United Nations *Convention Against Transnational Organised Crime* (Articles 15–42), its deterrent effect on economic criminals is expected to be limited because of defects in the structure of the Convention, which maintains a distinction between mandatory and non-mandatory crimes, such that the latter can be ignored and not incorporated into domestic law, and double criminality, required for an international claim, will be impossible to establish (UNODC, 2006).

Table 5.2: International anti-corruption law, codes of conduct and conventions

United Nations	Year
The United Nation Declaration against Corruption and Bribery in International Commercial Transactions	1996
The United Nations International Code of Conduct for Public Officials	1996
The United Nations Convention against Trans-national Organised Crime, (focus on organised crime, but deals with certain aspects of corruption)	2000
The United Nations Convention against Corruption	2003
Africa	
South African Development Community Protocol against Corruption	2001
Economic Community of West African States Declaration on Collaborating against Corruption	2001
African Union Convention on Preventing and Combating Corruption	2002
Economic Community of West African States Protocol on the Fight against Corruption	2002
The Americas	
Inter-American Convention against Corruption	1996
Europe	
The European Union Convention on the Protection of the European Communities' Financial Interests	1995
The Council of Europe Twenty Guiding Principles for the Fight Against Corruption	1997
The European Union Convention on the Fight Against Corruption involving Officials of the European Communities (Article K.3 of the Treaty of European Union)	1997
The Council of Europe Civil Law on Corruption	1999
The Council of Europe Criminal Law Convention on Corruption	1999
The Council of Europe Agreement Establishing the Group of States Against Corruption (GRECO)	1999
The Council of Europe Model Code of Conduct for Public Officials	2000
The Council of the Organisation of Economic Cooperation and Development Convention on Combating Bribery of Foreign Public Officials in International Business Transactions	2001
The European Union Framework Decision on Combating Corruption in the Private Sector	2003
Protocol to the Convention on the Protection of the European Communities' Financial Interests (Two)	1996

The solution to weak regulation is learning from the progress that has been made in the field of international criminal law. Thus, when confronting the problem of genocide after World War II, the Polish lawyer, Raphael Lemkin concluded that the term 'mass murder' did not adequately describe the crime which at that time 'had no name, and invented the word, "genocide" ' (Lemkin, 1944; Power, 2002). Since the anti-genocide convention was passed in 1948, the international community no longer expect genocidians to, in effect, prosecute themselves. A similar extra-territoriality is required in anti-corruption legislation, because again, many perpetrators are simultaneously law makers. Arguably, the tendency of donors to make bilateral treaties on anti-corruption within good governance policy, is insufficient, lacking commitment on both sides. Economic criminals can neuter or destroy, in some cases, physically, any 'capable guardian' (Jacob, 1961) likely to bring their reprehensible conduct to account. Occasionally, investigations or probes are conducted to stem the activities of the economic criminals; but these tend to be partisan, symbolic or vindictive (Akinseye-George, 2000: 56). This accounts for the persistence of corrupt environment in most countries, including Nigeria.

Credibility gap

To this day, economic criminals in Nigeria widely believe in the power of 'settlement' 'egunge' or 'dash' (all referring to bribery and dishonest conduct of public services) to further their crimes, despite the occasional exposure of a corrupt group who are regarded as careless enough to get caught. Those engaged in grand corruption are embedded in a cultural space where corruption is part of the background expectancy (Garfinkel, 1967) of holding a public office. It is almost a career failure if one's wealth is not furthered by public office, with such a person termed a 'ye ye', which in colloquial use means to have a lack of enterprise. With such pressures, Nigerian media, political culture and public debate are replete with allegations of corruption, counter-allegations, conspiracy, and ingenious scams of large financial magnitude, with large numbers of people accused of embezzlement of public funds (Transparency International (TI), 2004).

There also remains a credibility gap in how Nigeria attempts to combat economic crimes, with the current anti-corruption policy crusade being highly personalised. The president, the minister of finance and the head of the Economic and Financial Crimes Commission (EFCC) seem to embody the anti-graft crusade. Many Nigerians, however, behave as if they are spectators, watching who is going to be exposed next. There seems to be no groundswell of public opinion of zero tolerance of abuse of public funds, but instead a residual respect for criminality, sometimes justified within an anti-colonial or ethnic discourse.

For example, the federal government is obliged by law to allocate public office in line with the ethnic make-up of the federation. This cardinal rule of Nigerian politics is not always adhered to, giving rise to complaints of 'marginalisation'. In this context, when a public official is removed from public office because of corruption, the tendency is to view his or her removal as ethnic victimisation without regard to the justification or the evidence, so the Government's anti-graft crusade, overall, meets with a partisan response. For example, when the infamous, cross-dressing, bail-jumping governor from Bayelsa state was arrested and charged in London in 2005, a Professor Kimse Oko was reported to have said, 'the Ijaws cannot accept a situation where one of its most patriotic leaders is being vilified and humiliated without any shred of evidence' (cited in *Nigerian Tribune*, 30 September, 2005). According to the Chair of the EFCC, the Governor subsequently left Britain using a forged Nigerian passport and an illegal travel route (ibid.). Similarly, his predecessor from Plateau state was also depicted as a victim by eminent members of his community, who asked for him to be allowed to return to Nigeria as a 'birthday gift'. According to the Nigerian Tribune, the campaign was lead by a former governor of the state, Chief Solomon Lar and a former Head of State, General Yakubu Gowon (ibid.).

Despite his criminal behaviour, the governor of Bayelsa received a hero's welcome when he unexpectedly arrived in the state, by people 'agog with jubilations', and was hailed the 'conqueror of the British Empire'. Crowds of people cheered him as the 'local son' who had outwitted the British police. He 'drove into the state capital, Yenagoa, in a long convoy' (Oji and Okocha, 2005: 1), suggesting a degree of planning, organisation, the support of others (ibid.) and a penchant for public spectacle. The governor regaled the crowds with:

> Today, I am back at my desk, forever committed to serve the people of Bayelsa and Nigeria. I thank the Almighty God for his protection, I thank Bayelsans, the Ijaw Nation and indeed Nigerians for standing by me.

He then 'received in audience' a plethora of local dignitaries and office holders (ibid.).

This adulation of economic crime is difficult to explain. Oko has written that public officials commit crimes in Nigeria, secure that they will go unpunished, indeed 'cheered on by relatives and friends', in anything from 'over-invoicing to outright theft of government property' (Oko, 2002: 403). The EFCC has revealed the amount of money and property Governor Alamieyeseigha was alleged to have wrongfully acquired while in office[11] since his return, and public opinion has become more critical. As support for the governor waned, people came out to demonstrate against him, some with placards calling him a rogue. In fact, contrary to Governor Alamieyeseigha's expectation, he has been impeached and removed from office, thus losing his immunity, the first state governor to be removed in this way, and is now in custody, facing both criminal charges in Nigeria and possible extradition to London. The process of removing him from office was fraught with constitutional and logistical uncertainties. For example, after serving notice of impeachment on the governor, the majority of the state assembly members took refuge in Lagos because of concerns for their personal safety.

This impeachment has become a watershed event in the credibility of the current anti-corruption campaign, a critical moment when the federal government took an unprecedented response. Both the ICPC and the EFCC, the anti-graft agencies, realised they could not prosecute the governor for his economic crimes as long as he enjoyed immunity under section 308 of the constitution. They thus persuaded the majority of the state assembly members to take the uncertain risk of removing him from office, which action they confirmed by removing the speaker as well, since they believed him an accomplice. More importantly, this marks the de facto end of section 308, and its immunity protection, in so far as offenders will be permanently excluded from public office, and the 'rehabilitation' of the Babaginda regime, where offenders later reappeared in other public positions, is avoided (see Nwanko, 1999: 57).

The institutions of the anti-corruption campaign

The new civilian administration elected in 1999 (referred to as the Fourth Republic), set up two bodies, the aforementioned Independent Corrupt Practices Commission (ICPC) and the Economic and Financial Crimes Commission (EFCC). The ICPC has a general anti-corruption brief, but needs the Attorney General's approval to prosecute cases, whereas the EFCC concentrates on financial crimes. By all accounts, the EFCC is regarded as the more active and effective of the two, and has wider powers. It can prosecute cases without seeking the fiat of the Attorney General. The establishment of the ICPC and the EFCC mark a shift away from the use of probes or inquiries to combat corruption. This signalled a significant shift in policy and a greater willingness to use the criminal courts, although the number of people convicted by the courts remains small in comparison to the number of allegations.

The donors claim a large responsibility for this change in policy emphasis, with, for example, the US claiming their intervention:

was instrumental in pushing through legislation on money laundering, and the creation of an Anti-Terrorism, Economic and Financial Crimes Commission (EFCC) that responded to Financial Action Task Force (TATF) standards. (US State Department, 2005)

While this may overstate US influence *per se*, the institutional approach is certainly common to many other donor interventions and subsidised anti-corruption initiatives in Africa, and both the ICPC and the EFCC have received substantial grants in aid from external sources, including DfID, to provide a more effective service, which includes funding for the new EFCC training school to produce a cadre of investigators. The European Union (EU) has also been quick to praise the EFCC's record, asserting that it has led to 'a higher degree of financial probity' in critical economic sectors, with particular impact in the Customs Service, leading to over 1.2 billion euros of seized assets and 1080 arrested persons (EU, 2005: 3). The ICPC, in contrast, has been compared unfavourably with the EFCC, with the EU blaming the 'poor and corrupt judicial system' for ICPC's poor results (EU, 2005: 2). Its reliance on police to investigate cases certainly weakens its powers.

Constraints

The EFCC and the ICPC have both hinted that while they have *prima facie* evidence of wrong-doing against a majority of state governors, with the EFCC calculating that together they hold assets worth $17bn in foreign countries, the constitutional constraint of section 308 remains in place. In fact, the 1999 Federal Constitution confers immunity on a total of 74 public office holders: the President (1), Vice-President (1), Governors (36) and Deputy Governors (36), under section 308. The National Judicial Council have joined groups calling for the amendment of the section by removing the protection it offers for criminal offences potentially committed by the 74, but the situation still contains ambiguity and the Government seems under no hurry to repeal or amend it, despite the successful test case brought by the EFCC against the Governor of Bayelsa (above). In fact, the EFCC case itself wasn't without ambiguity in its result, as two separate Federal High Court opinions held diametrically opposite views of whether the action could proceed.

On the face of it, the legal opinion that prosecution could not be brought is the correct interpretation of section 308. However, the precedent of

Pinochet suggests that it is time for the Nigerian judges to be bold and apply similar logic: immunity is intended to facilitate the lawful performance of duties by the person on whom it is conferred; in other words, immunity was never intended to facilitate nefarious acts. As a common law jurisdiction, the decision of the UK House of Lords in the Pinochet case is of a persuasive authority in Nigerian courts, although it is unclear whether or not the Supreme Court of Nigeria will accept this interpretation, because the matter on which their Lordships deliberated was an egregious crime, whereas they may, wrongly in the authors' view, argue an exceptional case for 'economic' crime.

A shift in political perception may also be required to solve the immunity problem, a dual shift in which: economic crime is given its due weight for the adverse consequences it has on society; and a powerful (re)iteration of the argument that the purpose of the law is to further the common interest of the governed. A club membership for untouchable criminals is manifestly unjust in a democracy. It is time to heed the law enforcement agencies who believe that section 308 has been an obstacle against the prosecution of the most prolific abusers of public funds in the country.

Conclusion

Corruption is like an elephant; it is hard to describe but easy to recognise. In doing a literature search for the definition of corruption, there was, unsurprisingly, a lack of consensus. Yet, there is an agreement on the constituent elements of genocide and crime against humanity (see Rome Statute of International Criminal Court (ICC), 1998, article 5), and corruption as an economic crime against society should arguably be commensurate with these. As a global crime, it is critically important to find a new definition similar to that by Lemkin in respect of genocide (1944: 79). There are lessons that can be drawn from the work done by the international community to counter the commission of egregious crimes, including the production of the Rome Statute and the establishment of the International Criminal Court. Indeed, a legal definition, distilled from a consensus of civil and common law jurisdictions, would seem infinitely more achievable than relying on the vagaries of academic disciplines.

It is important therefore to draw attention to the report of the *Expert Working Group on Corruption* which influenced the wording of the UN Convention against Corruption. Although the Group chose not to include a definition of corruption in the Convention, their work provides a framework from which the international community can set about negotiating an agreed definition. As Costa, the Executive Director of the United Nations Office on Drugs and Crime, affirms,

> Since 1994, unprecedented efforts have been made to raise awareness about corruption, its insidious nature and the damaging effects it has on the welfare of entire nations and their peoples . . . There is now increasing recognition throughout the public and private sector that corruption is a serious obstacle to effective government, economic growth and stability, and that anti-corruption policies and legislation are urgently required at the national and international level.

But he also noted the difficulty in obtaining

> reliable information about the nature and extent of domestic and trans-national corruption . . . The problems are compounded by the very broad nature of the phenomenon and a lack of consensus about legal and criminological definitions. (UNODC, 2004b: 30).

Arguably, this is also the most salient problem remaining for Nigeria, where domestic institutions and cultural change urgently needs the validation and support of an international institutional effort, not least because a significant degree of economic crime in Nigeria is internationalised. It is convenient for economic principals to claim a lack of knowledge of the actions of their agents while accepting the lucrative contracts obtained by their agents or surrogates by dubious means. Economic agents, who prefer rectitude to corruption, garner little or no economic reward, such that the solution must lie in the establishment of an international court, an International Court for Economic Crimes, to which 'whistle blowers' can turn.

The donor community has claimed credit for encouraging anti-corruption reform within its good governance framework in Nigeria since the return to civilian rule. But it is also the domestic markets of the North, and the internationalised relationships of northern companies which are facilitative of economic crime, and it is in reference to reforming these that the donor community remains deafeningly quiet.

Notes

1. Chief DSP Alamieyeseigha, Governor of Bayelsa State in 2005, and Chief Joshua Dariye Governor of Plateau State in 2004.

2. For example, Mobutu went into temporary exile in Togo and later in Morocco; Alberto Fujimori, the ex-President of Peru, until his arrest in Chile (2005) was granted refuge in Japan. Jean-Claude Duvalier 'Baby Doc' was granted exile in France. Nigeria has granted diplomatic protection to Charles Taylor of Liberia.

3. United Nations Office on Drugs and Crime (UNODC) (2006) represents an important development here, in respect of mutual legal assistance and extradition (Article 44) and assets recovery (Articles 51–59) provisions.

4. Public Interest Deficiency can be defined as indifference to harm caused to the public interest because of preoccupation with self interest.

5. Justice Mohammed Bello Tribunal 1984.

6. The magazine claims to have published excerpts from the report, which include these figures, which have not been subsequently challenged by those named.

7. Ige (UNODC, 2002:113) lists locations of the money as Austria, the Bahamas, Brazil, Canada, Dubai, France, Germany, the Hong Kong Special Administrative Region of China, Italy, Kenya, Lebanon, Liechtenstein, Saudi Arabia, Singapore, Sweden, Switzerland, the United Kingdom of Great Britain and Northern Ireland and the United States of America.

8. After a plea bargain, he was fined N4m and given six months imprisonment. The Federal High Court judge justified the light sentence on the grounds that it was his first offence!

9. Other prominent unpublished reports include the Christopher Kolade panel of 1999 to review contracts awarded by the Abdulsalami Abubakar Regime between January and May 1999; the Oluwole Rotimi panel that investigated the Federal Government's property and the Oputa panel on rights violations in 2000.

10. The media and commentators expressed disbelief that such an important document could disappear from the national archives (see, for example, *The Punch*, 10 and 18 November 2003). This became the subject of editorials and letters to the President especially as the Secretary to the Government of the Federation, Chief Ufot Ekaette, was also the Secretary to the Okigbo Panel. Meanwhile President Obasanjo intimated that he might approach Dr Okigbo's widow for a copy!

11. In this case, the Nigerian authorities have subsequently revealed that Chief (*sic*) Alamieyeseigha has, or has recently had, bank accounts with Barclays, HSBC, National Westminster and UBS Warburg in the UK, an investment company called Santolina Investment Corporation, and an offshore company named Solomon & Peters Ltd. He also has additional personal and business accounts in Cyprus, with Barclays Bank, Denmark with JYSKE Bank, the Bahamas with UBS Trustees (Bahamas) Ltd, the US with Bank of America, and with Bond Bank and Oceanic Bank Plc in Nigeria. His properties include two prestigious addresses in London, registered to his offshore company, allegedly (by the EFCC) an oil refinery in Ecuador, and numerous luxury flats, mansions, estates and individual houses in Lagos, Abuja and Port Harcourt. His companies also include Pesal Nigeria Ltd; Salomein & Associates (Nigeria) Ltd; Kpedefa Nigeria Ltd; and Jety Properties Ltd (EFCC, cited in *The Punch*, 23 November 2005).

References

Adeniyi, Olusegun (2005) 'The Verdict: Too Late to Turn Back . . . (2)' *ThisDay*, Thursday 14 April, p. 64

Adisa, Taiwo (2005), 'Fresh Details of Alamieyeseigha's Money Laundering Scandal', *Nigerian Tribune*, Friday 30 September, pp. 15 and 17

Akinseye-George, A. (2000), *Legal System, Corruption and Governance in Nigeria*, Lagos: New Century Law Publishers Ltd

Attah, Obong Victor (2003), 'Allegation of Bribery: a Distraction', *The News*, 4 August, p. 10

Ayittey (2006), 'Looting Africa: African Kleptocracies' available from freeafrica.org/looting5.html, accessed on 11 December

Bianchi, A. (1999), 'Immunity versus human rights: the Pinochet case', in *European Journal of International Law*, 10(2): 237–77

Blair, D. (2005), '£220bn stolen by Nigeria's corrupt rulers', *Daily Telegraph*, London, 25 June

Ebelo, G. (2003), 'Tafa Fights Back', *The News*, 4 August, vol. 21, No.5, pp. 16–25

European Commission (2005), *Financial Proposal*, AIDCO/14106/05-EN, June, Internal Market Department

Federal Government of Nigeria (1983), Federal Government Views on the Report of the Republic Building Fire Incident Tribunal of Inquiry, para 16, Abuja

Garfinkel, H. (1967) *Studies in Ethnomethodology*, Englewood Cliffs, NJ: Prentice-Hall

Hussain, H. (1999) *The Detrimental Effects of Corruption in Developing Countries*, available from www.andover.edu/aep/papers/410/hhusain99.pdf (accessed on 3 July 2005)

Hussain, Mudashiru Oyetunde (2005) 'Obasanjo Not Sincere with Anti-Graft War', *ThisDay*, Thursday 14 April. p. 14

Huther, J. & Shah, A. (2000) *Anti-corruption Policies and Programs: a Framework for Evaluation*, Washington: World Bank Policy research Working Paper 2501

Ige, B. (2002), 'Abacha and the bankers: cracking the conspiracy', *Forum on Crime and Society*, Vol. 2 No. 3, December

Jacob, J. (1961) *The Death and Life of Great American Cities*, New York: Random House

Keeling, W. (2005) 'Lagos May Prove World Bank's Acid Test', as reprinted in *The News*, 23 May, originally in *The Financial Times*, 1 July 1991, London

Kolade, C. (1999), *Panel into the Award of Government Contracts*, unpublished

Le Billon, P. (2005), 'Corruption, Reconstruction and Oil Governance in Iraq', *Third World Quarterly*, 26, 4–5 , pp. 685–703

Lemkin, R. (1944) Axis Rule in Occupied Europe, Proposals for Redress, Washington DC: Carnegie Endowment for International Peace

National Conscience Party (2006), 'Probing Corruption in Nigeria' available at www.nigeriancp.net/tribune.html, accessed on 1 November 2006

Nnanna, Ocherome (2004), 'National or Presidential Awards? (Tintin and Picaros!)', Vanguard, Thursday 21 October, p. 41

Nwankwo, A. A. (1999) Nigeria: *the Stolen Billion Nairas*, Enugu: The Fourth Dimention, p. 56

Nwaobi, G. C. (2004) Corruption and Bribery in the Nigerian Economy, available from ideas.repec.org/p/wpa/wuwpdc/0401003.html, Quantitative Economics Research Bureau, Abuja, accessed on 1st November 2006

Obanikoro, Musiliu (2005), 'Corruption goes beyond National Assembly', *ThisDay*, Thursday 7 April, p. 14

Odekunle, F. (1986) 'Corruption in Development: Definitional, Methodological and Theoretical Issues', in Odekunle, F. ed. *Nigeria: Corruption in Development*, Ibadan, Ibadan University Press, ch. 1

Oham, Otei (2005), 'Osuji: Wabara, Others asked for N100m-Ex-Minister says N55m is no Bribe but Welfare', *The Comet,* Tuesday 12 April pp. 1 and 32

Oji, G. & Okocha, C. (2005), 'Alamieyeseigha in Dramatic Escape from London', *ThisDay*, 21 November, www.thisdayonline.com/nview.php?id=338 89, accessed November 2005

Okigbo, P. (1994), 'Report of the Panel on the Reorganisation and Reform of Central Bank of Nigeria' (unpublished report)

Oko, O. (2002), 'Subverting the scourge of corruption in Nigeria: a reform prospectus', *International Law & Politics*, August, vol. 34, pp. 397–473

Olubi, Olutayo (2003), 'Corporate Fraud', *The News*, 4 August, p. 12

Power, A. (2002) *A Problem from Hell: America and the Age of Genocide*, New York: Basic Books

Punch (2003), Editorial, 'The Missing Okigbo report', 18 November

Soniyi, Tobi (2005), 'Court Jails Balogun', *The Punch,* 23 November, p. 5

Transparency International (2004), *Country Study Report,* Nigeria

Transparency International (2005), *Corruption Perception 2005,* www.transparency. org/cpi/2005/cpi2005_infocus.html (accessed 5.11.05)

United Nations (2005) *Independent Inquiry Committee into the United Nations Oil-for-Food Programme,* available from www.iic-offp.org/story27oct05.htm accessed on 1st November 2006

United Nations Office on Drugs and Crime (UNODC) (2006), *Legislative Guide for the Implementation of the United Nations Convention Against Corruption*, New York, 2006

UNODC (2002), *Forum on Crime and Society*, vol. 2, no. 1, December

United Nations Organisation on Drugs and Crime (UNODC) (2004a), *'Manual on Anti-Corruption Policy, Part II,* Vienna, Austria

UNODC (2004b), *The Global Programme Against Corruption: UN Anti-Corruption Toolkit*, 3rd edition, Vienna, September

United States Senate (1999), Hearing of the Permanent Sub-committee on Investigations, of the Committee on Governmental Affairs, *Private banking and money laundering: a case study of opportunities and vulnerabilities,* (1999), 9 November, Washington DC, available from: frwebgate.access.gpo.gov/cgi-bin/ getdoc.cgi?dbname=106_senate_hearings&docid=f:61699.wais

US State Department Press Release (2005), April 2005, p. 3, www.state.gov./p/inl/ rls/ rpt/cbj/fy2006/51142.htm

Van Zant, Eric (2004), 'A Black and White Issue', Asian Development Bank, accessed from: www.adb.org/Documents/Periodicals/ADB_Review/2004/vol36_3/ black_white. asp

6
Challenges to the Philippine Culture of Corruption

Edna Estifania A. Co

Upon the suggestion of financing institutions such as the World Bank and the Asian Development Bank, corruption has taken centre stage in policy discourse, making corruption the locus of many re-engineering efforts in Philippine governance (Transparency and Accountability Network, internal documents, 2005). Although there are no systematic studies on the extent of economic losses due to corruption, the Ombudsman estimates that the Philippines has lost approximately US$48 billion during the last 20 years, while the Commission on Audit estimates a loss of $44.5 million each year and the World Bank argues that around 20 per cent of the annual budget is lost to corruption (Romero, undated article). Meanwhile, a Social Weather Stations (SWS) survey reports a popular perception of public institutions riddled with corruption, leading to low public confidence in government (SWS, 2005).

This high level campaign to reduce corruption is communicated to a public who put up with, or see no alternative to, low level petty corruption in daily life. Here, corrupt acts facilitate the daily transactions between citizens and institutions, providing a survival mechanism which serves as a palliative to the myriad inconveniences produced by public bureaucracies. This embeddedness of petty corruption complicates how an anticorruption campaign should proceed. How should one view corruption in the context of a developing society such as the Philippines? Is corruption centrally a cultural issue? What challenges does corruption pose for democrats and advocates of the rule of law and of democracy? This chapter addresses these queries in the context of the challenge to minimise corruption, and argues that where government is tasked with managing such an unequal society, with large centres of economic power, a long process of democratisation is required to change the whole culture of political life, as well as its institutional base.

Understanding corruption in the Philippines

Contemporary development works on corruption are largely operationally based, highlighting potential strategies to curb, reduce, and check corruption; voluminous works by scholars, donors, and development agencies, foremost of which are the World Bank, the Asian Development Bank, USAID, the UNDP and Transparency International. For example, Eigen (2000) tackles the role of civil society; Bolongaita and Bhargava produced a World Bank-commissioned study on cases and a framework for action (2003); Azfar and Gurgur (2000) discuss decentralisation and corruption; while Doig and Riley (2000) and the Transparent and Accountable Governance project (various documents) extensively discuss strategies to subvert corruption. Recent works in the Philippines by multilateral agencies fall within this genre of action-oriented, multi-stakeholder handbooks. Recently, the Development Academy of the Philippines or DAP (Romero, undated) prepared the most comprehensive framework to date, to 'combat' corruption in the Philippines. The DAP framework is derivative of the Hong Kong model of an anti-corruption campaign, and DAP's *Integrity Development Review* (IDR) is currently being piloted in a number of agencies, among which is the Presidential Commission against Graft and Corruption (PCGC), the Department of Education, and the Bureau of Customs.

Academic works have also proliferated, moving from the post-war view that corruption was principally sited within the public bureaucratic structure (See Carino et al., 1999), to the current consensus that it is a somewhat broader social malaise. Admittedly, government bureaucracy is still the central locus of corruption, being the seat of authority and the inevitable machinery of public transactions, but other disciplinary perspectives have also been applied to the study of corruption in the Philippines, and have been found to be severally illuminating. For example, the work of political economists such as Rose-Ackerman (2000), Nye (in Williams, 2000) and Alam (ibid.) have recently informed Philippine corruption studies, because of their particular salience and correspondence to understanding a historical culture of elite collusion and overlap between public office and private gain. The exclusive partnership, depicted by Rose-Ackerman (1996) in Williams (2000) as a type of buyer/seller relationship between business and a few individuals in the bureaucracy, explains how Philippine corruption emanates from high political collusion.

Filipino authors such as Mendoza, Jr. (2000) have focused on government procurement, bidding and award of contracts in the Philippines and illustrated how these are the bearers of corrupt practice, while de Dios and Ferrer (2001) have dissected the transactional corruption that takes place between government and business. The 'goods' in these transactions are bids, contracts, government purchases, and auctions, while opportunities for rules-evasion and the exchange of the 'goods' for illicit or opaque private benefits are found within government/business networks. These transactions sometimes result in political harassment of business by government, when the latter makes the granting of a permit or licence to the former particularly difficult. In the same environment of government–business transactions, Batalla (2000) observes the many acts involving unqualified and blacklisted contractors who continue to win bids, the payment of bribes in order to secure contract award, and the misrepresentation of labour costs in payroll, among other fraudulent practices.

Klitgaard's (1998) famous formula, explored in Chapter 3 of this book, that corruption is a result of the fatal combination of monopoly of power, wide latitude of discretion, and the absence of accountability, that is, $C = M + D - A$ where C is corruption, M is monopoly, D is discretion, and A is accountability has also been creatively reworked in Aquino (1999) who affirms Klitgaard's statement and provides an account of Asia's scandalous history of corruption in the political class (see also Werner (1983) and Carino et al. (1999)). Meanwhile, Hutchcroft's (1998) association between corruption and the politics of privilege, of rent seeking, and clientelism, where power and authority serve as a tool for coddling followers and supporters, who in turn demand political power holders to engage in corruption in exchange for votes is also evident in Filipino politics.

Historical roots of corruption

What is arguably missing, certainly from the action oriented development publications, but also from the disciplinary formulae, is historical perspective. Scott (2000) provided an explanation of corruption as an instrument of domination during colonialism, while Lim and Pascual (2000) have affirmed the continued role of biased international policies in the perpetuation of corruption, and Virtucio and Lalunio (2000), among others, the role of unregulated marketisation, discussed elsewhere in this volume, that is providing new opportunities for corruption. In the Filipino case, the legacy of colonialism and current processes of international inequality are fundamental to producing corruption, and relatively immutable in relation to the donor-sponsored quick fixes.

There is evidence that prior to the Philippine colonial conquest, that is, before the 1520s, Filipinos lived and believed in norms of honesty and fairness, evident in their 'dealings particularly with the Chinese traders who exchanged goods' (Carino et al., 1999). Norms of conduct upheld the accountability of public office by rulers, with rulers selected more on the basis of common acceptance by all, rather than on an individual's wealth and power (Carino et al., 1999). Acceptance was achieved through a process of consultations and pacts among groups, while replacement was a consequence of a leader not performing well, such that even without a written code, there were enforceable norms of conduct.

In contrast, during the Spanish colonial period, from the sixteenth to the late nineteenth century, public office was viewed and treated as the king's personal property and therefore depended on his discretion as to how to dispose of it – whether to award it or to grant it as a favour (Endriga, 2003). The king gave away lands, properties, including public office to anyone who showed loyalty to him. But it was not only a matter of philosophy that public office was viewed and treated in such a manner – it was also about distance. The management of the colonial government was effectively located 10,000 miles away, such that Philippine-based administrators could, and did use wide discretion: public offices were disposed of in a number of ways, including through award, or through sale, or through a bid, from which gains, monies were added into the colonial coffers. Thus, corruption was deemed as a natural process at that time.

Widespread corrupt practices were not noted under the American colonial government (from 1898 to 1941), since civil service was formally introduced by the Americans during this period and the inculcation of professionalism in government reduced corrupt acts. The introduction and the institutionalisation of the Civil Service Commission in 1900 was a transplant of the American-influenced Pendleton Act, the policy that tried to correct the spoils system under the Jacksonian democracy, and which led to the professionalisation of public office and public personnel management, such that arbitrary hiring and promotion of personnel was reduced and the merit principle became dominant. However, the period of meritocracy was short-lived and arrested by the Second World War during which time, force, coercion and death encouraged treason and loyalty to the Japanese imperial army, such that notions of loyalty and service became corrupted. The understanding of Filipinos was that loyalty, nationalism, and truthfulness meant punishment, while treason and betrayal would bring rewards by the Japanese colonisers.

After the Second World War the Philippines underwent a period of rehabilitation, where, besides technical assistance, international financial aids and grants flooded in for physical infrastructure and reconstruction thereby also providing the opportunities for public personnel to be vulnerable to corruption. Thus, by the late 1940s through to the early 1950s, one of the most outrageous issues that contributed to the fast expansion of the *Huk* rebellion in the countryside was the erosion of the people's trust in government, largely due to widespread corruption. Thus, five centuries of colonialism did not only wreak havoc on the patrimony of the country but it also paved the way for corruption as incoherent values under different colonial epochs suggested that corruption was a natural act and people fast gained tolerance for it. Public office had been a self-serving opportunity rather than an honourable position of service undertaken by those who have the merit and qualifications for it. Instead, those who purchased public office aimed to get back whatever they had 'invested' in the fastest time possible; an historical legacy which provided the institutional context for grand corruption to flourish.

The strong one-man rule and Marcos' plunder

Before President Ferdinand Marcos' declaration of Martial Law in 1972, Primitivo Mijares in *The Conjugal Dictatorship* recalled the transfer of PhP69 million, then a very large amount, by Marcos from the Malacanang Palace contingency funds to the House of Representatives to give allied congressmen who belonged to the same ruling party, campaign funds for re-election in 1969 (Coronel, 1998: 68). The scandal did not surface until 1972, when Marcos successfully ordered congress and other democratic, rule-making institutions to be simply shut down, removing constitutional checks and balances on the Executive, such that Marcos could effectively ignore any scandal. The declaration of Martial law meant rule was by Presidential Decree.

Aquino (1999: 49) outlines the sequence of business takeovers Marcos then conducted of the assets of other elite families, by extra-legal means and violence: the business empire of the Lopez family from 1972, when martial law was declared and when the head of the Lopez family, Eugenio Sr., was in the US, which included the 'nation's largest corporation, six television and 21 radio stations, one of the leading newspapers, and the Benpres Corporation', and eventually Meralco, with assets totalling more than $400 million, using allegations of complicity in an assassination plot, false arrest, and ultimately threats to the physical person and safety of his son's life.

Continuing in the process of extortion by extra-legal means, the Marcos–Romualdez group, headed by Marcos, and using the military, then seized all the corporations owned or controlled by another elite family, that headed by industrialist Fernando Jacinto (who was also out of the country at the time), without any settlement. These included:

> the Iligan Integrated Steel Mills, Inc. (IISMI) the only one of its kind in the country. Numbering 26 in all, they were worth $21 million (Coronel, 1998: 45)

These later became the government-operated National Steel Corporation. The excuse for not compensating Jacinto, had been that he owed money, and now numerous takeovers took place of banks, utilities, and other institutions, under the pretext of unpaid loans. In the case of the flag-carrier national airline, Philippine Airlines (PAL), the manager, Benigno Toda 'apparently incurred the ire of Imelda Marcos when he presented her with a million-peso bill for her constant travels abroad', which led to take-over and the company being placed with Roman Cruz, Jr., a key Marcos crony (Coronel, 1998: 58).

This process put large and profitable sectors of the Philippine economy into the hands of a small group of Marcos cronies,[1] creating state monopolies in most major industries and commodity sectors. Although backed by the government, the monopolies were formally private national cartels, controlled by the cronies, who with no experience of legal restraint, became audacious 'new oligarchs' in a system of 'crony capitalism' (Aquino, 1999: 89). This group were then joined by Marcos' military allies, notably General Ver, who, though historically excluded from the traditional elite, were now promoted to a new lavish lifestyle and social standing, symbolised by the development of the Corinthian Gardens in Metro Manila (Aquino, 1999).

The Marcos family and their cronies used the machinery of government to serve their private interests, committing acts of grand kleptocracy from 1965 to 1986, in an archetypal example of state capture (see Aquino, 1999 Table 1.1 this volume for definition of state capture), accompanied by extensive violation of human rights. 'Plunder' aptly describes the extent of this corruption, facilitated by unaccountable personal rule by Presidential decree: Marcos' absolutist power lead to coercive executive rule and consolidated and centralised business ownership, with corruption a somewhat inevitable consequence.

Anti-corruption measures in the post-dictatorship era

Marcos was finally unseated by people power in 1986, in a bloodless revolution, and the Marcos plunder of the nation then paved the way to a

Philippine lexicography of corruption, catalysing anti-corruption laws, policies, and programmes: if anything good arose from the Marcos plunder, it was that the Philippines learned to institute anti-corruption measures. From 1986, democratic institutions were reinstalled under the Aquino administration, and laws and policies were purposively introduced to both recover Marcos' ill-gotten wealth, and prevent and curtail corruption in the bureaucracy. Aquino vigorously eliminated anyone associated with the Marcos regime including those who performed well (Carino, 1986), which some viewed as over zealous. The intuitional and legal framework for anti-corruption is now comparable to international best practice, with a recognition that corruption is sited as much in the private sector as the bureaucracy (reflected in the latter Republic Acts 9184, 8792, 8799, 9160, 9194 and 8791) (Co et al., 2007).

More specifically, the 1987 Constitution established two special, independent bodies whose goals are to embed the principles of integrity and accountability in public office. These bodies are the Office of the Ombudsman (created under Republic Act 6770), and the Sandiganbayan (created under Republic Act 7975) for the offences of higher level officials, which are complimented by two other constitutional bodies, the Civil Service Commission (CSC) for value orientation, and the Commission on Audit (COA).[2] Various administrative orders were then issued to enforce the framing laws on anti-corruption bodies and programmes. Meanwhile, below these iconic institutions are the Department of Justice (DOJ), for the prosecution of lower level officials, and the Presidential Commission on Good Government (PCGG), to retrieve Marcos' spoils.

The institutional infrastructure is indeed extensive, and each new Administration, post-Marcos, has added new resources: the President's Committee on Public Ethics and Accountability (PCPEA) under President Aquino in 1987; the Presidential Commission against Graft and Corruption (PCAGC), charged with a Moral Recovery Programme, under Ramos in 1994; a new focus on the inter-agency body composed of the PCAGC, the Ombudsman, DOJ, and the Civil Service Commission under Estrada; and the Presidential Anti-Graft Commission (PAGC) under the Arroyo administration. However, whether these effectively curb corruption is questionable: numerous initiatives with overlapping mandates, comprehensive provision and wide-ranging functions, follow older initiatives which were inadequately implemented and did not work. Since corruption persists regardless, it can be argued that anti-corruption policy has rewards for its Presidential advocates beyond actually reducing corruption. Leaders have a greater proclivity for law making than law enforcement; for exhibition and grandstanding, not quite for accomplishment.

Different administrations pronounce their respective flagship programmes against corruption, without examining whether the creation of these bodies and policies, in themselves, contributes to a further diminished public perception of the public administrative system. In the meantime, public officials and bureaucrats, especially those in higher ranking positions, continue to stand above the law and its application, while specific discretionary powers in office insulate authorities from institutional accountability.

Different loci of corruption

Another explanation for the persistence of corruption despite an extensive and archetypal institutional anti-corruption campaign is that the type of corruption which is most prevalent has changed, with some types remaining uncontested: while systemic grand corruption is largely assigned to the Marcos past, the culturally embedded petty corruption, and the political economy corruption involving the political elite, who retain discretionary powers despite new institutions, remain.

In terms of culturally embedded petty corruption, the poll body Social Weather Stations (SWS), identifies most corruption-prone business–government transactions to be in the area of permitting and licensing (local and national), payment and collection of taxes, tax auditing and investigation, customs regulation, and procurement and government contracting, including supplying government with goods and services (SWS, 2005). The *modus operandi* is for the tax examiner and the subject taxpayer to come to an informal agreement, whereby the latter's tax due will be reduced in exchange for an illicit payment to the tax auditor. A popular adage is that more money goes to 'PR' (public relations) or to the tax examiner's pocket than to 'RP' (the Republic of the Philippines), a sentiment reinforced by wider SWS polling on businessmen's perception of likely solicitation by public officials, which recorded an expectation that an average of 26.7 per cent of officials would elicit a bribe over a range of six government services in 2005 (SWS, 2005).

There is also the commonplace 'sharing scheme' that occurs within the Bureau of Internal Revenue (BIR), where the examiner retains 30 per cent of the illicit payment while the remaining 70 per cent is shared by the regional director, revenue district officer (head of the BIR district office), and the chief of the assessment division. Meanwhile, Customs administration corruption falls into two categories, namely those that occur to facilitate and make possible illegitimate and illegal transactions, and virtual smuggling where there is collusion between smugglers and Customs personnel. Technical smuggling assumes the forms of under-valuation, misclassification, and/or misdeclaration of goods. In all cases, the national coffers are the ultimate losers and benefits narrowly accrue to both the clients (smugglers) and the bureaucrats. Corruption in these cases is transactional between the bureaucracy and society – it involves the bureaucrat and the client, government and business, or government and the citizen – as opposed to more strictly defined graft, which is theft without another's involvement. Corruption is not the monopoly of the bureaucrats because the act is committed by a process of osmosis within and without the bureaucracy, generating multiple high risk areas and 'objects of corrupt transaction' (de Dios and Ferrer, 2001).

A culture of corruption

Underpinning these transactional corrupt acts is a larger set of cultural institutions that persist in the Philippine political-administrative system, namely, gift giving, reciprocity, clientelism, the so-called 'dark side of social capital' or the network, fixing, and facilitation. Indeed, the stereotyped Filipino character is synonymous with generosity and gift-giving, with the latter commonplace to show appreciation, gratitude for a favour done, or to 'bridge' and reach out to a stranger or someone distant. The practice of gift-giving is carried into the political and administrative institutions, hence, when a job is done by a bureaucrat, the client often sends gifts as a way of thanking the employee for the service rendered, despite the passage of a Presidential Decree 46 in 1972 which forbids gift-giving in bureaucratic transactions. When gift-giving is constantly practised, certain expectations of regularity in the act grow on the bureaucrat until the habit is embedded in the office, in the transactions, and eventually in governance institutions. Similarly, reciprocity creeps into the electoral system through clientelism wherein a political candidate coddles the electorate through outright vote buying and the promise of favours at a future time in exchange for the vote.

A widespread view among aspiring politicians and candidates is that public office is an employment from which money, cars, travel abroad, wealth, a privileged lifestyle and social mobility result (Democracy Audit, 2005). Public office is therefore seen as an opportunity to reward one's self rather than as an apex of responsibility and public service, both legacy and reinvention of the colonial experience. Thus elections are an expensive occasion for political corruption. In 2001, the research institute of the Liberal Party estimated that it took between 25 to 50 million pesos to win a seat in the lower house of congress, with the variation depending on the size of the district, with the number of voters ranging between 10,000 to 20,000 nationally, and the intensity of the competition (interview with Chito Gascon, Liberal Party, 2005). For national positions, the figure can balloon to 5 billion pesos for a presidential post and 100 million pesos to run for Senate, according to former Commissioner on Elections, Christian Monsod (interview with Monsod cited in Democracy Audit, 2005). Once in office, the incumbent seeks to recoup election expenditures, in spite of the laws and institutions in place, to ensure reward, perceived as a return on investments.

A culture of dualism embedded in the Philippine administrative system, where junior officials are subject to accountability while higher ranking officials remain above it, also remains a major cause of contemporary corruption (Varela, 2003). For example, the discretionary funds of the Executive, particularly the intelligence funds, are spent without any scrutiny from the proper auditing body. More widely, many Filipinos want to feel they are in high, special positions which entitle them to exemption from the rules and the standard procedures. For example, a different set of traffic rules apply to high officials and police officers, as the traffic comes to a standstill and yields to a police car as it noisily escorts some Very Important Persons (VIPs). In the end however, this revered special treatment upholds dualism and subverts the rule of law and the equitable application of the rules.

The 'social bad' in social capital: networks, 'fixing', and 'facilitation'

Despite the formal rules, policies, and programmes against corruption, the informal networks and rules abound and operate more effectively than the formal ones, being therefore a conduit for petty corruption. Amorado (2005) argues persuasively that the purpose of the network is to 'fix' the complex ways of the bureaucracy, in exchange for a fee. The Filipinos, just like many others in Asia, have a predilection to informal networks and connections – 'bridge', 'connector', 'facilitator', 'fixer' – when things are difficult and complex to deal with or to reach, such as the bureaucracy. When the bureaucracy fails to achieve the Weberian goals of efficiency, effectiveness and order, it restricts services, providing simultaneously the conditions for 'fixing' and 'facilitation', between those inside the system and those who 'fix' outside.

Connections, networks, and links can be positive social bridges (Putnam, 2000), but not necessarily. Although fixers are sometimes recognised as trouble shooters who help clients in trouble, 'doctors' who fix the bureaucratic problems for the clients, fixers are also seen as 'bagmen' who deliver the illicit tariffs to their connections inside government agencies (Amorado, 2005). For example, based on a poll survey (SWS, 1999), 44 per cent of Filipinos believe that policemen ask for bribes. Fixing, bribery or outright extortion is commonplace, such as in the driving licence application process (Land Transportation Office), revenue collectors (Bureau of Internal Revenue), environmental inspectors and business assessors, land appraising, business permits, and travel packages, among others. The clients yield to fixing when the bureaucratic procedures are cumbersome, inefficient, and unfriendly to clients, using the dark side of social capital, which in turn leads to further bureaucratic pathology.

When fixing becomes deliberate, persistent, and organised, the corrupt act then becomes institutionalised and graduates into a syndicate, causing the respective bureaucrats to gradually refuse any attempts to remedy bureaucratic inefficiencies, introduce transparency, or simplify rules. Tolerance of fixing or bribery is nurtured by the culture of *pakikisama* (*esprit de corps*), the habit of conforming, laziness, and fear: systemic fixing networks embolden the syndicate to resist, even destroy, those who have the will to fight them (Santiago, 1991). As Varela (2003) insists, organisations are made up of individuals and their habits, such that anti-corruption reform requires changing the mindset of both the bureaucrat and the client toward gift-giving and fixing: it requires more than the constant reinvention of iconic governance institutions which has been the pattern of anti-corruption reform in the Philippines since 1987, and which is also, as discussed in this volume, salient in the current anti-corruption global campaign.

The political economy of corruption

Corruption also persists in the Philippines at the highest levels because discretionary power is embedded in central governance institutions whose personnel transact with flourishing, but opaque, economic cartels. For example, the Ramos administration was scarred by the PEA–Amari deal, between 1995 and 1997, which involved the sale of property along Manila Bay. Then Senator Ernesto Maceda investigated this 'grandmother of all scams' in Senate Committee, a deal which involved the payment by Amari of over PhP1.7 billion in cash and real estate commissions to a cast of dealmakers and officials (Coronel, 1998: 85). Coronel in the 1998 document claims that the government was defrauded of billions of pesos, and although there was no solid evidence of the involvement of high officials such as House Speaker Jose de Venecia and President Fidel V. Ramos, the conclusion of the senate committees was that collusion existed, since the deal could not have been clinched without their approval, while a key participant was indirectly related to Ramos. Moreover, the Senate felt that there were frantic attempts to derail full investigation (Coronel in PCIJ, 1998: 85). It was the usual blood-political links, a kin-associate who dabbled in independent ventures, and managed to 'get Malacanang approval for the Amari joint venture' (Coronel in PCIJ, 1998: 87) (Malacanang is the official residence of the President). Based on the PCIJ account, these business relationships were nurtured over a long time, at parties and social gatherings thrown by Malacanang, involving 'coffeeshop hustlers, with an instinct for a fast buck' (ibid.), who could easily construct corporations, such as the Amari Coastal Bay Development Corporation, which in 1994 partnered with an Ital-Thai development company, which had a track record of cornering huge construction projects in Asia. The cosy sociability and networking of the political elite was symbiotic to the Asian business networks that buttressed the 'Asian miracle'.

Despite regulatory bodies such as the Public Estates Authority (PEA), or the Office of the Government Corporate Counsel (OGCC), and the Department of Justice (DOJ), rapid opaque deals still occur. PEA management did not use open tender, but chose to negotiate with only two developers, one of whom was later paid off (Maceda in PCIJ, 1998: 96), and was convinced of the Amari's proposal based on three appraisals, despite indications that 'the appraisal process was clearly flawed and designed to justify . . . a flawed transaction' (Coronel in PCIJ 1998: 95). In short, favourable decisions were granted to officials who enjoyed informal approval by those 'upstairs'. This suggests that there are shadow decision makers around the official ones, and agents within the corridors of power who prove to be more influential in sealing contracts, by garnering the consent of top politicians, than those who officially define the rules of bids and contracts.

Indeed, the latitude of discretion of top authority is enormous, especially that which stems from the Office of the President, where accountability is only vaguely defined. Principals of executive agencies, who are the cabinet members and advisors of the President, serve at the pleasure of the Chief Executive and are not governed by performance indicators, or accountable within the wider democratic system. Instead, they consist of a cabal who answer only to the President, in procedures grounded in personal loyalty. For example, in the last 2004 national election, the sitting President is alleged to have used public resources in favour of her campaign: the use of social security funds to win the support of the electorate, and the use of road programmes to employ contractual street cleaners to advertise her campaign. Worse still, the President is alleged to have influenced a member of the Commission on Elections, himself a presidential appointee, to manipulate the outcome of the elections (Aquino, 2005: 26). The unaccountability of the Executive arm of government and the Office of the President in particular facilitates such abuses.

The Philippine administrative and political system has a leadership that is personality-centred rather than one that is rules-driven. Where the rule of law is not embedded within cultural norms corruption is likely to flourish (Kaufmann and Wei, 1998), such that this form of leadership authority is indicative of a wider malaise, where the rule of law is not seen as a universal principle but as a particularistic guide to behaviour. The culture tends toward special treatment and exceptions to the rule rather than submission to rules. Worse still, some practitioners view the rule of law as a failed principle if and when it does not respond to a particular context, and then go on to suggest that 'blind' and 'irrelevant' rules be reformulated, particularly where exemptions for high officials from the enforcement of routine procedures and rules are at issue. This proposition must be challenged because the principle behind the rule of law is precisely a universal application of the rules beyond person, stature, or specific circumstances.

Conclusion

If the number of anti-corruption laws, and corresponding institutional bodies, were to become the benchmark of an anti-corruption campaign, the Philippines would have ranked first among corruption-free countries in the region. Obviously however, the formulation, formalisation, and articulation of these laws have proved insufficient solutions to corruption, partly because they have been insufficiently implemented, but more fundamentally because of the persistence of a culture of dualism which has allowed universal principal to be corroded by particularistic and limited interpretation, and because of the forfeiting of immediate reward by officials that public integrity demands. Nonetheless, bureaucratic reform should emphasise the need for greater accountability of positions, especially those that hold immense discretionary power and authority, such as the Presidency, elected officials, and executives of government owned and controlled corporations. A more consistent pattern of sanction would also assist the anti-corruption effort: even when corruption has been detected and investigated, usually hyped by media, it is not always known whether prosecution and conviction result.

The continued blight of grand corruption, even post-Marcos, suggests that the Philippine political system conditions a process of leadership

selection which is fallible in democratic terms: all too often the Philippines has suffered leaders who were either incompetent, corrupt or unwilling to support anti-corruption efforts, even as their support has grown more critical to successful political reform. To produce good leaders, a wider democratic infrastructure is required: the effective and credible execution of democratic elections; competitive, fair political party competition and financing; and the permanent risk of public outrage, by a strong citizenship and responsible media, if rules are abused.

Thus other cognate reforms are required to reduce corruption. The Philippines currently counts among the 41 per cent of countries worldwide that have a prevalence of illegal political donations (World Economic Forum, 2004; Transparency International, 2004: 31), while serious flaws remain in the electoral system (Co et al., 2005), suggesting areas of essential reform. Arguably, however, legal reform is not enough, as cultural change is also necessary. Local government units, community organisations and small networks of organised citizens offer creative methods of embedding the rule of law into the social fabric, while educational institutions and the traditional culture-shaping institutions of the church and community remain critical constructors of social norms at the micro and meso levels. International interventions and proclamations, and the institutional projects of those in high office, are not enough, and have passed with little effect: successful anti-corruption campaigns require a mass social movement, since corruption is legitimised by popular social coding.

In this broad campaign, donors should support both public and private efforts. In their desire to remove corruption in government, and commensurate with the current action-oriented policy orthodoxy outlined above, some donors switched funding support from public organisations to the private sector, forgetting that corruption could flourish there to, and creating the illusion that bureaucratic corruption was reduced. As our examples show, corruption is not a monopoly of government; civil society and the private sector have their own share of accountability problems.

Notes

1. These included Roberto Benedicto and Benjamin Romualdez (together, mass media); Eduardo Cojuangco (athletics) and Juan Ponce Enrile (together, coconuts); Campos (pharmaceuticals); Floreindo (bananas, real estate); Geronimo Velasco, the Energy Minister (controlled oil and energy); Herminio Disini, a cousin-in-law to Imelda Marcos (tobacco); Ricardo Silverio (car assembly and retail inc. Toyotas); Roman Cruz, Jr. controlled two government corporations,

GSIS and PAL; Benedicto, Marcos' son-in-law Gregorio Araneta III, and Marcos' financial adviser Rolando Gapud (banking); Rodolfo Cuenca, Marcos' golf partner, (construction); Alfredo Romualdez, another Imelda brother, (casino gambling) (from Aquino, 1999: 49).

2. To achieve effective operation, these bodies were given fiscal and political autonomy as stated in Section 2, Article VIII, Section 14, Article XI and in Section B1, Article IX, and Section D1, also Article IX, and Section 11, Article XI of the constitution. The actions and decisions of these bodies can be appealed to the Supreme Court.

References

Amorado, R. V. (2005), *Fixing Society. An Ethnographic Study of Fixers in the Philippines*, Ateneo de Davao University, July, unpublished dissertation

Aquino, B. A. (1999), *Politics of Plunder. The Philippines under Marcos*, 2nd edn, University of the Philippines, College of Public Administration, Philippines

Aquino, Norman (2005), 'Corruption: Cultural or institutional?', in *Business World Anniversary Report 2005*, pp. 26–8

Azfar, O. and Gurgur, T. (2000), 'Decentralization and Corruption in the Philippines', Mimeo, IRIS Center, University of Maryland

Batalla, E. C. (2000), 'De-institutionalizing Corruption in the Philippines: Identifying Strategic Requirements for Reinventing Institutions', conference paper for the Konrad Adenauer Foundation and Yuchengco Center For East Asia of De La Salle University, Makati City, August

Bhargava, E. and Bolongaita, V. (2003), *Challenging Corruption in Asia: Case Studies and a Framework for Action*, Washington DC, World Bank Publications

Carino, L. (ed.) (1986), *Bureaucratic Corruption in Asia: Causes, Consequences, and Controls*, University of the Philippines Press, College of Public Administration, Philippines

Carino, L., Iglesias, Gabrielle, and Mendoza, F. (1999), 'Initiatives Against Corruption: the Philippine Case', *Occasional paper UP-NCPAG 99-1*, July

Co, Edna E. A., Tigno, Jorge, Lao, Ma. Elissa Jayme, and Sayo, Margarita (2005), *Philippine Democracy Assessment: Free and Fair Elections and the Democratic Role of Political Parties*, Friedrich Ebert Stiftung and University of the Philippines National College of Public Administration and Governance, Philippines. Distributed by Ateneo de Manila University Press

Co, E. E. A. Lim, M. O., Jayme-Lao, M. E. and Juan, L. J. (2007), *Philippine Democracy Assessment. Minimizing Corruption*. British Council, Friedrich Ebert Stiftung, Philippine Democracy Audit, and Transparency and Accountability Network. Manila, Philippines

Coronel, S. (ed.) (1998), *Pork and other Perks: Corruption and Governance in the Philippines*, Quezon City Philippine Center for Investigative Journalism

De Dios, E. and Ferrer, R. (2001), 'Corruption in the Philippines. Framework and Context', *Public Policy*, 5(1): 1–42, University of the Philippines Centre for Integrative and Development Studies

Democracy Audit (2005), *Notes from a Focus Group Discussion among key informants in Luzon*, Philippines, July

Doig, A. and Riley, S. (2000), *Corruption and Anti-Corruption Strategies: Issues and Case Studies from Developing Countries*, Washington DC, Work Bank

Eigen, P. (2000), 'The Role of Civil Society', in *Corruption and Integrity Improvement Initiatives in Developing Countries*, Washington DC, Work Bank

Endriga, J. (2003), 'Stability and Change: Civil Service in the Philippines', in *Introduction to Public Administration in the Philippines: A Reader*, Bautista, Victoria, Alfiler, Ma. Concepcion, Reyes, Danilo and Tapales, Proserpina (eds) UP-NCPAG Philippines

Hutchcroft, Paul D. (1998), *Booty Capitalism: the Politics of Banking in the Philippines*, Ateneo de Manila University Press, Quezon City, Philippines

Kaufmann, D. and Wei, S-J. (1998), 'Does Grease Money Speed Up the Wheels of Commerce?', World Bank Institute and Development Research Group, Washington DC

Klitgaard, R. (1998), 'International Cooperation against Corruption', RAND Graduate School, International Development and Security, Santa Monica, California

Lim, J. and Pascual, C. (2000), 'The Detrimental Role of Biased Politics: Framework and Case Studies', Study Paper 3 prepared for Philippine Centre for Policy Studies, Quezon City, Philippines

Mendoza, A. Jr. (2000), 'The Industrial Anatomy of Corruption: Government Procurement, Bidding and Award of Contracts', Study Paper 2a, Quezon City, Philippines

Pascual, C. and Lim, J. (2001), 'Corruption and Weak Markets: the BW Resources Stock Market Scam', in *Public Policy*, Center For Integrative and Development Studies, University of The Philippines, January–June, pp. 109–29

Putnam, R. (2000), *Bowling Alone: the Collapse and Revival of American Community*, New York, Simon and Schuster

Romero, S. (undated), *Civil Society Initiated Measures for Combating Corruption in the Philippines*, Development Academy of the Philippines, Philippines

Rose-Ackerman, S. (1996), 'Democracy and Grand Corruption' in *International Social Science Journal,* 149 September, pp. 365–80, also in *Explaining Corruption: the Politics of Corruption*, Robert Williams (ed.), Elgar Reference Collection UK and USA, pp. 321–36

Santiago, Miriam Defensor (1991), *How to Fight Graft*, Movement for Responsible Public Service, Manila, Zita Publishing Corporation

Scott, J. (2000), 'The Analysis of Corruption in Developing Nations', in Robert Williams (ed.), *Explaining Corruption. The Politics of Corruption*, Elgar Reference Collection UK and USA

Segundo, R. (undated), *Civil Society Initiated Measures for Combating Corruption in the Philippines*, Development Academy of the Philippines, Philippines

Social Weather Stations (SWS), *National Survey Report*, September–October 1999, 1999 and 2005

Transparency International (2004), *Global Corruption Report 2004*, Pluto Press, London and Virginia, USA

Varela, Amelia P. (2003), 'The Culture Perspective in Organization Theory: Relevance to Philippine Public Administration', in *Introduction to Public Administration in the Philippines: a Reader,* Bautista, Victoria, Alfiler, Ma. Concepcion, Reyes, Danilo and Tapales, Proserpina (eds) 2nd edition, UP-NCPAG, Philippines

Virtucio, M. A. and Lalunio, M. (2000), 'Tender Mercies: Contracts, Concessions and Privatization', Study Paper 26, Quezon City, Philippines

Werner, S. (2000), 'New Directions in the Study of Administrative Corruption', in Robert Williams (ed.), *Explaining Corruption. The Politics of Corruption*, Elgar Reference Collection UK and USA

Williams R. (ed.) (2000), *Explaining Corruption. The Politics of Corruption*, Edward Elgar, Cheltenham

World Economic Forum (2004), *Global Corruption Report 2004, Transparency International*, Pluto Press, London

7
Challenges of Anti-Corruption Policies in Post-Communist Countries

Anastassiya Zagainova

This chapter reviews corruption and anti-corruption policies in post-communist countries since the beginning of transition by reviewing authors who have identified corrupt characteristics specific to the post-communist countries (Mendras, 1998; Andreff, 2003; Satarov and Parkhomenko, 2001). As a group, the post-communist countries are considered among the most corrupt in the world. Indeed, according to Transparency International (2005), seven transition countries are in the 30 most corrupt of 159 countries in the index. The historical legacy of communism, the history of transition, and the adaptation of networks into modern clientelism emerge as powerful conditioning experiences in the types of corruption which emerge, with two conceptual types appearing as particularly salient: state capture or political corruption, and administrative corruption (Hellman, Kaufman and Jones, 2000; 2002). Using measurement and diagnostic tools from major donors, the World Bank (WB), Transparency International (TI), Political Risk Services and the European Bank for Reconstruction and Development (EBRD) the chapter then uses the prevalence of these corruption types to create a comparative typology of measurable corruption within the post-communist Eastern European countries. However, by using donor diagnostics this standardising methodology ultimately occludes a more diverse, historical and contextual picture.

Origins of post-communist corruption

Corruption in the soviet system emerged from an excess of bureaucratic control and the absence of private property, which in turn gave rise to clientelism and shortage. Kornaï (1992) showed that shortage acts as a mode of regulation, which creates a market dominated by sellers, a problem exacerbated by information deficits. The firm's adjustments to the

Plan's requirements used forced substitution, queues, the recruitment of sellers by bribery, and the related emergence of a parallel market.[1] To be able, despite its irrationality, to carry out the Plan's instructions, companies organised relations out-of-the-Plan, to the benefit of their directors. These networks of multilateral barter and illicit exchanges, which were often tolerated and even encouraged by the Party, have subsequently nourished the development of corruption (Duchene, 1987), as opportunities were expanded and diversified with liberalisation around discretion in the granting of credit, patents, and privatisation.

There are several characteristics of the soviet system which contributed to the modern system of clientelism, defined as where a political person or party increases its power based on clients gained and attached by the attribution of favours (Mendras, 1998). In the soviet system, economic power was concentrated in the Ministries' administration, which then obliged the economic actors and private individuals to be subject to the Plan. But there was also a conjunction of interests between companies and administration: to be able to survive within the Party's hierarchy, the state administrators needed to ensure the successful performance of 'their' production units, by whatever means, by creating faithful and loyal clients (Egnell and Pessik, 1974). Moreover, the soviet administrative and economic elites overlapped, and were sometimes embodied in the same person: one day a man was directing the committee of the city party and the following day he was a mayor, or a chief of a company, always closely related to the administration. This characteristic made it possible to accumulate functions, contacts and influence. Thus, informal networks mixed representatives of the Party, the directors of production units, and civil servants.

Practices during transition

The necessary complexity, but also non-transparent nature, of privatisations and the initial imperfections of the institutional system provided a wide range of discretion, creating opportunities for bribery. Privatisation transformed the positions of the former elite, who were deemed irreplaceable, because of the information, knowledge and specific awareness they held. Within most Eastern European countries, privatisation was transformed into what one may call *prikhvatizatsiya* (usurp the assets) where the 'crown jewels' were divided up between some oligarchs, causing a concentration of industrial and financial capital (Andreff, 2003). Countries that have chosen mass privatisation faced the most significant growth of corruption, as in Russia, Kazakhstan, Georgia or Azerbaijan. It is 'the paradox of mass privatization' described by Labaronne (2002): fast, badly prepared procedures in non-transparent institutional frameworks caused increasing corruption through state capture. Resistance to reform appeared in a great number of economies of transition, and was rooted in the rising social and economic inequalities which resulted.

Institutional change is central to the process of post-communist transformation (Samson, 1994), but often moves toward a market economy were made before institutions which are necessary to its operation, such as the right of ownership, a financial system and guarantees of transactions were properly in place (Stiglitz, 2000; Andreff, 2003; Samson, 1998). There occurred an institutional trap, as governments proved incapable of catalysing adequate institutional change, paying insufficient attention to arresting the legacies of the past, clientelism and the informal economy, which undermined new market regulating institutions. Djankov et al. (1998) put particular emphasis on the role of the 'concentration of corporate control' in determining 'the evolution of the legal system', such that ownership structures are seen to condition institutional development, leading to power struggles within the soviet mix of economic and political elites. Economic freedom proved not to be the first, or even a sufficient, condition for curbing corruption, a statement which can be validated by regression analysis using the WB *Governance Indicators* and the TI *Corruption Perception Index*, as there is a weak correlation between trade liberalisation and the incidence of corruption. A credible government is also required, such that early donor intervention failed its anticorruption objectives.

Corruption measurement in transition countries

An avalanche of studies analysing corruption in transition countries has occurred over the past decade (Boycko et al., 1995; Hellman and Kaufmann, 2004; Raiser, 1999; Stephan, 1999; Moran, 2001; Kaminski and Kaminski, 2001; Kotkin and Sajo, 2002; Karklins, 2002; Treisman, 2002), and a great effort of measurement has taken place by international institutions, academics and other specialists working on the problem. Three aggregate indicators from TI, the WB (2005) and Political Risk Services (PRS) (2004) strongly correlate and together indicate four clear groups of countries with discrete and different quantitative bands. The least corrupt are the Central Eastern European countries (CEEC) (Kaufmann, Kraay and Mastruzzi, 2005), whose adhesion to the European Union supported structural change. Among the most corrupt we find the ex-soviet countries of Central Asia and the Southern Caucasus, where the proximity of

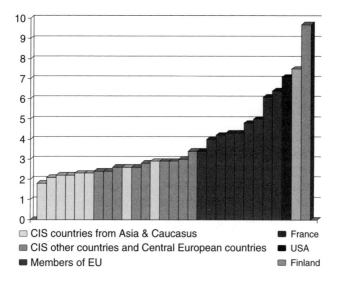

Figure 7.1: Corruption's level in the transition countries
Source: Compiled from CPI (TI, 2005)

economic and political systems with the old communist structure is correlated with a persistent high level of corruption (see Figure 7.1).

Different configurations

However, these trend results hide different configurations of historical,
economic and political causality, and different forms of resultant corruption. The WB and EBRD acknowledge this, and thus further classify
countries in transition into four groups according to the type of the
most active corruption: administrative, political, both or none (WB, 2000;
see Table 1.1).[2] Four institutional situations can then be distinguished
using this WB/EBRD conceptual categorisation triangulated with the
quantitative ranking from the three correlated indicators above (WB, TI
and PRS): countries with predominant endemic (Group 1), bureaucratic
(Group 2), or political (Group 3) corruption, and the countries which
have entered into a virtuous circle (Group 4), as illustrated in Table 7.1.

In the group of countries with *endemic corruption* the concentration of
political power militates against the emergence of institutional reforms.
For example, Moldova retains many structural and institutional features
of its soviet past, including elements of totalitarianism and 'socialist corruption'. In comparison, Georgia, in Group 2, enjoys the political

Table 7.1: Typology of corruption forms in post-communist countries

	High administrative corruption index	Characterised by	Medium administrative corruption index	Characterised by
High state capture index	*1) Endemic corruption* Azerbaijan, Moldova, Ukraine, Kyrgyz Rep.	strong bureaucratic corruption, significant state capture	*3) Political corruption* Croatia, Bulgaria, Latvia, Russia	strong concentrations of elite power, but not necessarily weak administration
Medium state capture index	*2) Bureaucratic corruption* Armenia, Kazakhstan, Belarus, Albania, Romania, Georgia	weak administrative reforms, underdevelopment of the private sector and legislative capacity	*4) Virtuous countries* Slovenia, Hungary, Estonia, Czech Rep, Poland, Lithuania, Slovak Rep.	strongest historical legacies of capitalist regulation, structural reforms condition of EU entry

Source: Compiled using Hellman, J. S., Kaufmann, D. and Jones G. (2000).

engagement of the new government and co-operation with the international community, but still suffers widespread bureaucratic corruption, whereas Russia, in Group 3, has endemic political corruption and state capture, thriving in the non-competitive climate of both politics and economy. The last group is the *virtuous countries*; the new member states of the European Union. The quantitative indicators support this classification, as illustrated in Table 7.2.

Table 7.2: Main indicators of countries by group

	Corruption perception index, TI 2004[a]	Corruption to administration as a proportion of sales, 2002[b]	Combined average rating of Freedom House, 2005[c]	Transition index, EBRD 2004[d]	Real GDP growth 2003 (Base 1989 = 100) EBRD[e]
Group 1					
Azerbaijan	2.2	5.7	5.5	2.5	71
Kyrgyzstan	2.3	5.3	5.5	2.9	75
Moldova	2.9	4	3.5	2.7	41
Ukraine	2.6	4.4	3.5	2.8	51
Group 2					
Albania	2.4	4	3	2.8	129
Armenia	2.9	4.6	4.5	3.1	89
Georgia	2.3	4.3	3.5	3	41
Kazakhstan	2.6	3.1	5.5	2.9	94
Romania	3	3.2	2.5	3.2	92
Uzbekistan	2.2	4.3	6.5	2.3	107
Group 3					
Bulgaria	4	2.1	1,5	3.4	84
Croatia	3.4	1.1	2	3.5	91
Latvia	4.2	1.4	1,5	3.6	83
Russia	2.4	2.8	5,5	3	77
Group 4					
Estonia	6.4	1.6	1	3.8	102
Czech Rep	4.3	2.5	1	3.8	108
Hungary	5	1.7	1	3.6	115
Lithuania	4.8	2.8	2	3.5	84
Poland	3.4	1.6	1	3.8	135
Slovakia	4.3	1.4	1	3.6	114
Slovenia	6.1	1.4	1	3.4	120

Sources: [a] TI Corruption Perception Index 2005. Scale: 1 very corrupt, 10 least corrupt
[b] Hellman, Jones and Kaufmann, 2002
[c] Freedom House Annual global survey 2005. Scale: 1 most free, 7 least free
[d] EBRD Transition report 2004. 1 unchanged planned economy, 4,5 + industry countries
[e] EBRD Transition report 2004.

Group 1: endemic corruption

Countries suffering from endemic corruption are principally those countries least advanced in marketisation and institutional reform, such that economic liberalisation has largely created new opportunities for bribes. These countries are among the 30 most corrupt countries of the world (Azerbaijan is the 10th most corrupt); with the level of profits devoted to bribes at nearly 30 per cent (50 per cent in Kyrgyzstan) (Hellman et al., 2000b); and weak civil freedoms (Freedom House, 2005), due to concentrated political power and arrested development.

For example, Moldova, which is not only the poorest country in Europe, with 80 per cent of the population falling below the poverty line and per capita income currently estimated at USD 890 in 2005 (CIA, 2006), but is also characterised by ethnic conflicts, and colloquially referred to as the 'museum of the USSR', indicating the persistence of soviet forms of political and economic organisation. While Moldova has a parliamentary system of government, adopted in 2000, the ruling Communist Party still monopolises power, achieving victory in flawed local and regional elections in 2005, due to weak political freedoms (Freedom House, 2005b). Judicial, legislative and executive powers, which have great discretionary scope, are not separated institutionally, but concentrated in traditional hands: it is the ex-Minister of Internal Affairs of the USSR who governs the country surrounded by the politico-economic elite of the soviet era. Attempts to liberalise prices and trade were undermined by political requests for intervention by the State in the economy, or their informal circumvention, while privatisations were derailed by cronyism, bureaucratic discrimination and a corresponding lack of international investors. Institutions function ineffectively because of the incompatibilities of their functional and institutional frameworks (GRECO, 2003).

Nonetheless, the Moldovan Parliament approved, in April 2001, a governmental programme for 2001–2005, against organised criminality and corruption, through reinforcement of a legal framework and more transparent financial environment. Several pillars compose this plan: the adaptation of legislation to control financial flows; improvement of prevention (criteria for public agents' selection and codes of conduct); improvement of the control system; and public education and international co-operation. A vibrant NGO sector and media, including the local TI and UN, have contributed to sensitising a population already disillusioned in Government, despite a difficult operating environment, which includes political pressure from national and local authorities. A further law of 2003 attempted some judicial reform, to define an independent prosecutor's office, but this and other reforms remain stymied

enterprises, and who then converted their de facto control of property into ownership rights on privatisation. The oligarchs subsequently built industrial and financial empires. They often captured state institutions where regulatory decisions are made and policy implementation carried out, working hard to reduce the cost of doing (their own) business in Russia (Boycko et al., 1995).

President Yeltsin's government introduced reforms which gave a greater autonomy to local government, in order to consolidate a federal system and reverse political concentration, but unfortunately this merely increased discretionary power, although with variations, within regional institutions and led to their greater capture by regionalised firms, aided by close ties between political and economic elites: the governors often head large companies.[3] In contrast, President Putin initiated centralisation processes, restricting the autonomy of regional political elites in order to reduce local capture (Yakovlev and Zhuravskaya, 2004). The relative power of firms to capture political and administrative decisions in their favour, quantified by Yakovlev and Zhuravskaya, shifted from a higher frequency in regional to a higher frequency at federal level, between the two periods 1996–99 and 2000–03. Preferential treatments for firms involved in 'loans for shares' decreased over the two time periods, ending roughly equal to the rate for all other firms (ibid). In the later period, the most lucrative capture, under the Putin regime, was found at the federal centre, particularly for larger financial-industrial groups, extractive firms, and enterprises which belong to federal government (ibid.).

Since 2000, the Russian government has introduced new laws to improve political accountability, including laws on political parties and election campaign finance, election procedures, and media coverage of elections. In 2002 the Duma drafted anti-corruption laws which, for the first time in post-soviet Russia, defined the terms 'corrupt act' and 'bribery'. They also extend criminal liability and require top federal bureaucrats to make annual financial declarations to the public, although this remains in draft form. In 2002 President Putin also issued a decree outlining a code of conduct for public officials, requiring them to obey the law, serve the public efficiently and courteously, remain politically neutral and avoid conflicts of interest. Putin's actions, in particular his attacks on oligarchs and consolidation of power in the hands of the federal centre, have led to real redistribution of political power and the fall of previous clients. Nevertheless, Information Science for Democracy (INDEM), in its studies of corruption from 2001 through 2004, show that 43 per cent of citizens and 37 per cent of firms' chief executives consider corruption to be more important during Putin's presidency than during Yeltsin's (2005: 18).

Meanwhile, reforms to administrative collection of revenue have served to merely change the type of concession available, rather than the overall volume, from a situation where tax breaks were the most preferred preferential treatment in the late 1990s, to one where subsidies, subsidised budget loans, budget guarantees of credits and subsidised energy prices have significantly increased (Yakovlev and Zhuravskaya, 2004).

During Yeltsin's presidency, in the urgency to develop the private sector, state assets were dishonestly acquired, indeed plundered, by those who became the 'new rich', the oligarchs who then became the effective creators of Russian economic policy. The arrival of Putin and the 'dictatorship of law' signalled a policy change towards anti-corruption, with rapid arrests of persons formerly close to Yeltsin and potential political rivals. A contradictory state and government has since emerged, signalling an uncertain trend for corruption: strong and credible yet still prone to increasing soviet style repression of political rights and civil freedoms.

Group 4: virtuous countries

This group of countries with relatively weak corruption is composed of the new member states of the European Union, countries considered to have completed transition to European capitalist democracies. Among these, the Baltic States of Slovenia and Slovakia showed a remarkable will to reduce corruption, no doubt favourably influenced by the importance of Finnish and Swedish direct investments (FDI). More proximate to the countries of Western Europe, with memories of capitalism and a shorter history of communism, these countries have, perhaps unsurprisingly, achieved the greatest progress in systematic institutional reforms, liberalising the economy, strengthening bureaucratic accountability and promoting political contestability – all factors that reduce the capacity of powerful firms to capture the state.

The emergence of new institutional standards was strongly stimulated from outside, through international co-operation and conditionalities applied to the prospect of joining the European Union. As members of the EU in 2001, these countries installed national programmes of adoption, or '*acquis*' [of the EU], which include reform of public administration, legislative development, wide-ranging economic and financial reforms and fixed priorities in anti-corruption (criteria imposed for the first time to applicant countries). However, this pressure weakened after accession, insofar as the European Union does not have measures to enforce anti-corruption policy on new member states, any more than it can on older members. Also, some of the remarkable earlier reforms have been offset by the growth of new forms of corruption, more correspondent with

Western practices, some more sophisticated and less easily detectable. For example, as elsewhere, political institutions are still closely networked with economic interests, with additional conflicts of interests inside the state between the government and the local authorities. Also, political financing remains a challenge, as the Polish example illustrates.[4]

Political corruption in the Central Europe and Baltic States has also been reignited by democratic instability. In Estonia for example, the champion among transition countries since it won independence in 1991, not a single ministerial cabinet has succeeded in completing a four year mandate, with most crumbling amid accusations of corruption. Elsewhere, corruption scandals brought down the Polish Prime Minister, Laszek Miller, and Roland Paksas, a President of Lithuania. The latter was found guilty by the Deputies of Parliament in 2004 of having taken electoral finance from a Russian businessman (Youriy Borisov), in return for supplying him with confidential information, the disclosure of which violated state security. Paksas also helped his friends acquire companies through privatisations.

Nonetheless, many Central European countries have sought to improve transparency in political party financing by fixing allowances from public resources and by demanding publication of annual financial statements. Also, widespread policy reform has taken place in the control of high officials using new supervisory structures, moral codes, obligatory declarations of assets, and by instigating rules governing conflicts of interests. Many of these initiatives are seen as global 'best practice', and were reinforced by international memberships. For example, all these countries are GRECO members, and have signed the Council of Europe *Civil and Criminal Law Conventions on Corruption*. Moreover, except Lithuania, they have signed the OECD *Convention* and, except Estonia and Slovenia, the United Nations *Convention against Corruption*. These changes in political culture are underpinned, in most countries, by NGO public awareness activities, and codes of conduct for politicians, civil servants and businessman. In certain countries, NGOs were created with the singular objective of 'tackling' or 'fighting' corruption, acting like independent auxiliaries or sentinels of the global campaign, by resisting politicians' attempts to either occult the problem or obstruct individual prosecution of cases. With international support, NGOs and journalists raised public awareness of corruption and encouraged political action, and have begun to lead anti-corruption agendas and benchmarking in the other 20 post-Communist states and territories, playing an increasingly active role in promoting democracy outside their borders.

Conclusion

While the origins of corruption, and some types most resistant to reform, are found in the soviet era, the social practices of transition have rewrought modern corruption in economic networks and relationships. Our review of measurement and quantification of corruption reveals fixed categories and a classification, but says little about underlying causation. Some observations can, however, be made. First, political corruption thrives in strongly concentrated political systems, such that anti-corruption policy must deconcentrate power, both between the three branches of the central state (horizontally), and by developing local institutions (vertically). Second, the liberalisation process can create market distortions and economic monopolies to form, as predicted theoretically in Chapter 3. Third, international co-operation has been beneficial in anti-corruption campaigns in European countries bordering the EU, as illustrated by our 'Group 4' countries above. However, fourth, anti-corruption policies require considerable investments and longevity of commitment which might be without precedent to the donor community.

Since the 1990s anti-corruption policies are '*à la mode*' in the world and nowhere more so than in the Eastern European countries. Each country aims to make a good impression on the 'international community' and produces anti-corruption action plans, constantly borrowing new initiatives from neighbours: in processes of imitation, each new measure in one country is immediately avowed by others. The international community has a central role in this process of policy adoption and transfer, recommending good practices that governments then absolutely seek to apply. However, governments often do this without any preliminary assessment of policy applicability in the national context, and with a subsequent weak commitment to implementation and results. Sometimes, anti-corruption policies set up by political leaders simply camouflage a desire to get rid of 'awkward' personalities and political opponents, or only go so far as to meet the conditionalities of lending financial institutions, but are not subsequently implemented. A policy will not be effective unless it catalyses significant cultural and social change. Thus, corruption in transition countries cannot be erased solely by good advice from foreign experts, strict sanctions or short-term activities (USAID, 1999; Steves and Rousso, 2003), but requires a coherent strategy, a fixing of clear objectives, and a firm, long-term government commitment (Pope, 2000; DAC, 2003; Gilman and Stout, 2005).

However, perhaps in a somewhat contradictory finding to the analysis stressing the importance of country ownership above, these qualities have been best approximated here by conditionalities to EU membership. Governments corroded by political corruption have little motivation to self-regulate, since comfortable spoils will be forgone. This is reflected in statistics which, overall, show little change in levels of corruption after ten or so years of permanent policy initiative, and fifteen or so years of transition. Only Lithuania, Croatia, Bulgaria, Poland and Byelorussia have succeeded in reducing corruption, the latter two countries by the greatest margin (TI, various). International solidarity is still important to social change, despite the flaws of the anti-corruption campaign, as discussed further in the concluding chapter.

Notes

1. Parallel market is used in preference to 'black market' to overcome the racialised geneology of the latter. The market it refers to is characterised by informality and/or illegality.
2. To define these conceptual forms, Shleifer and Vishny is used here: administrative corruption 'involves the abuse of power by officials to extract rents from private agents'; while political corruption or grand corruption 'involves collusion between officials and private citizens at the expense of the state' (Shleifer and Vishny, 1993; cited in Ahrend & Thompson, 2005: 48). It is possible to build an 'index of state capture' (Hellman et al., 2000b) which measures the degree of grand corruption in various public domains.
3. For example, Roman Abramovich in Chukotka, or Alexander Khloponin the former head of Norilsk Nickel and governor in Taimyr, or Tsvetkov Magadan's governor who was murdered in 2002 while the owner of a large share of the regions gold-extraction industry.
4. Polish political party funding is widely regarded as corrupt from the 1990s onward, due partly to the tendency of State-owned companies to provide money to parties in a disguised or illegal manner. Amendments to the Electoral Act came into effect in 2001, but scandals are still frequent. These include 'Rywingate' and 'Orlen', the former contributing to the resignation of then Prime Minister Leszek Miller in 2004 (see Surdej and Gadowska, 2005).

References

Ahrend, R. and Thompson, W. (2005), 'Fifteen years of economic reform in Russia: what has been achieved? What remains to be done?', *OECD Economics Department Working Paper*, 430

Andreff, W. (2003), *La mutation des économies postsocialistes: une analyse économique alternative*, Paris: L'Harmattan 'Pays de l'Est' Collection

Boycko, M., Shleifer, A., and Vishny, R. (1995), *Privatizing Russia* (Cambridge MA: MIT Press)

CIA (2006), *World FactBook*, accessed from: www.cia.gov/cia/publications/factbook/index.html, 30 November 2006

Development Assistant Committee (DAC) (2003), *Synthesis of Lessons Learned of Donor Practices in Fighting Corruption*, Paris: OECD

Djankov, S., Claessens, S., Fan, J. P. H., and Lang, H. H. P. (1998), 'Diversification and Efficiency of Investment by East Asian Corporations', The World Bank *Policy Research Working Paper* Series, 2033

Duchene, G. (1987), *L'économie de l'URSS*, Paris: Editions La Découverte

Egnell, E., and Pessik, M. (1974), *URSS: l'entreprise face à l'Etat*, Paris: Seuil Eds

Freedom House (2005), *Annual Global Survey 2005*, accessed from: www.freedomhouse.org on 30 November 2006

Freedom House (2005b), *Nations in Transit*, Budapest: Freedom House Europe

Gilman, S. C. J. and Stout, J. (2005), 'Assessment Strategies and Practices for Integrity and Anti-corruption Measures: a Comparative overview', in J. Bertok, *Public Sector Integrity: a Framework for Assessment*, Paris: OECD, pp. 75–122

Group of States Against Corruption (GRECO) (2003), *Rapport final du Premier cycle d'évaluation en Moldavie*, Strasbourg, October 2003 available from: www.greco.coe.int

Guriev, S. and Rachinsky, A. (2004), 'Ownership concentration in Russian industry', *CEFIR Working Paper*, 41, October, pp. 1–29

Hellman, J. and Kaufmann, D. (2004), 'The Inequality of Influence', in Kornai, J. and Rose-Ackerman, S., eds, *Building a Trustworthy State in Post-Socialist Transition*, Basingstoke, Palgrave Macmillan

Hellman, J. S., Kaufmann, D. and Jones, G. (2000), *Anticorruption in Transition: a Contribution to the Policy Debate*, World Bank, Washington, DC

Hellman, J. S., Jones, G., Kaufmann, D., and Schankerman, M. (2000b) 'Measuring Governance, Corruption, and State Capture: How Firms and Bureaucrats Shape the Business Environment in Transition Economies', World Bank Institute, Regulation and Finance BERD, *Policy Research Working Paper 2312*, April

Hellman, J., Jones, G. and Kaufmann, D. (2002), *Far from Home: Do Foreign Investors Import Higher Standards of Governance in Transition Economies?* Washington DC, World Bank

Hoffman, D. (2003), *The Oligarchs: Wealth and Power in the New Russia*, NY: PublicAffairs

International Monetary Fund (IMF) (2005), 'Georgia: Second Review Under the Three-Year Arrangement Under the Poverty Reduction and Growth Facility and Requests for Waiver of Performance Criterion and Conversion of an Indicative Target into a Performance Criterion', *Country Report No. 05/314*, Washington DC: IMF, September

Information Science for Democracy (2005), *Diagnostics of the Corruption in Russia: 2001–2005*, Moscow, available from www.indem.ru

Kaminski, A. and Kaminski, B. (2001), 'Governance and Corruption in Transition: the Challenge of Subverting Corruption', *Paper presented on Creating a Supportive Environment for Business Enterprise and Economic Growth: Institutional Reform and Governance*, UNECE Economic Analisis Division Spring Seminar

Kaufmann, D., Kraay, A., and Mastruzzi, M. (2005), *Governance Matters IV: Governance Indicators for 1996–2004*, World Bank, Washington DC

Karklins, R. (2002), 'Typology of Post-Communist Corruption', *Problems of Post-Communism*, 49, 4, pp. 22–32

Kotkin, S. and Sajo, A. (2002), 'Political Corruption in Transition: a Sceptic's Handbook', Central European University Press

Kornaï, J. (1992), *Growth, Shortage and Efficiency*, Oxford: Basil Blackwell and Berkeley and Los Angeles: University of California Press

Krueger, A. (1974), 'The Political Economy of the Rent-Seeking Society', *American Economic Review* no. 64, June, pp. 291–303

Labaronne, D. (2002), 'Privatisation et corruption dans les pays de l'Est: le paradoxe des privatisations de masse', in I. Cucui and I. Stregaroiu, *Le management de la transition*, Bucharest: Editura Economica, pp. 49–77

Mendras, M. (1998), 'Enrichissement et clientélisme en Russie', *Mondes en dévelopement*, 26, 102, pp. 83–93

Moran, J. (2001) 'Democratic transitions and forms of corruption: Corruption and democracy', *Crime, law and social change*, vol. 36, no 4, pp. 379–93

Political Risk Services Group (2004), *International Country Risk Guide 2004*, available from www.prsgroup.com/icrg/, accessed 1 December 2006

Pope, J. (2000), *Confronting Corruption: the Elements of a National Integrity System*, TI Source Book 2000, accessed from www.transparency.org/publications/sourcebook on 30 November 2006

Raiser, M. (1999), 'Trust in transition', *BERD Working paper No. 39*

Samson, I. (1994), 'The stabilisation of transition in post-communist societies', communication at PROMETEE seminar, Buenos Aires July 1994, presented also to the Conference 'Central Russia at the edge of the XXIth century' Orel (Russia) July 1995, p. 17 (published in Russia)

Samson, I. (1998), 'La Russie deviendra-t-elle une économie de marché?', in J. Fontanel, ed., *Où va l'économie de la Russie?*, Grenoble: PUG

Samson, I. and Zagainova, A. (2006), 'Transition and corruption lessons for Georgia', *Georgian Economic Trends Quarterly review, no 4*, Georgian-European Policy and Legal Advice Centre, pp. 62–76, geplac.org/files/english_2006_4.pdf

Satarov, G. and Parkhomenko, S. (2001), 'Raznoobraziye stran, raznoobraziye korupptsii: analys sravnitelnih issledovaniy', Moscow: INDEM

Selowsky, M. (2000), *Transition after a Decade: Lessons and Policy Agenda*, Washington: World Bank

Shleifer, A. and Vishny, R. (1993), 'Corruption', *Quarterly Journal of Economics*, 58, 3, pp. 599–617

Stephan, P. B. (1999) 'Rationality and Corruption in the Post-Socialist World', University of Virginia School of Law, Working Paper No. 99–11

Steves, F. and Rousso, A. (2003), 'Anti-corruption programmes in post-communist transition countries and changes in the business environment, 1999–2002', *EBRD* Working paper No. 85

Stiglitz, J. (2002), *Globalization and Its Discontents*, W. W. Norton & Company, New York

Surdej, A. and Gadowska, K. (2005), 'Political Corruption in Poland', Working Papers of the Research Centre for East European Studies no 65, Bremen, March

Transparency International (TI), *Global Corruption Report* (2005, 2004), accessed from www.transparency.org on 30 November 2006

Treisman, D. (2002) 'Postcommunist Corruption', Department of Political Science University of California, Los Angeles

USAID (1999), *Handbook on Fighting Corruption*, Washington: USAID Center for Democracy and Governance Technical Publication Series, February

Yakovlev, E. and Zhuravskaya, E. (2004), 'State capture and controlling owners of firms', Center for Economic and Financial Research, Working Paper No. 42, Russia

World Bank (2000), *Anticorruption in Transition: a contribution to the policy debate*, Washington, DC: World Bank

World Bank (2005), *Governance Matters: Worldwide Governance Indicators*, available from www.worldbank.org/wbi/governance

8
Political Corruption in Georgia
Nina Dadalauri

Poor governance provides opportunities for political corruption and undermines ongoing democratisation and economic liberalisation in the CIS region. A growing collection of research on corruption and democracy examines the institutional factors necessary for a corruption-free, democratic state and society (Shleifer and Vishny, 1993; Rose-Ackerman, 2004; see also Olson, 1996), concluding that poor governance and corruption are impediments to institutionalising democracy, promoting a free market economy and building a strong and 'corruption-free' political culture within the state (also Bohara et al., 2004). Missing from these texts, however, is the historical path dependence of social formations, and the role of international donor intervention in shaping these histories. This chapter reviews corruption in Georgia, a country which has had a revolution in the name of anti-corruption, subsequently rapidly adopted an archetypal package of anti-corruption policy and practice, but arguably still remains trapped by unsavoury structures of privilege which the donors have always been myopic towards due to geopolitical interest.

Soviet-era corruption

In Georgia political corruption was bred in early soviet times, infiltrated everyday life, became systemic, but eventually catalysed resistance to communism. The Georgian Soviet Socialist Republic (GSSR), as a part of the USSR, was the object of wide-spread embezzlement, bribery and nepotism from the side of public officials at all levels of the political system. Membership of the Communist Party meant involvement in vertical structures of corruption, brought social prestige, secured individuals' well-being, political power and access to profits. Party members and corrupt public officials were expected to act according to the unwritten 'rules' of their networks; otherwise, they could not sustain their positions among the political elite. This vertical structure of corruption worked as a patron–client relationship, as the patron provided favours in exchange for bribes (Crawford and Lijphart (1995, 181), citing Stefes, 2003). This created inequality in society, undermined the rule of law, and hindered the democratisation of governance within the State. Horizontal corruption was also systemic among administrative branches and other political institutions, securing the delivery of 'favours' among network associates ('clans'), by means of state embezzlement.

The post-soviet era

Soon after Georgia declared independence in 1991, the Government of Georgia, led by Zviad Gamsakhurdia, was overthrown in a bloody *coup d'état* which is often referred to as the Georgian Civil War. Soon after the turmoil, Edward Shevardnadze was invited by a Military Council, consisting of the very individuals who had carried out the coup, to chair the Council, which was later transformed into the State Council. Later on, following parliamentary elections, he became first Chairman of Parliament (from October 1992 until the presidential elections of 1995), and then (from 1995 to 2003) the elected President of Georgia. Initially, Shevardnadze was seen by a majority of citizens as a person who could help the State to become strong and to develop economically. This was because, even though all Georgians remembered Shevardnadze's past career in soviet times (he had been the First Secretary of the Georgian Communist Party from 1972 to 1985 and Minister of Foreign Affairs of the USSR under Gorbachev), he managed to portray himself as a promoter of democracy in the eyes of the international community, especially after his decision to support the fall of the Berlin Wall in 1989 (as a supporter of *perestroika* initiated by Gorbachov in the 1980s). However, both types of corruption continued to exist in the new political institutions of Georgia, as most high-ranking officials and members of clans and networks were merely reshuffled.

Shevardnadze governed the state by creating democratic institutions and thus acquiring legitimacy from both its citizens and the international community, who poured in significant amounts of development assistance according to geopolitical calculations. Relatively fair elections, free media, and party pluralism were present in Georgia, while the interests of Shevardnadze's clans were met by ratified laws in their favour, non-transparent political institutions, the absence of the rule of law, manipulated courts and the imposition of state control. Chrisophe defines adeptly the actual rules of governance in this period, arguing that state-building rested on five pillars: manipulation of conflicts, creation of insecurity, preventive co-opting of potential adversaries, destruction of interpersonal trust, and privatisation of risk (Chrisophe, 2004: 6).

Thus, though formally Georgia was moving from an autocratic regime towards a democratic political system, most of the institutional and legal initiatives were actually of singular benefit to the political elite, sustaining them in office with international money, while relegating other citizens to a continuance of autocratic governance. Informal institutions, or 'clans' remained a source of illegal income for politicians, while they provided a 'krisha' (roof)[1] for individuals who acquired astonishing wealth at the same time as the State budget suffered from a chronic deficit and poverty spread throughout Georgia (see Theisen, 2000). The pillars of a democratic state – democratic political institutions, democratic political culture, empowered and educated citizens – were illusionary or factually inefficient, the executive and judicial branches of power were interdependent with politics and porous to bribery (Stefes, 2004), public services were captured by crony networks with poor provision but guaranteed handouts (Antadze et al., 2005), while corruption in education surpassed its soviet manifestations (Rostiashvili, 2004). Corruption was endemic, particularly in the law enforcement sector, such that illegal smuggling and criminality were central to the national economy (see Siradze, 2004; Kukhianidze et al., 2004). Legal businesses were stymied by redundant, but bribe necessitating, paperwork, while connected businessmen prospered, sometimes with the help of state-guaranteed monopolies (for example, the insurance company 'Aldagi') (Siradze, 2004).

The Rose Revolution, also called the anti-corruption revolution

Although the donors funded Shevardnadze's chimerical attempts at democratisation, without undue illumination of the continuation of authoritarianism, eventually improvements in governance nevertheless contributed to his downfall. While Shevardnadze struggled to keep the power balance among different interested clans and groups, he also increased media freedom as part of his presentation of himself as a democrat to the international community. Then, spurred on by donor rhetoric and pent up frustration satiric shows on television convincingly exposed political corruption, with the media eventually playing a decisive role in the 'Rose Revolution' (Wheatley, 2004).

The events of November 2003 in Georgia were triggered by the gross falsification of votes in the parliamentary elections of 2 November 2003, in favour of Shevardnadze's supporters. However, the results of the parliamentary elections were denounced by international organisations, and electoral fraud was vociferously denounced by a powerful emergent opposition, in the persons of Saakashvili, Burjanadze and Zhvania and their associated parties. These opposition groups arranged rallies in the streets and finally forced Shevardnadze to resign, in a sequence of events nicknamed the 'Rose Revolution', which is often used synonymously with the 'Anti-Corruption Revolution'. Commitments were rapidly made to tackle the challenges 'inherited' from the former government, which included chronic political and bureaucratic corruption, poor governance, centralisation of power and financial resources, lack of democracy, and a distorted market economy (Haindrava, 2005).

The new government internationalised its campaign by developing memberships that Shevardnadze had courted from strategic reasons only. Being a member of the Group of States against Corruption (GRECO) and the Anticorruption Network for Transition Economies (ACN for Transition Economies) under the Organisation for Economic Collaboration and Development (OECD), Georgia ratified a number of international agreements against corruption and joined the Istanbul Plan – an action plan which aims to implement national anti-corruption policies, criminalise corruption, and make institutions and public services transparent (Government of Georgia (GoG), 2005). Currently, a *National Anti-corruption Strategy* is being penned, which must be implemented in accordance with the newly created *Action Plan*, public expectations are high, and donor conditionality on anti-corruption has been (re)asserted.

By making anti-corruption policy implementation its priority, the GoG has attracted the support and financial assistance of the international community. The GoG presented its 'Strategic Vision and Development Priorities in 2004–2006' at the *Joint EU–World Bank Georgia Donors' Conference* in Brussels in 2004, and Georgia was consequently awarded almost three time more than the Georgian government had received from the EU from 1992 to 2003 (approximately 1 billion USD, or 850 million Euro as compared to 370 million) (European Commission, 2004). In addition, the American Government has also chosen Georgia to be a recipient of five year's worth of financial assistance worth $295.3 million through the Millennium Challenge Account (MCA), aimed at improving governance and the rule of law, developing the country's infrastructure, fighting corruption as well as tackling the serious problem of poverty (*Civil Georgia*, 2005a). Such a great influx of foreign aid illustrates a new high level of confidence expressed in economic and political reform by the international community (see for example, EU, 2005; WB, 2006).

Progress of reform

Before turning its efforts to anti-corruption initiatives, the new government made constitutional changes which concentrated unprecedented powers in the President, justified as a precaution against losing power to anti-revolutionary forces (Khidasheli, 2004). As an anti-corruption measure, government officials received salary rises made possible by the establishment of Georgia's *Development and Reform Fund*, resources donated by Hungarian-born tycoon, George Soros and the Open Society Institute (OSI), the Swedish International Development Agency (SIDA) and the United Nations' Development Programme (UNDP) (Peuch, 2005). Some ministries were merged and unnecessary positions removed to increase resources. The second measure was to arrest high-profile former officials from Shevardnadze's government, including the former Minister of Energy (accused of misappropriating $6 million while in public office), the Chief of Georgian Railways, the former head of the Chamber of Control, the son-in-law of Shevardnadze (the owner of the cell-phone company MAGTI), and the former president of the Georgian football Association, Merab Zhordania. The latter was released after he paid 750,000 Lari to the budget (*Civil Georgia*, 2004). All in all, one year after the implementation of the anti-corruption law, $30 million had been confiscated from high-ranking officials for the good of the Georgian State (*Civil Georgia*, 2005b).

However, the mass-arrests of former officials were not all welcomed, as some in civil society perceived a pattern of selectivity which suggested political revenge, not least because even though the arrested officials were corrupt, they were also all Saakashvili's opponents (Esadze, 2004). Court practices also belied the social justice motive of restitution stated for the arrests and return of funds, with the lawyers of arrested officials complaining that judges were following 'political orders' when rendering their verdicts, sometimes leaving the impression that decisions had been made beforehand. The holding of suspects for up to three months' pre-trial detention became a kind of 'tradition' when it came to high-profile officials, even though the persons were not dangerous, and having them arrested before the Prosecutor's Office could gather all the required proof was not necessary. These sorts of proceedings shook the confidence of Georgians in their genuine hope for independent courts and made them suspicious that judges' decisions were dictated by the prosecutors. The results of one public survey pushed the President of Georgia to arrange a meeting with 33 new judges (those who had successfully passed their exams) where he indicated that the judiciary system was in crisis and that it had to gain back public trust by meeting its obligations and being free from executive persuasion (*Civil Georgia*, 2005c).

Not long after the high-profile arrests and the consequently shaken reputation of the courts, the post-revolutionary government progressed to more profound, systematic and institutional changes to eradicate corruption including downsizing of public administration. In June 2004, the Ministry of Interior Affairs (MIA) abolished the traffic police, notorious for embezzlement and extortion, to be replaced by a new, western-type patrol police. Approximately 16,000 policemen (among whom the Traffic Police account for 2,738 officers) were dismissed from the MIA, many of whom remain unemployed (MIA, 2005) (which some see as a risk for increasing crime rates), although allegations of nepotism in new appointments also arose (Siradze, 2004). Overall, however, and with increased salaries and television support (Siradze and Krunic, 2005), the new police have been a success, with public trust in police services increasing (ALPE, 2005).

The GoG has also attempted to free the army of corruption, although a lack of transparency in its expenditures from the Army Development Fund,[2] coupled with old scandals, give room to sceptics who argue that systematic corruption in the new army is still present. The Deputy Defence Minister, David Sikharulidze, himself argues that in light of the astonishing increase in funds (instead of the originally planned 137 million GEL that equals $74 million, the current budget has earmarked 317 million GEL to the defence budget, roughly $173 million more) for army reform as a result of the privatisation campaign and revenue generation from the anti-corruption campaign, the budget 'should be managed more transparently' (*Civil Georgia*, 2005d). Foreign experts helping the Georgian government with army reform are dissatisfied with the accelerated process that has been conducted without proper planning or grass-roots changes. In particular, insufficient attention has been paid to the education and training of young officers relative to spending on new equipment, which risks creating a 'broken military with fancy-looking brigades' (ibid.). This example also illustrates the potential moral hazard of accelerated donor financing in the early days of political reform.

Another step towards administrative reform was made in June 2005, when the Georgian Parliament passed a law to cut the number of permits and licences from 909 to about 156, with a one-stop shop for applications. Before the change took place, the required number of licences was artificially high, a system created to enable rent-seeking officials to demand bribes: on one estimate by the Georgian Young Lawyers Association, '83% of all papers requested by officials made no logical sense and were used solely for extortion' (*Civil Georgia*, 2005e). Thus, the new initiative was welcomed by the public, on the grounds that it would cut bureaucracy and give more freedom and help to entrepreneurs to start new businesses.

Political corruption in post-revolutionary Georgia

Inevitably, political corruption still exists in post-revolutionary Georgia, which does not itself indicate that the reforms have failed after such a short implementation period. However, there are also weaknesses in the initiatives which can already be identified as more serious to their sustainability, and other exogenous and deleterious aspects of political change which suggest that democratic structural reform is not being undertaken with the same zeal, or commensurate to, the anti-corruption package, including a worrying reigning in of media independence and a centralisation of power in the Presidency. That anti-corruption policy and democratisation more generally can diverge is worrying to prospects of political development and suggests that the former lacks structural roots.

For example, following November 2003, some media representatives were taken off air and open debates on some TV channels disappeared. In February 2005 the newspaper *Rezonansi* published an article saying that all the large television stations have been under government censorship and control (*Civil Georgia*, 2005f). The article attempted to find explanations for the compromises television stations have made in the choice of their owners.[3] In July 2005, 76 Georgian journalists signed a statement to express their discontent over government attempts to control editorial policy. This came after Giga Bokeria, MP from the ruling National Movement, criticised the talk-show 'Archevanis Zgvarze' (On the Verge of Choice) due to a portrayal of conflict between sportsmen and the police, after which the programme was closed down (*Civil Georgia*, 2005g). In August, events again belied reform, when Shalva Ramishvili, known for his critical political show 'Debates', and one of the co-founders of TV Station 202, was arrested on suspicion of extorting a bribe from MP Koba Bekauri (*Civil Georgia*, 2005h), who accused him of blackmail, asking for money to stop an investigative report going on air. This may have been preemptive, as the report, when it was aired, revealed the involvement of MP Bekauri in questionable commercial activities involving the Opiza customs terminal; an astonishing increase in the MP's assets by as much as 294,000 GEL (approximately 163,300 USD) in the year after he became a parliamentarian; and in a recorded interview with MP Bekauri that he somehow obtained an interest-free loan of 150,000 USD from a Georgian businessman based in Israel (*Civil Georgia,* 2005i). Ramishvili has received support from the opposition, who perceive his arrest as an attack on media freedom, while MP Bekauri has received strong support from key figures in the ruling party, although the opposition has won an investigatory parliamentary commission (*Civil Georgia,* 2005j).[4]

The law enforcement sector has also been host to corruption cases, involving high-ranking officials within the Tax Department, including its Chief, Temur Dvali, which lead to the resignation of the Minister of Finance (*Civil Georgia,* 2005k); the arrest of three Georgian Defence Officials for fraud (Radio Free Europe/Radio Liberty, 2005); and incidences of corruption, mostly smuggling, in the 'new' police force (Kupatadze, 2005). Against the backdrop of sporadic but persistent scandal, Georgia made a slight improvement in its TI perception ranking, 136th out of 146 countries listed, as compared to a ranking of 127th out of 133 the previous year (TI, 2004). Perhaps more worrying for the GoG, a Georgian Opinion Research Business International (GORBI) survey in March 2005 showed the popularity of the President plummeting (by 25 per cent in the preceding six months), frustration growing, a full 39 per cent believing the country was 'not developing in the right direction', while 34 per cent believing that life in Georgia had not improved since the 'Rose Revolution', a doubling of discontent. However, Saakashvili remains at the top of the list of most popular politicians (GORBI, 2005).

Conclusion

Political corruption existed at all levels of government during the soviet period, persisted in the post-soviet era, and remains a challenge in post-revolutionary Georgia. Political corruption in Shevardnadze's time was not only tolerated (as in soviet times), but used as a tool of governance, by the power it gave to the President to hold something over officials, in the form of *kompromats* (see Wheatley, 2005). In all these period, political corruption has been, and is, a consequence of undemocratic government, regardless of the fact that after the collapse of the Soviet Union, Georgian governments came to power via national-wide elections. Even though the elections were widely distorted by electoral fraud and falsification of votes, officially the governments were able to obtain legitimacy, at least in the international arena.

The lavish style of politicians' lives during the Shevardnadze era could be seen in the mansions they built for themselves, despite a wretched economy and overwhelming poverty. The new government has pursued an anti-corruption campaign, with key reforms including personnel change, downsizing administrations, eliminating traffic police, and, while not discussed here, changing University entrance examinations. Critics understand that the size of bureaucracy had to be decreased, but still criticise post-revolutionary employment policy, since many high-ranking officials are now very young, and lack experience and professionalism. The criteria for appointing them were partly based on their membership of the ruling party and on their activity during the 'Rose Revolution'. As for the rule of law in Georgia, institutional changes in law enforcement institutions have been made but continued scandals give sceptics the opportunity to claim that these are somewhat superficial.

Higher salaries as an incentive for high-level public office holders to refrain from corruption have been successfully introduced in Singapore and Hong Kong, and may yet prove successful in Georgia (Bohara et al., 2004). However, when set against higher unemployment, glaring poverty, and low salaries in budget funded institutions (apart from high-ranking governmental bodies), this new form of social distribution looks rather like the old, with a privileged elite and an impoverished majority. These rises in salaries have given the public the impression that social inequalities, popularly seen as evidence of corruption, have merely been legalised, with public offices still used for personal enrichment. In short, accusations against officials from the previous government aside, the post-revolutionary still has much to do to reduce corruption.

Notes

1. 'Krisha' is a Russian word and its original meaning is roof, though in Georgian it is being used as slang and is a synonym of 'patron'. However, the strong social networks of the corrupt political elite have little to do with Georgian culture and the traditionally strong family and friendship ties among Georgians. Clans and systematised corruption were an anomaly brought to the government by the soviet regime, although pre-existing bonds among friends and family may have made these easier to build.
2. The Army Development Fund was created after the 'Rose Revolution' to give a kick-start to Georgian military reform. The main contributors of the non-profit foundation are said to be 'businessmen living abroad who wanted to contribute to Georgia', Deputy Defence Minister, Sikharulidze (*Civil Georgia*, 2005d).
3. For example, the article in *Rezonansi* (Feb. 28, 2005) pointed out that the owner of Imedi is Badri Patarkazishvili, who is wanted by Russia for fraud allegations; that the owner of Rusatvi 2, the key television company in the events of

the 'Rose Revolution' is now owned by Khibar Khalvashi, a close friend of the Defence Minister; while Mze is 50 per cent owned by the brother of the Secretary of the Georgian National Security Council, Davit Bezhuashvili, while the other 50 per cent is owned by Vano Chkhartishvili, a parliamentarian.
4. In a similar case to Ramishvili-Bekauri, Revaz Okruashvili was arrested for alleged narcotics dealing, after publishing an article in the '*People's Newspaper*', in which he accused the governor and chief of the local police in Shida Kartli of being involved in illegal smuggling. The governor of Shida Kartli is a close friend of the then Minister of Internal Affairs and current Minister of Defence Irakli Okruashvili (Devdariani, 2004).

References

Abuladze, B., Antadze, N. and Dadalauri, N. (2005), *Corruption and Financial Mismanagement in Municipal Solid Waste Management in Tbilisi*, TraCCC-GO (text in Georgian)

ALPE – on Public Perception of the Police Performance (2005), [Online] www.alpe.ge/pdf/Patrol%20Police%20eng.final.pdf

Bohara, K. Alok, Mitchell, J. Neil and Mittendorff, F. Carl (2004), 'Compound Democracy and the Control of Corruption: a Cross-Country Investigation', *Policy Studies Journal,* 32, 4, 481–99

Christophe, B. (2004), Understanding politics in Georgia. *DEMSTAR Research Report No. 2,* Department of Political Science, University of Aarhus [Online] www.demstar.dk

Civil Georgia (2004), 'New Authorities Launch Fighting Corruption with High-Profile Arrests', 18 January, available from www.civil.ge

—— (2005a), 'Major U.S. Aid to Boost Georgia's Infrastructure', 14 September, available from www.civil.ge

—— (2005b), 'USD 30 mln Confiscated in Anti-Corruption Drive' 4 January, available from www.civil.ge

—— (2005c), 'Saakashvili: Judiciary System in Crisis', 10 October, www.civil.ge

—— (2005d), Freese, Theresa, 'Defence Reform Poses Crucial Civil Society Test for Georgia', 8 April, www.civil.ge

—— (2005e), 'Georgia Moves to Cut Red Tape in Licensing', 6 November, www.civil.ge

—— (2005f), 'Government Controls Editorial Policies of the Private TV Stations', 28 February, www.civil.ge

—— (2005g), 'Journalists Accuse Government of Pressuring Media', 7 August, www.civil.ge

—— (2005h), 'TV Co-Founder Arrested, Accused of Black mailing MP', 27 August, www.civil.ge

—— (2005i), 'Lawmakers to Probe into Ruling Party MP's Business', 15 September, www.civil.ge

—— (2005j), 'Top Official of Tax Department Arrested for Suspected Bribery', 28 June, www.civil.ge

Esadze, Londa (2004), *Organized Nature of Corruption in Post-Soviet Space and Challenges of Donors: the case study of Georgia*, presented at the Development Partnership Forum: Improving Donor Effectiveness in Combating Corruption (9–10 Dec. 2004), [Online] www.oecd.org/dataoecd/41/27/34097907.PDF

EU Commission (2004), 'International Donors give Extraordinary Financial Support to Georgia: approx. US$1 billion/E850 million pledged', Press Release, at europa.eu.int/comm/external_relations/georgia/intro/press170604.pdf

EU (2005) *Communication from the Commission to the Council: European Neighbourhood Policy Recommendations for Armenia, Azerbaijan, Georgia and for Egypt and Lebanon*, available at: www.delgeo.cec.eu.int/en/press/communication_0503_en.pdf

Haindrava, I. (2005), Georgia's Incomplete Democracy, Institute for War and Peace Reporting, *Caucasus Report, No. 285*, 5 May 2005, www.iwpr.net

Khidasheli, T. (2004), 'Georgia: the Rose Revolution has wilted', *International Herald Tribune* [Online] www.int.com/articles/2004/12/08/edkhidasheli_ed3_.php

Kukhianidze, A., Kupatadze, A. and Gotsiridze, R. (2004), Smuggling through Abkhazia and Tskhinvali Region of Georgia, TraCCC-GO [Online] www.traccc.cdn.ge/publications

MIA (2005) Statistics of Ministry of Internal Affairs 2004–2005, available online at www.police.ge , accessed on 11 December 2006

The National Anti-Corruption Strategy of Georgia (2005); available from nsc.gov.ge/download/pdf/ANTICOR_STATEGY_Eng.pdf, accessed on 11 December 2006

Olson, M. (1996), 'Big Bills Left on the Sidewalk: Why some Nations are Rich and Others Poor', *Journal of Economic Perspectives* 10: 3–24

Peuch, J-C. (2005), 'Georgia: Experiment On Averting Corruption Among State Officials', Radio Free Europe/Radio Liberty [Online] www.rferl.org/featuresarticle/2005/1/FB8ADBDC-E36E-4BB9-9FCA-5252B9E26825.html

Public Opinion Survey (2005) March, GORBI, Georgian Member of Gallup International [Online] www.gorbi.com

Rose-Ackerman, S. (2004), 'The Challenge of Poor Governance and Corruption', *Copenhagen Consensus 2004* [Online] www.copenhagenconsensus2004.dk

Rostiashvili, K. (2005), 'Problems of Corruption in the Higher Education System of Georgia', Starr Foundation and IREX, TraCCC-GO [Online] www.traccc.cdn.ge/publications

Shleifer, A. and Vishny, R. W. (1993), 'Corruption', *Quarterly Journal of Economics,* 108: 599–617

Siradze, G. (2004), *Corruption in the Ministry of Internal Affairs of Georgia,* Transnational Crime and Corruption in Georgia, TraCCC-GO [Online] www.traccc.cdn.ge/pulications (text in Georgian)

Siradze, G. and Krunić , Z. (2005), *The Ministry of Internal Affairs of Georgia – Report on the Current Situation with the Recommendations for its Reform – Summary*, The European Commissions' Delegation in Georgia [Online] www.delgeo.cec.eu.int/en/

Stefes, C. (2003), 'Can a Corrupt State Be Democratic? The political impact of Corruption on Democratic Development in Georgia' [Online] www.traccc.cdn.ge/publications

Theisen, S. (2000), 'Georgien-Klaners nationalstat: Post-electorale noter om State og Politik I Georgien' [Online] www.kaukasus.dk

Transparency International (2004), *Annual Report*, Berlin, see: legacy.transparency.org/in_focus_archive/AnnualReport04/download/TI%20Annual%20-Report%202004.pdf, accessed 18 May 2007

Wheatley, J. (2004), *Elections and Democratic Governance in the Former Soviet Union: the Case of Georgia* [Online] http://www.oei.fu-berlin.de/cscca/Publications/boi_jw_elections_and_democratic_governance.pdf

Wheatley, J. (2005), *Georgia from National Awakening to Rose Revolution: Delayed Transition in the Former Soviet Union* (Post-Soviet Politics), Aldershot, Ashgate

World Bank (2006) *Doing Business in 2006: CIS Economies Pick up the Pace of Reform:* web.worldbank.org/WBSITE/EXTERNAL/NEWS/0,,contentMDK:20643534~me nuPK:34466~pagePK:34370~piPK:34424~theSitePK:4607,00.html

9
Corruption Scandals and Anti-Corruption Institution Building Interventions in Jamaica

Philip Duku Osei

Introduction

In Jamaica since 1981, numerous institution building efforts have been undertaken aimed at improving administrative propriety, including but not limited to the establishment of the Office of the Contractor-General – an ombudsman of contracts (1983), the National Contracts Commission (1999), the Anti-Corruption Commission (2003), Public Management Accountability Act (2002) and several codes of conduct for ministers (2002), public officials and politicians (1973). However, despite these new anti-corruption institutional initiatives, there is a general public perception that corruption is endemic in Jamaica (*Jamaica Gleaner*, 2001), a view supported by public polling in February 2005, which found more than 90 per cent of respondents believing that corruption was rampant in society, with 70 per cent believing that most corruption resides in public sector agencies (Buckley, 2005; Hart, 2005). This view is supported by a falling ranking in 2004 for Jamaica on the Transparency International (TI) *corruption perception index* to 74 out of 146 countries, down 17 places from its position in 2003 (TI, 2005). This chapter presents an overview of the persistence and growth of corruption in Jamaica in spite of the plethora of anti-corruption policies and institution building that have been pursued by the state; and concludes that resolve, political will, and a change in political culture are additionally required to supplement the institutional response.

Perceptions of corruption and conceptual issues

Munroe (2002b: 272), a Caribbean scholar, has sought to broaden the definition of corruption from the abuse of public office for 'private economic gain' (Rose-Ackerman, 1999: 75), to include 'the abuse of office in spheres outside the public sector for personal advantage', a 'departure from rule governed behaviour' (Munroe 2002b: 272–3). In Jamaica, this broader definition fits the job of work that the concept is required to do, in that it covers the spread of specific corrupt behaviours apparent in both the public and private sectors. The findings of a number of Commissions of Enquiry have confirmed the endemic nature of corruption. In 1972, the DaCosta Commission identified political corruption in the form of 'venality, graft, sale of office, kick backs from state contracts and theft of public largess' (Jones 1992: 40). Jones argues that corruption has increased alongside the process of democratisation in the Caribbean region (a relationship first suggested by Huntington, 1968; and more recently explored by Moran, 2001 and Marquette, 2003), as democratisation opened up new opportunities for discretionary decision-making, which was facilitated by public servant's skewed and privileged access to information (Jones, 1992: 40). In Jamaica the growth of community-based self-management schemes since the 1970s augmented these opportunities.

There has also been a significant increase in the perception of corruption in Jamaica historically. Mills (1997: 24), writing in the mid-1990s stated that, 'from the end of the 1930s to the 1950s [before independence] – public service corruption was negligible. When cases came to light we were horrified.' This is in contrast to later years (the 1980s to the present) where:

> there is no doubt whatsoever that the incidence of unethical behaviour and corrupt practices has risen significantly . . . become[ing] so prevalent that it has become almost the norm; we now take it almost for granted. (ibid.)

This changing historical perception seems to strengthen the case that in Jamaica, corruption has become a perennial problem of public administration in the particular circumstances of the post-Independence period.

Causes of corruption in Jamaica

A number of reasons have been advanced to explain the perceived prevalence of corruption, which includes the wide publicity given to the phenomenon in the popular press, which in itself has contributed to anxiety about ethical standards in public life. However, the failure of successive administrations to deliver development and improved human welfare aggravates this lack of trust in politicians. Other causes of corruption include material scarcity, which generates social demands for a limited supply of valued resources, such that some 'clients' often pay to cut red tape in order to transform the distant public administrator into a friendly patron (Jones, 1992: 41). This represents bureaucratic clientelism, typical in a system of political clientelism more broadly, which Stone (1980) traced to the legacy of the truncated Westminster system in the Caribbean, in which the practice of competitive politics was expressed as a type of clientelism. Under this regime, the competitive milieu is said to have created:

> a degree of social acceptance of unethical behaviour rooted in strong partisan feelings that judge conduct according to partisan persuasion. To be sure, the public policy process is also embedded in a culture in which anticorruption deterrence is mainly symbolic and weak. (Jones, 1992: 41)

This might explain why the low public trust in politicians has not led to alienation from politics more broadly, since Jamaica remains highly politicised and polarised in relation to allegiances towards the two dominant parties – the People's National Party (PNP) the incumbent, and Jamaica Labour Party, the opposition. To a certain extent, the political fortunes of governing parties therefore hinge on the extent of political and administrative corruption that is deemed tolerable by the public.

The above features of the political culture have also been termed political tribalism in Jamaica, a generic term which refers to the legacy of the inherited Westminster system of governance found here in the concentration of political power over time. It is associated with a 'winner takes all culture' or a zero-sum game in which the party in power controls all the lucrative resources (especially procurement contracts) of the state and distributes them copiously to party supporters to the relative neglect of the opposition party and its supporters. This behaviour is reinforced by homogeneous voting in some constituencies during general elections (Figueroa and Sives 2003), which are garnered by enforcers of party loyalty within inner city communities dubbed as political garrisons. The high tolerance of corruption in Jamaican society (Jones, 1992), is partly due to the expectation within this model that electoral success should reap material reward, and may further contribute to the use of violence to protect political control (Ryan, 1999; Osei, from personal notes). Leaders will certainly go to almost any lengths to secure power and amass resources to allocate to party favourites or supporters, to bribe opponents, and to secure viable coalitions of important groups in society.

Apart from these directly political causes of corruption, there are also administrative factors that lead to corruption in the Jamaican public sector, including the hierarchical structure, lack of accountability, centralised decision-making and high discretionary power, lax rules of sanction, including weak or unenforced rules and regulations, an ineffective judicial system, poor internal and external monitoring systems, and cultural practices that lead to apathy and the absence of moral guidelines (Mills, 1997; Munroe, 2002a). For the individual, low civil service salaries, promotion unconnected to performance or merit, and inadequate human and financial resources, leads to increased work pressure to meet demands and deadlines. Staff members, in these circumstances, may see the opportunity to 'offer assistance' to members of the public who require an expedient service in return for compensation.

Types of corruption in Jamaica

Munroe identifies the most prevalent types of corruption in Jamaica as:

> petty (bureaucratic) corruption, political corruption and narcotics-related corruption, caused by a culture of tolerance towards beating the system, traditions of patronage and clientelism, the concentration of power of the executive and the geopolitical location of the state in relation to the drug traffic route of North America. (2003: 5)

Munroe sees the first of these, petty corruption, as the most prevalent in organisations that offer services directly to the public, such as the Registrar Generals Office, the National Land Agency (Titles Office) and the Inland Revenue Department (2003). Certainly, paying for services or bribing civil servants to 'get things done' was becoming common place in government organisations in Jamaica, in a model originally described by Lewis where 'either the civil service or the politicians or both consider themselves entitled to make fortunes out of bribery, embezzlement, nepotism or awarding themselves favourable contracts,' (1973: 409). More recently, Harriott (2000) has analysed this type of activity as 'entrepreneurial corruption', where the intended goal of the civil servant is not only to acquire additional income, but to amass capital.

Profit-making ventures have included (a) the selling of public services, such as expediting the provision of birth certificates, passports, drivers' licences, and motor vehicle certificates of fitness; (b) acceptance of bribes by some government employees, especially in the police force, the judiciary and customs; (c) the disposal of politically-owned assets, such as land

and other scarce benefits to relatives, friends and political supporters; (d) discrimination in the award of government contracts; (e) nepotism in appointments and promotions within the Civil Service; and (f) engaging in business activities which represent a conflict of interest (Mills, 1997: 25–6; Tindigarukayo and Chadwick, 1998). In the private sector more properly, Lindo noted corruption in the banking and financial sector in the 1990s, which 'contributed to the melt down of Jamaica's financial sector . . . (and) the associated multi-billion dollar increase in the national debt now on the backs of the Jamaican people,' (2002: 374).

A catalogue of corruption scandals

The perception amongst the Jamaican people that corruption has increased is validated by numerous scandals[1] and acts of corruption recorded in the last 15 years. In 2002 alone, corruption scandals (some of which are summarised in Table 9.1) cost over J $6 billion, and with the various cost-overruns, the total loss to Jamaica was estimated at over J $8 billion in November 2005. This is a cost that the country, which in any case spends over 60 per cent of its budget to service debts (which represented 151 per cent of GDP in 2003), can ill afford, while social welfare programmes are compromised.

For example, The Programme for Resettlement and Integrated Development Enterprise (PRIDE) was set up in 1995 by Prime Minister P. J. Patterson to provide housing solutions primarily for low-income earners. The programme was implemented by the National Housing Development Corporation (NHDC), which was then under the steward-ship of a portfolio minister, but was characterised by cost overruns, over-payments for work not done and budget difficulties. The report of a special committee of enquiry (also known as the Angus Report, 2002) concluded that approximately $1.6 billion had been squandered on Operation PRIDE projects; that Carl Blythe was a meddling minister whose interference went beyond policy direction; and that Operation PRIDE/ NHDC had an inner circle and was run more like a 'brotherhood' than as an accountable, government-supported project. Upon these find-ings several key figures in the Ministry and the entire board at NHDC resigned. However, a review of the Angus Report by former solicitor-general Ken Rattray (Rattray, 2002), claimed that the Angus team had made errors in fact and law and sought to exculpate Blythe (*Jamaica Gleaner*, 2003). In short, this scandal involved the setting aside of government procurement rules (established in 1983), in favour of contractors who were known to be activists of the ruling party.

Table 9.1:   Some corruption scandals in Jamaica

1989 The zinc scandal	A sum of JA $500 million of hurricane relief from overseas, which was destined for poor people, was diverted to political favourites. Some relief was sold.
1990 The furniture scandal	More than JA $10 million was spent to furnish, among other places, a town house for the then Minister of Foreign Affairs and Foreign Trade, Ben Clare (Daley, 2002).
1991 Shell waiver scandal	The sum of JA $29.5 million was waived on duties to the Shell Company in 1991 and subsequently led to the resignation of then Finance Minister, P. J. Patterson from the Cabinet (Daley, 2002).
1995 PRIDE	Sum of $1.6 billion squandered, project run like a 'brotherhood' (Angus report).
1998 Public sector salaries scandal	Some JA $60 million was lost when a number of top government executives were paid allowances above stated guidelines (Daley, 2002).
2001 The NetServ/Intech fund scandal	Development finance of US$ 380,000 misused with little result. Feeble sanctions response.
2001 Kingston public hospital	Renovations exceeded budget by JA $250 million, for which insufficient explanation was given.
2003 North coast highway	Set up to provide a highway from St Ann to Hanover in 2003. The project was reported to have exceeded its budget by JA $3 billion and is still uncompleted.
2005 National solid waste management scandal	Involved a loss of over J $1 billion.

In contrast the Netserv Global Communications Limited Company scandal involved lack of oversight and due diligence. The company was one of the beneficiaries of a fund created by the Government to create jobs in the IT sector using the US dollar windfall generated from the sale of cellular licences. Netserv was given an initial loan of $180 million and set out to create 3,000 jobs in the first year of operation, with the aim of increasing employment to 10,000 jobs within three years. However within months there were reports of problems with the company such as its inability to pay rent and to meet the wage bill despite the fact that the employment figure was nowhere close to what had been projected. The company received a further loan of Jamaican $200 million, but went into receivership almost immediately after, which represented a substantial loss of development funds (Ministry of Commerce and Technology, 2001). The misjudgement and failure of the portfolio minister to heed warnings, which led to a loss of millions of tax dollars, was regarded by the Prime Minister as due to 'youthful exuberance'. He escaped blame, retained his job and was never sanctioned by parliament (Bartley, 2003), such that an initial disregard of fiscal accounting was met with feeble sanctions.

The National Solid Waste Management (NSWMA) scandal of 2005 involved another disregard for established rules of public procurement, and involved a loss of over J$1billion. The establishment of NSWMA in 2001 caused a great disquiet in the local government fraternity, because it represented the recentralisation of an important function of the local authorities, particularly irksome since the architect of this recentralisation policy was the former local government minister, Arnold Bertram. The NSWMA subsequently became the only agency of the Ministry of Local Government that had ever been allocated funds in excess of requests in the history of budgeting in the ministry (Osei et al. 2005), an indication that the NSWMA enjoyed a most favoured agency status.

Parliament's *Public Accounts Committee* (PAC) eventually criticised the NSWMA for spending some $16.8 million on the repair and servicing of garbage processing equipment for the period 2002–2004 (Rose, 2006), eventually an enquiry was called, and reports by the auditor-general and the contractor-general were tabled in parliament in July 2005. These reports painted a picture of cronyism and mismanagement at the solid waste authority. Reports in the *Gleaner* newspaper revealed that the executive chairman of the agency was a personal friend of the Prime Minister, while the Prime Minister's son was also contracted to the agency as an information technology specialist (2005). Moreover, the same executive chairman of the NSWMA was campaign manager for the minister of finance who has declared his interest in becoming the new president of the People's National Party, to eventually replace Mr P. J. Patterson as premier before the general elections of 2007 (Reid, 2005a; 2005b). This scandal therefore resonates at the heart of political life in Jamaica, illustrating the functioning of the truncated Westminster system. In this case, a lack of vigilance and good management in the heart of government, or sheer neglect, has allowed a particular crony network and clientelism to function at the highest level, although specific responsibility remains ill-assigned.

In general, when scandals break out, there is a great frenzy to review institutions and introduce new ones, without a thorough assessment of existing institutions and their ability to contribute to anti-corruption enforcement across the system. In terms of Netserv, procedures were reformed, while in the solid waste management scandal the Opposition leader, Bruce Golding, argued that a systemic problem existed in the 'practice of appointing executive chairmen for public agency boards'. Golding, in his contribution to the 2005/2006 budget debate in parliament in April 2005, suggested the establishment of a new 'prosecutor-general' who would deal directly with corruption in the public sector by investigating and charging those who steal from government coffers. The Prime Minister was willing to agree – 'I am not prepared to rule out of consideration the creation of any office that may boost confidence in our ability to root out corruption' – but with a cautionary note that there was already an auditor general, a corruption prevention commission, and an integrity commission, which examine similar matters. This epitomises the tradition of additive institutional change, without examining the desired impact and implementation of policies already in existence and the cost of creating new institutions.

Debates about the appropriateness of anti-corruption institutions

Current anti-corruption policy centres on the two poles of institutional and behavioural change. In terms of the former, Ryan points to the powerful and independent committees in the American congress which probe deeply into decision-making processes at the executive, legislative and judicial levels (Ryan and Brown 1992: 37). Klitgaard (2000) emphasises the importance of creating Independent Anti-Corruption Commissions such as the *Independent Commission Against Corruption* in Hong Kong, which significantly reduced police corruption between 1960 and 1980, and became iconic within the anti-corruption literature (Caiden, 1991: 249). Also much copied is Singapore's *Corruption Practices Investigation Board*, which used anti-corruption legislation and the reorganisation of government agencies to minimise opportunities and incentives for corrupt activities while highlighting the negative results of corruption (Caiden, 1991: 250). Another initiative in wide use is the creation of an independent ombudsman to hear complaints of maladministration. This was largely confined to Scandinavian countries, but by the late 1960s and 1970s there was a burst of 'ombudsmania' in the Commonwealth countries, the Middle East, Asia, India and Latin America (Caiden, 1991: 251).

These institutional initiatives have been replicated in Jamaica from the early 2000s onward. Given their brief provenance, only rapid evaluation of institution building is possible here, but policy characteristics

Table 9.2: Post-2000 anti-corruption reform in Jamaica

Measure	Date	Provision
The Parliament (Integrity of Members) Act	1973	To prevent corruption by Members of Parliament. Established the Integrity Commission. Parliamentarians to submit annual declarations of their assets including those of spouse and children, in order to detect unexplainable wealth that cannot be justified by income. Offences that fall under this Act include failing to declare all assets, providing false information and failing to attend an enquiry.
Corruption Prevention Act and Commission for the Prevention of Corruption	2000 and 2003	To provide statutory declaration of asset and wealth by public servants who fall outside of the the Parliamentary (Integrity of Members) Act whose total emoluments are two million Jamaican dollars and above, and any body, whether public or private, providing public services.
The Public Bodies Management and Accountability (PBMA) Act	2002	Concerns corporate governance in public bodies, who must 'develop specific and measurable objectives and performance targets' (Section 6b). On the application of the Attorney-General, courts apply penalties and injunctions for contravention of rules concerning the (a) acquisition of shares and payment of dividends, (b) exercise of borrowing powers, (c) corporate governance, (d) general duties of auditors, (e) failure to furnish information to auditors, (f) levels of emoluments, (g) restriction on formation of new companies (Section 25 (1)).
Access to Information (ATI) Act	2002	To strengthen the constitutional rights already provided for in Section 22 of the Jamaican constitution (1962).
Code of conduct for Ministers, Ministry Paper 19/02	2002	To avoid conflict of interest between the parliamentarian's personal business interest and public responsibility. Also, outlaws the acceptance of gifts by a minister or any members of his/her family, in which an obligation to return a favour is perceived.
The Parliament (Integrity of Members) Act, Amendments Act	2002	To allow the commission to report non-submission to the Director of Public Prosecution. The amendments also established an *Integrity Commission* to investigate the assets, liabilities and income of parliamentarians (Barnett: 2000).

analysis[2] can still help explain their underperformance. From 2000, institutional responses have been exponential and reactionary, despite an already replete set of institutions, common law and statutory rules prohibiting corruption and illicit enrichment of government officials, including constitutional provisions regarding the governing of elections, taxes, customs and so on (Barnett, 2000). Table 9.2 summarises the measures that have been put in place, on an incremental basis in Jamaica, to combat corruption.

A rapid assessment of institutions installed since 2000

There have been over twenty-one policies, acts of legislation and organisational forms enshrined in statute added to the anti-corruption regulatory infrastructure since 2000, with salient measures including the *Corruption Prevention Act* 2000 and its organisational form – the *Commission for the Prevention of Corruption* 2003; the *Public Bodies Accountability Act* 2002; and the *Parliament Act (Amendments)* 2002, which set up the *Integrity Commission*. This latter is now core to the anti-corruption infrastructure, and is empowered to investigate the assets, liabilities and income of parliamentarians, to conduct independent enquiries and investigations relating to the declarations, and to summon witnesses, request the production of documents and to do all such things as it considers necessary or expedient for carrying out its functions (Barnett, 2000: Gager, 2001: 3).

The *Corruption Prevention Act 2000*, widened statutory asset declaration procedures to public servants outside Parliament with the definition of public servant broadened to include any person who is appointed, elected, selected or otherwise engaged to perform a 'public function'. The Commission for the Prevention of Corruption (CPC) was appointed on 1 May 2001, with a Justice as Chairman, and four members including the Auditor-General, under the Corruption Prevention Act 2000 to enforce the Act, by securing the annual declaration of assets by almost 17,000 public servants. However, a report of the CPC (2005), tabled in parliament in December 2005, covering the period January 2004 to December 2005, revealed substantial shortfalls in compliance, with non-compliance rising from 24 per cent in December 2003 to 31 per cent in 2004. Many forms were filed without validating documents, such as bank statements (Henry, 2005). In particular, for 2003, the CPC revealed that 62 per cent of the breaches were due to non-compliance by the security forces.

New accountability measures also included *The Public Bodies Management and Accountability (PBMA)* of 2001, a new instrument, which embodies New Public Management (NPM) principles for corporate governance, such as the request for public bodies or agencies' boards to 'develop specific and measurable objectives and performance targets' (Section 6b). The most interesting part of the PBMA Act relates to enforcement, where courts were left to provide remedies by imposing pecuniary penalty not exceeding one million dollars or granting an injunction restraining persons from engaging in certain conduct, on the application of the Attorney-General. Similarly, accountability was also at issue in the *Access to Information (ATI) Act* of 2002, although as law which contributes to anti-corruption provision, this has several weaknesses. While the Act is strong on granting of access to documents which contain material of a purely factual nature or reports, studies, tests or surveys of a scientific or technical nature, it is less powerful in relation to public interest documents, and only reforms The Official Secrets Act of 1911 at the margins.

For example, public access to Cabinet documents can still be withheld for 20 years (as in Canada and Australia), rather than the 10 years pertaining in neighbouring Trinidad and Tobago. Meanwhile, the public interest is referred to only twice, in Section 20 (2) 'Documents relating to Business Affairs'; and in Section 21 (2) 'Documents relating to heritage sites', which again contrasts sharply with Trinidad and Tobago's Freedom of Information Act, which directly covers 'Disclosure of exempt documents in the public interest', and provides that public authorities are mandated to produce, 'notwithstanding any law to the contrary' an exempt document where there is 'reasonable evidence that significant' abuse of public interest, including acts of corruption, has occurred (Section (35)). In short, the Jamaican ATI Act was intentioned to capture contemporary best practices in open government, to fend off international pressure for good governance, attend to modernisation and the influences of the information society, and generally help stem corruption and scandals, and yet this significant opportunity to reinstate clean government and strengthen law enforcement was not fully captured.

Conclusion

Public perceptions about corruption and actual corruption scandals have been trending upward in Jamaica in the last decade or so, as personal and political relationships within the Westminster democracy practised in the country and political tribalism have conspired to undermine the otherwise noble efforts at institutional developments for fighting corruption. A reconstituted culture of high politics and governance is required, to embed the institutional initiatives, some of which still lack prosecutorial backbone, while complementary reform in strengthening the justice system would assist in implementation. Most importantly, the way policy responses to corruption scandals have privileged adding institutions, instead of overhauling existing ones and examining corruption as a wider systemic and cultural issue, perhaps epitomises the high pitch of institutional failure. From a policy characteristics perspective, what the country needs urgently is not so much additions to laws, regulations and institutions, but a joined-up administrative process, or division for public accountability, for co-ordinating, evaluating and monitoring the already existing anti-corruption institutions and enforcement agencies.

While the international corruption campaign has created indices for corruption such as the CPI and the international country risk guide (ICRG); has produced codes of ethics and conventions as useful symbols; and produced broad agendas that are being pursued at the macro level, it is still micro level analyses that shed light on the effectiveness of specific anti-corruption initiatives. In the efforts of developing countries to please international observers, their attention to the effectiveness of individual policies has remained weak, as attention to monitoring and evaluation has often been sacrificed in favour of symbolism and gesture. This chapter contends that this lack of serial and regular attention to the effectiveness of policies at the micro level is the main reason why anti-corruption measures have performed dismally in Jamaica, and may be behind policy failures in other developing countries as well.

Notes

1. Some of these include:, the Zinc, Furniture, Fat Cat Salaries, the BOJ Foreign Exchange, the Motor Vehicle Importation, the Land Distribution, the NWC, and the Sand Mining Scandals. Also, the Rollins Land Deal, The Shell Waiver, Netserv, Kingston Public Hospital Renovation, North Coast Highway and Old Harbour Bypass cost overruns, Operation Pride and National Housing Development Corporation scandal and most recently the National Solid Waste Management Authority as well as allegations of corruption at the Sandals Whitehouse hotel development project. Some of these involved cost overruns, but are still perceived as corruption by the public and the media.
2. Policy characteristics analysis, developed in the 1990s, is an analytical tool embedded in the scholarship of policy implementation, which aims to improve the knowledge and understanding of policy reformers, and to facilitate a more systematic assessment of policy. Brinkerhoff and Crosby (2002: 153), who have done the most work in developing the methodology, suggest that the key focus of policy characteristics analysis is to examine the distribution and time frame for benefits and costs, asking 'what the policy is designed to do, the context in which the policy will be implemented, how the reactions of the public are likely

to be manifest, and how consequential the changes for the bureaucracy are likely to be' (Brinkerhoff and Crosby, 2002: 153).

References

Angus Report (2002), Report to the Honorable Prime Minister on the Operations of the National Housing Development Corporation Limited and Operation Pride April 05, 2002, submitted by the Special Investigative Commission

Barnett, L. (2000), *Proscribing Corruption under Jamaican Law, a legal Roadmap.* A Citizens guide, 'Combating Corruption in Jamaica', Carter Center and Sangsters Bookstore publication

Bartley, E. M. (2003), 'Patterson's administration from a world perspective', *Gleaner*, Sunday October 19, 2003. www.jamaicagleaner.com.

Brinkerhoff, D. W. and Crosby, B. (2002), *Managing Policy Reform: Concepts and Tools for Policy-Makers in Developing and Transitioning Countries,* Bloomfield, CT: Kumarian Press

Buckley, B. (2005), *Gleaner*/Don Anderson poll – 'A crisis in confidence', Sunday, March 27, 2005. www.jamaica-gleaner.com

Caiden, G. (1991), *Administrative Reform Comes of Age,* New York: Walter de Gruyter

Corruption Prevention Commission (2005) *Annual Report for Period January 2004 to December 2005,* Gordon House, Kingston, Jamaica

Daley, V. (2002), 'PNP Scandals send over $6 billion down the drain', *Jamaica Gleaner*, Tuesday February 19, 2002, www.jamaicagleaner.com

Figueroa, M. and Sives, A. (2003), 'Garrison Politics and Criminality in Jamaica: Does the 1997 Election Represent a Turning Point?' In Harriott, Anthony, ed. *Understanding Crime in Jamaica: Challenges for Public Policy,* Kingston, Jamaica: University of the West Indies Press, pp. 63–88

Gager, W. (2001), Jamaica Struggles with Accountability. Commonwealth Workshop on Accountability, Scrutiny and Oversight. Canberra, 23–5 May 2001. www.cdi.anu.edu.au/ . . . research_downloads/es.wyvolyngager.pdf. Accessed: June 20, 2005

Harriott, A. (2000) *Police and Crime Control in Jamaica,* Kingston, Jamaica: University of the West Indies Press

Hart, R. (2005), 'Corruption accusations loose', says Patterson. Kingston: *Jamaica Gleaner*, April 28, www.jamaica-gleaner.com. Accessed: October 28, 2005

Henry, Balford (2005), 'Civil servants snub Corruption Commission Anti-corruption commission says work hampered by lack of support staff', *Jamaica Observer*, Wednesday, December 07, 2005, www.jamaicaobserver.com. Accessed: January 17, 2006

Huntington, S. (1968), *Political Order in Changing Societies,* New Haven: Yale University Press

Jamaica Gleaner (2001), 'Rampant Corruption in Government, police force' – Anderson poll. Monday September 17, 2001, www.jamaica-gleaner.com

Jamaica Gleaner (2003), 'NHDC Report . . . Rattray defends', Sunday January 26, 2003, www.jamaica-gleaner.com/gleaner/20030126/lead/lead5.html

Jamaica Gleaner (2005), Editorial – Dealing with corruption. Sunday May 15, 2005, www.jamaica-gleaner.com. Accessed: May 20, 2005

Jones, E. (1992), 'Maladministration and Corruption: Some Caribbean Realities', In Ryan, Selwyn V. and Brown, Deryck R. (eds) *Issues and Problems in Caribbean Public Administration*, Trinidad and Tobago: ISER, pp. 39–41

Klitgaard, R. (2000), *Corrupt Cities: a Practical Guide to Cure and Prevention*, Institute for Contemporary Studies. World Bank Institute Washington DC, USA: ICS Press Oakland California

Lewis, W. A. (1973), 'The Development Process: the Lessons of Two Decades', published in *Sir William Arthur Lewis: Collected Papers 1941–1988, Vol. III*, edited by Patrick A. M. Emmanuel. ISER (Eastern Caribbean, University of the West Indies, Barbados)

Lindo, L. (2002), *Jamaica Betrayed – Institutional Failure in a Caribbean Setting*, Arawak Publications, Pear Tree Press, Kingston, Jamaica

Marquette, H. (2003) *Corruption, Politics and Development: the Origins and Development of the World Bank's Anti-corruption Agenda*, Basingstoke: Palgrave – now Palgrave Macmillan

Mills, G. E. (1997), Westminster Style Democracy: the Jamaican Experience. Grace, Kennedy Foundation Lecture 1997. Stephenson's Litho Press Ltd

Ministry of Commerce and Technology (2001), 'Netserv Scandal – Loan Policy Guide for Intec Fund', March 1

Moran, J. (2001), 'Democratic Transitions and Forms of Corruption', in *Crime, Law and Social Change*, 36 (4), pp. 379–93

Munroe, T. (2002a), 'Governance under Threat: the Impact of Corruption and the Fight Against Corruption', In *Governance in the Age of Globalisation, Caribbean Perspectives*, edited by Hall, Kenneth O. and Benn, Dennis. Kingston: Ian Randle Publishers, pp. 369–82

Munroe, T. (2002b), Transforming Jamaican Democracy through Transparency: a framework for Action. Fostering Transparency and Preventing Corruption in Jamaica. Carter Centre

Munroe, T. (2003), National Integrity Systems Transparency International Country Study Report Jamaica. Transparency International Secretariat, Berlin Germany

Osei, P. D. with Smith-Tennant S., Walters, D. and Breese, I. (2005), 'Financing Local Government in Jamaica: Policy and Praxis since 1993 and the Way Forward'. Report Submitted to the National Advisory Council on Local Government Reform, Task Force on Finance. Research supported by CIDA. Sir Arthur Lewis Institute of Social and Economic Studies, Mona, Kingston: Jamaica

Rattray, K. (2002), Assessment of the Culpability of Dr. Karl Blythe Former Minister of Water and Housing Arising From the Report of the Commission of Enquiry into Operation Pride

Reid, T. (2005a), Staff Reporter, 'Take the blame' – JLP wants Patterson to accept responsibility for NSWMA scandal', *Gleaner*: Wednesday August 3, 2005, www.jamaicagleaner.com

Reid, T. (2005b), Staff Reporter, 'Stewart quits as Davies' campaign manager – Haunted by solid waste saga', *Gleaner*, Monday October 31, 2005, www.jamaicagleaner.com

Rose, D. (2006), 'Public Accounts Committee raps National Solid Waste Management Authority (NSWMA) for waste', *Gleaner*, Wednesday February 15, 2006

Rose-Ackerman, S. (1999), *Corruption and Government: Causes consequences and reform*, Cambridge, UK: Cambridge University Press

Ryan, S. (1999), *Winner Takes All: The Westminster Experience in the Caribbean*, Trinidad and Tobago: ISER, University of the West Indies, St Augustine.

Ryan, S. and Brown, D. (eds) (1992), *Issues and Problems in Caribbean Public Administration*, Trinidad & Tobago: ISER

Stone, C. (1980), *Democracy and Clientelism in Jamaica*, New Brunswick and London: Transaction Books

Tindigarukayo, J. and Chadwick, S. J. (1998), 'Civil Service Reform in Jamaica', www.magnet.undp.org/Docs/psreform/civil_service_reform_in_Jamaica.htm, accessed: May 20, 2004

Transparency International (2005), *Global Corruption Reports 2002–2005*, www.ti.org. accessed: November 20, 2005

10
Governance, Neoliberalism and Corruption in Nicaragua

Ed Brown, Jonathan Cloke and José Luis Rocha[1]

Representations of Nicaragua's political health during the Alemán administration (1997–2001) were highly polarised. On the one hand, the period saw considerable inflows of international funds destined for governance reforms, the introduction of a range of anti-corruption measures and detailed governmental treatises and proclamations on how Nicaragua was becoming more transparent (e.g. Alemán, 1999). Nevertheless, at the same time, critical commentators (e.g. Envio, 1999: 7) lamented a continuing decline in integrity recorded in surveys of popular and business opinion (although the validity of such sources is of course open to debate).[2] At the time, there was little more than an increasing weight of accusation and a decline in Nicaragua's position, then 77th out of 91 on Transparency International's (TI's) corruption perception index (TI, 2001) to support claims of endemic corruption in Nicaragua. The administration of Enrique Bolaños (2001–2007), however, subsequently unearthed the extent of the corruption of his predecessor.[3] The reality was that, despite the evolution of internationally-funded anti-corruption programmes, the extent of corrupt personal enrichment and political manipulation that had occurred under the Alemán administration was extreme even for Nicaragua.

Nicaraguans are not the only Central Americans who would do well to question the sincerity of their governments' embracing of the anti-corruption agenda. At the end of the 1990s, most Central American leaders had been quick to assimilate the new anti-corruption discourse, as described in this collection for other regions. As a result, the language of transparency and accountability grew to be liberally scattered throughout government documentation and speeches. Accompanying the rhetorical flourishes new government departments, 'think tanks' and anti-corruption offices were created, national anti-corruption plans drafted and national institutions such as the offices of the Comptroller General or national ombudsperson strengthened (see Gutierrez, 2001; USAID, 1999). National initiatives were complemented by a range of activities at the regional level; the Carter Centre hosted a number of regional conferences; USAID initiated a website, whilst the OAS (through its foundation 'the Trust for the Americas') promoted the agreement of an 'Interamerican Convention against Corruption' which was adopted in 1997 (Robinson, 1998; Trust for the Americas, 2001; OAS, 2004; USAID 2004).

Despite the substantial sums now being spent on institutional reform, all of this activity appears to have been incredibly slow in producing results, fomenting fears that rhetorical commitments to combating corruption may be little more than cleverly constructed attempts to capture the international resources now available for institutional reform. Just to take one, admittedly flawed indicator (see Brown and Cloke, 2004), the Central American republics continue to perform poorly in indexes calculated by TI – in the 2001 Corruption Perceptions Index, for example, three Central American countries appear in the worst third of the 91 countries surveyed: Nicaragua (14th), Honduras (18th) and Guatemala (24th) (TI, 2001).

Corruption scandals continue to occur across the region with monotonous regularity, including that of El Salvador's finance secretary Miguel Lacayo (Gutierrez, 2001: 154), the 'boozegate' scandal and the growing number of cases being brought against high-ranking Guatemalan politicians (Hernandez, 2001; Gonzalez, 2003) and a range of allegations of impropriety in the post-Mitch reconstruction process in Honduras (Jeffrey, 1999; Rodgers, 1999 and TI, 1999). Our focus here, however, is placed specifically on Nicaragua and the initiatives and forms of discourse about corruption that took place during the government of Arnoldo Alemán. In particular, we explore how the chasm between rhetorical commitments to transparency and probity and a sharply contrasting Nicaraguan reality reflected interactions within a complex matrix of interests, which included the contradictory role of international donors.

The Alemán case: an overview

Former-President Alemán[4] of Nicaragua was sentenced to 20 years imprisonment in 2003 for the theft of public funds in excess of $100 million, the first time that any public figure had been sentenced to any custodial term for corruption in Nicaragua, so some progress is plainly being made.[5] At the same time, it has to be noted that the clientelistic political system that enabled Alemán to commit such grand larceny is still firmly in place and that whilst he was in the process of diverting such a huge quantity of money, aside from expressions of general concern by the Consultative Group and other international actors, a public façade was maintained (particularly by the The Interamerican Development Bank (IADB)) that the government of Nicaragua was making a determined effort to combat the corruption of which its own leader was the worst example.

The struggle against corruption had been a rallying cry of the opposition to the Somoza dictatorship since the misuse of reconstruction funds following the Managua earthquake of 1972 but the issue largely faded from view during the revolutionary years until the aftermath of the *piñata* in 1990.[6] Thereafter, questions of transparency and accountability gradually began to figure in the institutional reform programmes that accompanied the renewed access to international funding during the governments of Violeta Chamorro (1990–1996) and Arnoldo Alemán (1997–2001). It was, however, during the latter's administration that the funding and implementation of anti-corruption efforts really began to take off (Langseth and Pezzulo, 2000). This culminated in the formation of a National Integrity Committee, chaired by then vice-president Enrique Bolaños, which began operating in 1998 with input from the World Bank (through their Economic Development Institute's Governance team). This was intended to provide a forum where government and civil society could collaborate to promote 'integrity and openness at the national level, prevent and combat corruption and foster values of honesty, public spirit and ethics in the citizenry' (RN, 1999a: 4). This approach was coupled to externally-funded programmes of institutional modernisation, involving the reform of the Nicaraguan state's financial management and auditing systems, civil service reform, tax system reform and further privatisation initiatives.

The culmination of this two-track approach was the articulation of a National Integrity Plan presented to the Stockholm Conference of the Donor's Consultative Group in May 1999 (RN, 1999a), all of which earned the Nicaraguan government significant praise at the time from donors and observers (including from Seligson (1997, 1999) and, to a lesser degree, Langseth and Pezzullo (2000)). In April 1998, for example, USAID Nicaragua's budget application for the following financial year suggested that the Alemán government had initiated 'bold steps to increase openness and accountability . . . [taking] a very public stance on anti-corruption' (USAID, 1998: 12). Work on this National Integrity Plan accelerated in the aftermath of Hurricane Mitch, as donors sought assurances about the accountability of the use of reconstruction funds, which gave further impetus to the institutional reform process (see IADB, 1999b), leading to a system for monitoring implementation under the 'Group of Five' mechanism.[7] The international community seemed relatively optimistic about this enhanced focus upon transparency, with USAID using their Central American experiences as an exemplar in their 2001 Latin American budget submission (USAID, 2000) and some commentators suggesting that Central America might take on a leadership role in the development of mechanisms of accountability (CLACDS/HIID, 1998: 4).

Nonetheless, even as these measures were supposedly being implemented, the Nicaraguan government's ability to deliver on its promises of transparency was already being undermined when substantial quantities of the aid money donated for the relief of Hurricane Mitch victims were diverted by government officials into their own pockets. The most egregious example concerned the head of the Nicaraguan Inland Revenue, Byron Jerez Solis, a close friend of President Alemán. Jerez had used Nicaraguan tax revenues (via PETRONIC, the state petroleum company) to pay for the construction of a palatial summer house, as well as issuing cheques to a firm owned by his brother in Miami (Marenco, 2000). The work done on the Jerez summer palace was also paid for by donated funds from Hurricane Mitch reconstruction projects (Bodan, 2000a).

The formal case against Ex-President Alemán himself (and his thirteen co-accused, who included Jerez) sets out a whole catalogue of abuses over this period. These included irregularities in relation to a heliport, a television station and a cement company, tax evasion, lavish trips abroad, and widespread money laundering through front businesses and banks. The amount involved, $100 million (the sum of what has been detected to date) is the equivalent of $200 for every man, woman, and child in Nicaragua (CEPAD, 2002; see ODC, 2002). By the end of the Alemán presidency, one observer suggests that Nicaragua had descended into an 'advanced state of habitual corruption . . . [where] corruption is promoted, expedited and protected from the highest state levels, in this case the presidency itself, and from the different fiefdoms controlled by President Alemán's cronies' (Rafael Cordova, cited in Envio, 2002: 2).

The international dimension

As we have argued elsewhere (see Brown and Cloke, 2004), whilst corruption in any country has important internal dynamics, it is not singularly a domestic issue. The dynamics of corruption relate as much to the changing relationship between internal and external actors as they do to the arena of domestic politics and political culture. The inaction (or even active collaboration) of external actors under conditions of increasing international flows can provide great opportunities for illicit activity at the highest levels. Furthermore, such is the reciprocal onus on IFI and debtor country governments to provide positive assessments of the impacts of institutional reform, that important contradictions and inconsistencies can be buried under reams of cosmetic statistical information, positive action plans and well-meaning but often pointless documentation. It is this, as much as anything, that allowed the looting during the Alemán presidency to occur.

To explore these inconsistencies in a little more depth, it is worth looking at specific examples of the occasionally surreal communications passing between the government of Nicaragua and the IFIs on the subject of governance. Following the May meeting of the Donor's Consultative group in 2000 in Washington, the Nicaraguan government (RN, 2000a) wrote in a letter of intent to the IMF dated 30 August 2000:

> In the structural area, the National Assembly passed legislation to help improve transparency and efficiency in government procurement. Laws relating to the central bank, commercial banks and the Superintendence of banks approved in the fourth quarter of 1999 strengthened the autonomy of the central bank and improved the legal basis for prudential regulation and supervision of financial institutions.

This statement was clearly accepted at face value by the institutions (see IMF/IDA, 2000). At the time that it was written, however, Nicaragua was passing through a significant banking crisis (the Nicaraguan banks INTERBANK, BANIC, BAMER and BANCAFE all collapsed in the period 1999–2001) and yet there is no acknowledgement of this crisis and its impacts. The IADB, the World Bank and the US Drug Enforcement Agency (who designed the Nicaraguan regulations for controlling money-laundering) were all apparently very satisfied with the management of the Superintendence of banks and its norms for classifying portfolios. However, less than a month before its collapse, Interbank appears in the Superintendence's September 2000 report with 96.1 per cent of its portfolio classified in the 'no risk' category, a level higher than any other bank (Superintendecia de Bancos y Otras Instituciones Financieras, 2000: Table 23). There was also no comment from the IMF/IDA on the blatant lack of success of earlier commitments to banking reform, which had been articulated in a Letter of Intent and Memorandum to the IMF on 9 January 1998. Although banking oversight and regulation were apparently facilitated through international cooperation during this period, national systems for dealing with banking collapses remained fatally flawed, from the selection of the members of the 'juntas liquidoras' to the interest rates applied to state bonds and the reclassification of bank portfolios. Legal actions were finally initiated in 2006 against the persons implicated, although they will be heard in courts controlled by the political parties, which tempers the independence of proceedings.

Furthermore, legislation passed by Nicaragua's National Assembly in this period was controlled by a pact between the two major parties (FSLN and PLC), effectively dividing up the government between them. As a consequence, laws promoting the autonomy of the Central Bank and the Superintendence were effectively meaningless since the regulation and supervision of financial institutions was exercised in an arbitrary manner by political party executives, who simultaneously sat as board members. Thus between 1990 and 2002 at least six Nicaraguan banks went bankrupt and many of the chief debtors to those banks were members of the elite connected to the major political parties who were never brought to account for those debts, leaving the Nicaraguan people to foot the bill in the form of government-issued bonds (Acevedo, 2005).

In a similarly Orwellian fashion, at the same May 2000 meeting of the Consultative Group in Washington, Sr Enrique Iglesias, the president of the IADB, commented:

> we support the recently approved Law of State Contracting, which mitigates for a greater transparency in public acquisitions and contracting. At the same time, we also support the Law of Comptroller Reform, which makes for a greater independence and professionalism in the actions of this state entity. (Iglesias, 2000, authors' translation)

The reform of the Comptroller's Office had been demanded by the international community following Alemán's ousting of the former independent Comptroller General, Agustin Jarquin Anaya, who had shown an uncomfortable predisposition towards doing his job properly. This had resulted in his being briefly jailed by Alemán in November 1999 for enquiring too closely into the exponential enrichment of the president and his close circle of family and friends.[8]

The FSLN/PLC pact had then turned the Comptroller's Office into a college of comptrollers, individually picked by the two party leaders and led by an unconditionally loyal supporter of Alemán, and it was this 'reform' that was being praised. By creating this college of political appointees, the PLC and FSLN controlled enquiries undertaken by the state office responsible for ensuring the legitimate use of public funds, politicising the Comptroller's office. Moreover, those promoting the reform had themselves played invidious roles in effectively neutralising the independence of that office. In other words, the president of the IADB was praising the most corrupt members of the government of Nicaragua for the introduction of a law that had exactly the opposite effect of that which he claimed for it; demonstrating either a lamentable lack of understanding of the dynamics of Nicaraguan politics or a blatant lack of concern for the actual outcomes of the institutional reforms funded by his organisation.

International concern over the extent of corruption in Nicaragua under the Alemán administration was, however, not entirely absent, with individual donors expressing severe reservations in the initial months after Mitch (Vukelich, 1999). Indeed, a report from the External Cooperation Secretariat published scarcely two weeks after the hurricane, reveals that donors were willing to channel only 50 per cent of aid through the government, the other 50 per cent being directed through a diverse set of NGOs and civil society organisations (Envio, 1998). Moreover, following the Stockholm conference, several individual projects were also abandoned when donors discovered irregularities (e.g. Sweden and Germany – LADB, 2000) whilst the disbursement of other project monies was delayed mainly because of fears over corruption (Chamorro, X., 1999; Umanzor, 1999). Even the US ambassador, Oliver Garza, began to press Alemán over the growing charges against him in March 2000; although as late as mid-1999, USAID officials were still talking of the 'exaggerated' and politicised nature of the claims being made about high-level corruption in the Alemán administration. These contradictions were undoubtedly related to geopolitics, where the US was preoccupied with Alemán's unwelcome rapprochement with Ortega and the FSLN, which not unrelatedly affected property claims still being pursued by US citizens from the revolutionary years of confiscation. The muted censure that did occur, nonetheless, appears to have done little to influence the behaviour of the Alemán administration.

The unavoidable conclusion must be that as the centralisation of powers under the presidency, the corruption of the political process and the exponential growth in actual corruption continued in Nicaragua, all of the responsible authorities (domestic and external) abandoned responsibility in order to maintain the façade of a political and macro-economic *status quo*. For all of the IFI experience with, and insistence on, conditionality in relation to economic policy, their attempts to force the Alemán administration to respond to the corruption charges fell on deaf ears – for as long as the Alemán government was prepared to make the right noises and produce the right documents and figures, however concocted, the IADB and the IMF, under intense scrutiny by the US government, took everything at face value and maintained the flow of money. Thus, whilst in September 1999 the IMF had taken the unprecedented move of making its support for Nicaragua's accelerated inclusion into the HIPC initiative conditional upon progress in the fight against corruption (relating particularly to the Jerez case and the constitutional reforms of the PLC–FSLN pact), in December 2000 the country was allowed to enter without any demonstrable progress having been made. This suggests that to act on conditionality, rather than to merely threaten it, is fundamentally problematic, which is also illustrated in the case of Kenya (see World Bank, 2004).[9]

The absence of systematic IFI condemnations of corruption in Nicaragua stood in stark contrast to the critique of a fiercely partisan but independent press which regularly exposed it. The two daily newspapers, *La Prensa* and *El Nuevo Diario* (of diametrically different political orientations) kept up a constant barrage of revelations and exposés throughout the period 1996–2000. *La Prensa* in particular played a major role in bringing to light documentary proof of corruption in the Jerez case, publishing document after document in the face of an absolute refusal to investigate by the police, the judicial system and the responsible state authorities. The dailies were backed up by magazines such as *Confidencial* and *Envío*, whose commentary examined in minute detail the overt dishonesty of PLC officials. In sum, proof of corruption was everywhere, but subordinated to economic ideology and perceived geopolitical priorities.

The descent to the levels of corruption that occurred in Nicaragua under the Alemán administration was not the fault of the IFIs or the international community more generally, but the institutions' reluctance to broach the growing problems, and the economic priorities urged on Nicaragua by international pressure undoubtedly facilitated and exacerbated the looting. There was also a failure to make connections between the escalation of corruption problems and the evolution of other areas of policy under IFI control and influence, such that they continued to advocate policies that in many ways fuelled the problems. In particular, as has frequently occurred elsewhere, the corruption which so frequently impregnates or animates privatisation processes locally was disregarded. Despite the large amounts of international money ploughed into them (and despite the initial statements of praise and support), the anti-corruption efforts of the National Integrity Plan, the institutional strengthening and other 'good governance' initiatives, in at least some cases merely provided further sources of patronage for the clientelistic political system.

The Nicaraguan political system

The political realities of Nicaragua during this time rendered anti-corruption initiatives impotent, not just through the actions of a corrupt president and his circle, but also because of the way in which the Nicaraguan political system functions. Some of the worst features of this were magnified historically by processes of economic and political reform financed by the IFIs after 1990, particularly the liberalisation and privatisation processes which shaped the political economy into a clan-based patronage system. However, domestic conditions for this were also fuelled when Daniel Ortega (Sandinista, ex-President, now President once again) reached a political agreement with Alemán in the late 1990s, affected through a package of sixteen constitutional reforms approved by the national assembly of Nicaragua on 9 December 1999, which legitimised and accelerated his abuse of the Nicaraguan state. These reformed laws were key to the explosion of corruption in Nicaragua, and a big step backwards from the democratising changes to the constitution of 1995 (ICEP, 2000). Through them the *caudillos* of the PLC and the FSLN effectively constitutionalised the division of spoils of the *estado botín* (the booty state) between them.

The PLC–FSLN pact

For the FSLN, the reforms of 1999 guaranteed possession of a series of businesses, farms, agricultural co-operatives and residential properties that they had appropriated in the *piñata* of 1990. Rent arrears from some 240 state businesses in FSLN hands since 1992, a sum of some US$50 million, were also written off. The FSLN were guaranteed a seat on the managing committee of the Superintendence of Banks and the Central Bank, as well as seats in the Comptroller General's Office, the Supreme Electoral Council, and 40 per cent of all the offices in regional, departmental and municipal electoral bodies. They negotiated an alternation in the presidency of all of this state apparatus, a period of PLC rule, followed by a period of FSLN rule. They were further guaranteed 40 per cent of the electoral budgets for the general and municipal elections and a reduction in the number of votes required for a second round in the presidential elections from 45 to 35 per cent, a change important to Ortega's presidential aspirations (as proven in November of 2006). Managua was divided into three municipalities giving the FSLN a better chance of winning overall, whilst leaving the PLC in charge of the wealthy and rural areas from which their support was derived. The FSLN also gained seats on the ruling bench of the Supreme Court, posts in all the Appeals Tribunals, and took control of 80 per cent of the Criminal and Local Courts throughout the country and positions in the ruling committee of the national assembly, whilst FSLN-controlled banks were guaranteed participation in the potentially lucrative Wet or Dry transoceanic canal project.

For the PLC, the pact saw the FSLN agree to stop disruption of government, using its influence to dismantle unions in the state businesses earmarked for privatisation – ENITEL (the state telecoms company), ENEL (the state electricity company), INAA (state company responsible for bridges and aqueducts), the airport and the ports authority. Most importantly, the PLC gained control of the office of the Comptroller General at a time when it was becoming embarrassingly effective. As a failsafe, Arnoldo Alemán also attempted to secure his further immunity from prosecution upon leaving the presidency by the conferral of a deputy's seat in the national assembly as of right. The PLC also gained control of the Supreme Electoral Council, and thus the national electoral process (from the counting of votes, to setting the electoral budget and the constitution of the local electoral boards), the Supreme Court and other justice tribunals. Finally, the PLC achieved the promulgation of a series of laws privatising a series of state businesses whilst allowing members of the PLC government to work in them as shareholders or associates. The privatisation of electricity generation, the international airport and the state bank BANIC, together with the opening up of the telecommunications market, were all conducted in ways permitting the PLC and party functionaries to profit.

The pact and the above reforms were far more than a de facto recognition of the bipartite political divide that has been the political reality of Nicaragua since 1996; they wrote that political division into the constitution and into the legal system. Even more importantly, in dividing up the Supreme Electoral Council, they attempted to write all other political opposition out of official election processes.

Government transparency and accountability

Our concentration on the inadequacies of the interventions of the IFIs and the impacts of the broader political economy upon the path of institutional reform in Nicaragua should not be seen as suggesting that there is not a need for better governance and enhanced institutionality in Nicaragua. Quite the contrary, it is the lack of transparency of state institutions, the limited public access to government data and the lack of professionalism of the civil service which have facilitated the abuses that have occurred. These factors are gradually being approached by the outgoing Nicaraguan government, but its reluctance to embrace what would be difficult change in any circumstances, is further hindered by the fact that they too are beneficiaries of this system: that giving up these aspects of the Nicaraguan socio-cultural environment signifies the breaking-up of their gatekeeper role as regards state power.

Immunity from prosecution has been perhaps the single most effective block to transparency of government in Nicaragua. As of 1999, the Nicaraguan constitution allowed for immunity from legal action for the President and Vice-president, the magistrates of the *Consejo Supremo Electoral* and the *Corte Suprema de Justicia* and members of (*diputados*) the National Assembly, as well as members of the *Contraloría General*, ministers and vice-ministers of state (Ley de Inmunidad No. 83 of March 1990, Capítulo 1, Artículo 1). Section 3.1.2 of the National Integrity Plan dealt with reform of the executive branch of government and notes the passing of Law 290 in 1998 in order to promote efficiency and openness in the public sector. Nevertheless, far from making this situation better, Law 290 actually made the legal situation worse, by effectively conceding to the president the discretion to impart immunity to other functionaries where (s)he sees fit. Under this law, the president was given the right to create sectoral cabinets wherever and whenever it was deemed necessary, and to bestow official GON (Government of Nicaragua) rank to whoever it was deemed appropriate, with all the privileges that might entail including immunity from prosecution. In other words, the president arrogated to himself the right simply to bestow government patronage at will, a further centralisation of powers.

It is easier to understand how it was possible for Arnoldo Alemán and his family to have stolen over $100 million in a mere five years when these powers are taken into account; after all, this was a sum equivalent to the entire USAID budget for Nicaragua for the financial years 1998, 1999 and 2000, which averaged some $35 million per year (USAID, 2000). However, this sum deals only with that amount taken by Arnoldo Alemán and family. As a mere consequence of logic, hundreds if not thousands of his deputies, governmental appointees and party loyalists must also have been involved in their own corruption, petty and otherwise (for example through taking advantage of their position to extract bribes from private companies for granting operational permissions, forestry or mining concessions or avoidance of fines or other fiscal penalties). Plainly the amounts stolen from the Nicaraguan public purse during the Alemán presidency must have been several multiples of this $100 million figure; this without mentioning the quantities extracted by the FSLN for their support.

Ineffective freedom of information and transparency laws have also facilitated high-level corruption in Nicaragua. Information technology is still a rare commodity, and written and printed records often tend to be used to obscure fact rather than reveal it. These are frequently destroyed by the authorities responsible for them, as for instance when the financial files of the *alcaldía* of Managua from 1990–96 were destroyed by (then-*alcalde*) Alemán when they were requested by the Comptroller General as part of the investigation into the financial affairs of the *alcaldía* of Managua. The minimal transparency of government accounts sits as the most significant testimony to inadequate record-keeping and unaccountable power more generally, facilitating the *presidencia* to divert money where it wishes. In 1997, for instance, the budget for the Republic passed by the National Assembly contained a mysterious element for 'internal debt' of C$940 million, which no one could explain and which was therefore unaccounted for (Envío, 1997).[10] The government budget has frequently contained an element of the surreal, given that the budget submitted to the National Assembly for the following year is invariably far less than the actual total spent; 'slippage' is simply spent illegally. The budget for 2000, for example, increased illegally by C$1,404 million during the first few months of the year (Barbarena, 2000), an over-spend which was subsequently legalised by the National Assembly retrospectively.

Public service integrity, and patronage

Transparency of state functions clearly requires a system of laws and regulation that is understood, and the requisite people and mechanisms to operate it. The manual of accountability issued by the government of Nicaragua in November of 2000 recognises the need for a civil service career structure based in merit, the need for improvements in personnel administration in Nicaragua, and thus promises modernisation and measures to increase professionalism (RN, 2000b). However, the manner in which successive Nicaraguan governments have chosen to fulfill this promise has been to select only party members and in particular close relatives for the majority of state offices. This 'familiarisation' of the state essentially involves the suborning and disposal of offices in strategic positions as a direct personal favour to the donor; with beneficiaries of this personal largesse plainly owing no loyalty to the state or the people of Nicaragua. The employing of relatives and party workers therefore inflicts very real economic damage on an already desperately poor country.

President Alemán appointed numerous family members to various state posts, but Alemán was by no means alone in this. As of January 2001, for instance, the then-vice president and recent ex-President of Nicaragua, Enrique Bolaños Geyer, had at least sixteen members of his family in state posts of one description or another. Two of the assessors he appointed to the National Integrity Committee, for example, were nephews, whilst a further nephew was appointed as a delegate of the National Development programme in Carazo. In addition, one of his wife's nephews, Fernando Abauza Noguera, was appointed DGI (Inland Revenue) delegate for Masaya in January of 1997, some five months before he actually came back to live in the country in May 1997, having in the meantime obtained Canadian citizenship (Goitia, 1998; *El Nuevo Diario* 05/01/2001; Roiz Murillo, 2001).

In theory, all government action is governed by the constitution or respective laws and regulations passed by the National Assembly, but in practice this is frequently subverted by a 'Shadow State' (Reno, 2000) of the clientelistic structures, systems of personal obligation and political arrangements that supercede all democratic and juridical regulation. As an example, Article 5 of the *Ley de Contratacion* (the law governing contracting and licensing of purchases of services and goods by the state) of Nicaragua contains admirable considerations of convenience, cost, quality, efficiency, rationality and transparency of proceedings to obtain in quantifiable fashion to contracting activities in order to meet the general public interest (RN, 1999b). However, Article 3 gives a list of excluded goods, which, by itself, is comprehensive enough to remove most goods from formal regulation. Meanwhile, the reality of state contracting can readily be demonstrated by (for instance) the following, not untypical, example. On 25 September 2000 ex-minister of transport Jaime Bonilla, in his declaration to the investigating *Controloria*, stated that he had personally supervised the progress of a road built by the construction company MODULTECSA (which built the summer palace of Byron Jerez, using Hurricane Mitch disaster relief funds) from Masachapa to San Juan del Sur, frequently visiting the works at the weekends because it was in his native department. It was subsequently revealed that this road did not in fact exist, and that no traces could be found of any construction on the dirt road that did exist, despite C$277, 307 having been paid for its 'construction'. The ex-minister had been appointed on the basis of his friendship to Alemán, and the disappearance of the money remains a public concern.

Geopolitical context

Nicaragua is by no means unique in the frequent discovery of non-existent roads and infrastructure for which large sums of money have been paid; neither is it unique in the corrupt forms of clientelism and *caudillismo* taken by the political economy which disrupt the proper use of public funds. What makes Nicaragua different is its geopolitical situation (see Brown and Cloke, 2004), the causal links that corruption has had to the symbolic position it came to occupy in the Cold War, and the complex network of relationships that this position gave its political economy to the political establishment of the United States and, in particular (as the interference of Governor Jeb Bush of Florida in the elections of 2001 clearly demonstrates), to the Republican party. Much of Alemán's assumption of his own invincibility came from his prior enjoyment of US-support as the only figure in Nicaraguan politics deemed capable of 'dealing with' *Sandinismo*.

Conclusion

Our review of corruption during the Alemán administration in Nicaragua has illustrated that institutional reforms (and particularly anti-corruption efforts), can never be dealt with separately from the political economy that acts as host to them. In the case of Nicaragua and the other Central American countries, the complexity of governance and transparency issues are inextricably mixed up with Cold War and post-Cold War neoliberal *realpolitik* in a way that makes treating corruption as if it were a problem of economics or of jurisprudence a waste of time.

But the uniqueness of the Nicaraguan case, as of others, is found in specific historical roots that are not amenable solely to external effort. Even the international institutions promoting anti-corruption programmes, and good governance more generally, recognise that lack of *meaningful* public participation and embedding within local political systems remains an intractable problem (see USAID, 1999 and Langseth and Pezzullo, 2000). In Nicaragua, the liberal, conservative and leftist political factions are still beset with the clientelism and *caudillismo* that developed before and after the Somoza dictatorship, and unless there is a radical change in the internal structures and democratic proceedings of such parties, corruption will remain a legitimate form of social capital in the Nicaraguan political economy. Partly as a result (but also because) of trends in political economy that apply more generally, the state and private sector are not distinct and separate in Nicaragua, as IMF policy would dictate, but are a complex and intermingled mesh in which it is virtually impossible to distinguish boundaries. In short, the clientelistic networks which control government are inseparable from those which run the private sector.

Reform within the FSLN to rediscover the moral authority that *Sandinismo* used to enjoy seems key to political democratisation more generally. The revolutionary legacy of 1979–90, currently, is less the programmes and initiatives that were implemented during that period and more what has happened as a result of the *piñata* of 1990, and the decision of the FSLN to become a political party for which the use of power was its own justification. As Sergio Ramirez said in his book *Adios Muchachos*:

> The FSLN was not prepared, as a whole, to assume its role of party of opposition inside a democratic system because it had never been designed for this. Its vertical structure was the inspiration of Leninist manuals, of the impositions of the war and of caudillismo, our oldest cultural heritage. (Ramírez, 1999: 149, authors' translation)

The most striking confirmation of this is Daniel Ortega's continued domination of the party and his willingness to manipulate the democratic institutions of the country in the pursuit of personal and political gain. This manipulation is clear in his role in the release of Alemán from jail in December 2004, and most recently in the manipulative and criminal suppression of the right to legal abortion in Nicaragua and the suspicious delays of the *Consejo Supremo Electoral*, controlled by the FSLN and the PLC, in releasing the final results of the November 2006 elections which brought Ortega back to the presidency (Juarez, 2006a and 2006b citing the Carter Centre and the Nicaraguan NGI *Etica y Transparencia*).

Moving beyond the specifically Nicaraguan issues and returning to the general critique of anti-corruption initiatives which has been advanced in other chapters in this collection, it is clear that if the IFIs wish to confront corruption realistically, then questions of political and cultural context such as those explored here, must be taken into account when designing mechanisms to improve transparency and governance. However, these national considerations need to be combined with a whole host of other issues such as the proper and effective roles of conditionality, external intervention and transnational accountability. First, the ideological baggage that surrounds both IFI perception of the state and the beneficial effects of liberalisation and deregulation must be abandoned. Second, the IFIs must examine themselves and their own complicity in the development of corrupt systems, and encourage the strengthening of punitive measures to deter Northern bribe-payers and companies from corrupt behaviour. If it continues to be the case that aid/loan disbursement by IFIs, multilateral and unilateral donors is dominated by the geostrategic concerns of the rich north (for instance in favourable treatment of governments with oil, or mineral resources, or a 'strategic' geographical position) then all initiatives to stop the growth of corruption will fail, since they will be taking place in a system that is itself corrupt.

Notes

1. This chapter is a shortened and updated version of a paper 'Neoliberal reform, governance and corruption in Central America: Exploring the Nicaraguan case,' published in *Political Geography* in 2005 (Brown and Cloke, 2005). This version concentrates on the specific case of Nicaragua under the administration of President Arnoldo Alemán and has been improved greatly through the collaboration of our colleague José Luis Rocha.
2. Relevant surveys include Seligson, 1997, 1999 for USAID: CIET International, 1998, cited in Langseth and Pezullo, 2000 for the World Bank and Vice Presidency of Nicaragua; Bodan, 200b on business opinion; Instituto de Estudios Nicaraguenses (IEN), various). Some commentators (e.g. Seligson, 1999) have claimed rising perceptions of corruption may reflect greater awareness (and hence the success of the programmes), rather than a worsening of the problem itself.
3. Despite Bolaños own involvement as Vice-President in the earlier administration, and his own use of illicit funds during the 2001 election.
4. Arnoldo Alemán began his political career in opposition to the Sandinistas on Managua's city council from 1990, benefiting from support from Cuban and Nicaraguan exiles, and constructed an alliance of liberal parties to challenge for the presidency in 1996 with US government support.
5. However, while writing this chapter, Alemán was released from jail into 'departmental' arrest (meaning the whole of the Department of Mangua), a move orchestrated by Daniel Ortega via his control of the Nicaraguan judiciary, allowing Alemán to exert a great influence over the recent (November 2006) elections.
6. The *piñata* (named after a traditional party game in which children smash open a papier mâché toy filled with sweets or other treats) occurred in 1990 when, following electoral defeat, the FSLN, ostensibly to fund its democratic opposition, or simply for the benefit of individuals, systematically looted goods, money, properties and vehicles held by the state before handing over power to the incoming UNO government of Violeta Chamorro.
7. The 'Group of Five' is a group of five nations (Canada, Germany, Spain, Sweden and the USA) who agreed at Stockholm to monitor the transparency of reconstruction and transformation in the region. Later, the group also included Japan.
8. In 1990, when he became mayor of Managua, Alemán declared a patrimony of some $26,118, which had increased to $309, 993 when he left that office in 1995 and was over $990,000 by 1997 (*El Nuevo Diario*, 26/02/1999).
9. Where the IFIs do act against corruption it raises profound questions concerning national sovereignty and provides brief glimpses of the hidden political

economy that the current discourse on corruption acts to conceal, including, for example, the role of bank staff in corrupt allocation of contracts, the need for the Bank to appear successful and the political pressure brought to bear by richer countries with vested commercial interests.

10. Other examples of the *presidencia's* arbitrary spending are the unhindered access to $62 million granted in the budget of 1999 for use at the president's discretion; the calculated $17 million annually being paid by state companies direct to the *presidencia* and for which no account appears in the national audit; and indeed the $47 million, $87 million and $56 million which were paid to the Banco Central de Nicaragua under the mysterious title of '*política económíca*' for 1997, 1998 and 1999 (Téllez, 2001).

References

Acevedo, A. (2005) 'We must all demand the restructuring of the domestic debt' *Envio*, 24, no. 284

Alemán, A. (1999) Opening remarks from the Stockholm meeting of the Consultative Group, 25–28 May 1999, www.iadb.org/regions/re2/consultative_group/ speeches/arnoldo_Alemán.htm (last accessed 10/08/2004)

Barberena, E. (2000) 'Aprobado el Presupuesto General', *El Nuevo Diario*, 15 December, Managua, Nicaragua

Bodan, O. (2000a) 'Testigo clave confirma: Mitch financio obras de Byron Jerez', *Confidencial* no. 187, www.confidencial.com.ni (last accessed 10/08/2004)

Bodan, O. (2000b) 'Empresarios señalan focos de corrupcion', *Confidencial* no. 196, www.confidencial.com.ni (last accessed 10/08/2004)

Brown, E. and Cloke, J. (2004) 'Neoliberal Reform, Governance and Corruption in the South: Assessing the International Anti-Corruption Crusade', *Antipode*, 36(2), 272–94

Brown, E. and Cloke, J. (2005) 'Neoliberal Reform, Governance and Corruption in Central America: Exploring the Nicaraguan Case', *Political Geography*, 24, pp. 601–30

CEPAD (Council of Evangelical Churches of Nicaragua) (2002) 'Alemán on the ropes but not yet out for the count', www.cepad.info/report/02-08and09/1 (last accessed 10/08/2004)

Chamorro, X. (1999) 'Presidente acorralado: Fortuna de Alemán creció de 90 a 96 en 4 mil %', *El Nuevo Diario*, 26 February, Managua, Nicaragua

CLACDS/HIID (Latin American Centre for Competitiveness and Sustainable Development and Harvard Institute for International Development) (1998) *Strategy for Central American Reconstruction and Transformation after Hurricane Mitch*, proposal submitted to the Consultative Group Preparation and Follow-Up meeting, Washington (10–11 December), available on the internet at: www.incae.ac.cr/ES/clacds/investigacion/articulos/cen1101a.shtml

El Nuevo Diario (1999) (Editorial) 'BM suspende desembolsos? Presión para que gobierno cumpla compromisos', 23/10/1999, Managua, Nicaragua

El Nuevo Diario (2001) (Editorial) 'Vicepresidente siembra su árbol genealógico en todo el gobierno', 5/1/2001, Managua, Nicaragua

Envio (1997) 'Budget legislation leaves many mysteries', *Envio*, 16, no. 189, 16
Envio (1998) 'Hore de oportunidades y de oportunismos', *Envio*, 17, no. 201
Envio (1999) 'What's behind the IMF Pressure', *Envio*, 18, no. 220, 3–11
Envio (2002) 'Dilemmas in the fight against the cancer of corruption', *Envio*, 21, no. 248, 1–8
Goitia, F. (1998) 'Nada como la familia: El presidente nicaragüense cree que "siempre es más de fiar un pariente" y copa con ellos la Administración del país', *El País Digital*, 15/10/1998, www.udel.edu/leipzig/010498/eld151098.htm (last accessed 10/08/2004)
Gonzalez, D. (2003) 'Graft Aggravates Woes Plaguing Central America', *The New York Times*, February 25, 2003
Gutierrez, M. (2001) 'Central America, the Caribbean and Mexico', In *Global Corruption Report 2001* eds R. Hodess, J. Banfield and T. Wolfe, pp. 152–67, Transparency International, Berlin
Hernandez, J. (2001) 'Arduos efforts for Institutionality', *Envio* 20, no. 237, 47–54
IADB (Interamerican Development Bank) (1999a) *Central America after Hurricane Mitch: the Challenge of Turning a Disaster into an Opportunity*, www.iadb.org/regions/re2/consultative_group/backgrounder1.htm (last accessed 10/08/2004)
IADB (1999b) Workshop on Transparency and Governance held at the Stockholm meeting of the Consultative Group, 25–8 May 1999, www.iadb.org/regions/re2/consultative_group/groups/transparency_workshop_contents.htm (last accessed 10/08/2004)
ICEP (Instituto Centroamericano de Estudios Politicos) (2000) *Reporte Politico: Panorama Centroamericano, Balance politico del ano 1999 y principales tendencias para el 2000*. Ano XXIX, 3era. Epoca, Numero 155, January, Guatemala
IEN (various), accessed at www.ibw.com.ni/~ien/
Iglesias, E. (2000) *Intervencion del Presidente Enrique V. Iglesias en la Sesion Inaugural del Grupo Consultivo para la Republica de Nicaragua*, www.iadb.org/regions/re2/consultative_group/nicaragua.htm (last accessed 10/08/2004)
IMF/IDA (2000) Nicaragua: Joint Staff Assessment of the Interim Poverty Reduction Strategy Paper, 21/9/00 (IMF, Washington), poverty.worldbank.org/files/nicaraguajsa.pdf. (last accessed 10/08/2004)
Jeffrey, P. (1999) One Year Later, Central America still recovering from Hurricane Mitch, www.gbgm-umc.org/honduras/articles/hondoney.html (last accessed 10/08/2004)
Juarez, L. (2006a) 'Centro Carter alerta', *La Prensa* 15/11/06, Managua, Nicaragua
Juarez, L. (2006b) 'EyT: fraude en la RAAN', *La Prensa* 25/11/06, Managua, Nicaragua
Langseth, P. and Pezzulo, D. (2000) Corruption in Nicaragua: Analysis and Suggestions for next steps. Paper prepared for the Norwegian Agency for Development Cooperation (NORAD), www.norad.no/default.asp?V_DOC_ID=700 (last accessed 10/08/2004)
Latin America Data Base (LADB) (2000) 'Nicaragua: Appeals court frees Comptroller General', NotiCen: Central American & Caribbean Political & Economic Affairs, including Cuba, 13 January 2000
Marenco, E. (2000) 'DGI: "Bisnes familiars" y checazos', *La Prensa*, 3/4/00, Managua, Nicaragua
ODC (Officina de Distribucion de Causas) (2002) The full text of the case against Alemán and his associates can be found at: www.presidencia.gob.ni/

Presidencia/Files_index/Secretaria/Notas%20de%20Prensa/Presidente/2002/ag osto/070802/acusacion.htm (last accessed 10/08/2004)

The Organization of American States (OAS) (2004) Anti-Corruption website at www.oas.org/juridico/english/FightCur.html (last accessed 10/08/2004)

Ramirez S. (1999) *Adiós Muchachos: Una memoria de la revolución Sandinista.* Aguilar, México

Reno, W. (2000) 'Clandestine Economies, Violence and States in Africa', *Journal of International Affairs*, 53 (2), 433–59

Robinson, M. (ed.) (1998) *Corruption and Development.* Frank Cass, London

RN (Republic of Nicaragua) (1998) 'Letter of Intent to the IMF', 9 January 1998, www.imf.org/external/np/loi/010998.htm (last accessed 10/08/2004)

RN (1999a) *National Integrity Plan: a National Commitment for Transformation*, Paper presented at the Meeting of the Consultative Group for the Reconstruction and Transformation of Central America, Stockholm, Sweden, May 25–8

RN (1999b) *Ley de Contrataciones del Estado*, www.hacienda.gob.ni/sigfa/ sin_frames/ley_no_323/indice.htm (last accessed 10/08/2004)

RN (2000a) *Letter of Intent and Memorandum of Economic and Social Policies to the IMF*, 30 August 2000, www.imf.org/external/NP/LOI/2000/nic/01/INDEX.HTM (last accessed 10/08/2004)

RN (2000b) *Manual de Contabilidad*, www.hacienda.gob.ni/sigfa/tomoii/contabilidad/ (last accessed 10/08/2004)

Rodgers, M. (1999) *In debt to disaster: What happened to Honduras after Hurricane Mitch*, www.christian-aid.org.uk/indepth/9910inde/indebt1.htm (last accessed 10/08/2004)

Roiz Murillo, W. (2001) La verdadera historia de Enrique Bolaños G. *Bolsa de Noticias*, 5/09/2001, www.grupoese.com.ni/2001/bn/09/05/op2MN0905.htm (last accessed 10/08/2004)

Seligson, M. (1997) 'Nicaraguans talk about Corruption: A study of public opinion', report prepared for USAID Nicaragua, www.respondanet.com/english/gover nance/best_practices/Seligsons_First_Survey.PDF (last accessed 10/08/2004)

Seligson, M. (1999) 'Nicaraguans talk about Corruption: A follow-up study of public opinion', Report prepared for USAID Nicaragua www.respondanet. com/english/governance/best_practices/nicaragua_english.pdf (last accessed 10/08/2004)

Superintedencia de Bancos y Otras Instituciones Financieras (2000) *Informe del Sistema Financiera Nacional a Septiembre de 2000*, Managua: Nicaragua

Téllez, D. (2001) Nicaragua – Anteproyecto de Presupuesto General de la República 2001: Análisis. Managua, October 2001

Transparency International (1999), *Newsletter*, June, www.transparency.org/ newsletters/ (last accessed 10/08/2004)

Transparency International (2001) *Press release: New Index Highlights Worldwide Corruption Crisis*, www.transparency.org/documents/cpi/2001/cpi2001.html (last accessed 10/08/2004)

Trust for the Americas (2001) Transparency and Governance Initiative, www.trustfortheamericas.org/english/transparency/ (last accessed 10/08/2004)

Umanzor, S. (1999) 'Gobierno de Arnoldo Alemán salpicado de scándalos', *La Prensa*, Honduras C.A., 10/9/99

USAID (1998) FY 2000 R4. USAID document, Managua, Nicaragua, 10 September, 1998

USAID (1999) *A Handbook on Fighting Corruption*, www.usaid.gov/policy/ads/200/crpthdbk.pdf (last accessed 10/08/2004)

USAID (2000) LAC Regional: FY 2001 Program Description and Activity Data Sheets www.usaid.gov/pubs/bj2001/lac/lac/lac_ads.html (last accessed 10/08/2004)

USAID (2004) Nicaragua website, www.usaid.org.ni (last accessed 10/08/2004)

Vukelich, D. (1999) Exclusive: German Deputies to Protest Nicaraguan Aid Scandal at Stockholm Meeting. *On the Record* 8 (9), May, www.advocacynet.org/news_view/news_146.html (last accessed 10/08/2004)

World Bank (2004) Kenya, World Bank Take New Steps Against Corruption. News Release No: 2005/135/AFR, Nairobi, 27 October 2004. Available on-line at, web.worldbank.org/WBSITE/EXTERNAL/COUNTRIES/AFRICAEXT/KENYAEXTN/0,,contentMDK:20272567~menuPK:356516~pagePK:141137~piPK:141127~theSitePK:356509,00.html (last accessed 04/01/2005)

Part III
Development Policy and Anti-Corruption Initiatives

11
Fighting Public Sector Corruption in Ghana: Does Gender Matter?

Namawu Alhassan Alolo

Introduction

In pursuit of a sustainable anti-corruption strategy the development community has injected a plethora of reform ideas into the public sector of many African countries. Spearheaded by the World Bank, these attempts have met with modest results at best, as evidenced by the fact that current data suggests entrenched corruption in many African countries. More recently, the failure of previous anti-corruption strategies has led to the promotion of the integration of women as a possible panacea to reducing public sector corruption. In particular, the Bank is advocating for increased participation of women in the sector as a key component of any anti-corruption strategy. However, after the failure of previous strategies, legitimate questions abound: would the new gender sensitive approach to anti-corruption work? Are women necessarily less corrupt than men? This chapter draws on findings of a study in Ghana to argue that unless corrupt opportunities and networks are restrained, women may not prove any less corrupt than men, when exposed to public sector environments characterised by opportunities for corrupt behaviour. The chapter concludes that the policy to integrate women into the public sector, which some commentators refer to as 'gender mainstreaming',[1] will only be effective if implemented concurrently with other anti-corruption strategies.

Historical context of anti-corruption in the African public sector

Attempts at obliterating public sector corruption in many sub-Saharan African (SSA) countries have occasioned the implementation of numerous strategies ranging from legal, political to socio-ethic reforms. These reforms have, however, achieved limited success in reducing corruption, as borne out by current data suggesting entrenched corruption in many African countries (Lambsdorff, 2002). Failure of these anti-corruption strategies is provoking a gradual paradigmatic shift towards the integration of women into the public realm as a sustainable anti-corruption mechanism. Spearheaded by the World Bank (World Bank, 2001) and currently gaining currency in the development community, promoting women in the public realm is being advanced as a potential tool for curbing public sector corruption. As such, African Governments are being asked to integrate gender, which includes increasing women's representation in the public sector, into country development frameworks as a precondition for development assistance (World Bank, 2001). This is premised on the few studies positing that women are less corrupt than men (Dollar et al., 1999).

However, after the previous failure of anti-corruption strategies in SSA, one is tempted to wonder whether integrating women in the public sector is the key to public sector corruption. Indeed, is an increase in the presence of women likely to reduce corruption in public sector environments where networks and opportunities for corruption abound? Would women necessarily prove less corrupt in the public domain, in most SSA societies, where certain acts of corruption, such as nepotism and cronyism, are widely tolerated and respected? How would a researcher reconcile the methodological conundrum associated with undertaking research of this nature? This chapter summarises research undertaken on the gender–corruption nexus, which focused on two public sector institutions in Ghana – the Ghana Police Service (GPS) and the Ghana Education Service (GES).

Differential association and opportunity (DAO) theory

The Differential Association and Opportunity (DAO) theory, developed by Sutherland and Cressey (1977) was adopted to guide the research. This theory essentially explains the process through which an individual comes to engage in criminal behaviour. As its basic tenet, the theory argues that opportunity for criminal behaviour and networks that condone criminal behaviour are critical determinants of an individual's engagement in a criminal action. In other words, people who commit crime do not only have frequent interaction with those that condone such behaviour, but also have opportunities to do so (Sutherland and Cressey, 1977: 77–9). Based on DAO theory, the study's primary hypothesis was that gender differences will not exist in attitudes towards corruption when both sexes are exposed to similar opportunities and networks of corruption.

Methodologies of studying gender and corruption

In order to appreciate the methodological approach employed in the study, it is essential to highlight a few intractable methodological challenges confronting the study of gender and corruption. Some of these challenges that particularly confront researchers who seek the 'Holy Grail' of what will work to mitigate public sector corruption, are: 1) how does one measure the incidence and seriousness of corruption where the giver and the recipient are both accomplices? Owing to the fact that corruption, particularly bribery, involves mutually satisfying relations between the parties involved, it is often difficult to accurately capture its incidence or seriousness, as reportage is often low (Hellsten, 2003: 61). Another crucial challenge is 2) how to define corruption in much of SSA where legality and morality seem to converge markedly. In societies such as Ghana, where the collectivist culture requires public servants to bestow favours on kinship/community networks, as a moral obligation, officials are often faced with the dilemma of either succumbing to the requirements of their collectivist culture or submitting to the law. This creates a conflict between private and public requirements of morality. The biggest challenge to a researcher, therefore, is: do you define corruption to include or exclude actions that are pervasively accepted and respected, despite being at odds with the law? Finally, 3) is the research challenge of capturing the specificity of gender within a study of public sector corruption.

The author used a sample survey of 138 responses from public officials, aware of possible social desirability bias where respondents attempt to say what they think will put themselves in the best light. As the survey investigated male and female officials' attitudes towards corruption, there was a high probability of officials disclaiming corrupt practices in favour of socially desirable responses, biasing the study, and causing individuals to either under-report or over-report their actions (Nederhof, 1985: 263–80). There are two factors that account for distorted responses towards socially desirable traits. The first factor involves 'self-deception' (Paulhus, 1984: 598–609) where an individual actually believes an inaccurate statement about him/herself (Millham and Kellogg, 1980: 445–57), which has little compensating methodological response (Nederhof, 1985: 263–80). The second factor – 'other-deception' – involves a deliberately false response from an individual as some form of impression management to avoid his/her personality being judged (Millham and Kellogg, 1980: 445–57). Fortunately, because the 'other-deception' is a situational determinant of social desirability bias, the researcher can influence and manipulate the situation to moderate the impact of the 'other-deception' bias. In my study, the most effective method employed to reduce social desirability bias was the use of self-administered, anonymous questionnaires, which eliminate social cues by isolating study subjects from the interviewer/researcher. The whole survey instrument was further validated by triangulation, which included qualitative interviewing, focus group discussion and a public perception survey.

Are men more likely to use public funds for private gain than women?

To answer this question, data was collected on respondents' attitudes towards a vignette of a hypothetical Chief Director who hired a cheap contractor for a state building project in order to use the difference in cost relative to a more expensive contractor, to pay for his son's medical treatment. The data revealed that a total of 55 per cent of male officials and 37 per cent of female officials agreed with the hypothetical Chief Director's behaviour. Using Chi-Square statistical technique to explore differences in male–female attitudes towards the use of public funds for private gain in the whole survey, the analysis revealed a significant result. This implies that the proportion of male officials that claim they would use public funds for private gain are significantly higher than the proportion of female officials who claim they would do so.

  Since this result conflicted with the initial assumption of the study, that no difference would be apparent, it was crucial to interrogate the interview data to triangulate this result. However, interestingly, the interview data refuted the statistical result, as both male and female officials supported the action of the hypothetical Chief Director in interview, asserting their high probability of acting in a similar manner, especially where job security is not threatened. This underscores the importance of opportunities for criminal behaviour as argued in the DAO theory. With the presence of opportunities, such as weak monitoring and evaluation systems, both male and female officials are likely to use public funds to resolve private financial difficulties. The question remained, however, of how these behaviours were variously justified, and whether this justification was itself gendered.

Justifications for misappropriation of public funds: gendered dialectics?

The interviews revealed fundamental differences in male and female justifications for supporting the corrupt action of the hypothetical Chief

Director. While the core issue was the fact that the Chief Director's job security was not threatened, most male officials focused their reasons on the cost saved, by hiring a cheap contractor, while the majority of females focused on the Chief Director's ability to save a life. Some male respondents rationalised that by engaging the service of a low cost contractor, the director was, more or less, at liberty to use the difference in cost for other purposes. Thus,

> why cry foul when the building was effectively executed? Once the building was well constructed, there is no cause for alarm. After all, auditors are not checking him and he is able to save some money. (Mr DD)

Conversely, an almost universal justification provided by female officials for their support for the Chief Director was the fact that he was able to save his son's life. To many female officials, so long as there is a life at stake, the Chief Director should employ any means to secure funds, even if such means deviate from legal, or conventional methods. The fact that the Chief Director was able to minimise the risks of being caught and punished was an added advantage and tantamount to 'killing two birds with one stone', as 'human life is more valuable than a project. Nobody will sit and watch their son die when they have an alternative means to save them' (Ms BE).

Of course, most officials engaged in misappropriation of public funds for private gain will continually provide 'good' justifications for their actions, but under the general rubric of corruption in Ghana, are these 'good enough' reasons for misappropriating public funds when opportunities exist? When these questions were asked, respondents were quick to defend their position, opining that low government salaries compel even the most ethical official to bend the rules every now and then. Some argued, for instance, that had the hypothetical Chief Director's salary been sufficient, he would not have had to delve into public funds.

To summarise, it is evident that both male and female officials support the use of public funds for private gain, though their justifications differ. It should, however, be noted that the binary distinction in male–female justifications underscores a masculinised and feminised construction of behaviour. The notion of gender constructing women as compassionate, sensitive and emotional, while men, by contrast, are logical and objective (Steans, 1998: 11) is clearly depicted in these justifications, as male officials stressed the cost factor while female officials emphasised the life factor. Thus gender behavioural differences were embedded in polarised significations. While the majority of psychosexual development discourses tend to posit these behavioural differences as innate or natural (Freud, 1961), feminist social theorists have long held behavioural differences to be culturally mediated and socially situated (Chowdrow, 1978: 43–5, Steans, 1998: 11–18).

Misuse of public office for private sexual gain

A vignette was also designed to capture male and female attitudes towards the use of sex to transcend public sector barriers, including its use for gaining promotion. This scenario was motivated by informal discussions held with experts on the anti-corruption campaign and a wide range of public servants in Ghana. When asked about their opinion on the integration of women into the public sector as a possible anti-corruption remedy, many argued that for most women, apart from its traditional definition as embezzlement, bribery and cronyism, corruption also manifests in the politics of sexuality: the pressure to supply sex to a man because of his public status for his private pleasure. These discussions motivated the inclusion of a hypothetical scenario where a competent long serving female official, called Derby, was denied promotion by her boss until she sexually 'enticed' him to provide it. When respondents were asked to affirm their moral agreement with the use of sex to obtain job promotion, 58 per cent of male officials and 48 per cent of female officials agreed that it was acceptable, although these figures proved statistically insignificant for this sample size.

Again, however, during the interviews, the male/female difference dissipated, with the majority of male and female officials supporting the use of sex-for-promotion on the basis of a perceived prior injustice experienced by Derby. They asserted that since she was capable of the task, she should stop at virtually nothing to prove her capabilities. It should be mentioned here that despite convergence at this fact, a discernible difference emerged in emphasis between male and female officials. While many female officials, generally, highlighted the hierarchical barrier placed on Derby's advancement, the majority of male officials emphasised her capabilities and competence as the overriding factor in their agreement with her action. For most females,

> she [Derby] deserves to use any means to achieve her aim because of the duration of her service without promotion; who knows if she would have been promoted if she waited longer? (Ms GG)

Other female officials lamented,

> this is the plight of most women. What to do to stop it, I cannot pro-
> vide an answer. It is an unfortunate situation for women, yet it is very
> common and we have to deal with these things often.

On the other hand, for some male officials, Derby's action was the 'case of
the end justifies the means, as long as the end is good, then I support it'.
To other male officials, this was the case of 'sell your mother for power.
After you have obtained the power, use it to rescue your mother and
punish her buyers' (Mr CK).

This evidence lends credence to the fact that when faced with difficult
circumstances, and when appropriate opportunities exist, men and women
will act in similarly corrupt ways, though their justifications and approaches
may differ. Corruption emerges in this research as a function of opportunity, with femininity as one weapon among many, representing an
opportunity for females to advance either personal or career-related goals.
Valorising[2] women's bodies, which convey sexual promise for men, as the
locus of female power underscores the theoretical assumption that opportunities are a prerequisite for corrupt behavior. The fact that some women
perceive their bodies as an opportunity to advance personal or career-
related goals when necessitated by circumstances reinforces this point.

In Ghana, women have traditionally been marginalised in the public
sector, through masculinist construction of the wage sector, with ramifications in the sexual division of labour, where females serve in junior
capacities while males serve in senior capacities. The implication for some
women is the use of body politics to transcend these socially constructed
barriers in the sector. Explorations into why women have traditionally
been marginalised in the public sector point to transhistorical factors that
'essentialise' (stereotype) women as less aggressive, passive, submissive,
indecisive, lacking in confidence and thus less capable overall (Weedon,
1999: 10). These essentialist tropes are socially constructed, serving to
legitimise and perpetuate female subordination.

The gendered use of public positions in return for kickbacks

In order to explore whether there was a gendered distribution in the use
of public office for private monetary reward (kickbacks/gifts), officials were
asked to indicate their agreement or disagreement with the conduct of a

hypothetical Tax Officer, called Seas, who underestimated taxes for female traders, as he felt their tax code was too high, in return for which he received generous 'gifts' from the traders. A full 71 per cent of male officials and 67 per cent of female officials supported the tax officer's use of his position to grant favours in return for gifts. The difference was not statistically significant at this sample size, and interview statements included both male and female officials justifying their support for the Tax Officer's action.

However, although both male and female officials supported Seas' reciprocal gesture, the interviews unearthed a discernible difference in justifications provided by male and female officials. While the majority of male officials supported Seas for his mutually beneficial act, female officials justified their support for him on the basis of his assistance to the women traders. To the majority of male officials, by Seas' action, the government at least receives a fraction of the taxes which otherwise would have been defaulted by the traders. The traders are able to pay what they can afford without risking bankruptcy and Seas himself is handsomely rewarded by the traders. Some male officials believed that since the Constitution, which is the only institutional framework currently addressing public corruption in Ghana, fails to stipulate whether or not hospitality is lawful, Seas' action could therefore be subsumed under the general rubric of hospitality, which is constitutionally neutral.

Conversely, most female officials based their argument on Seas' sympathy for the traders. Some argued that the gender dynamics and socio-economic realities in Ghana are harsher for female traders than their male counterparts. To many, the dual roles of women, where they undertake all domestic chores *and* participate in the trading sector, conspire against women's effective generation of profits relative to men. The explanation offered was that female identified-roles have been the bane of women's economic marginalisation, leading to females being doubly disadvantaged.[3] First, by fulfilling their domestic obligations of managing the home in addition to trading, these traders are overburdened. Second, as these traders are mandated by their gender to execute household production functions, such as cooking, fetching water and other domestic chores, they are often last to open their shops/stalls and first to return home. Not only do female traders lose important customers in the process, but they also make marginal profits relative to their male counterparts. Hence, they, the female officials, pledge their support for Seas' 'positive' use of his position. After all,

> no one would like to do business and lose, so if payment of high taxes will leave the women traders bankrupt, especially after numerous petitions, then it [Seas' action] is the best alternative. (Ms DR)

That most female officials justified their support for Seas on the basis of sympathy does not entirely come as a surprise, as sympathy itself is feminised in Ghana, where social duty dictates that females should explicitly express sympathy and compassion for people, more so in desperate situations. Transgressing this gendered trait risks being stigmatised and stereotyped as a 'male in female body', implying an abnormal or deviant gender behaviour. Respondents would be variously conscious of the social construction of these gendered behaviours and sentiments, but simultaneously were acting as vehicles of gendered power relations. The evidence here suggests that rather than radically challenging the male-centric existing order, many Ghanaian women have not only accepted the status quo, but have also provided a support system for the nurturance of the gender system. It is not therefore surprising that Marxist feminists, among others, have criticised women for contributing to their own subjugation by supporting their roles as housewives and contributing to the maintenance of an exploitative socio-economic order (Abbot and Wallace, 1990: 147). Differing justifications aside, however, both male and female officials exhibited similar attitudinal tendencies towards supporting corruption in this scenario.

Gender differences in the use of public position to grant favours to kinship networks

A scenario was designed in which a hypothetical Chief Director, called Denzel, was pressurised by family and friends to use her position, as state protocol, to obtain visas for them to travel abroad, a scenario which strongly echoes with a key contemporary pressure on public officials in reality. In Ghana, where society's principle yardstick for measuring successful bureaucrats is the extent to which he or she uses their position to extend favours to kith and kin, it was important to design this scenario to capture male and female officials' attitudes towards societal pressure to use public positions unlawfully. When asked to register their agreement/disagreement with the hypothetical Chief Director's conduct, a total of 50.7 per cent of male officials and 47.7 per cent of female officials agreed with the use of public position to obtain visas for relatives, a difference not statistically significant.

This result is corroborated by the interview data, as male and female officials defended their support for the Chief Director, although again, their underlying reasons generally differed. Most male officials generally focused their reasons on the problems of obtaining visas for Western countries, with some arguing that recent tightening of controls to Western countries has led to denials of visas for many Ghanaians, regardless of whether, or not, they meet the visa requirement. As a result, they were willing to use their positions to influence visa decisions when called upon, as captured in this statement:

> I would do the same if I were in her position even if it seems wrong. For me, the reasons given for refusing visas to most western countries are frivolous and therefore I will see it as a way of getting back at them . . . Again, I have to meet the expectations of my family so in some instances where I have the opportunity, I will do it. (Mr TJ)

Female officials, on the other hand, generally placed their responses within the wider social problems faced by public servants. To many, a public servant cannot disconnect from societal pressures with its collectivist concept of 'help-thy-neighbour'. To some, the concept of 'help-thy-neighbour' (as I have chosen to call it) is a social responsibility bestowed on public servants by virtue of their ability to influence decisions. Captured concisely,

> Denzel is fulfilling her social responsibility to her community. This could have been in any other area, so if her people need visas, so be it. (Ms SS)

Some female officials asserted that though the 'help-thy-neighbour' concept is a social requirement for both male and female public servants, the impact on women who defy it is generally more profound than men, due to the stigma associated with women who transgress these familial/societal expectations. Women who refuse to compromise their positions for societal or familial obligations are often stereotyped as wicked, evil, 'iron lady', 'stone cold', and so on. As these 'unfeminine' attributes are perpetuated over time, some women tend to internalise the repercussions of defying the social system, and as such, will employ all means to fulfil their societal obligations, even if they deviate from public sector ethics.

Unlike women, 'wickedness' and 'iron-heartedness' are judged as masculine traits, and as such, expected of the male gender. In fact, these traits are sometimes celebrated as attributes of a 'proper' man. As a result, men may not experience the same degree of social sanction and disciplining as women, within the gender system. To a particular female, even though there is some element of abuse of public office . . . the socio-cultural environment of the Ghanaian is such that a woman must be helpful to her relatives both close and extended. If she [the Chief Director] failed to help her people, she will be deemed as wicked, and no woman wants to be called wicked, at least in the Ghanaian sense. (Ms KL)

These assertions underscore the importance of societal obligations and expectations on public servants, which may interplay to influence attitudes of both male and female officials towards corruption.

Gendered reciprocal favours in old-student networks

A scenario of an old students' association, which relies on reciprocal gestures to fast track employment opportunities for members and their relations, was designed to capture male–female attitudes towards nepotism within networks. A total of 41 per cent of male officials and 48 per cent of female officials generally agreed with reciprocal gestures of extending favours to those linked to the alumni network. This result corresponds with the interview data, although, unlike in previous scenarios, responses here were not gendered. During the interviews, many officials, including those who had originally disagreed on the questionnaire, supported the action of the alumni claiming that such a network should exist to support members based on 'trust, loyalty and individual empowerment' (Mr GM). Some argued that not only does their action foster stronger bonds and solidarity among members, but it also guarantees members a vibrant support mechanism for desperate times. Put concisely in an axiom, 'when your brother is on the pawpaw tree, there is no reason why you should eat unripe pawpaw' (Mr HM). This implies that once a person has links with networks that can support him or her, he or she should not be allowed to 'suffer' when the networks can assist, as:

society is made up of groups and associations which are necessary evils that should never be done away with. We all need associations to protect our common interest. (Mr WW)

These assertions demonstrate the importance of networks in providing a context for corruption, validating the research's original hypothesis that opportunity and networks are critical for an individual's engagement in corruption.

Same outcomes, different meanings

Indeed, opportunities and networks of corruption are critical for both male and female likelihoods of engaging in corruption, while simultaneously conditioning patterns of gendered justification. Gender informs male and female attitudes towards corruption, while differing pressures by sex are motivators of corrupt behaviour, as men and women try to conform to (different) societal expectations and obligations in the conduct of public duties. Thus, while both men and women support corrupt behaviours, their underlying reasons might differ in accordance with their gender roles, expectations and obligations. For instance, feminised traits, such as sympathy and compassion, underpin female officials' justifications for corruption, while masculinised traits, such as objectiveness and thirst for money, underline most of male officials' justifications for supporting corruption. In both cases, rather than being allowed to shape their own behaviour, men and women see themselves as fixed in socio-cultural and political environments that dictate their roles and responsibilities in accordance with their gender.

These findings do not only alert us to the elasticity between normality and abnormality caused by gender in Ghana, but also highlight the extent to which men and women have internalised their gendered behavioural traits. In essence, what is perceived as normal for men is grossly abnormal for women, yet, rather than defying these genderised traits, most female officials in the study, and for that matter many Ghanaian women, have internalised gendered expectation and behaviour, and thus perpetuate these understandings. This, in itself, conditions corrupt behaviour in women.

Based on these findings, this chapter illustrates a model of corrupt behaviour in male and female public officials, which is illustrated in Figure 11.1. This model of corrupt behaviour argues that corrupt behaviour (what I do) is a function of opportunity, as perceived by the individual, networks (who engage and condone corrupt behaviours) and societal expectations. While the underlying justifications for supporting or engaging in corruption may or may not be motivated by the need to conform and fulfill gender stereotypic obligations, this research suggests that there is a strong role for these latter in providing a legitimising language and conceptual framework for participants, conditioned by gender. However, overall, this research concludes that significant differences do not exist in male and female likely participation rates when exposed to like, hypothetical, opportunities and networks of corruption derived from scenarios typical of Ghana, where nepotism and cronyism are widely tolerated and respected.

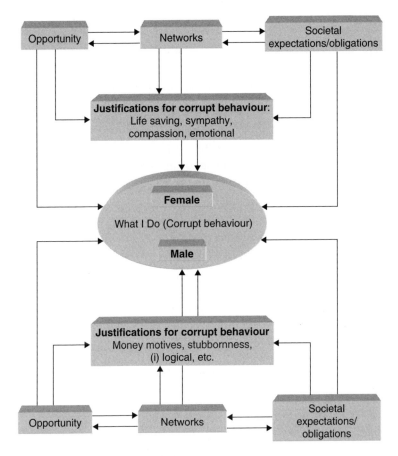

Figure 11.1:   Model for corrupt behaviour

Conclusion

Although this is not intended as a model for all public servants in sub-Saharan Africa, these findings may have resonance regionally, subject to the normal caveats on the limitations of case study research. There has been, to date, little work on a theory of gender and corruption (for overviews see Dollar et al., 1999, Swamy et al., 2001, Hung En, 2003), such that this study represents an addition to a small body of research within the gender–corruption discourse. It is clear already, however, that differences in the way men and women view their roles and social obligations will have a conditioning effect on their propensity to participate in corrupt behaviour in the workplace. By deduction, we can argue that understanding gendered motivations will be key to reducing corrupt behaviour in the public sector, even though the headline propensity to participate in corruption may be similar for men and women. In other words, merely increasing the numbers of women, though laudable in itself, who are public sector workers, will not necessarily decrease the incidence of corruption in and of itself, as the World Bank maintains: women are not a panacea for anti-corruption. Promoting women in the public sector as an anti-corruption strategy is not likely to reduce corruption unless corroborated with efforts at limiting opportunities and networks of corruption, as well as being accompanied by a wider challenge to address gender in societal relations more generally.

It should be emphasised that it is not the aim of this chapter to challenge any policy to integrate women into the public sector. Indeed, integrating women into all levels of public sector institutions renders development processes more complete and inclusive, is normatively correct, and translates into more vibrant and dynamic societies. An affirmative action to incorporate women into the public sector is the long awaited remedy to male-biased governance. Advocating for greater promotion of women in the public sector, should not, however, detract from the interrogation of implicit essentialised assumptions which are being made when this is unduly extended to other policy objectives, such as anti-corruption, such as that women have higher standards of honesty and ethics. It is not a simple or easily deduced step that more women will unproblematically lead to less corruption. In certain scenarios they will be less honest than men, depending on highly contextual, and gendered, pressures.

Hellsten (2003: 68) argues that in an entrenched institutional environment where social ethics are being challenged,

> those who . . . try to promote the public good and expose corruption and other forms of unprofessional behaviour may . . . find themselves in an unbearable position. Not going along with the commonly accepted unprofessional and corrupt practices may cost them their job, their social 'respect', their promotion . . . Reversed social ethics make those who fight against corruption easily . . . be seen as 'bad guys' who break 'the circle of trust' instead of seeing them as the 'good guys' who are the ones promoting the public interest.

This vivid picture portrayed by Hellsten underscores the fact that without restraining corrupt opportunities and networks, and without changing gender relations, women are likely to face all sorts of obstacles in serving as anti-corruption agents.

Notes

1. This author sees this as a problematic term because of its multiple uses and nebulous meaning, and will avoid it.
2. The use of valorising in this context is adopted from feminist discourse and defined as 'to give value to' or to 'privilege' (Andermahr et al., 1997: 286).
3. Feminists, particularly radical feminists, have challenged the feminisation of motherhood roles and the domestification of women on the basis that they are used to legitimise and perpetuate female subjugation and oppression at both the private and the public level (Abbot and Wallace, 1990: 86, Steans, 1998: 11–12).

References

Abbot, P. and Wallace, C. (1990), *An Introduction to Sociology: Feminist Perspectives,* London, Routledge

Andermahr, S. et al. (1997), *A Glossary of Feminist Theory,* London, Arnold

Bradburn, N. M. and Sudman, S. (1979), *Improving Interview Methods and Questionnaire Design,* San Francisco, Jossey-Bass

Chowdrow, N. (1978), *The Reproduction of Mothering: Psychoanalysis and Sociological Inquiry,* Berkeley, University of California Press

Dollar, D., Fishman, R. and Gatti, R. (1999), 'Are Women Really the "Fairer" Sex? Corruption and Women in Government'. *World Bank Working Paper Series: Policy Research Report on Gender and Development,* World Bank: Washington DC, Available online: www.worldbank.org/gender/prr/wp4.pdf. 03/11/03, 15:25

Edwards, A. L. (1970), *The Measurement of Personality Traits by Scale Sand Inventories,* New York, Holt, Reinhard and Winston

Freud, S. (1961), *The Standard Edition of the Complete Psychological Works of Sigmund Freud.* Strachey, J. (transl. & ed.), London, Hogarth Press

Hellsten, S. (2003), 'Trust me! My Hands are Dirty Also: Institutionalized Corruption and Competing Codes of Public and Private Ethics'. *Professional Ethics,*11: 1. 60–71

Hung En, S. (2003), 'Fairer Sex or Fairer System?: Gender and Corruption Revisited', *Social Forces,* 82, 2, 703–23

Lambsdorff, G. L. (2002) 'Corruption Perceptions Index', *Global Corruption,* 27/11. Available online: www.globalcorruptionreport.org/download/gcr2003/24_Data_and_research.pdf. 2/02/04

Millham, J. and Kellogg, R. W. (1980), 'Need For Social Approval: Impression Management of Self Deception?' *Journal of Research in Personality,* 14, 445–57

Nederhof, A. J. (1985), 'Methods of Coping with Social Desirability Bias: a Review', *European Journal of Social Psychology,* 15, 263–80

Paulhus, D. L. (1984), 'Two Component Models of Socially Desirable Responding', *Journal of Personality and Social Psychology,* 46, 598–609

Smith, W. H. (1981), *Strategies of Social Science Research: the Methodological Imagination.* 2edn, Englewood Cliffs, Prentice-Hall

Steans, J. (1998), *Gender and International Relations: an Introduction,* New Brunswick, Rutgers University Press

Sutherland, E. and Cressey, D. R. (1977), *Principles of Criminology,* 8th edn, Chicago, J. B. Lippincott

Swamy, A. Knack, S., Lee, Y. and Azfa, O. (2001), 'Gender and Corruption'. *Journal of Development Economics*, 64, 25–55

Weedon, C. (1999), *Feminism, Theory and the Politics of Difference,* Oxford, Blackwell

World Bank (2001), *Engendering Development through Equality in Rights, Resources and Voice,* World Bank: Washington DC, 2001, Available online: www-wds. worldbank.org/servlet/WDSContentServer/WDSP/IB/2001/03/01/000094946_ 01020805393496/Rendered/PDF/multi_page.pdf, 5/06/04

12
Upgrading Democracy in Mozambique: the Question of Party and Election Finance

Bruno Wilhelm Speck[1]

In December 2004 Mozambique held national multiparty elections for the President and National Assembly (*Assembleia da República*), ten years on from the first elections which signalled the end of the long civil war. The opponents are still the same as they were in the time of armed struggle: *Frente de Libertação de Moçambique* (*Frelimo*), the organisation which fought from the early 1960s for independence from Portugal, and subsequently held political power from 1975; and *Resistência Nacional Moçambicana* (*Renamo*), a movement of armed rebels against the *Frelimo* regime, initially sponsored by neighbouring countries, but more latterly emerging as a gathering point for internal opposition to the regime (Manning, 1998). The General Peace Agreement (*Acordo Geral de Paz*) was signed in 1992 by the emissaries of both parties in conflict, and initiated a new era of struggle for political power in Mozambique by the erstwhile warring factions. A one party regime changed to a pluralist and competitive political system (see Carbone, 2003), initiated unilaterally by *Frelimo* when the party abandoned its Marxist-Leninist one party doctrine in 1989, and later institutionalised in the new Constitution of November 1990. Given Mozambique's historical record, this move from war to peaceful power struggle, although with constrictions and setbacks, is a radical step forward.[2]

However, after a decade of peaceful power struggle at polling stations, the quality of Mozambique's democracy is still at issue (Cabaço, 1996). The process of political competition itself is still open to criticism, with international and national observers mainly questioning the openness and fairness of competition in the short run due to allegations of vote rigging (Hanlon, 2000). But a level playing field embraces issues beyond the process of voting and polling, and includes the provision of resources for political competitors, namely the funding of party organisations and electoral campaigns. This chapter reviews the question of political finance in Mozambique, focusing in particular on the 2004 elections, by illuminating the economic, social and political context. It argues that the concentrated economic and political power of *Frelimo*, and the influence and nepotism of its associated business and personal networks, undermines somewhat the quality of political competition and democracy more broadly.

Political party financing

In contemporary democracies parties and candidates resort to a wide range of possible funding sources, including candidates' personal resources, contributions from private donors and public subsidies (on southern Africa, see Southhall and Wood, 1998). Mobilisation of private or public funds for political competition can be an important step in fostering democratic competition by funding new competitors, where the political class is restricted to a small and wealthy elite. But there are risks for democracy: assuming financial support to candidates and parties influences the outcome of elections, large donations from individual or corporate donors undermines the democratic principle of equity ('one member, one vote'). Another risk is individual donors demanding compensation for their financial support, expecting favours such as contracts, access to information or favourable legislation, once the candidates they financed are in office. Meanwhile, allocating public resources to finance political competition can be supportive to democracy, but at the same time opens a Pandora's box of possible manipulations through or against the law. Thus, norms and rules on political finance are important guidelines for a political system to develop either towards competitiveness and openness or towards plutocracy and corruption.

Public political finance in Mozambique

The founding fathers of Mozambique's democracy produced rules on party financing, as a core element of the Rome Peace Process in 1992, when the military enemies decided in detail on the framework for political competition. Firstly, the parties agreed on elements of public funding in a number of fields. *Renamo* was entitled to support in order to have its combatants leave the battlefield and reintegrate into society. Complementary to this, the movement received subsidies in order to build up party structures and get democratic development on track. A second line of subsidies was directed at public institutions responsible for the organisation of the electoral process and conflict resolution as well as support to civil society oversight.[3] Finally, the Peace Agreement mentions all three versions of public support to parties, namely state subsidies, tax exemption and access to media, without specifying permanent amounts, but with clear and precise definition of the criteria for distribution of funds (with party funds proportional to parliamentary representation, and campaign support following criteria of equity). In addition, the peace agreement included financial transparency as one of the necessary requirements for party activity, although this has not been implemented.[4]

However, neither the Constitution enacted in November 1990 nor the revised Constitution of November 2004 mentions the issue of party or election finance.[5] Thus, the provisions within the peace protocols, signed in Rome 1990–92, the Party Law (*Lei dos Partidos Políticos*, 1991) and the Electoral Law (*Lei Eleitoral*, 1993) and its revisions (principally *Lei Eleitoral*, 2004), remain those by which funding of parties and elections are regulated.[6] Parties enjoy budget support in elections based on the number of candidates (amended later to include weighting according to representatives elected (*Lei Eleitoral*, Art. 36)), and free access to public radio and TV in election periods and tax exemption. Outside of elections parties also receive support proportional to their representation in the Assembly (*Lei dos Partidos*, Art. 17). Resources for presidential elections have to be allocated equally between all running candidates.

While Mozambique's model of supporting electoral campaigns sets incentives for new competitors by granting equal access to resources for all candidates, party finance is based on the idea of continuity, with only those represented in the *Assembleia da República* having access to continuous public funding outside electoral campaigns (the two main parties receive about 1.5 million USD per year).[7] Rewarding past electoral success as criteria for allocating public resources to parties tends to preserve the political landscape from innovations, although small parties can still reply on periodic campaign finance. Meanwhile the indirect public subsidies make parties exempt from customs duties and other taxes (*Lei dos Partidos*, Art. 15), while free public broadcasting access is regulated by the National Election Commission (*Comissão Nacional de Eleições, CNE*) (*Lei Eleitoral*, Art. 29).

Private political finance

Despite detailed rulings on access to public funds, the Rome Protocols did not touch the question of private donations to political competition,

which is contrary to other countries where rigid rules on private donations often exclude risk groups like public contractors, establish ceilings
for the amount of contributions or limit the campaign expenditure of
candidates. The *Lei dos Partidos* prohibits donations from state institutions
(except official funding), from foreign governments and from private
institutions of public utility (*Lei dos Partidos*, Art. 19), while *Lei Eleitoral*
follows these norms, except the last category, wherein, in fact, NGOs are
explicitly included as a legal source for campaign finance (*Lei Eleitoral*,
Art. 35, 40). Outside of these limited prohibitions, *Lei Eleitoral* defines as
legal revenues for campaign finance: candidates' and parties' own resources;
donations from national or foreign parties; from national or foreign
NGOs; from citizens and foreigners; campaign fundraising activities;
and public budget resources (*Lei Eleitoral*, Art. 35). Legal sources of party
funding listed by the *Lei dos Partidos* include membership fees; donations
and legacies; public funding, and a generous fourth category of 'other
sources' (*Lei dos Partidos*, Art. 17).

The Rome Protocols (1992) mention transparency requirements, stat-
ing parties have to render accounts on their funds and donations on an
annual base. The *Lei dos Partidos* obliges parties to report annually on
accounts, including detailed information on funding sources and disbursements; to publish the accounts in the official gazette; to register
before a public institution individually all donations and legacies; and
to hold internal records on all kind of properties (*Lei dos Partidos*, Art. 16,
18, 19, 20, 21). Meanwhile, the *Lei Eleitoral* states candidates and parties
have to render accounts on all revenues and expenditures, until 60 days
after the official announcement of the election result (*Lei Eleitoral*, Arts.
37), at which point the *CNE* has another 60 days to decide on the regularity of accounts and publish its decision in the official gazette *Boletin
da República* (*Lei Eleitoral*, Art. 39).

However, record keeping remains poor, not least because the regulatory
institutions of the electoral process as a whole – the *Secretariado Técnico
de Administração Eleitoral* (*STAE*), a branch of the government responsible for organising the electoral process, and the *CNE* – are not entirely
independent. The *STAE* is under the strong influence of the administration, including the heritage of a bias towards *Frelimo*, while the *CNE*
is a political institution *per se*, following the logic of proportional
representation of political parties for its membership, and following the
majority rule for decision-making typical of *Frelimo* politics in other institutions. Similarly, while Lei Eleitoral 2004 allows for sanctions, it is difficult to
identify any application since they came into place, while even the theoretical sanctions do not include imprisonment or fines; loss of registration

or representation, or the loss of public subsidies. Deprivation of the right to access public radio and TV free of charge during the electoral campaign seems the only deterrent against the abuse of campaign fund reporting.

Political finance in practice: party and election finance in 2004

Personal wealth

In a historical view, a candidate's own wealth has played an important role in political success, with active participation in politics remaining an occupation restricted to the upper social strata until quite recently, a situation which still prevails in many democracies today. Costs were carried by politicians who live 'for politics' and not 'off politics', in Max Weber's famous distinction. The electoral system, however, can mediate the extent of influence of private wealth. For example, in proportional elections with closed lists, individual candidates tend to play a minor role, since citizens place their vote for party lists, not for a person, which dilutes the benefits of personal engagement and the incentives for disbursement of private funds. Indeed, an important role of political parties is to facilitate the professionalisation of politics, and allow candidates to participate using party, rather than their own, funds.

In Mozambique both the social structure and the institutional environment conspire against the extensive use of individual private funds for politics. First, the economy and society are still stamped by recent history, including the nationalisation of private property. Although the country reversed this process step by step with a privatisation programme starting in the 1990s, Mozambique is still a very poor country, where doing business depends largely on the state. There is no large, powerful and thriving economic class of businesspeople with a vocation to engage in politics and lever their campaign resorting to private wealth. The second reason for the minor role personal wealth plays in politics is that legislative elections in Mozambique are based on large circumscriptions where candidates run for election on a closed list: parties rather than candidates are the centre of the campaign.[8]

However, the presidential campaign follows a different logic. With candidates running against each other candidates could invest personal wealth into the campaign, thus augmenting the chances of electoral success. Moreover, in the 2004 elections at least one of the candidates for the presidency, Armando Guebuza running for the *Frelimo* party is regarded as one of the richest businessmen in his country. However, since his party has substantial access to other resources, as shown below, the possibility that Guebuza injected personal funds in his campaign seems remote.

Membership funds

Indeed, in Mozambique only the ruling party *Frelimo* is able to raise a considerable amount of funds, which gives it some electoral advantage. The party has emerged from a cadre organisation into a mass party, with the number of party members rising from 100,000 before the political perestroika at the end of the 1980s to two million members today. Simultaneously, the party made a systematic effort to raise funds from party members, which now play a significant role for the funding of ordinary costs of the *Frelimo* party organisation [Field interviews, Mozambique, October 2004].

In many countries, parties charge special contributions from party members who hold public office, although this system is often criticised as compromising public service meritocracy and causing indirect subsidy. In Mozambique, there is no explicit spoils system in place at *Frelimo*, but the proper definition of membership fees (corresponding to one day's work in a month, about 5 per cent of salary) allows for a transfer to the party. Using this system the *Frelimo* party, with large representation in the state apparatus, guarantees part of its funding with public resources, estimated at 1,500,000 USD per year (Field interviews, Mozambique, October 2004). Meanwhile, by comparison, membership fees in other parties play only a symbolic role because their members are virtually banned from the state apparatus: since the state is a considerable employer in Mozambique, the capacity of citizens not employed by the state to make contributions to parties and other civic organisations is limited. In fact, most NGOs report that grassroots funding by private contribution to civic or voluntary organisations is not feasible in the country, given its extreme poverty rate. Even *Renamo*'s membership fees achieve only a symbolic value, though it is the second largest party. Members pay a monthly fee of just 1.000 Meticais, half a dollar per year.[9]

Commercial activities

Another source of party funds is commercial activities and sales of services to members. Once again, in Mozambique, *Frelimo* is the sole organisation with incipient experience in the field of quasi-economic activities. Although there is no consensus on whether *Frelimo* makes productive investments, a variety of sources reported that it holds real estate, including an impressive party headquarters in Maputo which is partially commercially rented. Information on the political transition in the city of Beira, one of the few places where the opposition seized power after winning the municipal elections in 2003, corroborates this information. When *Frelimo* yielded control over the administration, the party argued a number of buildings used by the local government were owned by *Frelimo* and thus charged the administration, now run by the former opposition, with rental costs. One analyst stated *Frelimo* has wide ranging economic activities and has centralised its investments in a holding company, although this remains uncorroborated.

Renamo also possesses some real estate, in the form of party headquarters in the capital and provinces. Some of these assets stem from the trust fund, responsible for financing *Renamo*'s transformation from a movement of armed rebels to a political party in the early 1990s. The *Renamo* party headquarters in the capital Maputo is a two-floor building with modest facilities, inconspicuously fitting into a middle-class neighbourhood and thus in sharp contrast with the impressive *Frelimo* building. There are no signs that *Renamo* or any other party, except *Frelimo*, is able to raise funds from (legal) economic activities.

Private donations

A fourth category of sources are donations from private donors. Again, international and national observers agree on the special position of *Frelimo* as the sole party with broad access to private sponsors, a position linked to the special protection the state – under *Frelimo* leadership – can give to private entrepreneurs. The group of private donors willing to contribute to party funds includes party members owning successful economic undertakings and willing to 'pay back' for their achievements. State credits to party members and friends of the party are just one example of economic benefits distributed selectively, and although subsequent repayments to the party are not documented, they are part of the logic of the system. For example, an analysis of state credits by a political scientist shows how these have been channelled selectively to party members (Mosse, 2004). One prominent beneficiary is Armando Guebuza, running for the presidency, who received a 2.5 million USD loan at interest rates below market conditions to purchase a fishing boat. Beyond the fact that this price is considered far beyond the cost for such an object, no purchase on this amount was reported at local shipbuilding facilities.

Another category of bountiful private donors are entrepreneurs in highly sensitive economic branches. Large parts of Mozambique's formal economy depend on government, a dependence which includes a need to secure licences, tax exemptions, subsidies and credits. The way government uses its discretionary power makes all the difference between the success or failure of an investment. Similarly, the criminal economy is another branch whose gains depend largely on the willingness of the government to turn a blind eye to activities like smuggling or drug trafficking. Individuals with links to this informal branch of the economy are reported to be part of the inner circle of donors and friends of the governing *Frelimo* party.

In the circumstances of an electoral campaign, this behaviour steps up to a more aggressive level, and the business community is invited to contribute to the campaign of the governing party. Fund raising events in the cities are disguised as invitations to discuss economic policies, while in the countryside businesspersons are approached door-to-door. Turning down these invitations tends to have negative consequences for business, while a further degree of non-cooperative behaviour would be to support opposition parties. Most of the interviewed experts said corporate donors to *Renamo* commit economic suicide. However, the picture is not that clear. Some specialist commentators report that *Renamo* still has traditional donors from private investors and merchants who oppose the *Frelimo* government, including the Portuguese business community and *Renamo* friends in neighbouring African countries. Seen from this standpoint, *Renamo* is thought to have access to a select group of private donors.

The *Partido para a Paz, Democracia e Desenvolvimento* (PDD) or *Partido Independente de Moçambique* (PIMO) seem to also possess unexpected resources. Several interviewees reported the managerial capacity of this new party, the extensive travel itinerary of its candidate and the quality of TV spots, concluding access to resources is one of the prerequisites for such development. PDD is a new party built up by the former *Renamo* leading politician Raul Domingos, who ran for the presidency in 2004. Domingos was the chief whip of *Renamo* in the *Assembleia da República* until he quarrelled with the party leader Affonso Dhlakama which ended with Domingos being sacked from the party. Domingos' experience and international contacts helped him build up a new organisation that soon outstripped the other newcomer parties of political amateurs and adventurers. Additionally, this social capital supposedly helped capitalise the campaign of the *PDD*, with two sources suggesting a donation above two million USD from a foreign bank, and another suggesting investments in real estate (Field interviews, Mozambique, October 2004). Meanwhile, the splinter party *PIMO* lead by Yaqub Sibindy is reported to count on the support of donors from the business community linked to a network of Muslims in and outside Mozambique.[10]

Resources for political competition in context

In Mozambique, while the formal provision of public funding forms the basis for political equality to prevail in electoral competition, as described above, private sources are allowed to differentiate the value of each party's resources considerably in practice. Mozambican parties and candidates gain access to public resources and then legitimately court private sponsors, such that the economic and political context of each party and candidate sets important conditions for political finance. There are also important inequities in practice to the public goods.

Budget subsidies to campaigns

During the electoral process parties receive additional funds, which in 2004 totalled about 45 billion Meticais (approximately 2.2 million USD), part of which came from international donors, the rest from the national budget. As defined by law the bulk of public funds for campaigns are allocated in equitable terms: one third of the total amount was reserved for the presidential campaign, with each of the five presidential candidate's parties receiving three billion Meticais (150,000 USD); one third sent to parties with candidates running for Legislative elections, proportional to the amount of candidates; one third went to parties represented in the *Assembleia da República*, following the proportion of seats.

Free media access was also provided as indirect public support, although free access does not mean equal ability to resource expensive programming. Expenses for producing sophisticated advertising neutralise the impact of savings on media time, with the quality of videos a good illustration of the financial capacity of a party. Only *Frelimo*, *Renamo* and *PDD* are able to produce TV spots of high quality, while other parties have produced either poor TV ads or do not use the space at all. However, one should bear in mind that the importance of mass communication in Mozambique is limited, since electronic media do not have far reaching coverage outside the cities, nor do print media reach out to the masses, who are to a large extent still illiterate.

Abuse of state resources

As elsewhere, unilateral public support to parties favoured by the government is illegal in Mozambique and any branch of government or state owned companies are prohibited to donate money unilaterally to candidates or parties. However, improper funding does exist, most inconspicuously when state bureaucracy delays payments and small parties flounder with no capital stock to pre-finance expenses. More critically, however, *Frelimo* is accused of using state resources on an ongoing basis for its own partisan interests, including use of public vehicles during the campaign (The Carter Centre, 2005: 39), and expensive travels of public authorities to distant places with a hidden or open campaign agenda. One emblematic situation was a so called 'goodbye trip' of president Chissano to all provinces, where he presented his candidate Guebuza as a natural successor whose election was above all doubt. However, these practices are deeply embedded in the political culture of Mozambique, and are not widely perceived as problematic.

Besides the improper use of public facilities, the abuse of tax exemption is reportedly a major source of improper revenue for some parties, particularly in import and export transactions, and in reselling imports on local markets (Field interviews, Mozambique, October 2004; see also USAID, 2005: 51–3). Parties are especially aware of the possibility of turning this form of 'legalised smuggling' into a source of funding for the party, although the opportunity is not equally available to all players since the state apparatus has discretionary power in either turning down or generously admitting applications for imports in the name of political parties. There is evidence of undue use of customs authority to favour *Frelimo* over other parties. A small party tried to import 500 TV sets, another construction material worth 600,000 USD, but the customs authority denied both applications. In contrast, *Frelimo* allegedly imported 300 tonnes of A4 paper for party use, but the material was later sold on the local market by a university paper store.

Political competition and organisational inequalities

The existing parties in Mozambique widely diverge concerning their organisational profile, managerial capacity and resources (including public and private donations, income-generating investments, equipment and other assets). The party system unfolds clearly into two main players, *Frelimo* and *Renamo*, and several much smaller parties, many of which have been absorbed by *Renamo*, since the barriers for entrance into the Legislature (5 per cent of votes nationwide) proved too high. On the other hand, a number of incentives (including the availability of public funding and the aspiration to tip the scales in the political struggle between *Frelimo* and *Renamo*) result in an increased number of parties in the pre-electoral period. Some small parties do seek to be a permanent third force in the political landscape, although many are driven by interests in personal promotion, economic speculation, or pure adventure.

Within this bipartisan reality, the governing *Frelimo* party has a clear advantage over its opposition party *Renamo*. For historical reasons, *Frelimo* reaches down to provinces and districts, nurtures cadre, and although the model of state socialism was rejected by the end of the 1980s, *Frelimo* never lost control over the state apparatus, such that the separation of party and state is still in many aspects more theory than reality. A large number of public officials are still party members, while there are close economic ties between the party and state resources. With its historical roots and privileged position in relation to the state, party and campaign finance is raised easier than within *Renamo*, whose main achievement was to transform a guerilla movement into a peaceful political organisation using international support, but which lacked a historical structure to absorb and transform these resources into productive long-term investments. *Renamo* remains on a low level of organisation and management capacity.

Renamo suffers from internal limitations to its efforts to modernise, including a centralised administrative structure and a personalistic leadership in Dhlakama, who allocates party funds with discretion. However, there are also clear signs that *Frelimo* uses its power over the state apparatus to hinder the economic consolidation of *Renamo*. State employees who join the *Renamo* campaign or run for office on the *Renamo* ticket are either fired or suffer setbacks in their career. Entrepreneurs who do support the party receive 'special treatment' by the state administration, including fierce control by tax collectors.

In contrast, *Frelimo* holds an overwhelming majority of votes in the southern and northern regions, where political identity stems directly from the fight for independence and nationality. The strength of these hegemonic associations goes as far as not allowing opposition candidates to campaign in these regions. By contrast, the identification with *Renamo* has its origin either in the historical support this movement had in specific regions in the centre of the country, or in the protest against *Frelimo*'s post-independence abuse of power. In these circumstances voting follows group patterns rather than individual choice, with areas of hegemony rather immune to incursions by political adversaries. Relatedly, following the established tradition of a *Frelimo* friendly bureaucracy, including in particular in the *STAE* and national and regional *Electoral Commissions*, and the extensive use of majority rule in proportionally composed institutions, some commentators assert that the outcome of the 2004 election was decided *not by voting but by vote counting* in some provinces.

Conclusion

Donations from the business community remain opaque, and party and campaign accounts rendered to regulatory authorities remain difficult to view publicly. Independent oversight is still a challenge for fair elections in Mozambique: any significant effort to reshape the patterns of political finance towards a more balanced access to resources has to include the de-politisation and institutional consolidation of the oversight bodies, *STAE* and *CNE* respectively.

The Mozambican system of party funding sets high entry barriers for small and new parties. New parties who remain below the threshold of 5 per cent of votes on a national average for the *Assembleia da República* do not get seats, to help consolidate majorities in the Legislature. However, parties not represented in the Assembly will then also find themselves outside the system of party finance, whatever their record of participation in the elections, which then unduly limits their potential to develop into political competitors. A system of political finance promoting political pluralism and committed to the consolidation of small parties does not contradict an electoral system that limits representation to larger parties. A reasonable alternative to the rule for the allocation of annual funds to parties would be an allocation proportional to the votes gained in national elections (instead of the current criterion of seats in the legislature).

In sharp contrast, the conditions of campaign funding are inviting for new competitors to participate in the contest, based on a principle of equity, but also fail for opposite reasons. Even unprepared newcomers encounter very favourable conditions during the elections. The presidential candidates have access to equal resources despite their highly uneven support by a solid party organisation. And most problematic, the access to indirect benefits like tax exemption for imports does not promote equal competition, but rather creates opportunities for manipulation and economic speculation. To promote serious electoral competition and avoid abuse by adventurers and con men, the system of campaign finance should be limited to qualified competitors. A requirement for candidates to be affiliated to a party long before the election could be a criteria for testing their political commitment.

The result of the above is that the Mozambican two-party system is strongly protected against innovation. The mix of incentives for unprepared ad hoc competition during elections, combined with a lack of support for solid party structures the rest of the time is questionable, resulting in a misleading picture of sustained political pluralism.

Another clear shortcoming of the systems of election and party finance in Mozambique is a lack of transparency and accountability, despite formidable legal provisions, with a wide gap between law and practice. The law imposes strict rules about transparency on the parties, and extensive rules for accountability, though different for public resources and non-public funds. But de facto public oversight is poor and transparency non-existent, with parties happy to flout legal provisions to render accounts on non-public resources. Where public funds are at issue, parties care about transparency requirements only to the extent that access to continuous public funding is linked to this condition, and transparency remains out of the focus of public awareness. The *CNE,* as the most important oversight body on the issue, does not publicise the reports delivered by parties on campaign finance, but only makes public its decision on whether accounts have been accepted or rejected. As far as parties' finance outside the electoral campaign period is concerned, they do not comply with the legal obligation of rendering accounts annually, nor do they register donations, as required by law. Reducing undue use of tax exemption privileges by parties, while simultaneously protecting them from arbitrary decisions by customs authorities, could also be achieved by increasing transparency, perhaps by means of a publication of imports so acquired, as well as applications turned down.

Most problematically, however, is the question of corporate donation, since this derives from social and cultural structures deeply embedded in the history of Mozambique and its current social practices. Extending transparency measures here, into a patently uneven playing field for private donations which benefits *Frelimo,* might have the perverse effect of increasing *Frelimo's* clientelist powers, further compelling donations to itself, and further discouraging donations to opposition parties as these became subject to public view and pressure. However, if the government is able to trace even hidden donations, then greater transparency could protect companies from abusive controls by state authorities. Corporate and political practices here have historically located and embedded meanings, with loyalty to the liberation party detracting from these practices being perceived as a problem, a historical legacy which might remain in place for some time. Conversely, when a critical mass of business people grow to perceive these donations as unfair taxes, probably spurred by perceptions of arbitrariness, the prospects of greater accountability and transparency in this critical area will increase.

Notes

1. This report is based on desk research, a field mission to Mozambique and interviews with national and international country experts, observers of elections, representatives from all mayor parties, activists from civil society, the head of the electoral management body, social scientists, journalists and donor agencies involved with projects funding democratic competition. A succinct version of this report was included in: *The Carter Center: Observing the 2004 Mozambique Elections*, Special Report Series, Atlanta, 2005, pp. 30–5.
2. For example, the second national election in December 1999 was questioned in court by *Renamo*, who then took protest to the streets in November 2000. The clashes with police forces killed 40 people, while another 119 riot detainees were killed by asphyxiation in an overcrowded prison cell. Violent incidents and intimidation are still part of political reality.
3. For a critical review of this early phase of funding re-democratisation in Mozambique since 1992 see de Tollenaere (2000) and Tollenaere (2006).
4. Protocol II of the Rome Peace Agreements, signed at 13 November 1991, settled questions of rights and duties of parties, making explicit reference to funding sources, private and public, of political parties (*General Peace Agreement of Rome*, 1992).
5. *Constituição da República de Moçambique, Novembro 1990*. The revised Constitution, approved by the National Assembly on November 16, 2004, entered into force after the 2004 elections.
6. In the following as *Lei dos Partidos* and *Lei Eleitoral* respectively. *Lei Eleitoral* (1993) governed the first multi-party elections, and has been adapted and complemented for every subsequent election, with laws on voter census and the *Comissão Nacional de Eleições*. The central text for the 2004 national elections was *Lei Eleitoral* (2004). For a discussion of rules and regulations of the 2004 elections, with a special focus on funding parties and candidates, see Nuvuunga (2005).
7. Estimation based on field interviews.
8. This is not to argue that the influence of personal wealth is eliminated entirely, since money is said to have influenced the composition and ranking of the candidate list during the convention of the *Renamo* party. According to field interviews, decision making inside *Frelimo* was not transparent, and personal networks also played a role.
9. There are reports that *Renamo* charges more significant amounts of money from elected deputies in the legislature, but these remain unconfirmed.
10. It is unknown if private donors make simultaneous donations to several competitors, a common feature in societies where large parts of the business sector depend on state contracts and where the outcome of elections is uncertain. The first condition applies fully to Mozambique, but the possibility of a regime change has gained credence only recently.

References

Cabaço, José Luís (1996), 'The long march of Mozambican democracy', in Brazão Mazula (ed.), *Mozambique: elections, democracy and development*, Maputo: Embassy of the Kingdom of the Netherlands, pp. 75–117

Carbone, Giovanni M. (2003), 'Emerging pluralist politics in Mozambique: the Frelimo–Renamo party system', LSE Development Research Center, Crisis States Programme, *Working Paper 23*

General Peace Agreement of Rome (1992), signed at Rome on 4 October 1992 by Joaquim Alberto Chissano, President of the Republic of Mozambique, and Afonso Macacho Marceta Dhlakama, President of Renamo (including Protocols I-VII signed between 18 October 1991 and 4 October 1992; the Joint Communiqué of 10 July 1990; the Agreement of 1 December 1990; the Declaration signed on 16 July 1992 in Rome and the Declaration signed on 7 August 1992 in Rome), original documents available at www.c-r.org/our-work/accord/mozambique/primary-texts.php

Hanlon, Joseph (2000), '1994, 1998, 1999', in *International Conference on Local Government Elections in Mozambique, Final Report*, edited by Obede Suarte Baloi and José Macuane, Maputo, Mozambique, pp. 83–93

Lei dos Partidos Políticos (1991), *República de Moçambique: Regulamento para a Formação e Actividade dos Partidos Políticos*, Imprensa Nacional de Moçambique, Maputo, Lei no. 7/1991, 23 de janeiro

Lei Eleitoral, Lei no. 4/1993, (1993) 28 de dezembro 1993 (apud: Ussumane Aly Dauto: Legislação eleitoral, Maputo, 1999, p. 4)

Lei Eleitoral, Lei no. 7/2004, (2004) 31 de maio 2004 (República de Moçambique: Lei Eleitoral, Imprensa Nacional de Moçambique, Maputo, Junho 2004)

Manning, Carrie (1998), 'Constructing opposition in Mozambique: Renamo as a political party', *Journal of Southern African Studies*, 24, 1, pp. 161–91

Mosse, Marcelo (2004) 'Guebuza e o combate à corrupção' (Guebuza and the fight against corruption), Weekly Newspaper *Savana*, 19 November, pp. 16–17

Nuvuunga, Adriano (2005), 'Multiparty Democracy in Mozambique: Strengths, weaknesses and challenges', *Eisa Research Report*, Johannesburg, South Africa, No. 14 pp. 56–79

Southhall, Roger and Geoffrey Wood (1998), 'Political party funding in southern Africa', in Peter Burnell, Alan Ware (eds), *Funding Democratization*, Manchester, Manchester University Press, pp. 202–28

The Carter Center (2005) *Observing the 2004 Mozambique Elections*, Special Report Series, Atlanta

Tollenaere, Marc de (2000), 'Sustainable electoral democracy in Mozambique – International support and self-reliance', in *Promoting sustainable democratic institutions in Southern Africa: Conference Proceedings*, Garbore, Botswana, International IDEA

Tollenaere, Marc de (2006), 'Apoio a redemocratização a Mozambique Pós-Conflicto. Intenções e Resultados', Netherlands Institute of International Relations, Clongendael, Conflict Research Unit, June 2006

USAID (2005), 'Avaliacao da Corrupcao: Mozambique. Relatório Final', 16 de dezembro, 2005, MSI, Washington

13
Accountability in Development Finance Projects: Between the Market and a Soft Place

Sarah Bracking

Development financed projects have a unique institutional context for the production of economic activities since accountability is enacted neither directly through the state nor the market. Most development finance institutions (DFIs) enjoy hybrid public–private status and weak lines of accountability to their underwriting Treasuries (Bracking, 2003). The market environment of DFI projects is also concessionary, without the accountability of competition, where often the participant companies are part of a small group of internationally networked enterprises, with close relations with contracting parties within the DFIs. This closed culture of large business enterprise is somewhat cronyistic, promoting a similar business culture in aid dependent countries, which resonates and reinforces historical and structural patterns of political economy in post-colonies (Bracking, 2006), often contributing to an enclave structure (see Mhone, 2001).

Anti-corruption policy is required to respond to this culture of patronage in institutional systems emanating from rich countries' DFIs, since it provides ample opportunity for corrupt business practice, while providing incentives for southern political elites to behave similarly, acting on behalf of, or within, subcontracted indigenous business enterprises. However, there remains a racialised contradiction within anti-corruption regulation, which militates against its effectiveness, between the positive view given to proximity and personal credential as a source of success and market intelligence (in the 'West'); and warnings of undue proximity in anti-corruption codes designed to impact on contracting behaviour (with the 'Rest'). This chapter explores these contradictions by examining contemporary regulatory codes, and some recent examples of corrupt practice, principally the Lesotho Dam (see also Bracking, 2001).

The chapter concludes that in aid dependent business environments there is an inevitable contest over resources and profits which can only be equitably regulated by democratically authored global regulation. However, current anti-corruption policy remains fatally embedded in racial and postcolonial discourse, and functions to discipline indigenisation processes by consigning local content rules to illegitimacy, while simultaneously occluding similar closed practices within DFI-underwritten markets.

Understanding corruption in development industry networks

This chapter concerns corruption in a political economy context, and in particular that found in aid-financed or aid underwritten business environments such as projects funded by bilateral and multilateral DFIs or Export Credit Agencies (ECAs), the latter of which fund collectively between US $50 and $70 billion worth of business annually (ECA Watch, 2006: 1). The Export Credit Guarantee Department (ECGD) is the British ECA. Cornerhouse have been assessing anti-corruption policy within these environments for some years, and were invited to submit comments to the Select Committee *Consultation on Changes to ECGD's Anti-Bribery and Corruption Procedures* in December 2004. They summarise the international obligations to which a national regulatory framework must correspond,[1] beginning centrally with Article 12 of the *UN Convention Against Corruption* (signed by the UK in December 2003, ratified in 2005) which deals with parties obligations on preventing corruption in the private sector. This states that

> Each State Party shall take measures, in accordance with the fundamental principles of its domestic law, to prevent corruption involving the private sector.

And includes Clause 2(d)

> preventing the misuse of procedures regarding subsidies and licences granted by public authorities for commercial purposes.

This covers the ECGD services to the private sector in terms of guarantee and investment insurance, which cost the UK taxpayer £150 million annually (Cornerhouse, 2004: 8), against £2 billion worth of new business in financial year 2004/05 (ECGD, 2006: 2).

The cornerhouse submission argues that the ECGD still maintains a corruption permissive regulatory framework in several respects, and that key businesses retain sufficient power to resist closer regulation, say on due diligence (Cornerhouse, 2004). In particular Cornerhouse are concerned that the ECGD regulations allow companies to not disclose commission payments which are less than 5 per cent of the contract price; are allowed to keep the name and address of an agent secret if they provide a written justification for doing so; are not required to state whether an agent has been previously employed by an affiliate such as a joint venture partner; do not have to explain commission payments made outside the Purchaser's country; are only required to declare that there is no relationship between the agent and the Purchaser 'to the best of their knowledge and belief' which does not require that they make any active enquiries as to whether there is such a relationship; agent's commission on contracts not related to the one ECGD is to underwrite do not have to be disclosed; and details of any payments not included in the contract price do not have to be detailed (Cornerhouse, 2004: 10).[2]

Cornerhouse's submission confirms that anti-corruption policy remains weak in the face of persistent corrupt practice, an observation which resonates with Michael (2004) on the lack of specificity and fit of anti-corruption donor policy, in this case, particularly where it concerns their 'own' companies. For example, the Africa Commission exhorts that:

> developed countries should encourage their ECAs to be more transparent and to require higher standards of transparency in their support for projects in developing countries. Developed countries should also fully implement the Action Statement on Bribery and Officially Supported Export Credits agreed by the OECD,

and asks that bribing firms be refused subsequent export credits (Commission on Africa, 2005: 12). However, transparency is a nebulous concept, particularly when Auditors Reports allow many opportunities for writing down discrepancy: financial oversight companies missed illegal payments entirely in recent scandals in Lesotho and Nigeria involving ECA-funded projects. Meanwhile, the retention of future credit, or temporary assignment to the World Bank's barred list, falls well short of what might be expected from activity deemed illegal by the OECD Convention. Thus, in general, very broad statements of purpose from key international regulators, combine with very weak punitive measures which lack a conclusive force of law.

Over and above laxity and ommission in the regulatory regime, however, there seem to be more fundamental contradictions within current regulation: that 1) given increased transparency, payments of an extra-contractual nature will, on the basis of a collusive understanding by two contracting parties, be merely incorporated into price unless effective competition is installed; 2) efforts to make companies contract only with 'reputable' agents and companies will have the perverse effect of increasing cronyism, and southern elites' resentment of being excluded from lucrative development projects; and 3) agents can still be used to avoid 'close' criminality, but are often found, later, not to be 'reputable'. Cornerhouse cite 78 per cent of respondents to a Control Risks Groups' 2002 survey, who believed that companies from OECD countries (including the UK, but excluding the US) used middlemen (*sic*) to cicumvent direct payment of bribes either 'occasionally' or 'regularly' (Cornerhouse, 2004: 11). Fundamentally, agents or 'middlemen' with market intelligence, or close proximity to contract providers, can be positively viewed and sought out by rational companies, primarily because of their preferential knowledge.

The CDC Group, for example, make much of their close relations with the companies they support, and even their close relationships, of a deep and historical nature, to governments themselves (CDC, 2005; Bracking 1997).[3] They state that

> CDC applies stringent criteria that require fund managers to be best of breed, either in their particular region or sector, (2005: 12)

and continue that:

> 'We look for track record, good deal flow, a serious and coherent fund strategy and ultimately a highly motivated team'. CDC has built up a growing database of specialist fund managers with deal history in emerging markets. 'We've met most, have done extensive due diligence on many of them ... Because developing markets are less mature, we have to be triply sure the fund manager is going to be reliable and a good investor and is prepared to follow sound business principles'. (2005: 12)

Similarly, the US *Foreign Corrupt Practices Act* (FCPA) requires a compliance regime, which includes well-documented, searching due diligence procedures on all business relationships including agents, such that

> An FCPA compliance regime would also require that a company establish business relationships only with reputable and qualified business partners. (cited in Cornerhouse, 2004: 11)

'Reputable', 'qualified' and 'best of breed' act as signifiers which preclude the corruptability of potential agents, without an assessment of proximity to government having to take place.

Now what is interesting to our analysis here, or perception of behaviour in business environments, is the contradiction between, on the one hand, the positive view given to proximity and personal credential as a source of success and market intelligence by market actors, as opposed to the warnings of undue proximity in anti-corruption codes designed to impact on contracting behaviour within markets. The CDC assume the best of breed have integrity, but for others a much more distal relationship is advised. For example, questions in other ECA best practice questionnaires on agents ask about undue proximity, such as whether the agent has a family member in a government position (Cornerhouse, 2004; 12),[4] but we can assume that in many countries 'best of breed' agents and government personnel are at least of the same social class, and in small or newly independent countries, probably also members of the same kinship, family or alumni networks. Regulating sociability is, in sum, inherently problematic.

Cornerhouse advise a number of actions which deepen interventionism and oversight into these national networks, including that companies ensure partners don't delegate substantial discretionary authority to individuals and have 'ongoing monitoring and oversight over joint venture partners' (Hildyard, 2000: 17). However, there is clearly an opportunity cost of such deepening oversight, which works inversely to promote companies' use of associates known to them, but not, as illustrated in the questions above, associates known to be 'too related' to government or indigenous political elites. Thus, these precautionary principles seem bound to encourage Western business cronyism, justified by 'successful track record' and 'best of breed' criteria, however culturally embedded and nebulous these might be.

The 'soft place' between the public and private sectors

Development projects are particularly prone to corruption because they involve large sums with little formal monitoring, in informalised networks of associates where participants are often purposely seeking out associates 'like them' (with inevitable ramifications for cultural and racial selection) in order to protect against non-payment. But the contradiction between protection offered by 'the known' and the moral hazard of 'the known too well' seems ubiquitous. As Heymans and Lipietz summarise:

> A common occurrence of . . . political and burueacratic corruption is where conflicts of interest are not managed, so that potential

beneficiaries of projects or resource allocations are directly able to control or influence decisions about those projects or allocations. (1999: 1)

They cite the Motheo housing development in the South African province of Mpumalanga, as an example where the friendship between the developer and the national Minister of Housing was at issue. They continue that:

Where corruption has become systemic, formal and informal rules that are at odds with each other become interchangeable and decisions increasingly arbitaray . . . [such that] corruption most often lies at the intersection of the public and private sectors. (ibid.)

This intersection is a whole spatial category in the development industry where network knowledge itself is a commodity that is bought and sold, through, for example, paid for places at elite conferences where 'contacts', often those in charge of dispensing contracts, can be made.

For example, at a recently advertised 'experts workshop' of the OECD *Development Centre* on 'governance–investment interactions' – which is modernised parlance for the older 'public–private partnership' – the proceedings are 'by invitation only' (closed for reasons of 'commercial confidentiality'), although the risks of collusion between public and private actors that such partnerships can promote was acknowledged, if obliquely and coyly:

The likelihood, in any country, that some investors (acting overtly or covertly, individually or collectively, through economic or political channels) are investing significant resources in attempts to shape and influence – including attempts to 'capture' – governance institutions and practices that impinge on their profits means there can also be an important reverse causal relationship between investors' behaviour and governance institutions and practices. (OECD, 2005b)

This oblique reference to the relationship between business profitability and government policy is the reason why companies invest in networking, expert workshops and sociability in its widest sense in the first place. Such behaviour, like corrupt behaviour, is linked to officials' discretion over rents and companies' need to secure contracts.

The normative morality of such relationships shape shifts in practice, in donor policy, and in official publications. For example, in an OECD working paper on Public–Private Dialogue, Pinaud seeks to

pinpoint . . . the institutional prerequisites (effectiveness of the bureaucracy, organisation and maturity of the local private sector, political environment) for a dialogue which avoids the pitfalls of an hazy and economically sub-optimal interaction between the State and the business milieu. (Pinaud, 2005: 1)

Which, roughly translated, implies that the relationships have a positive and profitable optimality found in close association. This European corporatist outlook compares with the *Joint Economic Committee* of the US Senate, using a neoclassical economic model, who warn:

> Research suggests that the more pervasive is the public sector's role in the economy, the more likely is corruption to flourish. Foreign assistance, however well-intentioned, can promote the very conditions fostering corruption. Such aid can strengthen existing public sector bureaucracry, result in larger government spending and a larger public sector (relative to the private sector), entrench a corrupt status quo elite, and foster delay in reforming existing corruption. (Saxton, 1999: 6)

Here all perverse incentive is located in the public sector, which is conceptually seen as a discreet realm, which interferes with the rather more pristine realm of the private which should remain separate.

As Polzer summarises of the World Bank's view of corruption:

> Rent, as defined by Gallagher, is 'the direct use or waste of economic resources for non-economic gains,' [1991: 31] and 'rent seeking' theories 'were employed to show that, *given any choice*, developing-country governments would only serve themselves and their (mostly urban) supporters.' [Schmitz, 1995: 64, emph in orig.]. Therefore, in the interests of equity, it was argued that development must be based on the market and not on the state. This conception, with minor variations, is still dominant today; it shows how deeply assumptions of the inherent corruptness of the state lie in the largely neo-liberal Bank. (Polzer, 2001: 7)

Here, the anti-corruption focus of the World Bank, is 'a logical further step in the neo-liberal trend of de-politicising the state apparatus for the advancement of the market', despite its debut coinciding with the 1997 *World Development Report* with which it 'clashes'.[5] This 'focus on "rent-seeking" and corruption . . . has given voice to the Bank's inherent mistrust of the state' (Polzer, 2001: 9; cites Ranis, 1997), even though, again in a contradictory fashion, the World Bank then calls on the state to solve the problem of corruption. This World Bank theorisation thus misses the interaction between the public and private as essentially a corruption permissive site, instead siting corrupt incentive singularly in the public sector.

Networks and sociability

The legal and formalistic definition of corruption as the use of public office for private gain is stretched, perhaps to breaking point, by anti-corruption policy designed to counter the corrupting effect of networks and personal business practices which themselves escape this dichotomy. For example, the issue of disclosure centres in ECGD guidelines on how far a UK company is responsible for others it deals with or is associated with; how far responsibility extends into its public–private hybrid network. According to Cornerhouse, the December 2004 ECGD procedures had reduced the scope of disclosure requirements too far by limiting them only to company directors (2004).

In general, the 'distance' between company and corrupt agent can be stretched institutionally, such that the company can appear not to be involved, but still arguably have responsibility and knowledge. This has been a recurring point of tension in the UK between the International Development Select Committee (IDC), who exercise oversight of bribe-paying and anti-corruption, the ECGD, and interviewed companies who maintain that facilitation payments are necessary in the environments in which they work (IDC, 1999; Hildyard, 2000, referring to IDC, 2001, paras. 62–81; 92–8). Related tensions have involved justifications by companies concerning bribe-paying that 'everybody does it', or 'if we don't do it somebody else will', with the result that a vital contract is 'lost' to a national competitor (IDC, 2001, paras. 181–192).[6] Companies are asked to step back from this environment and pursue ever greater due diligence across an ever extending network using profoundly limited criteria of who might or might not be trustworthy, to which their response is often to merely create institutional boundaries, 'stretch' their distance, and sub-contract.

Corruption permissible environments: the Lesotho Dam

For example, the International Rivers Network (IRN) summarise of the Lesotho Dam project, under their heading the *'Good Ole Boys' Syndrome,* that there was a tightly knit and mutually well-known network of people in their respective companies who were involved in the project:

> Funding for the project has come from the World Bank; the European Investment Bank; the German, British and French bilateral aid agencies;

the UK Commonwealth Development Corporation; commercial banks including Banque Nationale de Paris, Dresdner and Hill Samuel; and a number of export credit agencies (including Germany's Hermes, France's COFACE, South Afrikaans's SACCE and Britain's ECGD). The ECGD's support amounted to £66 million and went in loan guarantees to five UK companies: Balfour Beatty, Kier, Stirling, Kvaerner Boving and ABB Generation's UK subsidiary . . . Not one of these agencies however ever vetted the corruption records of the companies bidding for contracts.

But many companies later accused of corruption had prior histories of allegations of corrupt activity, which would include Spie Batignoles and Sogreah, for example, who

> were involved in Kenya's Turkwell Gorge Dam which, because of bribes reportedly paid to Kenya's president and energy minister, cost more than twice what the European Commission said it should have cost. (IRN, 2000, 3)

Also,

> Impreglio, Dumez and Lahmeyer were three of the principle firms involved in the Yacyreta Dam in Argentina and Paraguay, which Argentina's President Carlos Menem called 'a monument to corruption' . . . [while] Lahmeyer and Impregilio also had contracts on Guatemala's Chixoy Dam. Various sources estimate that between $350 and $500 million were lost to corruption on this project. (ibid.)[7]

Balfour Beatty was also famously implicated in corruption at the Pegau Dam in Malaysia.

British companies involved with the Lesotho Highlands Project were often funded by public development finance companies, as were the contracting authorities of the 'recipient'. According to the Department of Trade and Industry (DTI) in 1994, the UK provided consultancy support to the Lesotho Highlands Development Authority (LHDA) under technical co-ordination arrangements, which awarded contracts. At the same time, British consultants provided technical assistance, the ECGD provided export credit, while the CDC, European Investment Bank (EIB) (DTI, 1994: 64; see Bracking, 2001 for details), and International Finance Corporation (IFC) (House of Commons (HC), 1994: 65) provided investment capital. Bilateral development finance was funding UK companies

Sir William Halcrow, Balfour Beatty, Kier and Sterling International in dam construction, and Hill Samuel Bank, Coopers Lybrand & Deloittes and Price Waterhouse who were publicly paid for 'financial functions' (HC, 1994b: 95). In addition, Aid and Trade Provision (ATP) financing further supported Kvaerner Boving and Balfour Beatty. The Commonwealth Development Corporation (CDC) provided overall financial support to the LHDA (HC, 1994: 63; CDC, 1992: 31), and to the Lesotho National Development Corporation (LHDC), the overall control institution (CDC, 1992: 43), joined later by Overseas Development Administration (ODA)[8] funding to the LHDC (HC 1994: 63). The LNDC (supported by CDC and ODA) then lent the British loan on to the LHDA (CDC, 1992: 43), who commissioned the work and paid the UK construction and engineering firms (and possibly UK consultancy firms and banks), that part of the bill which wasn't already being paid from ATP finance. In sum, the institutional context acted as a recycler of public funds to multinational companies, as illustrated in Figure 13.1.

In the Lesotho Highlands project, multinational companies and private banks, technical co-operation assistance, export credit, soft finance and consultancy support were all used in the framework of provision for the project. In 1994, the Trade and Industry Committee summarised of Lesotho that:

It is a small economy with limited debt servicing capacity and in practice most business is done on concessional terms, but it is considered a reasonable risk for the relatively modest amounts of cover required. (HC 1994: 13)

The business environment was 'concessional': publicly subsidised credit was supplied to British companies; while these companies paid 'facilitation' to the LHDA Head, Mr Sole, who eventually appeared in court. Yet *no one*, it appears, provided effective oversight, while the companies largely escaped censure, although more than twelve multinational firms and consortia were found to have bribed the chief executive officer (CEO) of the project, three major international firms were found guilty, and one (Canada's Acres International) was subsequently debarred at the World Bank (Pottinger, 2005: 1).

Interestingly, to fund the Lesotho Dam project, when South Africa was still under apartheid and funds to it were thus politically sensitive, Chartered WestLB set up a London-based trust fund through which 'sanctions busting' payments could be laundered: of 'borderline' legality . . . [but] sanctioned at the highest level, not least through the Directors of

246

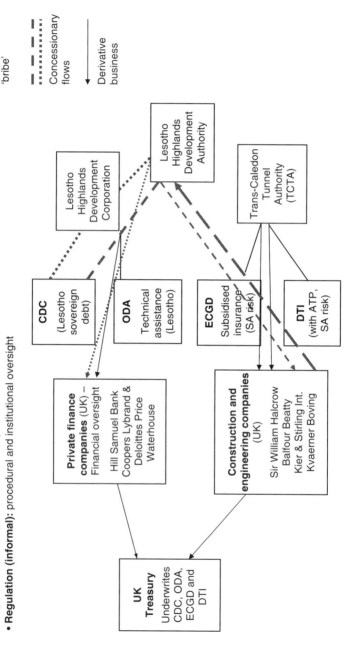

Figure 13.1: A concessionary business environment in Lesotho

the World Bank' (International Rivers Network (IRN), 2000: 1). A 'fiction' was also maintained that the money had been lent to the Lesotho-based Lesotho Highlands Development Authority, even though the South African government was responsible for repaying it (ibid.). By the time of the Chad Cameroon Petroleum Development and Pipeline Project, the convenience of a London-based 'clearing fund' for a donor-sponsored project in a 'difficult' country remained. In the latter case, the money was lent to Chad by the World Bank and EIB, who would take their repayments directly from the Bank account at Citibank in which ExxonMobil would make payments for the oil. After these deductions, under a 'Revenue Management Plan' agreed with the donors, and codified in Law 001, the remaining funds were earmarked for poverty reduction: 10 per cent to a Future Generations Fund; 72 per cent for capital investments in five 'priority areas' to fight poverty; 4.5 per cent to the oil-producing region in southern Chad (the indigenous people); and 13.5 per cent to Chad's treasury for 'discretionary spending' (Keenan, 2005: 396–7). Unfortunately, for the donors, who claimed this was a breakthrough in (variously) good governance, poverty reduction, breaking the 'curse of resources' and, according to the Central African representative of the IFC 'the model for every single project of this type worldwide' (cited in Keenan, 2005: 397), it is now clear that international environmental regulations have been seriously breached by the oil companies (Keenan, 2005: 399–402), while the Law passed to institutionalise the 'poverty reduction' arrangements is already subject to nullification by the new Chad government.

Multilateral development finance: a crony network?

The distribution of benefits deriving from the (aggregated) expenditures of the multilateral agencies suggests that the system of multilateral finance benefits a small number of rich countries predominantly, in terms of the derivative business that derives from it. For example, the US may spend the lowest proportion of multilateral aid relative to GNP, but in 1992 it still enjoyed 14.4 per cent of all derivative procurement business arising from the expenditures of the Bank, leading the ranking of recipients. Japan, likewise, leads funding of the ADB, but also enjoys 33.5 per cent of the derivative benefit, with the USA second at 30.6 per cent in 1992. Taken as a whole, just five core creditor states, the UK, US, Japan, Germany and France accounted for a massive 96.8 per cent of all derivative contract business of the Asian Development Bank, while with the addition of Italy, they also accounted for 96.5 per cent of business from the Inter American Development Band (IADB) in the early 1990s (Bracking, 1999: 220).

Thus the 'gift-giving' of aid is related to a strong expectation of reciprocal reward for the companies of that country, similar to gift-giving in personal networks (see Repetti, 2002). In Repetti's study of micro-business in Daka,

> Subordination and paternalism are not the prerogative of families. They are also found in the alliances and in client networks surrounding businesses. (Repetti, 2002: 55)

Here, relationships 'between commerce and sociability' are constantly converting social and cultural capital into economic capital, and vice versa (Repetti, 2002: 46), such that 'traditional and broader supportive networks are operating in an urban economy that is only partly governed by market relations' (Repetti, 2002: 43), In the case of development financed business and political networks similar processes can be observed.

The precedent for making such a comparison is theoretically justified. For example, Danby argues that:

> The anthropological literature on the gift has split the social and material world into a premodern realm of thick sociality where gift-giving is located, and a modern realm of thin sociality in which exchange occurs. It concedes the modern realm to the neo-classical economist. (2002: 13)

And by so doing, as Castree argues (2004) gives the concept 'economic' a power to signify things rational and beyond normative questioning. Instead, Danby argues against such a 'premodern/modern split' (2002: 13), and that 'neoclassical economic theory is too asocial to be an adequate description of material life anywhere, under any circumstances' (2002: 14). Restoring ideas of thick sociability to the networks here helps interrogate their avowed rationality.

Critically, the sociability of development finance networks acts to largely exclude companies from the South. For example, the CDC, largely through its equity fund Actis,[9] made 27 investments in the energy sector between 2001 and 2004 (Hansard, 2005), including the family of investments under the Globeleq company, which has controlling ownership of 20 projects in over 15 countries, including Kelvin Power (coal) in South Africa, Sidi Krir (natural gas) in Egypt, Songas (natural gas) in Tanzania, Azito Energie SA (natural gas) in Cote D'Ivoire, Tsavo Power Co. Ltd (fuel oil) in Kenya and Umeme Limited (supply and distribution) in Uganda. In-country, each of these investments proves critical to the national energy strategy as a whole; Songas the largest supplier of the national grid, Kelvin meeting the energy needs of Johannesburg; Sidi Krir supplying the majority of energy needed on the Egyptian national grid; Tsavo in Kenya owning the largest power stations (and also enjoying IFC support of $41 million in 2003).

But critically to our argument here, at the operational level it is key US and European multinationals, with empowerment companies sometime junior partners, who pick up the contracts, like Caltex in Kenya, who won a six-year contract to supply fuel to Kipevu 2, the power plant built by Tsavo, the largest contract 'ever won by regional Caltext in East Africa' (Caltex, 2003). Kipevu 2 was actually 'Kenya's first openly bid, project-financed independent power producer', with the Aga Khan Fund for Economic Development's affiliate the Industrial Promotion Services (Kenya) Limited (IPS) having a mediating role in the investment chain, with an 'international cast of financial institutions' (ibid).[10] Similarly, a cursory look at CDC investments in 2005 reveals a number of strategic partnerships with South African companies, including Eskom, the power giant, in a joint venture in Songas, Tanzania.[11]

In general, the high concentration of derivative business which Northern companies enjoy from DFIs, funded by Northern states, is due to their technical, spacial and financing advantages relative to companies from poorer countries. Their competitors, by comparison, are often labelled inadequate in a number of related respects; underdeveloped, subject to exchange, political, general country or investor risk, or other-wise, as 'corrupt' (see for example, the recent OECD, 2005). While regulations in DAC ensure controlled competition among members, opportunities to maintain a competitive edge nonetheless remain in place since the funding of research and consultancy relating to tendering for bids can be financed completely by the bidding company's government. Other technical and spatial advantages are enjoyed by companies from richer states, not least sophisticated contractor networks maintained by Government Departments and Commercial Officers in High Commissions.

These advantages, while legitimated through the language of efficient business, are also upheld in general for richer states by the procedures of the multilaterals themselves. For example, consultancy contracts derivative of aid projects funded by the European Development Fund (EDF) were distributed to short-listed, registered companies via a complex qualification procedure in the early 1990s (WAS, 1991). Articles 275–280 of Lomé IV 'set out the criteria for the selection of consultants – legal and financial status, qualification experience, independence and availability', with registration 'which is, of course, for Community consultants only', recorded on computer through the DACON system which 'the Commission has agreed with the World Bank to share' (WAS, 1991: 2). A preference for large companies is perennial while the use of open tendering is not practiced as a general principle by multilateral organisations.

The economic anthropology of the soft market for development finance

There is no 'free market' price for a development good, so that the monies paid to contractors are inevitably manufactured, which occurs elsewhere too, in the sense that 'free' markets are the exception rather than the rule in institutional market structures more generally. In fact a critique of the theory of 'free' markets, or of economic formalism from which they are asserted, is that utility maximisation is tautological in that whatever prices emerge are considered of the proper value: 'This post hoc reasoning back to a priori assumptions has minimal scientific value as it is not readily subject to falsification' (Prattis, 1982: 212). If the pricing is deemed concessionary, the loss in 'utility' is the price of Western benevolence and the development subsidy. If the price rises in construction, as often happens, this is judged as a rational response to hidden costs in a high risk environment. Either way, the assumption of economic rationality in donor-funded projects persists because it is derivative of the discourse of economic formalism in which the object, the project, is embedded. Thus, as Gudeman (1986) argues of Western economic anthropologists, but it is equally relevant to our development managers, 'rationally' will always be found, because that is what the model leads them to do.

In 'underdeveloped' countries anthropological formalists, or what political economists would term neoclassicists, often assume utility maximisation, but are thwarted in their expectations by perceived 'irrational individuals', but instead of rejecting the paradigm *per se*, take recourse in the idea of corruption. The individuals' rationality is then restored, but assumed to be centred outside the 'proper' market or public sphere, and solely apparent in individual self-seeking behaviour: it is, in short, the inappropriate context for the individual acts which denotes corruption, not that the individuals have stopped behaving as 'rational Man'. Thus, the corruption discourse here can contribute to the delegitimation of geographies and peoples, because of their assigned 'inappropriate behaviour', while ignoring that the problem of analysis is embedded in the paradigm of the observers themselves: the market rationality they hold as faith does not exist outside of its social construction, such that all prices, everywhere, are in fact socially constructed in context, by interested parties. In contrast, this would be the conclusion of a sub-stantivist economic anthropologist, who would be more comfortable with the premise that economic institutions and activites are embedded in the socio-cultural sphere (Granovetter, 1985; see also the formative Polanyi, 1968: 2001).

However, residual problems of substantivist analysis in anthropology still remain, not least the binary divide between 'primitive' and 'modern' economies, depicted as somehow distinct places, which was found in these texts, at least until recently. The divide is not theoretically sustain-able, and furthermore, serves to obscure the meaning of 'non-rational', or 'non-utility maximising' practices in the 'modern' space. Not only are non-Western spaces subject to differing and plural rationalities, but so too are Western ones, and it is in this sense that the development industry provides an interesting anthropological study since pure market exchanges are purposively vouchsafed for concessionary ones. The local here is an elite and transnational space, the network involved in development projects and consultancy.

Universalist discourses of economic rationality and Western benevo-lence combine to endow these 'localised' subjects with a unique justifi-cation for behaviour which, if practised elsewhere in concessionary space, would signify corruption. The worldviews of participants use ideas of competence and expertise (see also Kothari, 2005), technological capacity and experience, trust and reliability, and somewhat centrally, benevolence, to justify closed tendering, non-transparent accounts, price-setting, and concessionary contracting in a remarkably similar way to those subjects studied by anthropologists in networks of 'gift-giving' in non-monetised networks of social interaction and exchange. Thus the assumption that in the West the fit between formalism and substantivism is better than in the non-West (long held within substantivist economics and devel-opment studies) must be rebuked: instead, concessional spaces in the West, like the development industry, have grown apace with legimating discourses which constitute their subjects as 'non-political' rationalisers while simultaneously occluding issues of power and privilege. The Chad–Camaroon pipeline would be archetypal illustrative proof of such a proposition (see Keenan, 2005).

Through an anthropological lens, the argument here is that large devel-opment projects and the economic gifts of neo-patrimonial southern elites to their patrons look surprisingly similar in social arrangement. The construction of the meaning of each differs substantially, however, and it is here that a Foucauldian view of the construction of power and privilege can provide an explanation: constructing markets to fit the interests of privileged Western business can be legitimised through concepts of meritocracy and scientific expertise (see also Wallerstein, 1999 on the role of meritocracy in legitimating capitalism more generally); whereas constructing markets for the benefit of indigenous businessmen, the political elite and their associates is discursively constructed as corrupt by the same globally privileged class. However, between these constructed meanings we can place a third: both spaces correspond to processes of class reproduction, wealth accumulation and commodification, around which meanings are contested. Thus, eschewing an institutional definition of corruption in political economy we can reserve the normative for the observation that both concessionary spaces are referrent to the needs of privilege in parallel 'local' spaces.

Conclusion: the inevitability of politics?

The national elite response to the political economy of development, institutionalised in DFI-funded projects, which secures their relative exclusion, is at best a surge of autarchic nationalism and a favouring of indigenous business in competing regulation, such as rules on local sourcing. However, the racial inscription within current business codes of practice can also provoke more extreme responses. These include the denial of the inclusive basis of national development as the elite makes a Faustian pact with big business; a withdrawal from neoliberal norms of behaviour as contracts are retrospectively renegotiated or bilateral investment guarantees subsequently ignored; an increase in domestic 'cronyism' to compete better within the political economy of development; patriotic or racial nationalism; or economic redistribution by extra-liberal means. It is plausible to argue that the current Zimbabwean elite, for example, learned the 'winner takes all' nature of development economics during the colonial period, and have since developed the model into a particularly venal extractive nationalism (Bracking, 2005). These possible responses make it imperative that anti-corruption codes of conduct for development-financed business should better reflect global public interest, rather than the inscriptions of privilege they currently protect, and the incentives for southern elites to indulge in corruption that they currently catalyse.

Discourses around corruption act to fix its meanings spatially, with coordinates within related ideas of race, space, and nationality. These are complex, embedded, and entangled, as Moore (2005) argued elsewhere in relation to land. The depiction of the development finance market as competitive and reactive to the merits of firms in an anonymous and self-regulating way acts discursively to meet the interests of elite business classes from the West. However, elites in new state formations now also use the language of business, of expertise, success, 'best of breed', market knowledge and market opportunity to justify and explain their own routes to privilege. Both use the concept of corruption to undermine their competitors, and put their own behaviour in a better light. Re-presenting the corruption discourse on behalf of the dispossessed majority would fundamentally entail dislodging ideas of a neutral market, and would inevitably invoke wider political questions over the nature of privilege and governance: liberal democracy (which underpins current governance orthodoxy) only regulates privilege within the law, it can not protect against the immoral acts of a self-aggrandising elite using 'corrupted' market structures, as experienced by the majority. A long political contest over the normative basis of corruption and the construction of privilege more generally can be expected.

Currently, the political economy of development discourse inscribes different meanings for similar anthropological practices of business behaviour, while simultaneously *obscuring* these differences, pretending universality. Thus, developmental concession (closed tenure systems for development projects for western experts) is coded as benevolent expertise; while Southern state policy on empowerment (closed tenure systems for development projects which build African economic and political elites) is labelled as corruption.

Notes

1. Other international initiatives of best practice listed by Cornerhouse include The 2005 World Economic Forum's *Partnering Against Corruption: Principles for Countering Bribery* (PACI); The International Federation of Consulting Engineers (FIDIC) *Business Integrity Management System*, plus model representative agreement; The International Chambers of Commerce (ICC) *Rules of Conduct* (1998 revision); The UN *Global Compact*, whose 10th principle reads 'businesses should work against all forms of corruption, including extortion and bribery'; and Transparency International's *Business Principles for Countering Bribery*.
2. Some of these were later addressed during 2005, others remain the subject of controversy.
3. The CDC Group are underwritten by the UK Treasury to finance projects in the south with a developmental element. It was established in 1997 as a UK government-owned company, from its forerunner the Commonwealth Development Corporation (CDC).

4. International best practice on due diligence of agents are laid out by the ICC, the International Federation of Consulting Engineers, TI and Transparent Agents and Contracting Entities (TRACE).
5. This report called for a 'strong' state, not a minimal one (which is the default policy of neoclassical definitions of corruption, based in rent-seeking).
6. There is a resonance between the companies understanding of 'out there' and how 'deep corruption' is described as a systemic mode of everyday life in academic texts on neo-patrimonial African regimes (for example in Bayart et al., 1999; Chabal and Daloz, 1999; Médard, 1995).
7. ABB and Dumez worked on the Itaipu Dam on the Brazil/Paraguay border. The dam was originally projected to cost $3.4 billion, but the final cost came to around $20 billion. Numerous corruption allegations surround the project. (IRN, 2000, 3).
8. The ODA was renamed Department for International Development (DfID) in 1997.
9. But also African Lion, Aquarius Platinum, East African Gold Mines, and Platmin are listed as investments in the minerals, oil and gas sector.
10. The final consortium for Tsavo Power Company saw IPS join with Cinergy Global Power, a subsidiary of Cinergy Corp (a US energy company) to take 49.9 per cent, 30 per cent went to the CDC, 5 per cent to the IFC, and US-based Wartsila Development and Finance Services took 15.1 per cent. In summary, a total of US$65 million of debt financing was provided by IFC, CDC and Deutsche Investions-und Entwicklungsgesellschaft (Caltex, 2003).
11. Exceptions to the overall pattern do occur, such as the recent sale of CDC's holdings in Protea Hospitality to empowerment companies, allowing the latter to singularly surpass the ownership empowerment targets for the leisure industry in South Africa.

References

Bayart, J-P., Ellis, S., and Hibou, B. (1999), *The Criminalisation of the State in Africa*, Oxford: James Currey Press for the International African Institute

Bracking, S. (1997), 'Expanding markets and regulating dependency under structural adjustment: business and the case of Zimbabwe from 1991', University of Leeds, Ph.D

Bracking, S. (1999), 'Why structural adjustment isn't necessary and why it does work', in *Review of African Political Economy*, vol. 26, no. 80, pp. 207–26

Bracking, S. (2001) 'The Lesotho Highlands Corruption Trial: Who has been airbrushed from the dock?' vol. 28, no. 88 of the *Review of African Political Economy*, June, pp. 302–08

Bracking, S. (2003), 'Regulating capital in accumulation: negotiating the imperial "frontier"', in *Review of African Political Economy*, Spring, vol. 30, no. 95, pp. 11–33

Bracking, S., (2005) 'Development Denied: autocratic militarism in post-election Zimbabwe', *Review of African Political Economy*, 32, 104/5, 341–57

Bracking (2006), 'Contemporary political economies of sub-Saharan Africa: the post-colonial legacy of multiple narratives', *Afriche e Orienti*, Special Issue II, Occidente e Africa: Democrazia e nazionalismo dalla prima alla seconda transizione, pp. 85–102

Caltex (2003), 'The power and the glory' at www.caltex.com/magazine/articel_power_and_glory.htm

Castree, N. (2004), 'Economy and culture are dead! Long live economy and culture!', in *Progress in Human Geography*, vol. 28, no 2, pp. 204–26

Chabal, P. and Daloz, J-P. (1999), *Africa Works: Disorder as Political Instrument*, Oxford: James Currey for the International African Institute

Commission on Africa (2005), *Our Common Interest: a Report of the Commission for Africa*, Commission for Africa

Commonwealth Development Corporation (1992), *Annual Report*, London

Commonwealth Development Corporation (2005), 'Making Commercial Sense of Development', in *Emerging Markets Report*, Issue 2, October

Cornerhouse (2004), *Submission by the Corner House to the ECGD Consultation on Changes to ECGD's Anti-Bribery and Corruption Procedures Introduced in December 2004*

Danby, C. (2002), 'The curse of the modern: a post-Keynesian critique of the gift/exchange dichotomy', in *Social Dimensions in the Economic Process*, 21, pp. 13–42

Department of Trade and Industry (1994), in House of Commons (HC) (1994) Trade and Industry Committee, Fourth Report, *Trade with Southern Africa*, Vol. II, Memoranda of Evidence, London HMSO, no. 220-II

ECA Watch (2006), 'Export Credit Agencies Explained', available from www.eca-watch.org/eca/ecas_explained.html accessed on 20 December

ECGD (2006), *ECGD's 2005 Sustainable Development Action Plan*, available from www.ecgd.gov.uk/sd_action_plan_2005.pdf accessed on 19 December 2006

Gallagher, M. (1991), *Rent-seeking and Economic Growth in Africa*, Boulder/Oxford, Westview Press

Granovetter, M. (1985). 'Economic action and social structure: the problem of embeddedness', *American Journal of Sociology*, 91: 481–510

Gudeman, S. (1986), *Economics as culture: models and metaphors of livelihood*, London; Routledge

Hansard, (2005), *Written Answers* 27 January, pt. II

Heymans, C. and Lipietz, B. (1999), Corruption and Development: Some Perspectives, *Monograph No. 40*, September 1999, Institute for Security Studies, available from www.iss.co.za/Pubs/Monographs/No40/ConseptualIssues.html

Hildyard, N. (2000), *UK's role in promoting corruption, cronyism and graft*, The Corner House, October 23 accessed at www.probeinternational.org/pi/od/index.cfm?DSP = content&ContentID = 1439) on 3 July 2001

HC (1994), Trade and Industry Committee, Fourth Report, *Trade with Southern Africa*, Vol. II, Memoranda of Evidence, London HMSO, no. 220-II

HC (1994b), Trade and Industry Committee, Fourth Report, *Trade with Southern Africa*, Minutes of Evidence, 15 June, no. 220-IV

International Development Committee (2001), *Corruption*, Fourth Report, 4 April, HC 39-I Report and Proceedings of the Committee, and HC-39 II Minutes of Evidence and Appendices, accessed at www.publications.parliament.uk/pa/cm/cmintdev.htm 20 June 2001

International Development Committee (1999), *The Export Credits Guarantee Department – Development Issues*, First Report, 20 December, HC 73

International Rivers Network (2000), 'LHWP: What Went Wrong?' Presentation to Chatham House Conference, July 10 2000, 'Corruption in Southern

Africa – Sources and Solutions', by Nicholas Hildyard available from www.irn.org/programs/lesotho/index.php?id = chatham.01.html

Keenan, J. (2005), 'Chad-Cameroon Pipeline: World Bank and ExxonMobil in 'Last Chance Saloon'' in *Review of African Political Economy*, 104, 5, 395–477

Kothari, U. (2005), 'Authority and Expertise: the professionalisation of International Development and the Ordering of Dissent', *Antipode*, *37* (3), pp. 425–46

Médard, J-F. (1995), 'La corruption politique et administrative et les différenciations du public et du privé: une perspective comparative', in Borgi, M. and Meyer-Bisch, P. (eds) *La corruption ou l'envers des droits de l'homme*, Editions Universitaires, Fribourg, Suisse, pp. 37–46

Mhone, G. (2001), *Labour Market Discrimination and its Aftermath in Southern Africa*, United Nations Research Institute for Social Development, Conference Racism and Public Policy, Durban, 3–5 September

Michael, B. (2004) 'What Do African Donor-sponsored Anti-corruption Programmes Teach Us about International Development in Africa?' in *Social Policy and Administration*, 38, 4, 320–45

Moore, D. S. (2005), *Suffering for Territory: Race, Place, and Power in Zimbabwe*, Weaver Press, Harare

OECD (2005), *Guaranteeing Development? The Impact of Financial Guarantees*, by James Winpenny, Development Centre of the Organisation for Economic Cooperation and Development

OECD (2005b), 'Experts' Workshop: Governance-Investment Interactions in Developing Countries', available at www.oecd.org/document/49/0,2340,en_2649_33731_35553521_1_1_1_1,00.html

Pinaud, N. (2005), 'Public–Private Dialogue in Developing Countries: Risks and Opportunitites', *Working Paper*, OECD Development Centre, pp. 1–4

Polanyi, K. (2001) *The Great Transformation: the Political and Economic Origins of Our Time*, Beacon Press, Boston, 1st pub. 1944

Polanyi, K. (1968), 'The Economy as Instituted Process', in *Economic Anthropology* E. LeClair, H. Schneider (eds) New York; Holt, Rinehart and Winston

Polzer, T. (2001), Corruption: Deconstructing the World Bank Discourse, Destin, Working Paper Series, no. 01–18, London School of Economics

Pottinger, L. (2005) 'Lesotho Highlands Water Project: Corruption and Impoverishment' in *In Large Dams and the OECD*, ECA Watch, available from www.eca-watch.org/problems/dams/ECAW_trojan_horse_report_2sept05.html accessed on 20 December 2006

Prattis, J. I. (1982), 'Synthesis, or a New Problematic in Economic Anthropology', *Theory and Society* 11: 205–28

Ranis, G. (1997), 'The World Bank Near the Turn of the Century' in Culpeper, R., Berry, A. and Stewart F. (eds) *Global Development Fifty Years after Bretton Woods*, London, Macmillan

Repetti, M. (2002), 'Social Relations in Lieu of Capital' in *Social Dimensions in the Economic Process*, 21, 43–59

Saxton, J. (1999), 'Can IMF Lending Promote Corruption?', Vice Chairman, Joint Economic Committee, United States Congress, pp. 1–8, available from www.house.gov/jec/imf/corrupt.htm accessed on 20 December 2006

Schmitz, G. J. (1995), 'Democractization and Demystification: Deconstructing "Governance" as Development Paradigm' in Moore, D. B. and Schmitz, G. J. (eds) *Debating Development Discourse: Institutional and Popular Perspectives*, London, Macmillan

Wallerstein, I. (1999) *Historical Capitalism with Capitalist Civilisation*, London, Verso

World Aid Section (WAS) (1991) *European Community-Funded Aid Projects in Developing Countries: Consultancies*, compiled by the UK Permanent Representation to the European Communities, January, EDF 08

14
Why Anti-Corruption Initiatives Fail: Technology Transfer and Contextual Collision

Richard Heeks

This chapter examines an archetype of anti-corruption reforms – new technology-based 'e-transparency' initiatives in developing countries – analysing them as 'technology transfers' in the broadest sense of ideas conceived in one context and implemented in another. A model is presented of how transfers are mediated in practice between the two contexts, which can be applied more broadly to all types of anti-corruption intervention. The chapter examines how a system of tools, processes, values, and resources designed in one context can carry with it inscribed assumptions – values drawn from designers' backgrounds; assumptions about the skills, values, and resources of the user context; requirements needed for the proper implementation of the initiative – which may undermine its suitability, or which contain elements that may be appropriated by local users.

The contextual collision between context of design and context of use is a frequent source of failure of anti-corruption interventions, although other ameliorating outcomes include 'reciprocating accommodations' between the two contexts that lead to a viable intervention, albeit one that may compromise on its ability to address corruption. The issues of failure, transfer and context will be investigated using commissioned case studies of new technology designed to foster transparency and address corruption in developing and transitional economies (eGov4Dev, 2004),[1] and some conclusions on what causes certain outcomes will be made.

Public sector anti-corruption reforms as technology transfer

Anti-corruption reforms in the public sector are part of a more general global flow of knowledge, skills and artefacts from perceived epicentres in the industrialised world to transitional and developing economies. These flows – more uni-directional transfers than bi-directional exchanges – are but the latest example of a far longer transfer process that has characterised all efforts at public sector reform (Minogue, 2001). Anti-corruption reforms are thus part of a global project of technology transfer, conceiving technology in its broadest sense as a system of tools and techniques for undertaking a particular process, such that the technology transfer literature has value in illuminating experiences within the anti-corruption campaign (see Braa et al. 1995 on this literature).

Perhaps, above all, one of the themes of technology transfer has been failure, which is certainly a theme found in evaluations of anti-corruption intervention at various levels. For example, Siddiquee argues that in Malaysia anti-corruption 'institutions and mechanisms have performed poorly in arresting the erosion of moral values in society and administration.' (2005: 118); while a regional review of sub-Saharan African initiatives concluded that, in general, 'legal and administrative reform has produced disappointing results and corruption has flourished and even increased' (Szeftel, 1998: 221). Meanwhile, in a global review, Bertucci concluded that anti-corruption initiatives 'often fail to win lasting victories' (2000: 1).

The context of anti-corruption initiatives

Any anti-corruption initiative is connected to the social context in which it is deployed, rather than simply an isolated artefact of tools and techniques. Indeed, the relationship between initiative and context is bi-directional, with the latter altering the former during deployment, and changing itself as a consequence of the new technology. For example, a new personnel and payroll management system was introduced into the Cameroon Ministry of Public Service and Administrative Reform to try to address a number of corruption issues, including the common problem of 'ghost workers' (Kenhago, 2003), but staff were unhappy about the new approach to decision-making that the system supported and refused to use it, such that deployment was a partial failure. Meanwhile, in South Korea, anti-corruption initiatives since the late 1990s have resulted in dozens of prosecutions and disciplinary actions, changing the social context (rather than being stymied by it), and leading to improvements in South Korea's scores in both its *Corruption Perceptions Index* and *Bribe Payers Index* (Park, 2005).

The inter-relation between initiative and social context is not a simple duality, as this lacks any chronological perspective, since any initiative is designed in a context prior to, and separate from, that of use. Also, once transferred the initiative becomes part of, and changes, the context in which it resides, while prior context is also resident in the initiative. Theories of the social construction of technology help us understand the latter; again, conceiving technology in its very broadest sense of not just physical tools but also social techniques. Using these ideas anything designed contains within it an inscribed 'vision of (or prediction about) the world' (Akrich 1992: 208). This 'world-in-miniature' includes inscriptions of how processes will be undertaken; of the values that people will have; and of the structures in which they are to be placed. Anti-corruption initiatives must therefore be viewed not in a uni-dimensional, reductionist manner but in a systemic manner as a group of related dimensions that are drawn from the context within which that initiative is designed.

More specifically, there are various ways in which we can conceive the contextual dimensions that are inscribed into anti-corruption initiatives, including a checklist – ITPOSMO – that has already been used quite widely in relation to public sector reform initiatives (Heeks, 2006): information (data stores, data flows, etc.); technology (any physical artefacts including information technology); processes (the activities of users and others); objectives and values (the key dimension, through which factors such as culture and politics are manifest); staffing and skills (both the quantitative and qualitative aspects of competencies); management systems and structures; and other resources (particularly time and money).

For example, a democracy initiative was introduced in West Africa with the intention of making the electoral process more transparent (Boateng & Heeks, 2003). Inscribed within that initiative's design were a number of inherent assumptions or requirements, which are summarised in Table 14.1, using the ITPOSMO checklist. Some of these are explicit and overtly laid out, such as the information and technology requirements; others are more subtle and implicit, such as those about the values involved; while some lie in between, such as the required skills which are not designated in an explicit way but are referred to in general terms.

Many of these elements are what Latour (1992: 256) refers to as prescriptions: requirements, assumptions, or expectations about the context into which the initiative is going to be deployed. This includes assumptions about the activities, skills, culture and objectives of the public servants involved, and assumptions about their organisation's infrastructure and organisational culture (Suchman, 1987; Clemons et al. 1995).

These prescriptions do not draw directly, or even predominantly, from the world of the actors who deploy and use the initiative, but from the world of the designer, which conditions the perceptions of the designer

Table 14.1: The design inscriptions of a democratisation project in West Africa

ITPOSMO Checklist	Inscribed assumptions in the design
Information	The information set would consist of the traditional set of constituency results
Technology	The presence of an electronic scoreboard at national headquarters plus around 350 networked PCs, one in each constituency office
Processes	A new process of disintermediated reporting, by which results were sent direct from constituencies to the central headquarters of the National Election Commission
Objectives and values	Elections should be determined on fair and rational grounds
Staffing and skills	The presence of various technology installation skills prior to election, and of data entry skills and network operation and maintenance skills at election time
Management systems and structures	The usual hierarchical management structures of the National Election Commission
Other resources	20 million US$ to be available to cover total costs

about the world of the user. The design of anti-corruption initiatives is thus a situated action, an action 'taken in the context of particular, concrete circumstances' (Suchman, 1987: viii), which draws elements of that context into the design. In other words, designers themselves are part of and shaped by context, such that their own cultural values and objectives will be inscribed in their work, as illustrated in Figure 14.1, which in turn can cause problems of commensurability with the context in which the work is deployed.

The designers of anti-corruption initiatives

Anti-corruption initiatives are designed by many different groups, but a common pattern is for them to be, in some way, external to the context of deployment and use. These externalities can take various different forms. For example, there may be a 'disciplinary externality' when the designer is drawn from a different work domain to that of the focal public servants, such as an accounting rather than public management background or unit. The designer will characteristically have a different educational background, a different departmental culture, even a different

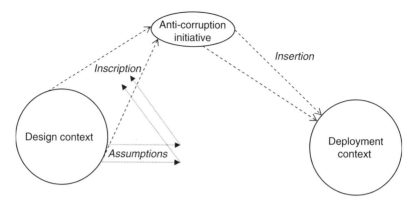

Figure 14.1:   Anti-corruption initiatives and context – inscription and insertion

'language' from those who are supposed to adopt the new initiative. There is also a 'sectoral externality', as the outsourcing of public sector reform projects grows and private sector designers are increasingly creating systems for public sector users, with similar problems of differing values, knowledge, structures, and culture between the two sectors.

In addition, public sector reform projects in developing and transitional economies are dominated by a process of global transfer, as described above. The carriers for these transfers are three main groups (Common, 1998): *international donor agencies*, principally as part of new public management and good governance agendas, with powerful leverage garnered from their role as fund providers; *consultants*, working to compensate for weak or absent local skills, to legitimise pre-determined changes, or as a required component of donor-funded change; and *Western-trained civil servants*, influenced by Western ideas on new public management, transparency and corruption.

These carriers may often be part of a 'country externality' where the designer is from a different national context to that of the users. The most extreme form of this occurs when industrialised country designers create an anti-corruption system within and for an industrialised country context, which is subsequently transferred to a developing country. Less extreme country externalities are present when the groups identified above work locally, or when Western influence is present. This latter can be due to patterns of elite education, who then act as Trojan horses for Western-inspired anti-corruption designs, and because of the leverage gained by Western domination of economic, political and cultural resources more generally.

Whatever the nature of the externality of design – disciplinary, sectoral or country – varying degrees of regard for locality, from a 'If it works for us, it'll work for you' mentality through to more local-oriented approaches, will then occur, although, as discussed above, thinking of the local does not imply its accurate incorporation into design. For example, in one South Asian Planning Ministry, a system was introduced to help make budgeting decisions more transparent (Anonymous, 2003a). An overseas consultant led a design team who inscribed a set of assumptions about the processes and culture of the Ministry into the system, including the assumption that decision-making about project and programme budgets was formal, open and rational. In reality, decision-making in the Ministry had quite different qualities – it was informal, closed, and highly politicised – and this mismatch compromised the system being able to function effectively.

These design failures can be attributed to thoughtlessness, shortage of time or lack of competence on the part of designers. However, they may also relate to the three externalities and arise in part from the nature of discourse in public sector organisations and the way in which that discourse can be disconnected from the organisation's underlying realities. Argyris' idea of two levels of theory, espoused theory and theory-in-use (see for example Argyris, 1985), applies here, where

> Espoused theory represents the values and beliefs individuals claim to hold and publicly support, while theory-in-use represents the values and beliefs individuals actually follow. (Clemons et al. 1995: 11).

Public discourse therefore differs from private motivations and actions (Suchman, 1987), or the privatised behaviour of public sector workers. Such patterns seem likely to be found everywhere but they have particularly been noted in the public sector in developing and transitional economies where there are 'strict formalities covering a substantially different reality of informal behaviour, or where political behaviour takes place under the cover of a formal bureaucracy' (Avgerou, 1990: 237). Reference to a guiding framework of formal, organisational-level rationality is included in public discourse but personalised and politicised rationalities may guide decision-making in practice. Similarly, critical or highly-sensitive issues such as corruption or performance may be excluded from public discourse, and deemed 'undiscussable'.

All these issues arose in the South Asian case described above. The image portrayed is that of the 'rotten coconut', where on the outside, the organisation appears hard and normal, like any other example of its kind, whereas on the inside there was a politicised inner reality. The designers stood on the outside, from different disciplines, from outside the Ministry and with leadership from overseas. Where they did engage with Ministry staff, that interaction was within the public discourse of organisational rationality, talking only about the 'shell' of the coconut not the fruit inside, thus invoking a fiction that bore little relation to the true functioning of the organisation.

These cases seem to reflect a wider picture, where designers inscribe within their anti-corruption initiatives contextual elements related to modernity, rationality, formality and efficiency (for example, Szeftel, 1998; Harrison, 1999; Williams & Beare, 1999), which then conflict with the reality within some public agencies, which beneath a veneer of formal rationality, remain traditional, self-interested, informal and politicised. Such a tension in the public sector – between the 'techno-economic rationality of western modernity' (Avgerou, 1999: 1) and a more traditional and politicised worldview – is neither new nor unique to anti-corruption initiatives. It has antecedents in conflicts within colonial and post-colonial bureaucratic systems (see Berman & Tettey, 2001), and is more broadly resident within policy transfers of new public management; the Western-context component conveyed into different contexts by the carriers identified above.

Contextual collisions

There are three main types of outcome which arise from the differences, misperceptions and inscribed meanings between design and deployment contexts: failure, local appropriation, and reciprocating accommodation. All of the formally-evaluated cases used to illustrate this paper were seen as either partial failures or as largely unsuccessful when judged against their stated objectives. For example, a project in India sought to bypass corrupt government officials by setting up a chain of village-level Internet kiosks that could be used to directly deliver government services such as land registration or issuance of certificates (Sanjay & Gupta, 2003). The project's design inscribed an explicit contextual requirement for both electricity and telecommunications infrastructure to be available on a regular basis. In reality, in quite a number of the villages, this requirement was not met, and as a result, the kiosks fairly quickly moved into a self-reinforcing spiral of low availability, declining use and declining income that led to closure.

In other cases, more subtle and implicit dimensions of inscription are involved in contextual collision and failure. For example, the police force in Andhra Pradesh state, India, introduced a network-based information system (eCOPS) to help improve the transparency of handling criminal cases (Anonymous, 2003b). The project's design inscribed an implicit contextual requirement for police officers to be honest, efficient and rational in their work, which collided with the real context of use in which many officers are highly politicised and self-interested. As a result, the inscribed contextual requirement was not met and police use of the system has been very low, leading eCOPS to be largely unsuccessful.

The second outcome type is a more subtle reaction in which there is some form of assimilation and appropriation of the anti-corruption system by key stakeholders within the context of deployment and use, where some inscribed features are commandeered, while others are left aside. For example, the eCOPS system was mooted in response to a high-profile crime case, where the identified perpetrators were closely associated with the incumbent political party in the State, such that a politicised police force had done nothing to secure arrests (ibid.). There was a public furore which threatened serious political damage for senior officials of the ruling party, who then spearheaded the introduction of eCOPS as an attempt to lessen this damage. The senior officials were able to appropriate important contextual inscriptions from eCOPS to serve their political purposes; inscriptions of objectivity, fairness, and rational justice, during a forcefully publicised planning, design and initial installation phase. After the initial phase, however, the system had served its political purpose: an actual change to local contextual reality was not required, merely a temporary appearance of potential change. From then on, there was little attempt to overcome operational resistance, and existing institutional values and procedures were able to continue largely unchallenged.

The third type of outcome, of reciprocating accommodations, acknowledges that local contexts will more than likely change, and that neither the design nor deployment context need necessarily be dominant. Instead, we see contextual collisions in this case leading to reciprocation with first one context, then the other, making incremental accommodations. Indeed, in some cases, one can see reform designers allowing local appropriation of new initiatives with the deliberate intention that appropriation will change the deployment context. For example, donor-funded consultants in Bangladesh had been asked to place information from departments of the Ministry of Communication on the Web, in order to improve transparency through better data flows from government to citizens (Ahmed, 2003). They knew that the design requirements of such a project were quite seriously mismatched to realities within the Ministry, where staff were averse to the new technology, lacked skills in using the Web, and had little or no ownership of the Web project. The consultants therefore intentionally helped key officials to appropriate Internet-based technology to their own purposes, allowing them to create personal Web pages, to chat online and send informal email messages, and to participate in unofficial discussion fora. At one level, this could be seen as a simple appropriation of the transparency initiative by user stakeholders, but accommodation was facilitated as the deployment context changed and attitudes grew more positive in relation to the project.

Accommodations such has these can be envisaged as continuous reciprocating improvisations between design and reality that, if success is to be achieved, will seek accommodation and adaptation between design and reality sufficient to achieve workable closure (Orlikowski, 1996). In more complex situations, one may find a mix of accommodations, as depicted in Figure 14.2 (adapted from Leonard-Barton, 1988). An example can be taken from the Indian Railways, where a computerised system for train reservations was introduced to reduce corruption in their allocation (Heeks, 2000). This initially met strong resistance from all groups involved until a set of design accommodations was undertaken that then led to reciprocating changes in the context of deployment. For example, a redesign decision was made during implementation to provide railway clerks with a white 'lab coat' as a uniform, which encouraged clerks to view themselves as computing professionals, part of India's burgeoning IT elite. This, together with a redesign

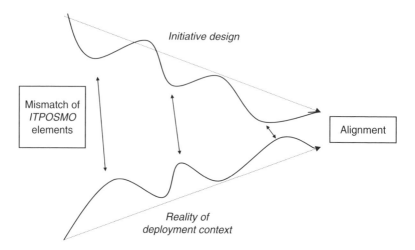

Figure 14.2:   Reciprocating accommodations between initiative design and reality of deployment context

that allowed additional payments for some new clerical activities, altered the clerk's values and interests to the extent that their initial resistance to system introduction was significantly reduced, despite the fact that it would reduce their opportunities for corrupt income generation. As another example, the designers agreed to remove procedures that automated the allocation of reservations controlled by the railway stationmasters. The stationmasters thus retained manual control over this pool of reservations (something from which they could derive corrupt income or other *quid pro quo* favours). This led to a reciprocal change in their attitudes from resistance to either indifference or even grudging support (since it reduced the opportunities for clerical corruption, something with which their own activities were somewhat in competition). The system was able to proceed albeit with some compromise with respect to its anti-corruption aims.

Understanding the pattern of types of outcome

The literature on technology and information systems suggests a set of factors which may help understand which of the three outcomes occurs. These ideas suggest ways in which risks in anti-corruption projects can be reduced; they are ideas that increase the chance of accommodations that lead to a workable system. However, it should be noted that such 'accommodations' may include compromising anti-corruption objectives, such that operational 'success' is not necessarily the same as 'success' in meeting these objectives.

First, the depth of the design inscription affects outcome, and we can conceptualise a continuum of anti-corruption initiatives based on Akrich's (1992) notions of obduracy and plasticity of artefacts (see Figure 14.3). At one end of the continuum, *design-imposing applications* can be seen as largely constraining, containing 'deep inscriptions' which – to be successful – either require or impose a strong set of requirements concerning processes, values, and competencies. An example would be the South Asian planning system described above. Such deep designs – which often

Figure 14.3: Deep- vs. shallow-inscribed anti-corruption initiatives

have many strong implicit elements – are obdurate and will resist attempts at improvisation during deployment, thus reducing the chances of local appropriation or accommodation. Public servants are obstructed by the initiative's matrix of 'contextual concrete', in which elements are bound together on a take it or leave it basis: they must either reject it (as they mainly did in the South Asian case), or accept the totality of its contextual prescriptions and change their own practice dramatically. In many anti-corruption projects there seems to have been a deliberate focus on the design-imposing approach; seeking to choke off opportunities for staff appropriation and improvisation. For example, most of the reviewed cases of e-transparency incorporated a conscious decision to reduce design flexibility because staff autonomy was associated with corruption and self-interested behaviour.

At the other end of the continuum, *reality-supporting applications* can be seen as more enabling, containing relatively 'shallow inscriptions' which impose few systemic contextual components. They are often more explicit in inscription, more plastic and more amenable to improvisation within, appropriation by and accommodation by the user. However, they are likely to be relatively rare in anti-corruption cases for the simple reason that corruption – as a key element within the context of deployment – is not something that is going to be supported. Instead, as just noted, designers are more likely to try to impose a change through their designs.

A second factor affecting successful outcomes will be the way in which the overall anti-corruption project is designed. One aspect of this is opportunity to expose designers to deployment context realities. For example, the Sri Lankan State Accounts Department decided to introduce a more transparent approach to publication of financial statements, enabled by the Web (Chandrasena, 2003), which specifically included the long-term presence of design consultants, enabling them to move beyond the 'discourse of rationality' to a closer contextual understanding. There was also a strong commitment to continuous staff participation and project communication, while the capacity for reciprocating accommodations was enhanced by the division of the project into a series of sub-elements. High divisibility in an anti-corruption project is thus a further project design aspect: it reduces barriers to improvisation, increases opportunities for learning, and limits the extent of change during any given time period to manageable levels, by means of either *modularity* (addressing just one government function at a time), and/or *incrementalism* (addressing government functions in one-at-a-time stepped levels). Finally, local accommodation is also enhanced if local capacity exists to facilitate (allowed) appropriation. This happens particularly through the development of hybrid individuals (Earl, 1989) who straddle the design and deployment contexts.

Drivers to accommodation: using actor-network theory

These three factors – initiative design, project design, and local capacities – are enablers that facilitate accommodations, but it is networks of interest, as outlined in actor-network theory (for example, Latour, 1992), which condition, or 'drive', certain outcomes. In brief, different groups of actors create and maintain networks of aligned interests, and the dominant network (among potentially conflicting ones, and within both contexts) will tend to condition the outcome of an anti-corruption project. The particular nuance of actor-network theory is that the actors within a network are not merely human beings but also nonhuman actors including artefacts such as the anti-corruption initiative itself.

In the case of the eCOPS system discussed earlier, the dominant network of senior politicians ensured that an objective and rational set of police procedures was inscribed into the design, but on implementation the network dissipated, having fulfilled its political function. From that point, a new dominant network emerged: of serving police officers resistant to the system because it ran counter to their interests, coupled with a population of distrustful and thus apathetic citizens. The initial network of interests had a momentum sufficient to get the system installed. The emergent network of interests ensured that no further accommodation was possible.

By contrast, in Romania after 2000, a powerful network of interests was created around the issue of tackling corruption in government (Ailioaie & Kertesz, 2003). This included senior government officials, EU commission representatives, key foreign ambassadors – all concerned with EU accession and good governance – plus some citizen and business groups. This network's drive led, among other things, to the development of the *e-licitatie* system: an e-procurement system to handle purchases of various types of goods by public agencies. The network of interests led not merely to the inscription of various passive anti-corruption values within *e-licitatie*, but to the active inscription and delegation of previously-human agency to the computing application, which undertook automated decisions about contract allocation that had formerly been undertaken by (fallible, corruptible) humans. The strength of this combined network of people and application was sufficiently strong that it forced an accommodation of the user context – combining both public servants and private sector suppliers – to the design of the system. This e-procurement system now handles hundreds of millions of US$-worth of transactions annually and appears to have significantly reduced opportunities for corruption.

The dominant network of interests within the context of design not only determines what contextual elements are inscribed into the anti-corruption initiative, but also those which are not. For example, the activities of stationmasters in the Indian Railways example were placed outside the scope of the initiative as part of a redesign process. The stationmasters thus supported the redesigned system, which would automate the larger set of reservations previously controlled by railway clerks. This is one instance of a broader pattern by which senior officials can be recruited into networks of support for anti-corruption initiatives when they see that initiative will shine more of a spotlight on the corruption of junior staff and thus, potentially, cast their own misdeeds deeper into the shadows (Frasheri, 2003).

Conclusion

This chapter has approached corruption from a novel angle, drawing insights from the informatics and technology transfer literature to provide a new insight on anti-corruption initiatives. Initiatives are seen to transfer between two contexts: one of design and one of deployment/use. Initiative designers are typically external to the context of deployment, thus inscribing assumptions that may mismatch the latter context. This helps us understand the outcome of anti-corruption initiatives – the total failure of implacable 'contextual collision'; the partial failure of local appropriation of inscribed elements; or the relative success of reciprocating accommodations between contexts of design and use. In practical terms, one can make recommendations about how anti-corruption initiatives or their project superstructures are designed. This can make a workable initiative more likely but we have also seen that such initiatives may water down initial corruption objectives.

Note

1. The 'eGovernment for Development Information Exchange' project is coordinated by the University of Manchester's Institute for Development Policy and Management. The project was initially funded and managed by the Commonwealth Telecommunications Organisation as part of the UK Department for International Development's 'Building Digital Opportunities' programme. The views expressed here are those of the author and not those of the funding/facilitating organisations.

References

Ahmed, M. (2003) *Publishing Bangladesh Government Information via the Web*, eTransparency Case Study No. 5, eGovernment for Development Information Exchange www.egov4dev.org

Ailioaie, S. & Kertesz, S. (2003) *E-licitatie: Transparency of Romanian Public Procurement Through ICTs*, eTransparency Case Study No. 9, eGovernment for Development Information Exchange www.egov4dev.org

Akrich, M. (1992) The de-scription of technical objects. In *Shaping Technology/ Building Society*, eds. W. E. Bijker and J. Law. Cambridge, MA, MIT Press

Anonymous (2003a) *Laying Foundations for Transparency of Development Project Finances in a South Asian Ministry of Planning*, eTransparency Case Study No. 16, eGovernment for Development Information Exchange www.egov4dev.org

Anonymous (2003b) *eCOPS: More Open Handling of Criminal Cases in India*, eTransparency Case Study No. 7, eGovernment for Development Information Exchange www.egov4dev.org

Argyris, C. (1985) *Strategy, Change and Defensive Routines*, Pitman, London

Avgerou, C. (1990) Computer-based information systems and modernization of public administration in developing countries, in: *Information Technology in Developing Countries*, S. C. Bhatnagar & N. Bjorn-Andersen (eds), North-Holland, Amsterdam, 243–50

Avgerou, C. (1999) *Recognising Alternative Rationalities in the Deployment of Information Systems*, mimeo, Dept. of Info. Systems, LSE, London

Berman, B. J. and Tettey, W. J. (2001) African states, bureaucratic culture and computer fixes. *Public Administration and Development*, 21: 1–13

Bertucci, G. (2000) Why anti-corruption crusades often fail to win lasting victories, paper presented at *Anti-Corruption Summit 2000*, Arlington, VA, 21 September

Boateng, K. & Heeks, R. (2003) *Computerising Election Results Management in West Africa*, Real-World Design-Reality Example 2, eGovernment for Development Information Exchange www.egov4dev.org

Braa, J. et al. (1995) Technology transfer vs. technological learning. Information *Technology for Development*, 6(1), 15–23

Chandrasena, A. M. S. K. (2003) *Web-Based Access to User-Friendly Government Financial Statements in Sri Lanka*, eTransparency Case Study No. 10, eGovernment for Development Information Exchange www.egov4dev.org

Clemons, E. K., Thatcher, M. E. & Row, M. C. (1995) Identifying sources of reengineering failures: a study of the behavioral factors contributing to reengineering risks. *Journal of Management Information Systems*, 12(2): 9–36

Common, R. (1998) The new public management and policy transfer, in: *Beyond the New Public Management*, M. Minogue, C. Polidano and D. Hulme, eds, Edward Elgar, Cheltenham, UK, 59–75

Earl, M. J. (1989) *Management Strategies for Information Technology*. Hemel Hempstead, UK: Prentice-Hall

eGov4Dev (2004) *Using ICTs for Public Sector Transparency*, eGovernment for Development, IDPM, University of Manchester, UK www.egov4dev.org/ topic2.htm

Frasheri, N. (2003) *Re: eTransparency: Hiding Big Corruption?*, personal communication with author, 13 December

Harrison, G. (1999) Clean-up, conditionality & adjustment: why institutions matter in Mozambique. *Review of African Political Economy*, 81: 323–33

Heeks, R. B. (2000) Information technology and the management of corruption, in *Development and Management*, T. Wallace (ed.), Oxfam Publishing, Oxford, 252–60

Heeks, R. B. (2006) *Implementing and Managing eGovernment*. London, Sage

Kenhago, O. (2003) *SIGIPES & Aquarium: More Transparent Handling of Personnel Files in Cameroon*, eTransparency Case Study No. 4, eGovernment for Development Information Exchange www.egov4dev.org

Latour, B. (1992) Where are the missing masses? The sociology of a few mundane artifacts, in: W. E. Bijker & J. Law (eds), *Shaping Technology/Building Society*, MIT Press, Cambridge, MA, 225–58

Leonard-Barton, D. (1988) Implementation as mutual adaptation of technology and organization. *Research Policy*, 17, 251–67

Minogue, M. (2001) The internationalization of new public management, in: *The Internationalization of Public Management*, W. McCourt and M. Minogue, eds, Edward Elgar, Cheltenham, UK, 1–19

Orlikowski, W. J. (1996) Improvising organizational transformation over time: a situated change perspective. *Information Systems Research*, 7(1): 63–92

Park, Y. S. (2005) International efforts to combat corruption and Korea's anti-corruption drive. *Korea Observer*, 36(2): 323–48

Sanjay, A. K. & Gupta, V. (2003) *Gyandoot: Trying to Improve Government Services for Rural Citizens in India*, eTransparency Case Study No. 11, eGovernment for Development Information Exchange www.egov4dev.org

Siddiquee, N.A. (2005) Public accountability in Malaysia: challenges and critical concerns. *Journal of Public Administration*, 28(1–2): 107–29

Suchman, L. (1987) *Plans and Situated Actions*. Cambridge, UK: Cambridge University Press

Szeftel, M. (1998) Misunderstanding African politics: corruption & the governance agenda. *Review of African Political Economy*, 76: 221–40

Williams, J. W. & Beare, M. E. (1999) The business of bribery: globalization, economic liberalization, and the 'problem' of corruption. *Crime, Law & Social Change*, 32(2): 115–46

15
Strengthening Checks and Balances in Financial Governance: the Evolving Role of Multilateral Banks in Latin America[1]

Carlos Santiso

> Constant experience shows us that every man invested with power is apt to abuse it . . . it is necessary from the very nature of things that power should be a check to power.
> (Charles de Montesquieu, *The Spirit of the Laws,* 1748: XI, 4)

It is increasingly acknowledged that improving economic governance and fostering fiscal responsibility, as well as securing effective aid delivery, necessarily require greater transparency and accountability in the management of public finances. These twin objectives have led to a renewed interest in the institutions overseeing the budget, in particular legislatures and external audit agencies, and as a result, the governance of the budget is the subject of renewed scrutiny (Schick, 1998; Santiso, 2006a).[2]

This study reviews a decade of support by the World Bank (WB) and the Inter-American Development Bank (IDB) to legislatures and external audit agencies in Latin America. It underscores recent developments in development finance, reflecting a learning curve in multilateral assistance to budget oversight institutions leading to a broader understanding of the determinants of fiscal credibility and financial integrity. However, tackling the underlying political economy of financial accountability and the political context of public budgeting is more challenging.

Changes in approaches to financial governance

While first-generation fiscal reforms in the 1990s centred on strengthening the executive functions of government in the management of public finances, often advocating a greater centralisation of budgetary systems and the adoption of numerical and procedural constraints, second-generation fiscal reforms increasingly emphasise the importance of transparency and accountability and underscore the value of external scrutiny, legislative and societal oversight. Whilst these two approaches are mutually reinforcing, the former centres on financial management within the executive and the bureaucracy, in particular finance ministries, central budget offices, central banks and tax authorities, with interventions around cash-management, treasury, accounting and statistical functions. In contrast, the latter approach to the reform of fiscal institutions necessarily requires engaging with a broader set of organisations and processes beyond the executive, in particular legislatures, external audit agencies, and civil society, in the broader context of the political economy of executive-legislative budget relations. This widens traditional modernisation programmes of financial management systems, to a broader institutional approach, as policymakers increasingly acknowledge wider democratic contributions to financial accountability (see Santiso, 2006a, 2004e; Schick, 2002, 1998; Wehner, 2004; Manning and Stapenhurst, 2002; Petrei, 1998).

The recent awareness of the international financial institutions (IFIs) of the limitations of an exclusive focus on the executive, and the need to balance executive discretion with external accountability, has prompted some discussion of the institutions of 'horizontal accountability' in fiscal policy and financial governance, especially in presidential systems of government (O'Donnell, 1999; Mainwaring and Welna, 2003).[3] Mitigating the risks associated with excessive executive discretion necessarily requires reinforcing countervailing mechanisms. Indeed, the central challenge of financial governance in emerging economies is to reconcile fiscal responsibility with political accountability and achieving a delicate balance between executive power and legislative oversight: how to retain the advantages of strong executive authority required to ensure fiscal responsibility, while providing the institutional checks and balances that ensure accountability and prevent corruption. This requires a system-wide approach to the institutions and incentives shaping fiscal behaviour in different phases of the budget process and conditioning the interactions between the different actors of the budgetary game. In democratic regimes, national legislatures and external audit agencies are key institutions of budget oversight and fiscal control (Stapenhurst, 2004).

This chapter reviews the decade-long multilateral assistance provided by the WB and the IDB to Latin American countries in order to strengthen budget oversight institutions, notably national legislatures and external audit agencies, although space prevents review of the promising initiatives in civil society (see Open Budget Initiative, 2006; Lavielle et al. 2003). The article focuses on lending, technical assistance and policy advice, in a subset of emerging economies where presidential systems of government combine with highly centralised budgetary systems, in order to assess whether this delicate balance has been achieved.

Understanding and strengthening financial accountability

Sound management of public finances and efficacious oversight of the budget are key dimensions of good governance, which, according to the standard WB definition, captures 'the manner in which power is exercised in the management of a country's economic and social resources for development' (WB, 1992: 1). Additionally, the IFIs recognise that strengthening of public finance accountability is a critical institutional reform required to consolidate second-generation economic reforms (Santiso, 2004c.)

In the first generation of economic reforms, Washington Consensus policy advocated a predominant role for the executive in the budget process and the insulation of economic policymaking in the finance ministry, leading to an increasing centralisation of the budgetary process within the executive branch, which positively influenced fiscal outcomes and fiscal discipline (Stein et al. 1998; Alesina et al. 1999). The prevalent view posits that concentration of budgetary powers within the executive is 'more likely to enforce fiscal restraint, avoid large and persistent deficits and implement fiscal adjustments more promptly' (Alesina and Perotti, 1996: 7). It warns against the dysfunctional fiscal effects of unrestrained legislative budgetary powers and consequently favours the insulation of economic policymaking within the executive (Alesina et al. 1999; Stein et al. 1998).

However, while these arguments are substantiated by empirical evidence, recent experience reveals the risks of excessive executive discretion in public budgeting (Santiso, 2006a). Admittedly, immature legislatures and unstable party systems can be the source of dysfunctional economic governance, budget deficits and fiscal imbalances. At the same time, however, autocratic presidents can accumulate excessive executive discretion, abuse the prerogatives of executive decree authority and the delegation of legislative authority and, left largely unchecked by impotent legislatures, cause serious economic mismanagement, pervasive corruption and even state capture. Autocratic presidents can neutralise accountability mechanisms.

It is increasingly acknowledged that greater transparency and accountability in financial governance will improve the quality and legitimacy of fiscal governance. While existing empirical evidence on the impact of legislative oversight and external scrutiny on fiscal outcomes remains largely inconclusive, partly due to the unavailability of comparative data, evidence exists on the positive contribution of legislative oversight and external auditing to fiscal governance. A review of external audit agencies in Latin America reveals a positive correlation between external auditing, corruption control and budget transparency (Santiso, 2006b).

Revisiting assistance strategies

The IFIs have both a fiduciary and a developmental interest in improving transparency and accountability in public finance management. Often, large policy-based loans and direct budget support grants integrate components specifically aimed at strengthening transparency and accountability in public financial management, in order to provide reasonable assurances that the funds are adequately spent on their intended purposes. Second-generation institutional reforms in the 1990s lead to increasing attention by government to the strengthening of financial governance (Santiso, 2004b, 2004c), which in Latin America translated into WB and IDB support for integrated financial management systems in Argentina, Bolivia, El Salvador, Honduras, Guatemala, Nicaragua and Venezuela (Dorotinsky and Matsuda, 2002; Santiso, 2004d).

Undeniably, the introduction of the governance agenda, with its principles of transparency, oversight, and accountability, has led the IFIs to broaden the scope of their interventions (Santiso, 2004a, 2001). In 1996, the International Monetary Fund (IMF) was urged by its governors to promote good governance (IMF, 1996), nevertheless restricting itself to those economic aspects of fiscal governance that could have a significant macroeconomic impact and could affect the implementation of economic reforms. Nevertheless, the IMF's role in fiscal governance has expanded considerably, integrating concerns over transparency, accountability and predictability of fiscal policy (IMF, 1997, 2001a; Op de Beke, 2002; Abed and Gupta, 2002).

In the mid-1990s, the WB began supporting programmes to strengthen accountability institutions, such as the legal and judicial reform and financial management systems. In 1997, it adopted an anti-corruption strategy and, in 2000, guidelines to orient its involvement in governance issues (WB, 1997 and 2000). Between 1996 and 2000, it supported over 600 governance-related projects in 95 countries. Between 1982 and 2002, it carried out 126 public sector reform projects totalling US$12 billion in Latin America and the Caribbean alone (Fuhr and Krause, 2003). A majority of these projects, usually policy-based loans with a marked emphasis on fiscal reform, included a component on public budgeting and financial governance.

Nevertheless, the IFIs have yet to clarify their approach to the strengthening of budget oversight institutions, in particular national legislatures and external audit agencies, although important progress has taken place in the past few years. Legislative strengthening remains a controversial and contested area of engagement for the WB (Pelizzo and Stapenhurst, 2004; Manning and Stapenhurst, 2002). The 2000 governance strategy remains ambivalent in this regard, in particular as it concerns the oversight functions of legislatures in public budgeting. It acknowledges the importance of achieving 'greater cognizance and support of the role and functioning of legislative oversight bodies, ombudsman offices, public audit institutions' (WB, 2000: 60). Similarly, the draft governance and anticorruption strategy of 2006 commits the WB to 'work in partnership with other donors, more systematically help legislatures [external audit agencies] and other formal oversight institutions develop the capacity to oversee public expenditure' (WB, 2006: 14). The WB nevertheless appreciates that any engagement in legislative strengthening is intrinsically political (Messick, 2002). Therefore, the WB underscores that:

> for reasons of either limited mandate or limited expertise, we do not envision the Bank becoming involved in some other areas of public sector reform, such as [. . .] general legislative processes or political governance. (2000: 62)

The WB's approach to external audit agencies has traditionally focused on fiduciary risk aspects for its own lent funds (WB, 2003b), although it is increasingly emphasising the development objectives of its engagement with external audit agencies in developing countries. In 2003, the WB reviewed its audit policy in order to better link fiduciary and development objectives, indicating that the WB would include measures to address weaknesses found in its initial audit of public financial management (WB, 2004a). Furthermore, in 2004, the WB adopted a strategy delineating its approach to the strengthening of external audit agencies (WB, 2004b), seeking

> to place greater reliance on the normal financial reports and audit processes of borrower countries when these are considered to meet acceptable standards. Where weaknesses are identified, the Bank supports programs to build capacity. (WB, 2003b: 7; Wolfensohn, 2004)

Regional development banks are also broadening their support to budget oversight institutions (Santiso, 2004e). In Latin America, the IDB, which does not have the political restrictions of the WB, has developed lending programmes specifically designed to strengthen legislative budget institutions. The Eighth Replenishment of IDB resources in 1994 mandated it to contribute to the consolidation of democracy in the region (IDB, 1999), such that the IDB explicitly recognises the representative, legislative and oversight functions of legislatures and pursues legislative strengthening within its strategy to strengthen democratic consolidation. The role of legislatures and external audit agencies in public budgeting, financial accountability and corruption control figure prominently in the strategy on the modernisation of the state adopted in 2003 (IDB, 2003), where the IDB stresses the need to 'strengthen the institutional capacity of the legislative branch', and 'help ensure budgetary, monitoring and oversight functions are performed based on objective and technical criteria' (IDB, 2003: 12).

Improving fiscal standards and financial diagnostics

The main channels through which the IMF promotes good fiscal governance are surveillance, lending and technical assistance (IMF, 1997, 2001b). In terms of surveillance, the IMF promotes standards and codes of good practice thorough its Article IV consultations in fiscal matters, including on fiscal transparency and the strength of the 'assurances of integrity,' such as external audit offices (IMF, 2001b). Since the late 1990s, it has acknowledged the importance of transparency in monetary and financial policy management, adopting a Code of Good Practices on Fiscal Transparency adopted in 1999 and updated in 2001, which includes anti-corruption among twelve areas of financial management (IMF, 1999, 2001b).

In recent upgrading and review of procedures, IFIs are attaching greater importance to the contribution of legislative budget institutions to fiscal policymaking and budget oversight. While the IMF's *Code* tends to restrict itself to fiscal governance within the executive, the OECD *Best Practices for Budget Transparency* includes consideration of the role of legislatures in the budget process (OECD, 2001). However, the IFIs continue to show restraint in their approach to budgetary reform, in that technical assistance tends to concentrate either on the expenditure side (providing assistance to the finance ministries or the central budget offices), or the revenue side, (providing tax reform advice and strengthening the capacities of tax authorities). It seldom addresses the budget cycle as an integrated holistic process.

The IFIs have also upgraded their diagnostic instruments to assess compliance with international standards. A country's observance of IMF standards is regularly assessed in the Reports on the Observance of Standards and Codes (ROSCs), 264 of which had been completed for 80 countries by the end of June 2002. Recent fiscal ROSCs, along with second generation reform initiatives more generally, have not only included considerations about the strength of financial accountability mechanisms, but also about the quality of executive-legislative budget relations. For example, the 2004 report on Peru underscored the dysfunctional links between the executive and the legislature in the budgetary process and recommended the strengthening of external auditing (IMF, 2004). Similarly, in 2001, the IMF advised Brazil to strengthen the functional linkages between external and internal auditing in governmental financial administration at the different levels of government (IMF, 2001c). In the case of Chile, the IMF (2003), as well as the WB and the IDB (2004), underscored the need to improve state accounting and review institutional arrangements for external auditing.

The WB uses different diagnosis instruments to inform country strategies, investment lending operations and the conditionality attached to policy-based loans, as summarised in Table 15.1. The recent addition of Institutional and Governance Reviews (IGRs) reflects the second-generation reform agenda. Examples include the IGR for Peru in 2001 (WB, 2001b), which contained an assessment of the institutional context and political constraints informing public expenditure management and accountability; and the IGRs for Paraguay (WB, 2005) and Argentina (WB, 2003c), which focus on the institutional context of financial management and fiscal control. As the WB notes,

> The IGR relates to the CFAA in its diagnosis of the shortcomings of formal public finance management systems that are due to inadequate capacity, incentives, or signals. (WB, 2003a: 2–3)

Indeed, there is a gradual convergence between the traditional economic approach to public finance management and the political economy approach to public finance accountability, which partly captures the influence of political influences, party systems and electoral rules on the structure of incentives.

Although they possess different mandates and perform different functions, the IFIs are seeking to coordinate their approaches to public finance reform and harmonise their assessment standards and instruments (OECD, 2003). In 1995, the IMF and WB issued guidelines to improve

Table 15.1: WB diagnostic instruments in public financial management

Instrument	Role	Outcome	Frequency
Country Assistance Strategy (CAS)	Informed by, in particular, the CFAAs.	Decisions on size of the lending programme, the selection of lending instruments, and approaches to risk management.	Every 4 years
Country Policy and Institutional Assessments (CPIAs)	Assess a country's policy and institutional framework in terms of poverty reduction and effective use of development assistance.	Inform the allocation of concessional resources by the International Development Association (IDA) (IDA 2002).[4]	Annual
Public Expenditure and Financial Accountability (PEFA) reviews	Assess the quality of a country's public financial management systems against 28 performance indicators and 3 indicators of donor practices (PEFA 2004).	Support borrower in the design and implementation of financial management reform programmes and donors' coordinated support programme.	Every 3 years (introduced in 2005)
Public Expenditure Reviews (PERs)	Analyse fiscal and expenditure policies; evaluates the robustness of public expenditure management systems. They may also examine institutional arrangements for public expenditure management, civil service reform, and revenue administration (WB 2001a).		Occasional

Instrument	Purpose		Frequency
Public Expenditure and Institutional Reviews (PEIRs)	Assess the institutional foundations of public expenditure management.		Occasional
Public Expenditure Tracking Surveys (PETS)	Assess the capacity of borrowing countries to track spending and reduce leakage of public funds.	Joint WB/IMF in Highly Indebted Poor Countries (HIPCs).	Occasional
Country Financial Accountability Assessments (CFAAs)	Assess a country's financial management . system (WB, 2003a); assists in risk management, that public funds will be used other than for agreed purposes (the fiduciary objective).	Support borrower in the design and implementation of financial management capacity-building programmes (the developmental objective).	Occasional
Institutional and Governance Reviews (IGRs)	Assess key governance issues, including the institutional arrangements for economic governance and fiscal policymaking and the political economy of public finance accountability (WB, 2002).		Occasional (introduced in 1999)

operational coordination based on an evaluation of their complementarities, a commitment that was subsequently reaffirmed in 1998 and 2003 (WB and IMF, 2003). Similarly, since the early 2000s, bilateral donors have sought to promote greater alignment and harmonisation amongst themselves, in the context of the Development Assistance Committee (DAC) of the OECD, in particular as it pertains to their approach to aid instruments, diagnostic tools and fiduciary risk management (OECD, 2003). Through the 2005 Paris Declaration on aid effectiveness, donors committed themselves to 'increasing alignment of aid with partner countries' priorities, systems and procedures and helping to strengthen their capacities' and 'using a country's own institutions and systems' for public financial management and accountability (OECD, 2005:1 and 4).

Similarly, the *Public Expenditure and Financial Accountability* (PEFA) programme, a multi-donor initiative established in 2001, aims to promote greater harmonisation in international public sector standards in accounting, auditing and internal control in developing and transitional countries. This effort has resulted in the development of a common framework, the *Public Financial Management Performance Measurement Framework*. Adopted in June 2005, it contains 28 indicators of financial management, as well as three indicators of donor practices. Interestingly, it concedes a greater role for legislatures in ensuring fiscal transparency and financial accountability (PEFA, 2004).

Multilateral lending to budget oversight institutions

These developments are, in turn, informing the lending strategies of multilateral development banks to strengthen legislatures and external audit agencies, although these differ by institution. The WB does not directly assist legislatures through targeted investment lending, and its diagnostic instruments only partially address legislative governance and the dynamics of executive-legislative budget relations. Only the World Bank Institute (WBI), through a small legislative programme, provides technical assistance and professional training to legislatures. However, the WB's diagnostic instruments increasingly acknowledge the importance of checks and balances in public financial management, the political determinants of policy reform and the political economy of institutional development (WB, 2006).

By contrast, the IDB provides investment loans specifically designed to strengthen legislatures in borrowing countries, sanctioned explicitly in its 2003 governance strategy. Since 1994, the IDB has approved or designed thirteen lending operations, totalling over US$100 million (as part of legislative reform programmes totalling over US$150 million), most of which were disbursed over a four-year period. These loans are predominantly aimed at the greater 'modernisation', or institutionalisation of legislatures, improved legislative quality, enhanced legislative processes, and better interactions with civil society, although the bulk of financing is directed at 'hardware investments,' such as development of physical infrastructure, improvements in information technology, and human resources management. The role of legislatures in the budget process was a salient feature in all these loans, with the inclusion of components to improve the work of specialised standing committees and strengthen strategic planning and research capacities.

Within these loans for legislative strengthening one focus was to reform the internal structures, rules and procedures shaping the legislative process, with a marked emphasis on those legislative committees involved in the budget process, either at the approval or the oversight stages. The roles of budget and public accounts committees receive special attention, including legislative rules regulating their organisation and functioning. For example, the IDB's Fiscal and Financial Management Programme in Guyana approved in 2004 includes a component specifically designed to strengthen legislative capacities for budget oversight, through its assistance to the Economic Services Committee, the Public Accounts Committee and the Public Procurement Commission.

A second focus was to enhance the capacities of legislatures for independent budget analysis. This is the case, for example, of the IDB loans to Brazil, through the strengthening of legislative information systems, and Peru, through support to the legislative research office. In a few instances, such as with the 1996 Budgetary Process and Economic Policy Analysis Support Programme in Venezuela, the IDB has been instrumental in the creation of a legislative budget office. In that context, the contribution of legislative budget offices to budget oversight is increasingly recognised, in particular as it concerns access to independent and impartial sources of fiscal information (Santiso, 2006a; Stapenhurst, 2004). The lack of professional legislative staff and the weaknesses of legislative advisory services often hinder effective legislative oversight. With the possible exception of Brazil, standing legislative committees in Latin America often lack the necessary research and advisory capacity with the required technical expertise to become a credible counterpart to the executive in budget debates. However, this is gradually starting to change, and although not as powerful as their US counterpart, the Congressional Budget Office, incipient legislative budget offices are gradually emerging, in, for example, Chile, Mexico and Venezuela, while Argentina and Colombia are considering establishing them (Santiso, 2006a, 2005; Uña, 2005).

Legislatures are key budget institutions, both in the making of budget policy (through the budget committee) and the oversight of budget execution (through the public accounts committee) (Santiso, 2005, 2004e). Within this, independent sources of analysis allow legislatures to partially redress the abysmal asymmetries of fiscal information with the executive branch. Independent budget analysis is also strategic for political reasons, as it is the legislative opposition that has the greatest incentives to require it to better oversee the government (Messick, 2002). Indeed, the strengthening of legislative budget capacity in Latin America coincides with the gradual reassertion of the legislature's budgetary authority throughout the region (Santiso, 2006a), associated with a greater assertiveness of legislative opposition (Stein et al. 2005); since the importance of the opposition is positively associated with more assertive legislative oversight of the budget (Messick, 2002). For example, the surge of legislative activism in the budget process in Mexico is partly the result of the emergence of an assertive opposition since the long-time ruling party, the Institutional Revolutionary Party (PRI), lost its legislative majority in 1997 (Carbonell, 2002; Weldon, 2002). It is probably not a coincidence that the Mexican legislative budget office emerged in 1998.

The case of Venezuela is particularly interesting, as the IDB became, willingly or not, an actor in the struggle between the executive and the legislature over the distribution of budgetary powers. In 1997, an Economic and Financial Advisory Office was created within the National Assembly, with support from the IDB, to enhance the technical advisory services of the legislature in public finance. Nevertheless, increasing tensions between the executive and the legislature since President Hugo Chávez took office have undermined the functioning of this office. It was closed in February 2000 to be subsequently reopened in June of the same year, as part of the reactivation of the suspended loan by the IDB. In 2003, the office was under renewed pressure (Rojas and Zavarce, 2004).

Unsurprisingly, the IFIs increasingly acknowledge that the influence of politics, the quality of the political party system and the incentives provided by the electoral code are key variables for effective legislative oversight of the budget. In many parliamentary systems, the main opposition chairs the public accounts committee, while the discipline of political parties determines, to a great extent, the quality of executive-legislative relations. The political nature of executive-legislative budget relations makes this a contentious area for IFI involvement. As such, lending operations tend to focus on specific components of the system and individual budgetary organisations within legislatures, rather than addressing the political economy of the budget process as a whole. As a result, however, loan operations often fail to generate the systemic impact they potentially could have on the budget process and legislatures' role in its oversight (Santiso, 2004d, 2004e).

Lending to external auditing institutions

Less contentious is WB's support for external audit agencies, as part of its policy dialogue with borrowing countries and through the conditionality attached to its policy-based loans. According to a recent WB estimate, between 1997 and 2002, policy-based loans included about 90 conditions requiring borrowing governments to improve external auditing, while a review of all 1479 adjustment lending conditions that referred to public sector governance shows that about 90 of them (or 6 per cent) addressed the external audit arrangements of 38 borrowing countries (WB, 2004b: 10). The WB also provides technical assistance through small grants, at times supporting larger policy-based loans or preparing the ground for investment loans. According to one estimate, in 2003, more than 30 such grants, with a value of US$10 million, were made to strengthen public expenditure management and financial accountability (Wolfensohn, 2004: 3). In 2000, for example, the WB provided a grant to Mexico to improve the auditing capacities of sub-national governments and, in 2003, another such small grant to strengthen the Argentinean external audit agency. In 2001, it approved a regional-wide initiative to support external audit agencies in Central America.

In the recent past, the IFIs have also started to provide investment loans specifically designed to strengthen external audit agencies, which from 1993 to 2004, numbered 15 in total, 11 by the IDB and four by the WB. These operations represent an investment of almost US$115 million, as part of modernisation programmes totalling over US$184 million, with increasing numbers in recent years.[5] However, even with the new emphasis on investment loans, differences remain between the WB and IDB, as the former tends to confine itself to advisory and analytical work, and small technical assistance operations, while the IDB privileges investment loans specifically designed to strengthen external audit agencies. More recently, as IDB's four loan operations to Ecuador, Haiti, Honduras and Bolivia show, it is integrating its support to external auditing into larger operations designed to improve public financial management systems.

Multilateral loans focus on improving the administrative efficiency of external audit agencies, focused principally on improving operational auditing of specific government programmes and agencies, especially in the social sectors, rather than on strengthening agencies' institutional role in auditing public accounts and the certification of government accounts by the legislature. Arguably, this latter core function would be naturally enhanced as a result of general capacity building, albeit not automatically as reformers tend to expect. Similarly, investment loans tend to confine themselves to the strengthening of external audit agencies in isolation of the rest of the public sector they are embedded in, rather than seeking to enhance the inter-institutional linkages and functional relationships between the different components of the systems of fiscal control. These two features of lending inhibit its efficacy, as in Latin America it is precisely these dysfunctional relations within systems of fiscal control that hamper fiscal management.

The paradox of audit institutions lies in the fact that they both need to be independent to adequately and responsibility perform their tasks, yet they are dependent on other state institutions to have a meaningful impact and to enforce accountability. For instance, reports and recommendations are ineffective if they are not acted on by, in particular, the public administration itself (administrative accountability), the judiciary (criminal accountability) and the legislature (political accountability). Ultimately, the effectiveness of national systems of integrity largely depends on the quality of inter-institutional linkages and the strength of the synergies between their different components (Diamond, 2002), a point recognised by the IDB (Stein et al. 2005: 258). In particular, this includes a symbiotic relationship between the external audit agency and the legislature's public accounts committee (Stapenhurst et al. 2005; Wehner, 2003; McGee, 2002; SIGMA, 2002). But critically, legislators must want to invest in reform, which in turn may require changing political and electoral incentives (Santiso, 2005).

Multilateral lending operations are only gradually addressing these dysfunctional institutional links, by integrating programmes for external audit and legislative oversight, with the IDB loans to the Dominican Republic in 2000 and El Salvador in 1999 good examples of this trend. In Colombia, the IDB took a further step to a systemic approach, undertaking a decade-long financing cycle of modernisation of agencies of financial oversight and law enforcement, which included a US$9.5 million loan to the General Prosecutor's Office in December 1995; a US$23 million loan to the Office of the Comptroller General, and Office of the Auditor General in March 2000; and a US$14 million loan to the Office of the Attorney General in 2003.

Conclusion: political will and policy efficacy

> He who lives outside the budget lives in error.
> (Carlos Fuentes, *La Silla del Águila,* 2003)

Countries have increasingly realised that achieving fiscal discipline requires strong checks and balances in financial governance and robust budget oversight institutions. The subscription of multilateral lending constitutes an important signalling mechanism that can strengthen the hand of reformers. These considerations, along with the pressure from external audit agencies for more resources, partly explain why governments accept to underwrite loans designed to strengthen those institutions tasked with overseeing and constraining them. Indeed, that governments subscribe to such loans is, in itself, an indication that some commitment to anti-corruption and democratic consolidation is in evidence, since multilateral lending to oversight institutions necessarily requires the consent or ascent of borrowing governments.

However, formal consent hides differing degrees of political commitment, and agreements to strengthen technical capacity *per se* do not necessarily, or automatically, improve the effectiveness of external audit agencies, nor prevent them from being captured. The case of Nicaragua is symptomatic in that regard (WB, 2004c; see Chapter 10), where the constitutional reforms of 2000 resulted in the division of key state institutions along party lines, including the external audit agency, the *Contraloría General de la República* (CGR). Pre-existing capacity constraints and organisational dysfunctions are now compounded by the politicisation of the agency and the neutralisation of the external audit function.[6]

More fundamentally, the case of Nicaragua illustrates that increasing technical capacity and enhancing analytical capabilities are likely to remain ineffectual as long as there does not exist the political space for them to be exercised effectively. Overwhelming adverse political incentives against sound financial management can emasculate technical improvements. Reform efforts fail not only because they are incomplete, but because they are designed to solve technical shortcomings when problems lie in institutional arrangements and political incentives structures, in short in the political economy of the policy process more broadly. While the IFIs increasingly acknowledge the centrality of political economy factors in initiating, pursuing and sustaining institutional reform, they remain, for various reasons, resistant to confronting the broader governance context in which legislatures and external audit agencies operate and the structure of incentives conditioning their efficiency.

In terms of strategies, the review of lending undertaken in this chapter indicates a WB preference for integrated support for improving financial management systems within the executive branch, while the IDB more often uses focused support to enhance the role of legislatures and external audit agencies in the budgetary process. Both the WB and IDB use different lending instruments which have different operational efficacies: the conditionality attached to larger policy-based loans is more effective at reforming institutions, while investment lending and technical assistance are more effective at strengthening already capable institutions. There thus exists scope for further enhancing the synergies between available instruments, and adopting sequenced approaches to, first, the reform of fiscal institutions and, then, their strengthening. This approach was evident in IFI relations with Guyana from 2001 to 2004, which sought to sequence the 'stick' of conditionality in a policy-based component to the 'carrot' of technical assistance grants and investment lending.

However, and perhaps more critically than issues of sequencing, multilateral lending operations often fail because they are tempted to address political problems with technical solutions (Girishankar, 2001). As Stein et al. (2005: 259) aptly note, 'It is important to understand that contributing financial resources does not change institutions *per se.*' Multilateral support to budget oversight institutions should more purposefully seek to enhance the functional linkages between institutions of fiscal control. More fundamentally, it ought to give greater consideration to the structure of incentives affecting institutional performance and influencing institutional change, in particular the role of political competition, party systems and electoral rules on the functioning of legislatures and external audit agencies in the oversight of the budget. Whether IFIs are willing or able to take on a wider political purview remains an open question.

Notes

1. This chapter is an abridged and edited version of a more technically detailed article in *Public Budgeting & Finance*, vol. 26, no. 2 (2006): 66–100, 'Banking on Accountability? Strengthening Budget Oversight and Public Sector Auditing in Emerging Economies.' The usual caveats apply. The findings, interpretations, and conclusions expressed in this paper are entirely those of its author. They do not necessarily represent the view of the institutions he is affiliated with.

2. The governance of the budget refers to the institutions, individuals, interest, and incentives governing the formulation, approval, execution, oversight and control of the budget. 'External audit agencies' refer to offices such as the Comptroller General, the Auditor General, Auditing Office or similar. They are autonomous state agencies tasked with overseeing the government's management of public finances (Santiso, 2006b).

3. 'Horizontal accountability' is hereby defined as: 'The existence of state agencies that are legally enabled and empowered, and factually willing and able, to take actions that span from routine oversight to criminal sanctions or impeachment in relation to actions or omissions by other agents or agencies of the state that may be qualified as unlawful' (O'Donnell, 1999: 38).

4. They contain twenty equally weighted criteria grouped in four clusters, one of which is 'public sector management and institutions' which includes an indicator of the quality of budget and financial management, and a further explicit indicator on transparency, accountability and control of corruption in the public sector.

5. Loans made to Brazil (2), Haiti, Peru, Chile, Ecuador, Nicaragua, Colombia, Dominican Republic, Honduras (2), El Salvador, Bolivia, Uruguay, and Caribbean countries.

6. The IDB nevertheless designed a US$5.4 million loan for a US$6 million programme to modernise the external audit agency. However, the question arises as to whether the agency needs to be strengthened, or whether it should be reformed and, therefore, whether the choice of instrument was correct.

References

Abed, George, and Gupta, Sanjeev (eds) (2002) *Governance, Corruption, and Economic Performance* (Washington, DC: IMF)

Alesina, Alberto, and Perotti, Roberto (1996) *Budget Institutions and Budget Deficits* (Cambridge, MA: NBER Working Paper 5556)

Alesina, Alberto, Hausmann, Ricardo, Hommes, Rudolf and Stein, Ernesto (1999) *Budget Institutions and Fiscal Performance in Latin America* (Washington: IADB OCE Working Paper 394)

Carbonell, Miguel (2002) 'Los Conflictos entre el poder legislativo y el poder ejecutivo en México,' *Contribuciones*, 3/2002: 11–24

Dorotinsky, William, and Matsuda, Yasuhiko (2002) 'Reforma de la gestión financiera en América Latina: Una perspectiva institucional,' *Reforma y Democracia*, 23: 141–66

Diamond, Jack (2002) 'The Strategy of Budget System Reform in Emerging Economies,' *Public Finance and Management*, 2(3): 358–86

Fuhr, Harald, and Krause, Philipp (2003) *Overview of Core Public Sector Reform Projects 1982–2002* (Washington: WB)

Girishankar, Navin (2001) *Evaluating Public Sector Reform: Guidelines for Assessing Country-Level impact of Structural Reform and Capacity Building in the Public Sector* (Washington: WB OED)

IDA (2002) *Linking IDA Support to Country Performance – Third Annual Report on IDA's Country Assessment and Allocation Process* (Washington, DC: World Bank)

IDB (1999) *Renewing the Commitment to Development* (Washington, DC: IDB.)

—— (2003) *Modernization of the State: Strategy Document* (Washington, DC: IDB 7/03, GN-2235-1)

IMF (1996): *Partnership for Sustainable Global Growth: Interim Committee Declaration* (Washington, DC: IMF)

—— (1997) *Good Governance: the IMF's Role* (Washington, DC: IMF)

—— (1999): *Code of Good Practices on Transparency in Monetary and Financial Policies: Declaration of Principles* (Washington, DC: IMF)

—— (2001a) *Review of the Fund's Experience in Governance Issues* (Washington, DC: IMF)

—— (2001b) *Manual on Fiscal Transparency* (Washington, DC: IMF)

—— (2001c) *Brazil: Report on the Observance of Standards and Codes – Fiscal Transparency*, 01/217 (Washington, DC: IMF)

—— (2003) *Chile: Report on the Observance of Standards and Codes – Fiscal Transparency*, 03/237 (Washington, DC: IMF)

—— (2004): *Peru: Report on the Observance of Standards and Codes – Fiscal Transparency*, 04/109 (Washington, DC: IMF)

Lavielle, Briseida, Pérez, Mariana and Hofbauer, Helena (2003) *Latin America Index of Budget Transparency* (Mexico and Washington DC: International Budget Project)

Mainwaring, Scott, and Welna, Christopher, (eds) (2003) *Democratic Accountability in Latin America* (Oxford: Oxford University Press)

Manning, Nick, and Stapenhurst, Rick (2002) *Strengthening Oversight by Legislatures* (Washington DC: World Bank PREM Note 74)

McGee, David (2002) *The Overseers: Public Accounts Committees and Public Spending* (London: Commonwealth Legislative Association and Pluto Press)

Messick, Richard (2002) *Strengthening Legislatures: Implications from Industrial Countries* (Washington, DC: World Bank, PREM Note 63)

OCDE (2001) *Budget: Towards a New Role for the Legislature* (Paris: OECD)

—— (2003) *Harmonizing Donor Practices for Effective Aid Delivery* (Paris: OECD)

—— (2004) *Budgeting in Chile* (Paris: OECD Working Party of Senior Budget Officials)

—— (2005) *Paris Declaration on Aid Effectiveness* (Paris: OECD)

O'Donnell, Guillermo (1999) 'Horizontal Accountability and New Polyarchies,' in Andreas Schedler et al. (eds) *The Self-Restraining State*, 29–52

Op de Beke, Anton (2002) *IMF Activities to Promote Good Governance and Combat Corruption – An Overview* (Washington DC: Policy Development and Review Department, June 7)

Open Budget Initiative (2006) *More Public Information is Needed to Hold Governments to Account* (Washington, DC: International Budget Project)

PEFA (2004) *Revised Consultative Draft PFM Performance Measurement Framework* (Washington, DC: PEFA)

Pelizzo, Riccardo, and Stapenhurst, Rick (eds) (2004) *Legislatures and Oversight* (Washington, DC: WBI Working Paper)

Petrei, Humberto (1998) *Budget and Control: Reforming the Public Sector in Latin America* (Washington, DC: IDB)

Rojas, Edgar, and Zavarce, Harold (2004) *Instituciones para la coordinación de la política monetaria y fiscal: Un enfoque transaccional para el caso venezolano*, paper presented at the XVI Regional Seminar on Fiscal Policy of ECLAC, Santiago de Chile, 26–9 January

Santiso, Carlos (2001) 'Good Governance and Aid Effectiveness: the World Bank and Conditionality', *Georgetown Public Policy Review*, 7(1): 1–22

—— (2004a) 'Development Finance, Governance and Conditionality: Politics Matter,' *International Public Management Journal*, 7(1): 73–100

—— (2004b) 'Re-forming the State: Governance Institutions and the Credibility of Economic Policymaking,' *International Public Management Journal* 7(2): 271–98

—— (2004c) 'The Contentious Washington Consensus: Reforming the Reforms in Emerging Markets,' *Review of International Political Economy*, 11(4): 827–43

—— (2004d) 'Lending to Credibility: the Inter-American Development Bank and Budget Oversight Institutions in Latin America,' *CEPAL Review*, 83: 171–90

—— (2004e) 'Legislatures and Budget Oversight in Latin America: Strengthening Public Finance Accountability in Emerging Economies,' *OECD Journal on Budgeting*, 4(2)

—— (2005) *Parliaments and Budgeting: Understanding the Politics of the Budget*, paper presented at the III Annual Meeting on Governance of the IDB, Hamburg, Germany, 12–13 December

—— (2006a) *Budget Institutions and Fiscal Responsibility: Legislatures and the Political Economy of the Budget Process* (Washington, DC: World Bank Institute Working Paper 37253)

—— (2006b) 'Improving Fiscal Governance and Curbing Corruption: How Relevant are Autonomous Audit Agencies?' *International Public Management Review*, 7(2): 97–107

Schedler, Andreas, Diamond, Larry and Plattner, Marc (1999) *The Self-Restraining State: Power and Accountability in New Democracies* (Boulder: Lynne Rienner)

Schick, Allen (1998) *A Contemporary Approach to Public Expenditure Management* (Washington, DC: WBI)

—— (2002) 'Can National Legislatures Regain an Effective Voice in Budget Policy,' *OECD Journal on Budgeting*, 1(3): 15–42

SIGMA (2002) *Relations Between Supreme Audit Institutions and Legislative Committees* (Paris: OECD SIGMA Paper 33, CCNM/GOV/SIGMA(2002)1)

Stapenhurst, Rick (2004) *The Legislature and the Budget* (Washington, DC: WBI Working Paper)

Stapenhurst, Rick, Sahgal, Vinod, Woodley, William and Pelizzo, Riccardo (2005) *Scrutinizing Public Expenditures: Assessing the Performance of Public Accounts Committees* (Washington, DC: WB Policy Research Working Paper WPS3613)

Stein, Ernesto, Talvi, Erneto and Grisanti, Alejandro (1998) *Institutional Arrangements and Fiscal Performance: the Latin American Experience* (Washington, DC: IDB OCE Working Paper 367)

Stein, Ernesto, Tommasi, Mariano, Echebarría, Koldo, Lora, Eduardo, and Payne, Mark (eds) (2005) *The Politics of Policies: Economic and Social Progress in Latin America* (Washington, DC: IDB)

Uña, Gerardo (2005) *El Congreso y el Presupuesto Nacional: Desempeño y Condicionantes de su Rol en el Proceso Presupuestario* (Buenos Aires, Argentina: Fundación Konrad Adenauer)

Wehner, Joachim (2003) 'Principles and Patterns of Financial Scrutiny: Public Accounts Committees in the Commonwealth,' *Commonwealth and Comparative Politics* 41(3): 21–36

—— (2004) *Back from the Sidelines? Redefining the Contribution of Legislatures to the Budget Cycle* (Washington, DC: WBI Working Paper 37230)

Weldon, Jeffrey (2002) 'Legislative Delegation and the Budget Process in Mexico,' in Scott Morgenstern and Benito Nacif (eds) (2002) *Legislative Politics in Latin America* (Cambridge: Cambridge University Press), 377–412

Wolfensohn, John (2004) 'Accountability Begins at Home,' *International Journal of Government Auditing*, 31(1): 1–3

World Bank (1992) *Governance and Development* (Washington: WB)

—— (1997) *World Development Report 1997: the State in a Changing World* (New York: Oxford University Press)

—— (2000) *Reforming Public Institutions and Strengthening Governance: a World Bank Strategy* (Washington, DC: WB Public Sector Group)

—— (2001a) *Guidelines for the World Bank's Work on Public Expenditure Analysis and Support* (Washington, DC: WB Public Sector Group)

—— (2001b) *Peru: Institutional and Governance Review* (Washington, DC: WB, Report 22637-PE)

—— (2002) *Institutional and Governance Reviews – A new type of economic and sector work* (Washington, DC: WB PREM Note 75)

—— (2003a) *Country Financial Accountability Assessment: Guidelines to Staff* (Washington, DC: WB Financial Management Sector Board, May 27)

—— (2003b) Audit Policies and Practices for World Bank-Financed Activities (Washington, DC: WB OPCS R2003-007 and IDA/R2003-0013)

—— (2003c) Argentina Institutional and Governance Review: Concept Paper (Washington, DC: WB draft)

—— (2004a) *From Adjustment Lending to Development Policy Lending: Update of World Bank Policy* (Washington, DC: WB OPCS)

—— (2004b) *Supporting and Strengthening Supreme Audit Institutions: a World Bank Strategy – Draft* (Washington DC: WB OPCS)

—— (2004c) *Nicaragua: Country Financial Accountability Assessment* (Washington, DC: WB Report No. 27922-NI)

—— (2005) *Paraguay Institutional and Governance Review - Breaking with Tradition: Overcoming Institutional Impediments to Improve Public Sector Performance* (Washington, DC: WB Report No. 31763-PY)

—— (2006) *Strengthening Bank Group Engagement on Governance and Anticorruption* (Washington, DC: World Bank, draft, 8 September)

World Bank and IDB (2004) *República de Chile: Evaluación de la responsabilidad financiera pública* (Washington, DC: WB)

World Bank and IMF (2003) *Bank/Fund Collaboration on Public Expenditure Issues* (Washington, DC: IMF FAD and WB PREM)

Part IV
Conclusion

16
Conclusion

Sarah Bracking and Kalin Ivanov

While this book has illustrated the varied experiences of political reform and anti-corruption policy which are currently underway, some patterns have nonetheless emerged. The central recurring theme is that relatively full implementation of the anti-corruption governance package can be associated with varying, and often low, degrees of actual reform in practice. The Nicaraguan, Philippine and Jamaican cases all illustrated that institutional reform and right-sounding rhetoric can litter government programming, but scandal and theft continue regardless. This suggests, in turn, that political and economic elites can covertly resist reform in a variety of situations: where the governmental façade and actual exercise of power differ in practice, as in the clientilist systems of Nicaragua and Malawi; where political parties and machine politics pervert government spending to captured vote banks, as in Jamaica or Nigeria; or where other considerations weaken the resolve of the international community to apply conditionality and punitive measures, as in Nicaragua and Georgia. We return to the problems this poses for the donors in our concluding remarks.

Our country studies uncover divergent, but sometimes cognate narratives, of what is perceived to be the problem and by whom. Sometimes donors pay little attention to corruption, despite its high prevalence, where it is found within donor practice (Bracking on development contracting); sometimes donors insist on the salience of corruption, only to withdraw from decisive action where other strategic objectives rank higher (Hall-Matthews, Brown et al. on Malawi and Nicaragua respectively); while in certain cases donor-prescribed institutional reforms have been followed quite faithfully, but corruption continues regardless (Osei on Jamaica). In other places, public policy on anti-corruption is leading to the desired changes in governmentality, relatively autonomously from international pressure, although not without setbacks and sporadic scandal (Dadalauri, Co on Georgia and the Philippines respectively). As indicated in the Introduction, contrary to development discourse we have found no singular or universal donor approach to correspond with the universal donor policy package. There is some evidence of donor learning and success, as in external auditing (Santiso), adaptation in technology transfer (Heeks), and political financing (Speck).

Post-communist and post-colonial trends in anti-corruption

The experiences of Central and East European anti-corruption campaigns have manifold ramifications for African expectations, being historically their predecessors in the form of holistic programmes. One such ramification is that 'too much' anti-corruption 'talk' can pathologise public policy and degenerate political culture, with little absolute benefit to government accountability. That anti-corruption policy can increase cynicism and detract from democratisation processes was presciently analysed by Szeftel (1998). We may now be approaching the prospect of regional processes of autarchy catalysed by ever deepening interventionism by the IFIs, implemented in the absence of sufficient legitimacy. The recurrent scandals and risks of corruption within aid-financed projects (Cooksey, 2003), the problems and cronyism within project contracting (see Bracking this volume), and the failure to adequately punish companies found to be engaged in bribery, even by means of domestic law on fraud in the North, all contribute to waning legitimacy for externally led governance and anti-corruption reform. To be credible, existing mechanisms for combating corruption, such as the World Bank's blacklist of corrupt companies, must impose meaningful penalties. As Brown et al. intimate (this volume), reducing corruption within a system which is corrupt is particularly problematic.

Exhortations for developing and post-communist countries to fight corruption will increasingly ring hollow if the self-styled mentors – Western governments and organisations – fail to set the right example. For reasons of economic interest and national prestige, a number of Western countries have been reluctant to investigate their own companies involved in the Iraq oil-for-food case. During its eastward enlargement, the European Union required Central and East European candidates to ratify anti-corruption conventions that not all member states had ratified. And in late 2006, Britain controversially (and expediently) ended an investigation into bribes paid by BAE Systems to secure military procurement contracts in Saudi Arabia. Appeals by Western governments and institutions to fight corruption will become more compelling if they begin at home.

While not the subject of this book, certain aspects of global capitalism undermine and stymie anti-corruption reform and good governance programmes. Examples abound of processes that are authored in the North, or have a primary residence in the practice of Northern institutions with bilateral outliers in the South: the privatisation of security and export of mercenaries; arms exports and arms recycling; money laundering; oligopolistic cartels in primary goods sectors; non-transparent governance of international debt; arbitrary foreign policy practices and abrogation of international law in territorial invasions and conflict.

All chapters on Central and Eastern Europe underscore the dissembling effects of marketisation that have provided a fertile ground for non-accountable behaviour. Anti-corruption policy emerges as a weak palliative to such immanent political economy processes. Meanwhile in Africa, anti-corruption policy has equally dissembling performative effects: it justifies the view of government policy as dysfunctional and illegitimate, regardless of any actual evidence of corrupt behaviour (although much exists, of course). Anti-corruption policy in Africa also unnecessarily restricts the discretion of the professional civil service and reduces issues of governance to banal public management frameworks. At a more profound level, the discourse reinforces negative perceptions and representations of African reality as deficient and dysfunctional while catalysing little actual change toward democratic governance.

Another pattern to emerge from the separate accounts is that adherence to institutional reform can leave patrimonial politics relatively untouched (Hall-Matthews, Speck and Osei, on Malawi, Mozambique and Nicaragua respectively), or criminal and/or elite nepotism largely functional (Dadalauri, Co and Zagainova on Georgia, the Philippines and various ex-communist countries respectively). In other words, constructing a liberal state alongside a capitalist market within the neoliberal governance package can be pursued with great apparent zeal by performing elites, confident that patronage and spoils will remain hidden from view. Whether accountability as social practice will 'catch up' and inhabit these spaces and institutional mechanisms as the populations grow more accustomed to exercising it; or whether the institutional forms will merely crumble for lack of meaningful use remains an open question. It is certainly not desirable that institutional reform should at this stage be abandoned because it is slow to take effect, or difficult to measure 'results' (which would ironically replicate a common mistake in development practice). However, there are also few historical examples of political elites who decide to unilaterally give away greater accountability and transparency to populations (whatever the subsequent historical transcript may suggest). Instead, political reform is normally won by people against the odds and with threats of oppression and political violence hanging above their heads.

We have also shown that much behaviour which is termed corruption is instead, or simultaneously exists, as embedded social processes with several explanatory and performative aspects. Thus, the 'problem of corruption' is sometimes needlessly foregrounded, when the behaviour in question is more accurately symptomatic of discrete or individual acts of theft or fraud, or more morally ambiguous, but universal, practices of networking or cronyism (Alolo on Ghana; Bracking on development contracting). The hazards of this foregrounding, and the instrumental reasons for privileging corruption in political discourse in particular contexts are evident throughout the volume, not least to slate one's political opponent (most obviously in Hall-Matthews's account of Malawi).

Hazards of the donor approach

The most obvious hazard is that economic conditionality may be misconceived or arbitrary. It also has an economy wide effect on the population of a state, who are not themselves the corrupt, as Ivanov's figures on Kenya (Chapter 2) illustrate. The effect of what is a qualitative measure, and thus subject to racial interpretation, is becoming more instrumental in the lives of southern populations (Ivanov, this volume), which entails significant moral hazard when the judgement is subject to error. Not only is development assistance tied to perception measurements of corruption, but FDI, savings, liquidity and overall economic variables are also affected.

Political hazards, some of which are mentioned above, include the holistic delegitimisation of southern states and polities. In turn, this affects the realm of governmentality and functioning of governments. For example, if a state is seen as systemically corrupt, the pursuit of objectives such as decolonisation, empowerment, and indigenisation, which may involve widespread wealth redistribution, are inevitably viewed as illegitimate acts of graft, punished by international investors and the IFIs. One could argue that the South African government is increasingly characterised as corrupt as a consequence of its redistribution policies post-apartheid, particularly the land reform process and Minerals Act of 2002. In short, legitimising redistributive economic policy becomes a problem when one's polity and economy are seen as inevitably corrupt. Further political hazards such as the degeneration of political

culture from discussions of substantive policy into accusations of corruption and promises of integrity, are described in Ivanov's chapter.

The particular measures within the anti-corruption campaign package
are also not without their hazards and perverse effects, which we have
summarised in Table 16.1, and which are evidenced by several of our
contributors. The final row of the table, however, outlines a broader
approach to anti-corruption which we propose would work better than
the current policy package, but which fundamentally relies on a consistency of moral position within global institutions and within Northern
policy. Thus currently, there are three central problems with the anti-
corruption campaign: 1) it neglects internationalised networks and incidence in the North (*an insight from the discipline of global political economy*);
2) it adopts the language of moral crusade, not democracy (*an insight
from the discipline of politics and development*); and 3) it requires the regulation of sociability, but this differs by spatial location (*informed by economic anthropology*). Consistent policies of democratisation and solidarity
would serve to remedy these, at least in part.

Problematising donor agency

It is, however, too simplistic to leave the impression that donors have
just got it wrong, or are applying the wrong strategies and that new policies
or new fashions will be sufficient to justify continuing the 'war against
corruption'. There are more fundamental problems with donor agency,
its effectiveness and representation. Indeed, another conclusion we can
draw from our chapters is that the self-representation of development
practice by donor governments and IFIs inflates their own moral consistency and effectiveness.

As indicated in the chapters on Nicaragua (Brown et al.) and Malawi
(Hall-Matthews) donors prefer not to talk about corruption and not to
be reminded of the sanctions they once threatened to impose, when
other geopolitical and strategic concerns prevail. Such inconsistencies
have historically served to maintain many a dictatorship, but they sit
more uneasily with current norms of neoliberalism and they are more
difficult to justify transparently. Corruption may also be overlooked if it
involves MNCs and domestic firms of the donor states (see Brown et al.
Bracking) or if it highlights the more morally questionable features of
global political economy. In addition, corruption may be downplayed in
the interests of stability, to avoid conflagration and state collapse, or
where donors find it difficult to withdraw for humanitarian reasons
(Hall-Matthews). When states are particularly nefarious, but donors still

Table 16.1: A summary of the global anti-corruption policy package

Measure	Geography	Epistemology	Disadvantages	Advantages
Anti-corruption Commission, establishment of external agencies	Inspired from Hong Kong and Singapore	Institutionalist	Parallelism in government, fuzzy accountability creates impression of inevitable dysfunction	Creates oversight facility when corruption endemic in mainstream government ministries
Integrity workshops and ethical codes of conduct	TI, Europe	Normative, moralism	Easy to adopt without policy change; shallow interventionism	Changes behaviour; reduces resistance to reform; changes organisational culture
Raising salaries of top civil servants	Hong Kong, Singapore	Neoliberal, econometric	Creates impression that public office remains the site for rapid private gain; large inequality justifiable	Reduces incentives for corruption. Allows civil servant to feel valued and respond with loyalty
Public service downsizing	UK, US	Neoliberal, new public management	Loss of seniority and experience; disrupts state-class reproduction and can cause social instability	Reduces ghost workers and loss of public revenue to corrupt payrolls. Can increase meritocratic criteria of appointment
e-technology	European	Technocist	No necessary human attitude change	Can reduce opportunities for corruption in discretionary decisions

Anti-corruption campaign	IFI	Postcolonial, interventionist	Symbolic violence and 'Othering'; pathologises politics of majority South; creates distrust of indigenous institutions; fuels a political culture based on scandal	Can package a set of reforms into one appealing discourse and raise political consciousness, knowledge and support for reform
Conditionality	IFI	Realist	Blunt instrument subject to geopolitical abuse	Allows for punitive basis for incentive where necessary
International Conventions	Global	Liberal	Judicial reach is poor when conventions not domiciled	Allows reformers to internationalise their efforts and recruit cosmopolitan support and solidarity. Creates norms of behaviour
Democratisation	*Global*	*Solidarist; social democratic*	*Long term policy; requires consistent policies of social justice and resource distribution; North needs to change too.*	*Embeds permanent values of accountability and transparency and the institutional means to achieve them*

want to save lives, such as in Zimbabwe currently, talk of corruption is deferred.

Also, as Brown and Cloke (2004) and Doig and Marquette (2004) suggest, donors may not have sufficient power or influence to pursue an anti-corruption model within a democratisation paradigm. Doig and Marquette neatly summarise that:

> Developed countries' promotion of a geo-commercial sphere of influence means that the politics of integrity may be a negotiated rather than an absolute public good depending on funding leverage and corporate influences. (2004: 205)

And even when integrity is negotiated and privileged, we can add that international actors have limited budgets and influence. In sum, anti-corruption coverage remains both sporadic and contradictory, despite recent improvements.

Concluding remarks

In 1996, World Bank president James Wolfensohn broke a longstanding taboo on discussing corruption, bringing the issue to the top of the international development agenda. Under his successor Paul Wolfowitz, the Bank has become even more outspoken against corruption, and even less hesitant to cut off borrowers seen as corrupt, raising concerns that it may paralyse lending, or target countries arbitrarily. Debates within the Bank's governing body and increased vigilance by shareholder governments are an encouraging sign that policies can no longer win automatic approval under the label of anti-corruption. Debates within the Bank may help to replace initial zeal with more fine-tuned approaches, based on clear and consistent criteria. As a component of these ongoing debates, the full range of perverse effects, hazards and opportunities presented in this book could usefully be considered.

Setting debates about anti-corruption policy within the wider democratisation agenda remains a priority, not withstanding the problems of the latter. Genuine anti-corruption practice requires systemic global change, which would deconstruct, in theory and in practice, Western/Northern double standards embedded in old-style realpolitik, and aspire to a consistent governance morality. While some donors do endorse 'democratisation', the current thin definition is not a panacea against corruption – especially if it simply means awareness campaigns by Western-funded NGOs. There are also high levels of corruption in countries commonly considered to be democratic. But currently, the anti-corruption campaign is chimerical in hiding these global inconsistencies and Northern problems of democratic accountability, and has thrived in the dissembled social fabric of post-communist and impoverished African societies. In other words, for anti-corruption policy to work, and for the global public to enjoy the fruits of their own energies without seeing them disappear into the pockets of political and economic criminal elites, there needs to be a return to the ideals of social justice and elite accountability. There are no quick fixes in the current anti-corruption package, but a set of inscribed meanings that further the cultural, economic and political domination of the North. Corruption can be better addressed within a morally consistent agenda of political and economic solidarity.

References

Brown, E. and Cloke, J. (2004), 'Neoliberal Reform, Governance and Corruption in the South: Assessing the International Anti-Corruption Crusade', *Antipode*, 36, 2, March, 272–94
Cooksey, B. (2003), *Aid and Corruption: a Worm's-Eye View of Donor Policies and Practices*, 11th International Anti-Corruption conference, Seoul, South Korea, May, 26–9
Doig, A. and Marquette, H. (2004), 'Corruption and democratisation: the litmus test of international donor agency intentions?' *Futures*, 37, 199–213
Szeftel, M. (1998), 'Misunderstanding African Politics: Corruption and the Governance Agenda', *Review of African Political Economy*, 76, June, 221–40

Index

Abacha, S.   105
accountability   233; in development
    finance projects 236–57; of public
    office 124
Acquis (of the EU)   148
activity   65
actor-network theory   269
administrative corruption   138
Administrative Panel of Inquiry   109
Africa   17, 36, 78; dictators 16;
    sub-Saharan 12
African Network for Environmental
    and Economic Justice   106
African public sector   21
aid; dependence   98
Aleman, A.   183–5, 192, 193;
    administration 187–9
allowances to MPs   98
Amari Coastal Bay Development
    Corporation   132
American colonial government   124
Andhra Pradesh state; India   264
anti-corruption: adverse side effects
    38–41; agenda 36–8; campaign
    114; campaign in Malawi 77–102;
    case study 18–20; intervention in
    21; measures 126; policy 68–9,
    236; post-communist and post-
    colonial trends 296–8; strategies
    58–62
anti-corruption agenda; origin   28,
    29–32
Anti-Corruption Bureau (ACB)   79,
    87, 88
anti-corruption initiatives: designers
    261;   failures 258–72
anti-corruption institutions; Jamaica
    174–7
Anti-Corruption Toolkit; UN Office
    Drugs and Crime (2004)   32
anticipatory award   107
Aquino, C.   127
Army Development Fund   160, 163

Asia; central   140, 145
Asian Development Bank   31, 122,
    247
Asian miracle   132
assistance strategies   276–8
auditing institutions; lending to
    285–6
Australian approach   59
Austrian economics   64
Azerbaijan   139

Banda, H. K.   78
Bangladesh   13, 31, 265
banking crisis; Nicaragua   186
Becker, G.   34
Bell, M.   97
Berlin Wall   40
Blantyre   87
Brazil   49, 279, 283
Bretton Woods Institution (BWI)   31,
    36, 46–7
British High Commission   86
budget: oversight   277; subsidies 229
Bulgaria   28, 36, 38, 151
Bureau of Internal Revenue (BIR)
    128
bureaucratic corruption   145
bureaucratic rules   13
Burkino Faso   38
Business Week   34
businesses; earmarked for
    privatisation   191
Byelorussia   151

Cameroon   259
capitalism; global   297
capture activity   50
capture theory of regulation   48
Caribbean   276
Caucasus; Southern   140, 145
Central Bank of Nigeria   109
Central Eastern Europe   52, 140
Chakuamba, G.   90

checks and balances 273–94
Chikakwiya, J. 85
Chile 279
China 52; authoritarian regimes 41;
    Peoples Republic 52
civil society; quantifications of
    corruption 32–6
clientelism 123, 138–9, 169;
    networks 195
Code of Good Practices on Fiscal
    Transparency (1999) 278
Cold War 37; end 31
colonialism 123
commercial activities 226
Commission on Africa 14, 238
Commission for Africa report 12
commission payments 238
Common Approach to Budget
    Support group (CABS) 98
Communism 39
constitution 223
constitutional constraint 115
consumer equilibrium principles 67
contextual collision 258–73, 264–7
Corner House 14
corporate donation 233; to *Renamo*
    228
corrupt leaders; private wealth
    accumulation 52
corruption 7, 10; by UDF politicians
    81; connection to national levels
    of income 53; cost 55, 55–8;
    culture 129; definition 4, 4–10, 56,
    167; in development industry
    networks 237; donor views 15–17;
    economic effects 53–5; economic
    models 46–74; efficiency wage
    model 58; fighters 38; Latin
    America 29; linked to regulation
    69; Malawi implications 93–9;
    model 216; permissible
    environments 243–7; permissible
    regulatory framework 237; petty
    and systemic 83; problem of the
    state 70; rational-legal paradigm
    12; scandals 171; tollbooth view of
    49; zero tolerance for 30
Corruption Perception Index (CPI)
    14, 28, 32–3, 34, 95, 140

Corruption Prevention Act (2000) 176
Council of Europe; Civil and Criminal
    Law Conventions on Corruption
    149
country externality 262
Croatia 151
crossover 65
current Zimbabwean elite 252
Czech Republic 38, 52

DaCosta commission 168
deception 207
demand countries 42
democracy: and autocracy 18;
    initiative 260
Democratic Progressive Party (DP)
    80
democratic state; pillars of 157
democratisation 121; Third Wave 9
Denmark 36
derivative business 247
design-imposing applications 267
development 95; finance 22, 250;
    finance institutions (DFIs) 236;
    projects 240; studies 7
differential association and
    opportunity (DAO) theory 206
direct investments; Finnish and
    Swedish 148
discourse theory; and corruption 14
Domingos, R. 228
donor 41, 96, 112; logic 82; policy
    20–3; to Malawi 96
donor agency; problematising
    299–302
donor approach; hazards 298
dualism; culture 132

e-transparency initiatives 258
Econometric research; corruption 35
Economic anthropology 12, 250–2
economic corruption 51–2
economic crime 103; adulation 113
economic criminals 103
Economic and Financial Crimes
    Commission (EFCC) 114
economic rationality 251
Emergency Drought Recovery
    Programme 97

endemic corruption   141, 144
endemic domestic corruption   98
Enhanced Highly Indebted Poor
   Country initiative   96
Enron   34
Estonia   149
Europe   9; Central 33, 40; Eastern 33,
   40, 138, 145; Western 148
European Bank for Reconstruction
   and Development (EBRD)   138
European Commission   36
European Union   148
European Union (EU)   36, 115
Expert Working Group on Corruption
   116
Export Credit Agencies (ECAs)   237

Federal Government of Nigeria (FGN)
   103
financial accountability   275
Financial Times   109
fiscal standards; improvement
   278–82
fixing   131
foreign corruption; threat to US
   security   29
free markets theory   250
free-market policies   46
Frelimo   221, 222, 224, 225, 228, 229,
   230–2

Gaddafi, M.   88
Galtung, F.   33
Geldof, R.   97
gender: dialectics   208;
   mainstreaming 21, 205
gendered kickbacks   211
gendered reciprocal favours; student
   networks   215
genocide   112
Georgia   13, 17, 19, 20, 139, 141,
   145, 155–66; Civil War 156;
   Development and Reform Fund
   159; post-revolutionary 161
Geyer, E. B.   194
Ghana   17, 21, 38, 57; gender 205–20
gift-giving   13, 129
global anti-corruption campaign   20
global integrity policy   23

global regulation   237
good governance   78, 275, 276;
   agenda 38; campaign 31; criteria 97
Gore, A.   30
governance: financial   273, 273–94;
   rules of 157
governance-investment interactions
   241
government: attempts to control
   editorial policy   161; procedure
   122
Gowon, General Y.   104
grease money   47
Greece   30
Guebuza, A.   227

Heisenberg effect   33
higher salaries   163
Hong Kong   163; model of
   anti-corruption 122
horizontal accountability   274
Huk rebellion   125
hypothetical case studies   208–15

illegitimate ('destructive') activity   65
Illovo Sugar Corporation   78
immunity; from prosecution   192
impeachment   114
income levels; and corruption   54
Independent Commission Against
   Corruption; Hong Kong   174
Independent Corrupt Practices
   Commission (ICPC)   114
independent ombudsman   174
India   36
Indian civil servant   13
Indian Railways   266
informal institutions   157
informal networks   130
information; ineffective freedom of
   193
Information Science for Democracy
   (INDEM)   147
institutional change   140
Institutional and Governance Reviews
   279
institutional infrastructure   127
institutional reform   297
institutionalisation   131

International Court for Economic Crimes (ICEC) 103, 117
International Criminal Court 116
International Development Select Committee; UK 14
international financial institutions (IFIs) 15, 16, 19, 22
international inequality 123
International Monetary Fund; surveillance 278
International Monetary Fund (IMF) 28, 31, 80, 276; guidelines 31, 42
international regulation 110
Istanbul Plan 158
ITPOSMO checklist 260

Jacinto, F. 126
Jafarey, V. A. 32
Jamaica 19, 167–81; anti-corruption institutions 174–7; causes of corruption in 168–70; types of corruption in 170
Joint EU–World Bank Georgia Donors' Conference; Brussels 158, 2004
Judicial Commission of Inquiry 109
Jumbe, F. 86

Kenya 35; loans 32
Keynesian interventionist theory 48
Keza Business Park 87
kinship networks; favours to 213
Klitgaard, R. 60; formula 123
Kutengule, M. 92

La Prensa 189
Latin America 9, 17; corruption 29; fiscal governance 22
law enforcement 162
legislative strengthening 283
legitimate ('productive') activity 65
Lesotho Dam 243–7
Libya 88
Lithuania 151
London 103

Malawi 17, 18, 20; anti-corruption 77; Congress Party (MCP) 84; Corrupt Practices Act 95; corruption; implications 93–9; development potential 95; Housing Corporation 84; Revenue Authority (MRA) 87; Schools Certificate of Education (MSCE) 89; Telecommunications Limited 92
Manila Bay; sale of property 131
Marcos, F. 125
Marcos–Romualdez group 125
market failure 36
marketisation; dissembling effects of 297
membership funds 226
Mexico 284
Millennium Challenge Account 35
Miller, L. 149
minor infringements 89
mobilisation fees 107
modernisation; by-produce of 7
Moi, D. A. 32
Moldova 141, 144
monopolisation 61
monopoly service 52
Morocco 88
most corrupt countries 144
Motheo housing 241
Mozambique 21, 221–35; party and election finance 221; party financing 22, 221; presidential campaign 225; public political finance in 222; struggle for political power in 221
Mpasu, S. 84
multilateral banks; role in Latin America 273–94
multilateral development finance 247
multilateral lending; budget oversight institutions 282–5
Muluzi, B. 77–99
Mutharika, B. W. 77, 80–99, 95
mutual legal assistance treaty (MLAT) 106
Mvula, H. 83
Mwanawasa, L. 78
Mwawa, Y. 91

National Integrity Committee 184
National Integrity Plan 189

National Solid Waste Management
(NSWMA); scandal   173
neoliberal: economic policies 58;
economists   70
Nepal; parliamentarians   36
Netser Global Communications
Limited Company   172
New Institutional Economics (NIE)
47, 49; developments within 64–6;
shortcomings in 67
new institutionalism   65
Nicaragua   20, 22, 182–201; banking
crisis 186; geopolitical situation 195
Nigeria   17, 18, 28, 103–20;
Economic and Financial Crimes
Commission (EFCC) 112;
Independent Corrupt Practices
Commission 109; regulation of
corruption 109
North Atlantic Treaty Organisation
(NATO)   29

Observance of Standards and Codes;
reports on   279
OECD   29, 32; Best Practices for
Budget Transparency 278;
Convention 30, 149; members 54
Oko, K.   113
oligarch   146
Oputa Report   110
organisational inequalities   230
Ortega, D.   190, 196

Pakas, R.   149
Pakikisama (esprit de corps)   131
Pakistan; authoritarian regimes   41
Paraguay   279
Patron–client relationship   156
Patterson, P. J.   171
pays legal   8
pays réel   9
Pearey, D.   96
Pendleton Act   124
personal wealth   225
Peru   57, 279, 283
phantom projects   105
Philippine Airlines (PAL)   126
Philippines   13, 18, 19, 121–37;
Development Academy of 122

Pinochet, A.   116
planning gaps   52
Poland   52, 149, 151
policy efficacy   287–8
political accountability   147
political competition   230; resources
for 229
political corruption   146
political economy   11, 131–3
political party financing   222
Political Risk Services (PRS)   140
political will   287–8
politics 4; of privilege   123
post-Keynesian economics   64
post-structuralist political economy
11
Poverty Reduction and Growth
Facility   80, 96
Poverty Reduction Strategy   16
power; abuse of   87
Press Trust Corporation   78
prikhvatizatsiya   139
priority   95
private donations   227
private political finance   223
private sexual gain   210
private wealth; accumulation by
corrupt leaders   52
privatisation   20, 41, 52, 139; of state
assets 146
privilege   18
procurement   50; scams 83
Programme for Resettlement and
Integrated Development Enterprise
(PRIDE)   171
Public Bodies Management and
Accountability (PBMA)   176
public budgeting; executive discretion
275
Public Expenditure and Financial
Accountability (PEFA)   282
public expenditure tracking surveys
(PETS)   57, 61
Public Financial Management
Performance Measurement
Framework   282
Public Interest Theory (PIT)   48
public office; abuse   4
public resources; theft   85

public sector: anti-corruption as technology transfer 258; integration of women 218; reform 262
public services 56; dishonest conduct of 112
pursuit of profit 70
Putin, V. 146–8

real world phenomena 11
reality-supporting applications 268
reform: fiscal 274; institutional 297
regulatory codes 236
regulatory environment 50
Renamo 221, 222, 229, 230–2; membership 226
rent seeking 10, 49, 65, 123
Romania 36, 40, 269
Rome: Peace Process (1992) 22–4; Protocols 224; Statute 116
Rose Revolution 157, 163, 164, *see also* anti-corruption revolution
Russia 13, 17, 139, 143; transition 62
Rwanda 88

Saakashvili, M. 145
Sandinismo 195, 196
Scottish Parliament 82, 97
Second World War (1939–1945) 124
Seko, M. S. 30
shadow prices 48
shadow state 9, 194
Shevardnadze, E. 59, 145, 156–8, 162
Shire Buslines Company 78, 83
Sibindy, Y. 228
Singapore; Corruption Practices Investigation Board 174
Slovakia 38, 148
Slovenia 148, 149
social capital 130–1
Social Weather Stations (SWS) 128; survey 121
socialist corruption theories 9
South American countries 51
South Korea 259
soviet: era 150; system 138
Soviet Union 16
soviet-era nomenklatura 146
Spanish colonial period 124

special client account 91
Sri Lanka; State Accounts Department 268
state: abuse of resources 229; capture 138; failure 36
Strategic Grain Reserves (SGR) 86
Swedish businessmen 33

Taiwan 88
Tanzania 57
tax: deductible expenses 110; revenues 71
technology transfer 258–73
Third World 31
transparency 191, 233
Transparency International (TI) 28, 32, 37, 106, 110, 122, 138; Corruption Perception Index (CPI) 53, 104, 167, 182
Tribunal of Inquiry Act 109
Trinidad and Tobago; Freedom of Information Act 177

Uganda 57
Ukraine 38
United Kingdom (UK) 63; Department for International Development (DFID) 16; legal system 59
United Nations (UN): Convention against Corruption 30, 116, 149, 237; Convention Against Transnational Organised Crime 110; on Drugs and Crime (UNODC) 104
United States of America (USA) 37, 195; central 182; and European multinationals 249; Foreign Corrupt Practices Act (FCPA) 29, 239; foreign policy 62; Senate Report (1999) 106
unregulated marketisation; role of 123
USAID 37, 122; anti-corruption strategy 61; World Bank and enviromental models 62–4
Uzbekistan 145

Venezuela 283, 284
Vietnam; authoritarian regimes 41

virtuous countries   143, 148
Volcker, P.; report into 'oil for food'
  programme in Iraq   110

Washington   29; Consensus policy
  275; institutions 70
Weberian goals   130
Weberian model; public
  administration   12
West Africa   260
Western benevolence   251
Westminster: model of executive
  government   19; system 169

Wolfensohn, J.   29, 31
women; promotion of   206
World Bank   11–12, 28, 31, 32, 97,
  122, 138; Anti-corruption in
  Transition report (2000) 63;
  barred list 238; fiduciary 277;
  governance indicators 140;
  Institute (WBI) 110, 282; view of
  corruption 242

Yeltsin, B.   146, 147

Zambia   57, 78